Using Common Core Standards

TO ENHANCE CLASSROOM INSTRUCTION & ASSESSMENT

Robert J. Marzano
David C. Yanoski
Jan K. Hoegh
Julia A. Simms

with Tammy Heflebower & Phil Warrick

555 North Morton Street
Bloomington, IN 47404

888.849.0851
FAX: 866.801.1447

email: info@marzanoresearch.com
marzanoresearch.com

Printed in the United States of America

Library of Congress Control Number: 2012918885

ISBN: 978-0-9833512-9-0 (paperback)

17 16 15 14 13   3 4 5

Editorial Director: Lesley Bolton

Managing Production Editor: Caroline Wise

Copy Editor: Rachel Rosolina

Proofreader: Elisabeth Abrams

Text Designer: Amy Shock

Cover Designer: Rian Anderson

Marzano Research Laboratory Development Team

Director of Publications

Julia A. Simms

Staff Writer/Researcher/Editor

Nancy L. Winter

Marzano Research Laboratory Associates

Elliott Asp
Tina Boogren
Bev Clemens
Jane K. Doty Fischer
Maria C. Foseid
Mark P. Foseid
Tammy Heflebower
Mitzi Hoback
Jan Hoegh
Russell Jenson
Jessica Kanold-McIntyre
Sharon Kramer
David Livingston
Pam Livingston
Beatrice McGarvey
Margaret McInteer
Diane E. Paynter
Debra Pickering
Salle Quackenboss
Laurie Robinson
Ainsley B. Rose
Tom Roy
Gerry Varty
Phil Warrick
Kenneth Williams

Teacher Reviewers for MRL's Scales for the Common Core State Standards

Delise Andrews
Cynthia Bauman
Kathy Christensen
Kristy Diehl
Abby Edwards
Kris Farris
Mitzi Hoback
Terri Jelinek
Cheryl Krafka
Kim Larson

Rhonda Martin

Amy Ruisinger

Melissa Schroeder

Terri Schuster

Alinda Stelk

Stacy Sullivan

Lenny VerMaas

Kristy Voigt

Suzanne Whisler

Amy Wilson

Visit **marzanoresearch.com/commoncore**
to access materials related to this book.

Table of Contents

Part I: Applying the Common Core State Standards

Part II: Scoring the Common Core State Standards

About the Authors

Robert J. Marzano, PhD, is the cofounder and CEO of Marzano Research Laboratory in Denver, Colorado. Throughout his forty years in the field of education, he has become a speaker, trainer, and author of more than thirty books and 150 articles on topics such as instruction, assessment, writing and implementing standards, cognition, effective leadership, and school intervention. His books include *The Art and Science of Teaching*, *Leaders of Learning*, *On Excellence in Teaching*, and *The Classroom Strategies Series*. His practical translations of the most current research and theory into classroom strategies are known internationally and are widely practiced by both teachers and administrators. He received a bachelor's degree from Iona College in New York, a master's degree from Seattle University, and a doctorate from the University of Washington.

David C. Yanoski, MA, is associate director of research and development for Marzano Research Laboratory in Denver, Colorado. He has worked in K–12 education as a classroom teacher, mentor coach, and teacher leader and has served on curriculum and assessment development teams. He has facilitated the development of proficiency scales with state departments of education, districts, and schools across the United States. He received his bachelor's degree from Midland University in Fremont, Nebraska, and a master's degree in education from the University of Phoenix.

Jan K. Hoegh, MA, is associate vice president of Marzano Research Laboratory in Denver, Colorado. She has been a classroom teacher, building-level leader, professional development specialist, high school principal, and curriculum coordinator during her twenty-eight years in education. Prior to joining Marzano Research Laboratory, Ms. Hoegh was assistant director of statewide assessment for the Nebraska Department of Education, where her primary focus was Nebraska State Accountability test development. Ms. Hoegh has served on numerous statewide and national standards and assessment committees and has presented at national conferences. As associate vice president of Marzano Research Laboratory, Ms. Hoegh works with districts across the country as they strive to improve student achievement. Her passion for education, combined with extensive knowledge of curriculum, instruction, and assessment, provides credible support for teachers, leaders, schools, and districts. A primary training focus for Ms. Hoegh is the transition to Common Core State Standards. An active member of several educational organizations, Ms. Hoegh was president of the Nebraska Association for Supervision and Curriculum Development. She is a member of the National Association for Supervision and Curriculum Development and the Nebraska Council of School Administrators. Ms. Hoegh holds a bachelor of arts in elementary education and a master of arts in educational administration, both from the University of Nebraska Kearney. She also earned a specialization in assessment from the University of Nebraska–Lincoln.

Julia A. Simms, EdM, MA, is director of publications for Marzano Research Laboratory in Denver, Colorado. She has worked in K–12 education as a classroom teacher, gifted education specialist, teacher leader, and coach. She is coauthor of *Coaching Classroom Instruction* and has led school- and district-level professional development on a variety of topics, including literacy instruction and intervention, classroom and schoolwide differentiation, and instructional technology. She received her bachelor's degree from Wheaton College in Wheaton, Illinois, and her master's degrees in educational administration and K–12 literacy from Colorado State University and the University of Northern Colorado, respectively.

Tammy Heflebower, EdD, is vice president of Marzano Research Laboratory in Denver, Colorado. She has served as a classroom teacher, building-level leader, district leader, regional professional development director, adjunct professor, and national trainer and has experience working in urban, rural, and suburban districts. She began her teaching career in Kansas City, Kansas, and later moved to Nebraska, where she received the District Distinguished Teacher Award. She has worked as a national educational trainer for the National Resource and Training Center at Boys Town in Nebraska. Dr. Heflebower has served in numerous leadership capacities at the state and regional levels. Recently, she was named Outstanding Alumni from Hastings College. She is a contributor to *The Teacher as Assessment Leader*, *The Principal as Assessment Leader*, *Becoming a Reflective Teacher*, and *Coaching Classroom Instruction* and a coauthor of *Teaching and Assessing 21st Century Skills*. Her articles have been featured in the monthly newsletter *Nebraska Council of School Administrators Today* and in *Educational Leadership*. Dr. Heflebower holds a bachelor of arts from Hastings College in Hastings, Nebraska, a master of arts from the University of Nebraska at Omaha, and an educational administrative endorsement from the University of Nebraska–Lincoln. She also earned a doctor of education in educational administration from the University of Nebraska–Lincoln.

Phil Warrick, EdD, is associate vice president of Marzano Research Laboratory in Denver, Colorado. He was an award-winning school administrator in Waverly, Nebraska, for nearly twelve years. In 2008, he was named campus principal at Round Rock High School, a school of nearly three thousand students in Round Rock, Texas. Dr. Warrick has been an adjunct professor at Peru State College since 2005. In 2010, he was invited to participate in the Texas Principals' Visioning Institute, where he worked with other principals from around the state to begin identifying model practices for Texas schools as they educate students in the 21st century. He is a past regional president for the Nebraska Council of School Administrators (NCSA). He also served on the NCSA legislative committee and was elected chair. In 2003, he was one of the first participants to attend the Nebraska Educational Leadership Institute, conducted by the Gallup Corporation at Gallup University in Omaha. Dr. Warrick was named 2005 Nebraska State

High School Principal of the Year, 2004 Nebraska Secondary School Principals Region One Principal of the Year, and 1998 Nebraska Outstanding New Principal. He is a contributor to *Coaching Classroom Instruction*. He earned a bachelor of science degree from Chadron State College in Chadron, Nebraska, and master's and doctoral degrees from the University of Nebraska–Lincoln.

About Marzano Research Laboratory

Marzano Research Laboratory (MRL) is a joint venture between Solution Tree and Dr. Robert J. Marzano. MRL combines Dr. Marzano's forty years of educational research with continuous action research in all major areas of schooling in order to provide effective and accessible instructional strategies, leadership strategies, and classroom assessment strategies that are always at the forefront of best practice. By providing such an all-inclusive research-into-practice resource center, MRL provides teachers and principals with the tools they need to effect profound and immediate improvement in student achievement.

Introduction

The History of Standards-Based Education in the United States

The discussion of standards is not new. As explained by Robert Marzano and Mark Haystead (2008), awareness of the need for national standards in the United States dates back to 1989, when President George H. W. Bush met with governors at an Education Summit in Charlottesville, Virginia. The group adopted six education goals for the nation, one of which was that "all children will leave grades four, eight, and twelve having demonstrated competency in challenging subject matter" (Rothman, 2011, p. 30). Two groups were subsequently formed to facilitate the implementation of these goals: the National Education Goals Panel and the National Council on Education Standards and Testing.

Recognizing that the federal government did not have the expertise internally to identify what students needed to know and be able to do in each content area, the Bush administration issued grants to subject-matter organizations to develop standards in their content areas. The first organization to develop standards was the National Council of Teachers of Mathematics (NCTM), whose standards identified "what it means to be mathematically literate . . . in a world where mathematics is rapidly growing and is extensively being applied to diverse fields" (NCTM, 1989, p. 1). In 1989 (six months before President Bush's Education Summit), NCTM published *Curriculum and Evaluation Standards for School Mathematics*, which specified the math knowledge and skills that students should know and be able to do by the end of grades 2, 5, 8, and 12. According to Robert Rothman (2011):

> The NCTM standards were . . . significant because in many ways they represented a sharp departure from conventional mathematics programs in use at the time. They placed a greater emphasis on the ability of students to solve problems and demonstrate their understanding of mathematics. (p. 32)

Other groups followed suit, and over the next decade, various organizations published standards for English language arts, science, social studies, history, civics, government, geography, foreign languages, business, health, physical education, technology, and the arts (dance, theater, visual arts, and music).

Through legislation and grants, the federal government encouraged states to adopt the subject-matter organizations' standards or develop their own sets of standards. In 1994, the reauthorization of the Elementary and Secondary Education Act (ESEA) required all states to "develop challenging standards for student performance in at least mathematics and English language arts and assessments to measure that performance against the standards" (Rothman, 2011, p. 42). The federal government further incentivized standards-based reform in 2002, when President George W. Bush signed No Child Left Behind (NCLB).

Problems With Previous Standards Efforts

Although NCLB encouraged states to set standards and define proficiency for their students, it also highlighted flaws in the system of individual state standards, as discussed by Willard Daggett and Susan Gendron (2010):

> NCLB left it to states to determine what students ought to learn in reading, math, and science; how they ought to be tested; and what levels of achievement determine proficiency. For example, what constitutes proficiency for grades 4, 8, and 10 in one state might be lower or higher than in another state. State benchmarks vary so significantly that it is difficult to compare test scores from different states. . . . To compound the problem, many states have lowered their proficiency levels in recent years to make it easier for schools to avoid sanctions under NCLB. (p. 3)

This state-to-state variance of standards and proficiency levels was just one of the problems that plagued early standards-based education efforts. Attempts during the 1990s and early 2000s to create state and national standards suffered from several flaws, including too much content (Marzano & Haystead, 2008); multidimensionality (Marzano & Haystead, 2008); too many standards (Kendall, 2011); too little curriculum (Kendall, 2011); too little alignment among standards, curriculum and instruction, and assessments (Loveless, 2012; Polikoff, Porter, & Smithson, 2011); and state-to-state variance (Porter, Polikoff, & Smithson, 2009).

Too Much Content

As different subject-matter organizations developed standards for their specific content areas, each group of specialists identified *everything* they thought students should know and be able to do in their fields. As a result, the standards developed by subject-matter organizations presented "far too much content to be effectively integrated into K–12 education" (Marzano & Kendall, 1999, p. 74). John Kendall and Robert Marzano (2000) identified 200 separate standards and 3,093 benchmarks in standards documents from 14 content areas at the state and national levels. Marzano and Kendall (1999) estimated that it would take 15,465 hours for a teacher to cover all of those standards and benchmarks. They also estimated that there are only 9,042 hours of available instructional time across grades K–12. Although only an estimate, this discrepancy was significant enough for them to conclude that "the answer to the question of whether the standards documents considered as a group contain too much content from an instructional perspective . . . is an unqualified 'yes'" (p. 104).

Multidimensionality

According to measurement theory (Hattie, 1984, 1985; Lord, 1959), "a single score on a test should represent a single dimension or trait that has been assessed" (Marzano & Haystead, 2008, p. 8). Therefore, an ideal standard would describe only one thing that students are expected to know or do, making it easier for teachers to assess students' level of performance on that individual skill or dimension of knowledge. However, state and national standards in the 1990s and 2000s often mixed multiple dimensions of knowledge or skill in the same standard. Marzano and Haystead presented the following benchmark statement (from a mathematics standards document published by NCTM) as an example: "develop fluency in adding, subtracting, multiplying, and dividing whole numbers" (NCTM, 2000, p. 392, as cited in Marzano & Haystead, 2008). This benchmark contains at least four dimensions of mathematics: adding, subtracting, multiplying, and dividing. To effectively use standards and benchmarks of this sort, teachers had to unpack each statement, identify the individual pieces of content within it, and determine the order in which each piece of content should be taught.

Too Many Standards

In spite of the existence of national-level standards documents from subject-matter organizations, individual states decided to define—for their unique populations and communities—what students in their specific state needed to know and be able to do. The national-level standards were a natural resource to draw from, having been created through "a process that pooled the cumulative wisdom and opinions of literally thousands of subject-matter experts" (Marzano & Kendall, 1999, p. 71). Instead of paring those unwieldy documents down to an instructionally manageable number of standards, however, "states tended to accept too many standards from each discipline—often, more than could be realistically addressed in the instructional time available" (Kendall, 2011, p. 6). Once again, teachers were left with two choices: unpack the standards, picking and choosing what they thought was the most important content, or race quickly through the standards, trying to touch on all of them but not teaching any in depth.

Too Little Curriculum

Before the standards-based education movement, decisions about what students should know and be able to do were often made by individual teachers and driven by textbook selection: the information and skills in the adopted textbook were what students were expected to learn. As Kendall (2011) observed, "the textbook *was* the curriculum" (p. 6). Unfortunately, the introduction of standards created a disconnect between expectations for students and the curriculum materials available for instruction. Kendall (2011) described the situation as follows:

> Standards were out in the front, while curriculum built to support these standards trailed behind. This lag crippled districts' and schools' attempts to implement standards-based instruction and has been counted by many as the single greatest failing of the standards movement. (p. 6)

Although curriculum publishers responded by creating versions of their products that were "aligned" to each state's standards, many questioned the rigor and accuracy of those alignments (Kendall, 2011).

Too Little Alignment

In addition to having too little curriculum to support standards-based instruction, the standards movement suffered from too little alignment among standards, curriculum and instruction, and assessments. Ideally, all three elements are aligned, as shown in figure I.1.

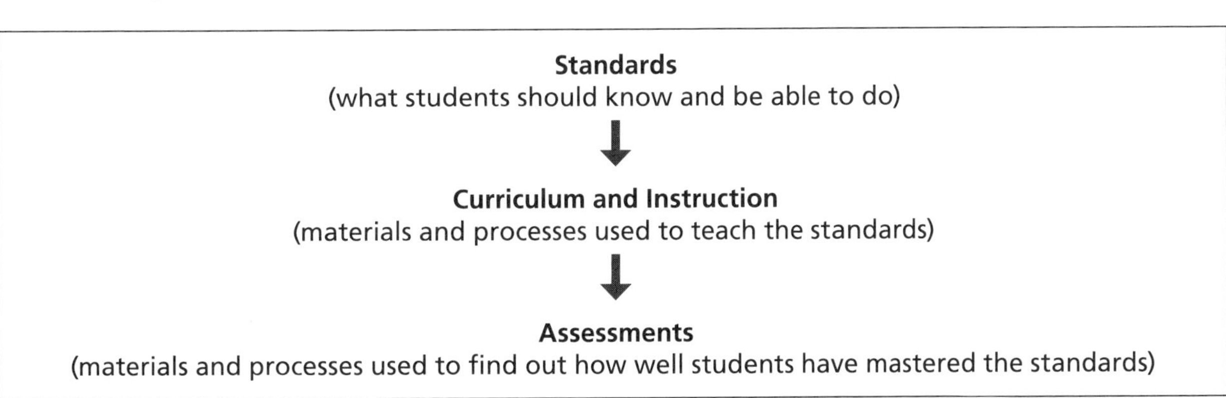
Standards
(what students should know and be able to do)
Curriculum and Instruction
(materials and processes used to teach the standards)
Assessments
(materials and processes used to find out how well students have mastered the standards)

Figure I.1: Alignment among standards, curriculum and instruction, and assessments.

Because standards were so numerous and multidimensional, however, teachers interpreted them in widely differing ways. According to Rothman (2011), "some saw [the standards] as substantial changes in practice and made corresponding adjustments to their instruction, while others viewed them in a relatively superficial way, making few changes" (p. 18). In other words, the *intended* curriculum (what the state wanted students to learn) didn't always match the *implemented* curriculum (what teachers taught), which didn't always match the *attained* curriculum (what students learned).

Misalignment between state standards and state assessments further exacerbated the problem. Morgan Polikoff, Andrew Porter, and John Smithson (2011) examined how closely state assessments were aligned to the state standards they were meant to measure and found that "standards and assessments in the observed states are not as well aligned as they could or were intended to be" (p. 992), a situation they described as "unfair to teachers and students" (p. 993).

State-to-State Variance

Prior to the Common Core State Standards, each state in the United States defined its own unique set of standards. This individualized approach led to several problems: (1) what one state expected of students in a specific grade might be higher or lower than what another state expected of students in the same grade, (2) each state had to shoulder the cost of creating an assessment for their standards, (3) in some states, districts were allowed to further personalize state standards, creating the same problems among districts that already existed among states, and (4) different states provided different levels of support to schools and teachers.

Porter, Polikoff, and Smithson (2009) measured this state-to-state variance and found that "the alignment among state content standards is no better than moderate for standards aggregated across grade levels and low when looking at a specific grade level. . . . States' content standards are, on the whole, different one from another" (pp. 263–265). Additionally, states often chose different score levels to define proficiency. This state-to-state variance led to two related problems: student mobility and national comparisons.

Regarding student mobility, one study found that over a two- to three-year period, 30 percent of students change schools (Reynolds, Chen, & Herbers, 2009). Although not all students move from state to state, some do, and the standards may be different in their new state. For example, if, during the summer after fourth grade, a student moved from a state where multiplying decimals is taught at fourth grade to a state where it is taught at fifth grade, he or she might learn the same content twice. Conversely, if the student moved from the state where decimal multiplication is taught at fifth grade to the state where it is taught at fourth grade, he or she might not have a chance to learn that content at all.

State-to-state variance also prevents national comparisons of students across states. One state might call its students "proficient" if they achieve a relatively easy score on state assessments, while another state might require its students to achieve a relatively difficult score on their state assessments to be proficient. When states used different assessments with different scores for proficiency and possibly even different measurement scales (for example, a 300-point scale versus a 500-point scale), there was no easy way to compare the achievement of students.

In summary, previous efforts to create national and state standards for education were well-meant but did not achieve the desired objectives.

Support for Common National Standards

Although the flaws in the early standards efforts caused some to question the validity of standards-based education, many recognized that creating a common set of U.S. national standards could remedy many of these issues. Specifically, many agreed that national content standards could be written to alleviate the problems of too much content, too many standards, and multidimensionality. Porter and Polikoff (2009) stated that "a common set of standards would allow for improvement in the quality of standards" and "allow the standards-setting process for each subject area to essentially start over again, informed, but unencumbered by, the mistakes and the inadequacies of past state efforts" (p. 2). Rothman (2011) stated that new national content standards should be "parsimonious, coherent statements of what students need to know and be able to do at each grade level" that "set out a logical learning progression over time" (p. 27).

Porter and Polikoff (2009) explained that a set of national content standards would remedy the issue of state-to-state variance by helping align curriculum and assessments, thus ensuring that "*all* students are expected to have an opportunity to learn rigorous content in academic subjects" (p. 2). Tom Loveless (2012) explained:

> The push for common education standards argues that all American students should study a common curriculum, take comparable tests to measure their learning, and have the results interpreted on a common scale, with the scale divided into performance levels to indicate whether students are excelling, learning an adequate amount, or falling short. Past experience with standards suggests that each part of this apparatus—a common curriculum, comparable tests, and standardized performance levels—is necessary. No one or two of them can stand alone for the project to succeed. (p. 7)

Rothman (2011) also argued that common national standards and assessments aligned to those standards would allow for better-quality tests, which "include a greater use of new formats, including performance tasks that will take place in classrooms over more than one class period, and thus are more likely than most state tests to measure the full range of the Standards" (p. 27).

In addition to these benefits for students, Porter and Polikoff (2009) recognized that "creating and re-creating standards for from eight to 12 grades in multiple subjects across 50 states is time-consuming and wasteful" (p. 2). Kendall (2011) described how common standards would be more cost-effective, "not only because publishers will focus their efforts on one set of standards rather than 43, but also due to the likely explosion of shared resources that will emerge once state boundaries are porous" (p. 55).

Not all were supportive of the idea of common standards, however. Loveless (2012) explained that those who believe that "local school governance is preferable to governance by larger entities" (p. 9) were critical of the idea of national standards. Loveless also predicted that common standards would not help rectify variation within states. He said:

> Within state variation is four to five times larger than the variation between states. Put another way, anyone who follows NAEP scores knows that the difference between Massachusetts and Mississippi is quite large. What is often overlooked is that every state has a mini-Massachusetts and Mississippi contrast within its own borders. Common state standards only target the differences between states, not within them, sharply limiting common state standards' potential impact on achievement differences. (p. 4)

Rothman (2011) cited further skepticism about the standards, including the idea that "a national effort to develop consensus could end up with the least common denominator" (p. 63), an inferior product that would then be "imposed on states that already had high standards" (p. 64).

Despite these reservations, two groups of national leaders decided that the benefits of common national standards would outweigh the challenges involved in creating and implementing them and decided to pursue the creation of common national standards, an effort they called the Common Core State Standards Initiative (CCSSI).

The Common Core State Standards Initiative

Although some think that the Common Core State Standards (CCSS) were a product of the federal government, the effort to create them was actually led by governors and chief state school officers from each of the fifty states. The National Governors Association (NGA) and the Council of Chief State School Officers (CCSSO) met in 2009 and agreed to take part in "a state-led process that will draw on evidence and lead to development and adoption of a common core of state standards . . . in English language arts and mathematics for grades K–12" (as cited in Rothman, 2011, p. 62). Other organizations also contributed to the effort, among them Achieve, the Alliance for Excellent Education, the James B. Hunt Jr. Institute for Educational Leadership and Policy, the National Association of State Boards of Education, the Business Roundtable, ACT, and the College Board (Rothman, 2011). These organizations created a set of three criteria that would guide the design of the CCSS:

1. The new standards should be fewer, clearer, and higher than previous standards. That is, there should be *fewer* standards statements, they should be *clearer* (unidimensional and concrete), and they should encourage students to use *higher*-level thinking.
2. The new standards should be based on research about what students need to be ready for college and/or careers after high school.
3. The new standards should be internationally benchmarked (that is, be comparable to standards from high-performing countries all over the world).

The leaders of the CCSSI convened a group of representatives, teachers, and researchers from both K–12 and higher education to draft the Common Core State Standards. The work was divided into two phases: (1) drafting a set of standards that describe what students should know and be able to do in English language arts (ELA) and mathematics by the end of high school, and (2) drafting grade-level standards that specify what students should know and be able to do by the end of each grade level, from kindergarten through twelfth grade. For the first phase, the CCSSI enlisted the help of organizations such as Achieve and the College Board, along with other experts in the field of college and career readiness. For the second phase, however, they enlisted "a different and larger work team of fifty-one people in mathematics and fifty people in English language arts. . . . The groups included individuals with expertise in assessment, curriculum design, cognitive development, child development, and English-language acquisition" (Rothman, 2011, pp. 70–71). After each phase, the CCSSI submitted drafts for public comment and revised them based on the feedback. Additionally, the CCSSI formed a validation committee to examine the final product and "determine whether it reflected the research on college and career readiness and international expectations" (Rothman, 2011, p. 71). This group concluded that the CCSS were:

- Reflective of the core knowledge and skills in ELA and mathematics that students need to be college- and career-ready;
- Appropriate in terms of their level of clarity and specificity;

- Comparable to the expectations of other leading nations;
- Informed by available research or evidence;
- The result of processes that reflect best practices for standards development;
- A solid starting point for adoption of cross-state common core standards; and
- A sound basis for eventual development of standards-based assessments. (NGA & CCSSO, 2010e, p. 3)

CCSS Adoption and Implementation

Adoption of the CCSS was voluntary; in other words, states could not be forced to adopt the CCSS. However, the federal government *strongly* encouraged states to adopt the CCSS by making it one of the factors that determined the success of their applications for federal education funding in a competition called Race to the Top. In some states, the state school board made the decision about whether or not to adopt; in others, the decision involved the state legislature. By the middle of 2012, forty-five states and the District of Columbia had adopted both the ELA and mathematics CCSS, one state had adopted the ELA CCSS only (Minnesota), and four states (Alaska, Nebraska, Texas, and Virginia) had not adopted either the ELA or mathematics CCSS.

To study states' progress and challenges in implementing the CCSS, Nancy Kober and Diane Stark Rentner (2011) surveyed a nationally representative sample of school districts during the winter of 2010 and spring of 2011. They reported that a majority (55–58 percent) of school districts viewed the CCSS as more rigorous than their old state standards and agreed that the CCSS would improve students' skills in their district. A majority (56–64 percent) also agreed that the CCSS would require "new or substantially revised" (p. 4) curriculum materials. However, only half of the districts surveyed agreed that the CCSS would require "fundamental changes in instruction" (p. 5).

The Future of the CCSS

Even as they were creating the CCSS, the NGA and the CCSSO acknowledged that their work would not be final and would probably require revision in upcoming years. In the validation committee's 2010 report, they stated:

> The certification and release of the Common Core State Standards is a historic milestone; however, it does not mark the end of the work. Standard setting is an iterative process; there is no finish line. . . . The standards will need to be continuously updated through processes that may, on occasion, pull stakeholders in opposite directions as consistency competes with the inevitable calls for changes or adjustments. (NGA & CCSSO, 2010e, p. 3)

Two consortia of states were tasked with designing new large-scale assessments aligned to the CCSS: the Partnership for Assessment of Readiness for College and Careers (PARCC) and the Smarter Balanced Assessment Consortium (Smarter Balanced). Each consortium planned to offer several different kinds of assessments aligned to the CCSS, including year-end summative assessments, interim or benchmark assessments (used throughout the school year), and resources that teachers could use for formative assessment in the classroom. In addition to being computer-administered, these new assessments would include performance tasks, which require students to demonstrate a skill or procedure or create a product. As of the writing of this book, both consortia planned to pilot and conduct field testing of their test items and assessments during the 2012–2013 and 2013–2014 school years. The full release and administration of both consortia's assessments were scheduled for the 2014–2015 school year (K–12 Center at ETS, 2012).

Kober and Rentner (2012) followed up their 2011 report with a second survey administered in the fall and winter of 2011. This second survey found that of the thirty-two responding states, two planned to fully implement the CCSS by the 2011–2012 school year, four by the 2012–2013 school year, nine by the 2013–2014 school year, and sixteen by the 2014–2015 school year. Although most of the states surveyed agreed that the CCSS were more rigorous than previous state standards, the majority of states identified finding adequate resources and providing appropriate professional development as the most pressing challenges facing their implementation of the CCSS. In this book, we seek to help teachers understand and apply the CCSS to their current practice through the use of proficiency scales designed to measure students' performance with the knowledge and skills identified in the CCSS.

Organization of This Book

Using Common Core Standards to Enhance Classroom Instruction &Assessment is composed of two parts. Part I, Applying the Common Core State Standards, consists of four chapters. These chapters outline practical steps that teachers can take to integrate the CCSS into their classroom practices. Part II, Scoring the Common Core State Standards, provides proficiency scales that teachers can use to measure their students' progress on the CCSS.

In chapter 1, we divide the CCSS into two categories: *practice standards* (represented by the college and career readiness anchor standards in ELA and the Standards for Mathematical Practice in math) and *content standards* (or grade-level standards). Then we walk teachers through the organization of the content standards, first by looking at the individual standards and then at the overarching learning progressions. Our goal in this chapter is to help teachers understand the organization of the content standards from which the proficiency scales in part II of this book were created.

In chapter 2, we focus on the ELA and mathematics practice standards and explain how teachers can use them to infuse 21st century thinking and reasoning into their instruction of the CCSS. Our goal in this chapter is to help teachers understand how to combine the thinking and reasoning skills outlined in the CCSS with the content standards.

In chapter 3, we describe how the content standards can be used to create learning goals and proficiency scales, with which teachers can measure and track students' progress on the CCSS. We also describe the process that teachers and researchers from Marzano Research Laboratory used to create the proficiency scales in part II of this book, Scoring the Common Core State Standards. Our goal in this chapter is to describe a process that educators can use to unpack and translate standards into useful learning goals and proficiency scales and explain how that process was used to create the scales presented in part II.

Finally, in chapter 4, we explain how the proficiency scales in part II can be used to assess students' progress on the CCSS, assign grades to students, and track students' progress with the knowledge and skills from the CCSS. Our goal in this chapter is to describe how teachers and schools can communicate with students and their parents about their growth and status on the CCSS.

As previously mentioned, part II, Scoring the Common Core State Standards, provides hundreds of ready-to-use scales created from the CCSS. We have separated part II into ELA scales and mathematics scales, and each section includes its own table of contents for easy navigation.

Part I

Applying the Common Core State Standards

1

Understanding the Common Core State Standards

As the authors of the Common Core State Standards (CCSS) in English language arts and mathematics sought to define what students needed to know and be able to do in the 21st century, they found themselves confronted with two broad categories of knowledge and skills. One of these categories (which we label *content standards*) involves relatively concrete knowledge and skills, such as "ask and answer questions about key details in a text" (NGA & CCSSO, 2010a, p. 11) or "solve word problems that call for addition of three whole numbers whose sum is less than or equal to 20" (NGA & CCSSO, 2010d, p. 15). The other category (which we label *practice standards*) involves relatively abstract skills, such as "students are engaged and open-minded—but discerning—readers and listeners" (NGA & CCSSO, 2010a, p. 7) or "students try to communicate precisely to others" (NGA & CCSSO, 2010d, p. 7). To their credit, the authors of the CCSS included both categories of knowledge and skills in their set of standards.

The content standards, which are discussed in this chapter, are easy to find: they are the grade-level standards that make up the bulk of the CCSS documents in ELA and mathematics. The practice standards require a bit more exploration. In mathematics, the practice standards are found on pages 6, 7, and 8 of the main standards document under the heading "Standards for Mathematical Practice." In ELA, they are described in the text on page 7 of the main document and are embedded in the college and career readiness anchor standards that precede each section of the content standards. Essentially, the practice standards outline the mental and interpersonal skills, processes, and habits that allow students to use content-specific knowledge and skills most effectively. The practice standards will be discussed in more depth in chapter 2.

We begin our exploration of the CCSS by looking at the organization of the content standards.

Organization of the ELA Content Standards

The authors of the ELA and mathematics standards used slightly different organizational schemes to present each subject's content standards. In ELA, the authors separated the grade-level standards into grades K–5 and 6–12. For grades 6–12, the authors further split the standards into two categories: "ELA standards" and "standards for literacy in history/social studies, science, and technical subjects." In the standards documents, the authors explained that they split the standards for grades 6–12 in this way in order "to facilitate a comprehensive, schoolwide literacy program" (NGA & CCSSO, 2010a,

p. 6). In other words, they wanted to emphasize the responsibility of *all* teachers in a school to teach literacy skills and support students' reading and writing in history, social studies, science, and other technical content areas. Vicki Phillips and Carina Wong (2010) provided a biological analogy for this idea: "Think of literacy as a spine; it holds everything together. The branches of learning connect to it, meaning that all core content teachers have a responsibility to teach literacy" (p. 41). For grades K–5, the authors of the ELA CCSS left content-area literacy and general ELA skills together, reasoning that many teachers at the elementary level teach all subjects to one group of students and are more likely to incorporate literacy across the content areas. Figure 1.1 depicts the organization of the ELA CCSS.

Figure 1.1 shows the strands into which the grade-level ELA standards are arranged. There are five strands for grades K–5: Reading (literature and informational text), Reading Foundations, Writing, Speaking and Listening, and Language. The same strands appear at grades 6–12 for ELA, with the exception of Reading Foundations. This is because the Reading Foundations standards are aimed at helping students learn to read and are therefore only included for grades K–5. Literacy for grades 6–12 contains standards in two strands: Reading and Writing.

The authors of the CCSS created a numbering system to use when referring to the ELA content standards. The scales in part II of this book use that same numbering system to cite the standards used to create each scale. Briefly, ELA standards are identified by strand initials, then grade level, and finally, standard number. The strand initials are as follows:

- Reading Literature = RL
- Reading Informational Text = RI
- Reading Foundations = RF
- Writing = W
- Speaking and Listening = SL
- Language = L

As an example of how a specific ELA standard would be cited, consider the following. In writing (W), the first kindergarten (K) standard (1) would be numbered W.K.1.

Organization of the Mathematics Content Standards

In mathematics, the content standards are arranged into domains (groups of related standards, such as *counting and cardinality*, *number and operations in base ten*, *operations and algebraic thinking*) at each grade level up through grade 8. For high school (grades 9–12), the authors chose to organize the standards according to five conceptual categories (Number and Quantity, Algebra, Functions, Geometry, and Statistics and Probability) rather than by grade. These conceptual categories are designed to facilitate different mathematics course offerings at the high school level (for example, algebra I, algebra II, geometry, trigonometry). Figure 1.2 depicts the organization of the mathematics content standards.

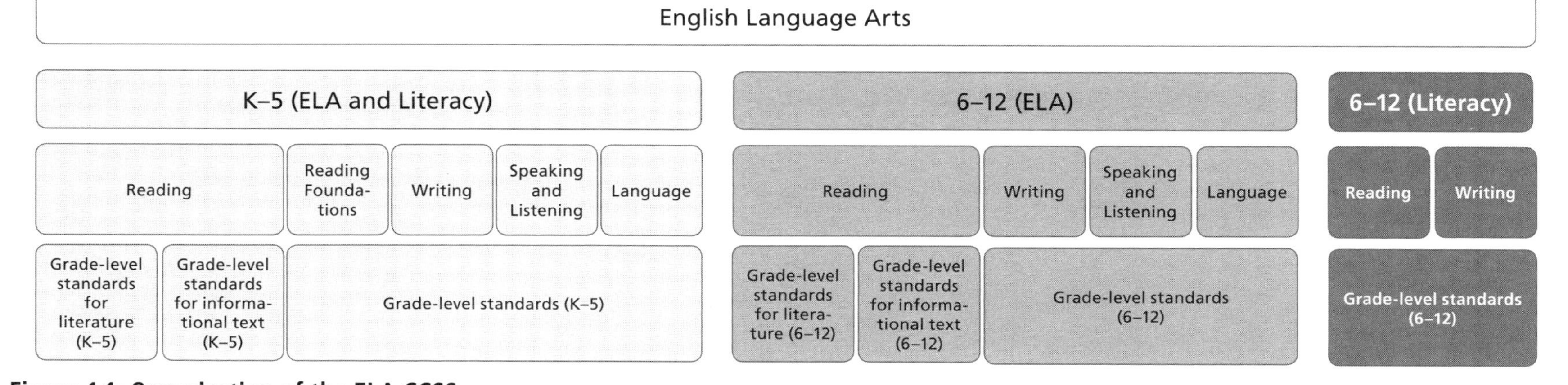

Figure 1.1: Organization of the ELA CCSS.

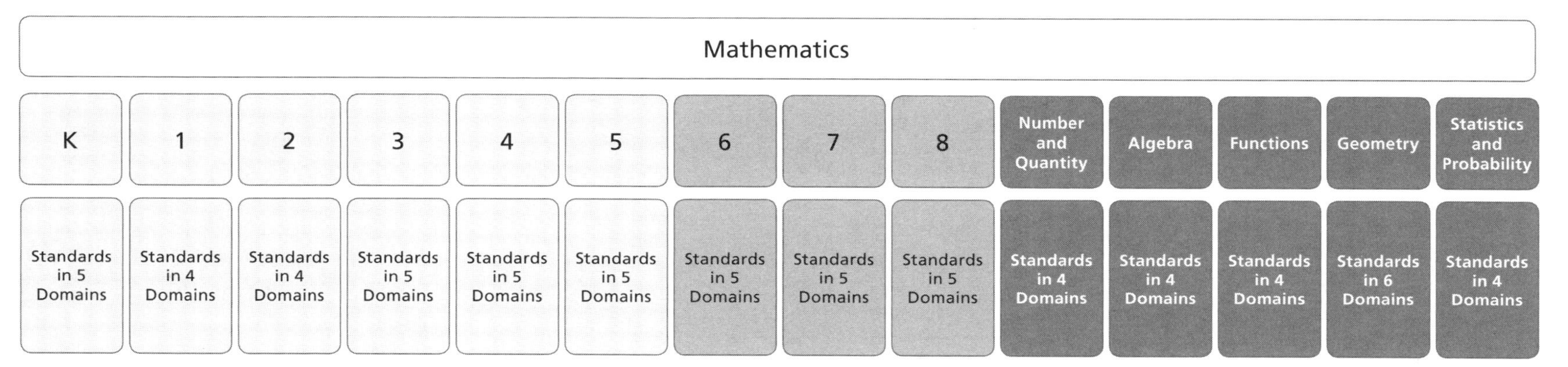

Figure 1.2: Organization of the mathematics CCSS.

The mathematics standards use a slightly different numbering system than ELA to reference individual standards. Mathematics standards are identified by their grade level first, domain name initials next, cluster letter next, and standard number last. The domain name initials are as follows:

- Counting and cardinality = CC
- Operations and algebraic thinking = OA
- Number and operations in base ten = NBT
- Number and operations—fractions = NF
- Measurement and data = MD
- Geometry = G
- Ratios and proportional relationships = RP
- The number system = NS
- Expressions and equations = EE
- Statistics and probability = SP
- Functions = F

Clusters within each domain are lettered using A, B, C, or D. Therefore 6.NS.A.1 (grade, domain, cluster, standard) represents the first standard of the first cluster in the domain *the number system* for sixth grade. At the high school level, the letters HS, a conceptual category initial (followed by a dash), and domain name initials are listed first. The initials for the conceptual categories and domains at the high school level are as follows:

- Number and Quantity = HSN
  - The real number system = HSN-RN
  - Quantities = HSN-Q
  - The complex number system = HSN-CN
- Algebra = HSA
  - Seeing structure in expressions = HSA-SSE
  - Arithmetic with polynomials and rational expressions = HSA-APR
  - Creating equations = HSA-CED
  - Reasoning with equations and inequalities = HSA-REI
- Functions = HSF
  - Interpreting functions = HSF-IF
  - Building functions = HSF-BF
  - Linear, quadratic, and exponential models = HSF-LE
  - Trigonometric functions = HSF-TF

- Geometry = HSG
    - Congruence = HSG-CO
    - Similarity, right triangles, and trigonometry = HSG-SRT
    - Circles = HSG-C
    - Expressing geometric properties with equations = HSG-GPE
    - Geometric measurement and dimension = HSG-GMD
    - Modeling with geometry = HSG-MG
- Statistics and Probability = HSS
    - Interpreting categorical and quantitative data = HSS-ID
    - Making inferences and justifying conclusions = HSS-IC
    - Conditional probability and the rules of probability = HSS-CP
    - Using probability to make decisions = HSS-MD

For example, HSN-RN.A.1 denotes the high school conceptual category of Number and Quantity (HSN-), the domain of *the real number system* (RN), and the first cluster's (A) first standard (1) in that domain.

The numbering system described here is referred to as the *dot notation system*. The authors of the CCSS also created specific URLs (uniform resource locators) and GUIDs (globally unique identifiers) for each standard to facilitate use of the CCSS in databases, gradebook applications, and online versions. However, the authors of the CCSS recommended that educators use the dot notation system (for example, W.K.1, 6.NS.A.1, HSN-RN.A.1) when referring to the CCSS in conversations. In part II of this book, the dot notation system is used to identify the CCSS standards used in each proficiency scale.

Learning Progressions in the CCSS

As previously stated, the NGA and CCSSO strove to create standards that were "fewer, clearer, higher," a phrase that they adopted as their motto. By *fewer*, they meant the CCSS should be fewer in number than previous sets of standards. By *clearer*, they meant they should be more focused and unidimensional. By *higher*, they meant they should require students to think at a higher cognitive level. One way the CCSS authors sought to achieve these goals was by writing and organizing the CCSS according to learning progressions. Learning progressions describe how students should develop increasingly sophisticated levels of understanding and expertise in an area of learning over time (Daro, Mosher, & Corcoran, 2011; Heritage, 2008; Nichols, 2010).

Learning Progressions in ELA

In ELA, learning progressions are seen in the grade-level standards, which are based on and build toward the overarching college and career readiness (CCR) anchor standards. Maryann Wiggs (2011) explained that:

> The CCR standards serve as the central points or significant learning expectations toward which all grade-specific standards aspire. As students move along the plane of a particular

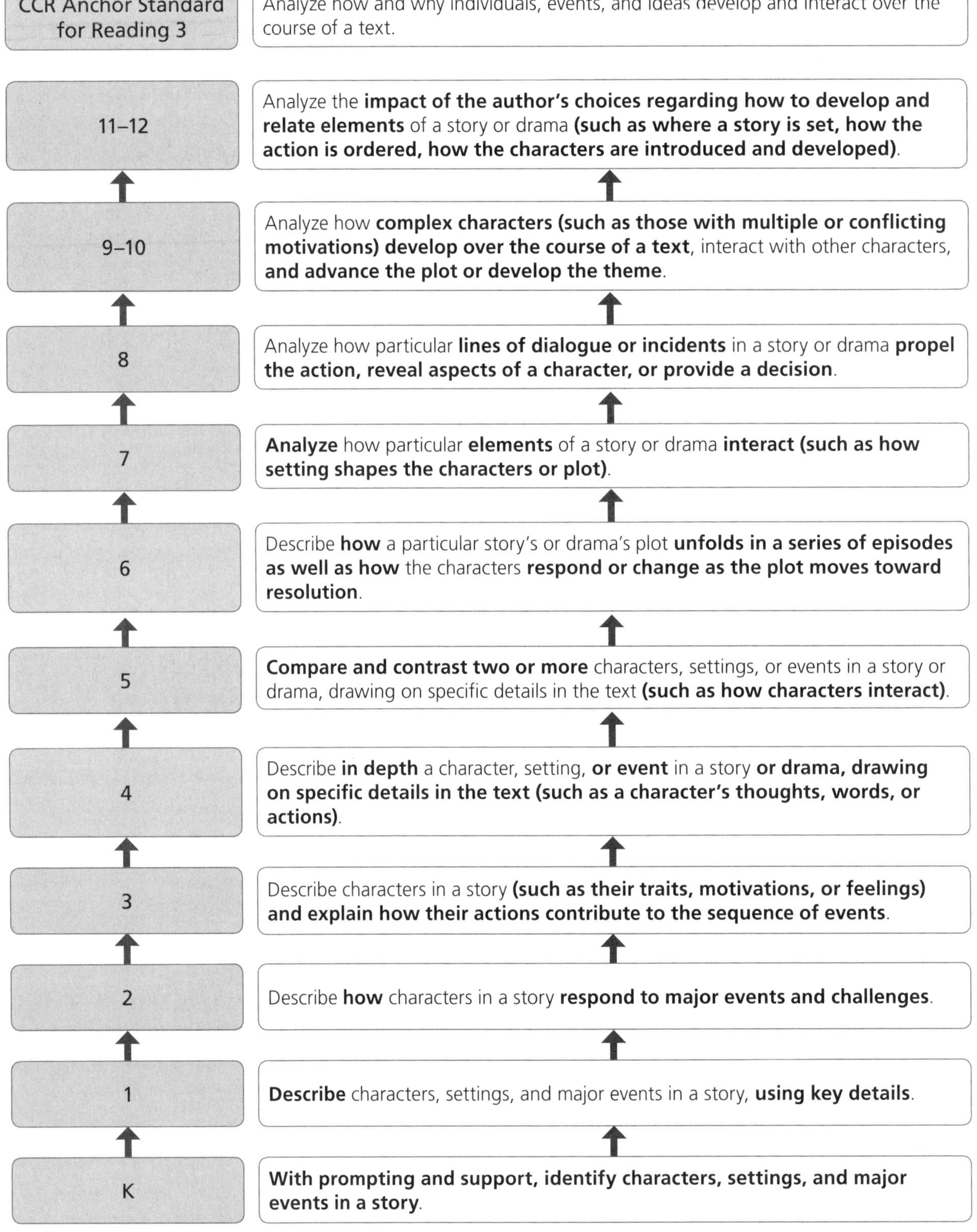

CCR Anchor Standard for Reading 3
Analyze how and why individuals, events, and ideas develop and interact over the course of a text.
11–12
Analyze the **impact of the author's choices regarding how to develop and relate elements** of a story or drama **(such as where a story is set, how the action is ordered, how the characters are introduced and developed)**.
9–10
Analyze how **complex characters (such as those with multiple or conflicting motivations) develop over the course of a text**, interact with other characters, **and advance the plot or develop the theme**.
8
Analyze how particular **lines of dialogue or incidents** in a story or drama **propel the action, reveal aspects of a character, or provide a decision**.
7
Analyze how particular **elements** of a story or drama **interact (such as how setting shapes the characters or plot)**.
6
Describe **how** a particular story's or drama's plot **unfolds in a series of episodes as well as how** the characters **respond or change as the plot moves toward resolution**.
5
Compare and contrast two or more characters, settings, or events in a story or drama, drawing on specific details in the text **(such as how characters interact)**.
4
Describe **in depth** a character, setting, **or event** in a story **or drama, drawing on specific details in the text (such as a character's thoughts, words, or actions)**.
3
Describe characters in a story **(such as their traits, motivations, or feelings) and explain how their actions contribute to the sequence of events**.
2
Describe **how** characters in a story **respond to major events and challenges**.
1
Describe characters, settings, and major events in a story, **using key details**.
K
With prompting and support, identify characters, settings, and major events in a story.

Source: Adapted from Wiggs, 2011, p. 32. Presented by permission of The Leadership and Learning Center, © 2012. Copy only with permission.

Figure 1.3: Learning progression in ELA.

learning trajectory they study the same expectation each year at ever-increasing increments of complexity and sophistication. Gradual cycling through repeated exposure to iterations of the same concepts and processes each year breaks complex learning expectations into manageable teaching and learning targets. (p. 31)

Wiggs (2011) provided an example of a learning progression by identifying the new, more challenging content added to an ELA anchor standard at each grade level. Figure 1.3 details the grade-level progression of skills and concepts associated with the third anchor standard for Reading: "Analyze how and why individuals, events, and ideas develop and interact over the course of a text." It starts with the kindergarten standard and builds up to the standard for eleventh and twelfth grades. In figure 1.3, the new skills and concepts at each grade level are in bold. As noted, students in kindergarten are expected to identify character, setting, and major events in a story when prompted. Expectations jump to describing how characters respond to major events by grade 3; comparing and contrasting two major characters, settings, or events in grade 5; and so on.

In certain cases, such as for the CCSS strand of Language, learning progressions aren't quite as linear. The authors of the ELA CCSS explained, "While all of the Standards are cumulative, certain Language skills and understandings are more likely than others to need to be retaught and relearned as students advance through the grades" (NGA & CCSSO, 2010b, p. 29). For example, a student's understanding of subject-verb agreement develops over the elementary and middle school grades. Table 1.1 illustrates this progression (the subject and verb are underlined in each example).

Table 1.1: Learning Progression for Subject-Verb Agreement

Example (from student writing sample)	New Learning	Approximate Grade Levels
Horses are so beautiful and fun to ride.	Subject and verb next to each other	Grades 3–4
When I started out the door, I noticed that Tigger and Max were following me to school.	Compound subject joined by *and*	Grades 3–4
A mother or female horse is called a mare.	Compound subject joined by *or*; each subject takes a singular verb	Grades 3–4
The first thing to do is research, research, research!	Intervening phrase between subject and verb	Grades 3–4
If the watershed for the pools is changed, the condition of the pools changes.	Intervening phrase between each subject and verb suggesting a different number for the verb than the subject calls for	Grades 5–7
Another was the way to the other evil places. All his stories are the same type. All the characters that Roald Dahl ever made were probably fake characters. One of the reasons why my cat Gus is the best pet is because he is a cuddle bug.	Indefinite pronoun as subject, with increasing distance between subject and verb	Grades 5–7

Source: Adapted from NGA & CCSSO, 2010b, p. 30.

As seen in table 1.1, students develop an understanding of subject-verb agreement by correctly applying it in increasingly complex situations. First, they use proper subject-verb agreement when the subject and verb are next to each other. Next, they learn to use a plural verb when two subjects are joined by *and*, as well as a singular verb when two subjects are joined by *or*. Then they learn to use appropriate subject-verb agreement when a phrase intervenes between the subject and the verb in a sentence. Finally, they learn to use a verb that agrees with subjects that are indefinite pronouns (*another*, *all*, *one*), regardless of whether or not intervening phrases are present.

Learning Progressions in Mathematics

In mathematics, the writers of the CCSS also sought to base their work on learning progressions, while acknowledging that all of the learning progressions in mathematics have not yet been identified:

> The development of these Standards began with research-based learning progressions detailing what is known today about how students' mathematical knowledge, skill, and understanding develop over time. . . . What students can learn at any particular grade level depends upon what they have learned before. Ideally then, each standard in this document might have been phrased in the form, "Students who already know . . . should next come to learn . . ." But at present this approach is unrealistic—not least because existing education research cannot specify all such learning pathways. Of necessity therefore, grade placements for specific topics have been made on the basis of state and international comparisons and the collective experience and collective professional judgment of educators, researchers and mathematicians. (NGA & CCSSO, 2010d, pp. 4–5)

Like the ELA CCSS, the mathematics standards show evidence of learning progressions. In a broad sense, the progression of the mathematical domains across grade levels illustrates how knowledge builds on itself as students advance through school. Figure 1.4 shows this progression.

The kindergarten standards are organized into five domains: (1) *counting and cardinality*, (2) *number and operations in base ten*, (3) *operations and algebraic thinking*, (4) *geometry*, and (5) *measurement and data*. One domain, *counting and cardinality*, ends after kindergarten. The four remaining domains continue through to fifth grade, meaning that students learn increasingly complex content in those areas at each grade level. In grade 3, *number and operations in base ten* splits into two separate domains: *number and operations in base ten* and *number and operations—fractions*.

At the middle school level (grades 6–8), the names of the domains change to reflect the increasing complexity of the standards therein, but they still focus on the same general areas as the elementary standards. For example, at grade 6, standards related to *measurement and data* are labeled *statistics and probability*, a phrase used to describe more sophisticated ways to measure and collect data. At grade 8, *ratios and proportional relationships* ends and *functions* is added.

As mentioned previously, at the high school level, the mathematics CCSS are organized into five conceptual categories. Figure 1.4 shows how the CCSS authors designed each of the domains at the middle school level to progress into one of the high school conceptual categories: *ratios and proportional relationships* and *the number system* lead into Number and Quantity, *equations and expressions* leads into Algebra, and so on.

An example of a specific learning progression in mathematics involves students developing understanding of *number* throughout elementary school, middle school, and high school. In kindergarten, students learn that numbers are used for counting (that is, 1, 2, 3, 4, and so on). Soon after, they encounter zero. By adding zero to the set of numbers they already use for counting, students become familiar with the set of whole numbers. Later in elementary school, students extend their understanding of *number* to include fractions and decimal numbers. In middle school, as students come to

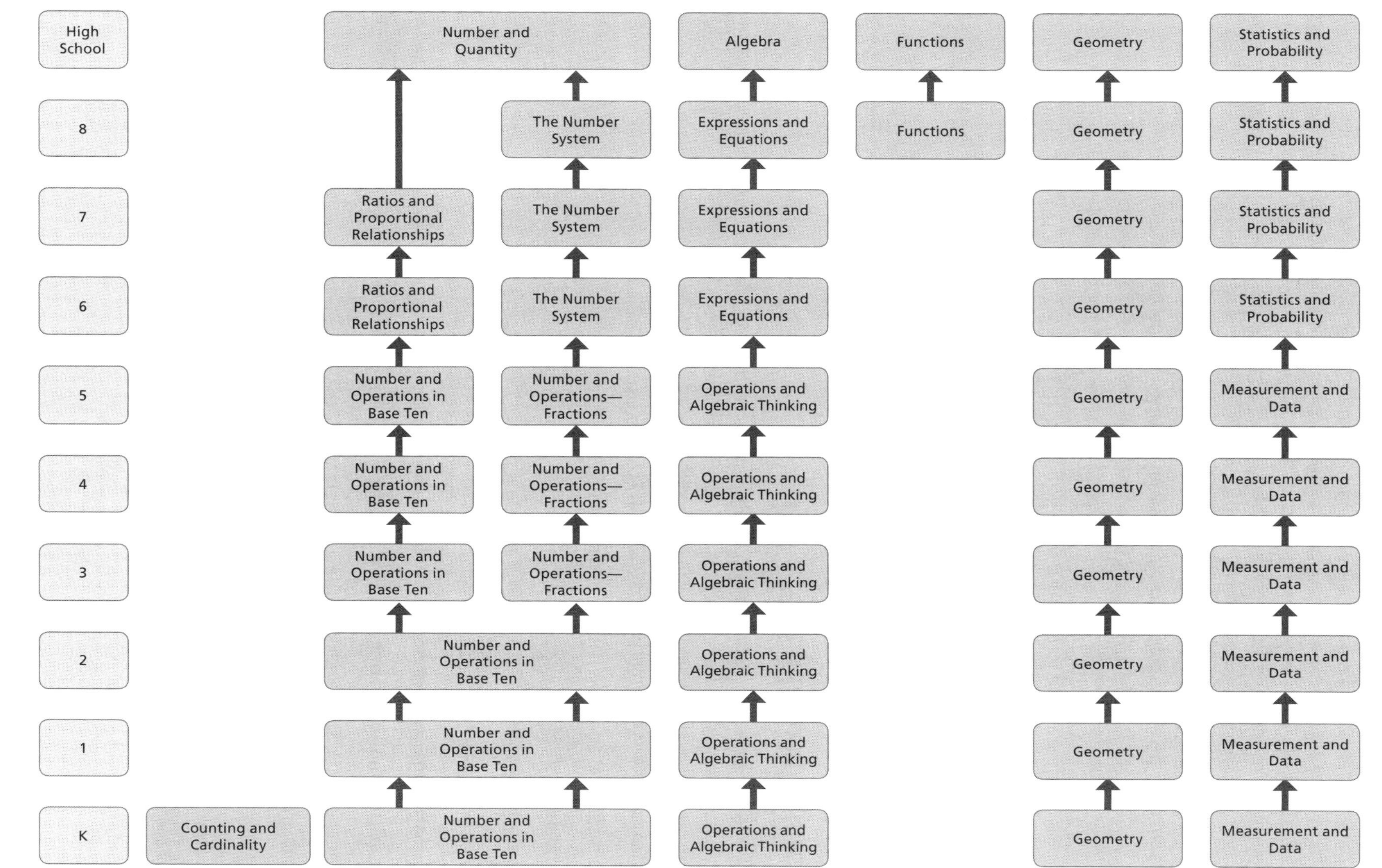

Source: Adapted from Wiggs, 2011, p. 47.

Figure 1.4: Learning progressions in the mathematics CCSS.

understand the concept of negative numbers (including negative fractions), they can then conceive of the rational numbers. In late middle school or early high school, when students encounter the idea of irrational numbers, their understanding of *number* is further extended to include the entire system of real numbers. Finally, students in high school learn about imaginary numbers and extend their idea of *number* to include the entire set of complex numbers. This learning progression intertwines with and supports other learning progressions, as the mathematics CCSS authors noted:

> With each extension of number, the meanings of addition, subtraction, multiplication, and division are extended. In each new number system—integers, rational numbers, real numbers, and complex numbers—the four operations stay the same in two important ways: They have the commutative, associative, and distributive properties and their new meanings are consistent with their previous meanings. (NGA & CCSSO, 2010d, p. 58)

Despite these examples of learning progressions in the CCSS, Andrew Porter, Jennifer McMaken, Jun Hwang, and Rui Yang (2011a) echoed the concerns of the mathematics standards writers, observing that "research that documents learning progression in mathematics and ELAR [English language arts and reading] is limited" (p. 187). In response to this limited amount of research, the NGA and CCSSO (2010d) stated that "one promise of common state standards is that over time they will allow research on learning progressions to inform and improve the design of standards to a much greater extent than is possible today" (p. 5).

Other Elements of the CCSS

In addition to the elements described previously, the CCSS offer a variety of supporting information and details related to the ELA and mathematics standards. For example, the ELA CCSS contain sections pertaining to:

- Progressive skills in language, by grade
- Measuring text complexity and matching texts to students
- Building knowledge systematically by using texts on the same topic across grade levels
- Research supporting key elements of the standards
- Key ELA terms (in glossary form)
- Exemplar texts and sample performance tasks for those texts
- Samples of student writing in different genres for each grade level

The mathematics CCSS provide additional information about:

- Modeling mathematical principles at the high school level
- Key mathematics terms (in glossary form)
- Common addition, subtraction, multiplication, and division situations
- Properties of operations, equality, and inequality
- Designing high school mathematics courses based on the CCSS

Although this additional information is interesting and useful, in this book we focus on the practice and content standards in ELA and mathematics and provide practical strategies that teachers can use to implement the CCSS in their classrooms. To this end, we now turn our attention to the practice standards in ELA and mathematics and discuss how teachers can use them to infuse 21st century thinking and reasoning skills into content-area instruction.

2

Teaching the Common Core State Standards

As seen in chapter 1, the ELA and mathematics CCSS can be divided into practice and content standards. In ELA, the practice standards are embedded in the introduction to the standards (on page 7 of the ELA standards document) and in the CCR anchor standards. The practice standards in mathematics are relatively easy to find because they appear under the heading Standards for Mathematical Practice on pages 6–8 of the mathematics standards document. Here we explain how we analyzed the practice standards in ELA and mathematics to make them immediately useful to classroom teachers.

The authors of the CCSS stated that the purpose of the Standards for Mathematical Practice was to "describe varieties of expertise that . . . educators at all levels should seek to develop in their students" (NGA & CCSSO, 2010d, p. 6). A similar logic guided the design of the college and career readiness skills in the ELA standards. In effect, the authors of the CCSS were attempting to articulate mental processes that could be directly taught to students and then used to apply mathematics and ELA content in meaningful ways.

This endeavor is not new or unique to the CCSS. Over the past few decades, mental processes that could be used to apply content in meaningful ways have been called by many other names, such as thinking and reasoning skills (Marzano & Pollock, 2001), habits of mind (Costa & Kallick, 2009), learning and innovation skills (Partnership for 21st Century Skills, 2012), workplace demands (U.S. Department of Labor, 1991), dimensions of learning (Marzano & Pickering, 1997), and dimensions of thinking (Marzano et al., 1988), among others.

To obtain a sense of the mental processes implied and stated in the CCSS, we began by identifying key words and phrases from the ELA and mathematics documents. To find these key words and phrases, we looked specifically for verbs that described mental processes or habits of thinking—practice standard skills—that students needed to develop (such as *comprehend*, *evaluate*, *establish*, *communicate*, and *employ* in ELA and *analyze*, *persevere*, *reason*, *quantify*, *construct*, *critique*, and *model* in mathematics). In ELA, we gleaned these skills from the introduction to the ELA CCSS and from the CCR anchor standards. In mathematics, we took them from the Standards for Mathematical Practice. We then eliminated repeated words or phrases and sorted the remaining entries into overarching categories. (Please reference the online table at **marzanoresearch.com/commoncore** to see these key words and phrases and how we categorized them.)

Table 2.1 (page 24) shows the categories identified.

Table 2.1: Categories of Skills Identified From the Practice Standards

ELA		Mathematics	
Argumentation	Interpretation	Analysis	Perspectives
Communication	Investigation	Application	Problems
Comprehension	Perspectives	Argumentation	Procedures
Defense	Questioning	Communication	Reasoning
Evaluation	Self-regulation	Data	Relationships
Information	Technology	Decision making	Representation
		Estimation	Self-regulation
		Knowledge	Tools

Using these categories, we looked for a framework that could be used to combine and integrate these mathematics and ELA practice skills into a unified whole that teachers could easily implement in their classrooms. We settled on one created by Robert Marzano and Tammy Heflebower (2012) that has been used to describe 21st century skills. That framework employs two broad categories of skills: cognitive and conative.

Cognitive skills are traditionally defined as those needed to effectively process information and complete tasks. Cognitive skills are required for tasks involving retrieval, comprehension, analysis, and utilization of knowledge. The majority of the practice standard skills from the CCSS are best classified as primarily cognitive in nature.

Conative skills are traditionally defined as the skills that allow a person to examine his or her knowledge and emotions in order to choose an appropriate future course of action. A useful way to think about conative skills is in terms of interacting with others and controlling oneself. For example, a student who understands effective communication techniques (knowledge about interacting with others) and recognizes that she feels tense (a personal emotion) because she and her friend have conflicting points of view might paraphrase what her friend is saying in order to defuse the tension.

Within the framework, Marzano and Heflebower (2012) identified specific classroom strategies that teachers can employ to teach cognitive and conative skills in their classrooms. From these strategies, we selected ten cognitive strategies and seven conative strategies that seemed most useful for teaching the practice standard skills we identified from the CCSS. For example, one of the categories of practice skills we identified in both the ELA and mathematics CCSS was *argumentation*. This category included key words and phrases such as:

- Construct arguments
- Develop ideas
- Build on others' ideas
- Integrate information
- Respond to others' arguments
- Compare arguments
- Explain flaws in arguments

- Decide if arguments make sense
- Decide if arguments are correct
- Determine domains to which an argument applies
- Clarify arguments
- Improve arguments
- Draw conclusions
- Justify conclusions

To help teachers address this category of skills, we identified three specific cognitive strategies from the Marzano and Heflebower (2012) framework:

1. Generating conclusions
2. Identifying common logical errors
3. Presenting and supporting claims

Another category of practice skills that we identified was *perspectives.* This category included key words and phrases such as:

- Points of view
- Open-minded
- Divergent cultures, experiences, and perspectives
- Varied backgrounds
- Collaborate
- Interact with others
- Reflect
- Step back
- Shift perspective
- Different approaches

To help teachers address these skills, we identified four specific conative strategies from the Marzano and Heflebower (2012) framework:

1. Becoming aware of the power of interpretations
2. Taking various perspectives
3. Interacting responsibly
4. Handling controversy and conflict resolution

In effect, we selected specific classroom strategies for each of the categories of practice standard skills that we identified in the CCSS. Many of the strategies we selected are useful for teaching more than one category of practice standards skills. For example, the cognitive strategy of "identifying common logical errors" applies to *argumentation*, *evaluation*, *defense*, *investigation*, *reasoning*, *analysis*, and *data*. As we will explain in chapter 3, teachers can use these cognitive and conative strategies and the words that prompt students to use them to compose complex learning targets and activities for the 4.0 level of each proficiency scale presented in part II. These cognitive and conative strategies can be used in both ELA and mathematics instruction.

Cognitive Strategies

Teachers can use the following ten strategies in the classroom to embed the cognitive strategies found in the ELA and mathematics practice standards into instruction:

1. Generating conclusions
2. Identifying common logical errors
3. Presenting and supporting claims
4. Navigating digital sources
5. Problem solving
6. Decision making
7. Experimenting
8. Investigating
9. Identifying basic relationships between ideas
10. Generating and manipulating mental images

Here we consider each briefly. Each strategy also includes a list of words and phrases to prompt students.

Generating Conclusions

Generating conclusions involves combining pieces of known information to form new ideas. Often, the pieces of known information are called premises, and they lead to a conclusion. For example, a student reading *Tuck Everlasting* observes that the Tuck family, although immortal, does not seem completely happy. In other words, he generates the following two premises.

- **Premise 1:** The Tucks are immortal.
- **Premise 2:** The Tucks are not very happy.

When working with students, it is important to help them clearly articulate the premises they are using to generate conclusions. Once the premises are recorded on the board, the teacher has students generate and defend conclusions such as the following.

- **Conclusion:** Being immortal doesn't necessarily make you happy.

For strategies that involve more detailed analyses of conclusions, see Marzano and Heflebower (2012).

In mathematics, a student learning about statistics and probability tracks the outcomes of a series of dice rolls (using the sum of two dice), as follows:

5, 4, 5, 9, 6, 8, 3, 7, 7, 3, 5, 6, 9, 7, 6, 10, 11, 3, 6, 11, 5, 7, 5, 10, 7, 7, 7, 8, 9, 4, 10, 11, 8, 6, 9, 7, 9, 7, 10, 9, 5, 9, 8, 3, 7, 10, 9, 4, 4, 6, 5, 5, 10, 8, 8, 5

The student observes that certain numbers occur more frequently than others, as shown in table 2.2.

Table 2.2: Frequency of Dice-Rolling Outcomes (Two Dice)

2	3	4	5	6	7	8	9	10	11	12
	IIII	IIII	IIIIIIIII	IIIIII	IIIIIIIIII	IIIIII	IIIIIIII	IIIIII	III	

He also observes that the most frequently occurring numbers are in the middle of the range of possible outcomes. Using these observations, the teacher helps the student articulate the two following premises.

- **Premise 1:** Certain numbers occur more frequently than others when rolling two dice.
- **Premise 2:** Numbers toward the middle of the range of possible outcomes occur more frequently than those toward the outer edges of the range.

The student then combines the two premises to try to explain his observations, generating a conclusion such as the following.

- **Conclusion:** Certain numbers occur more often when rolling two dice because there are more possible ways to roll those numbers.

He might even create a chart to support his conclusion, like the one in table 2.3.

Table 2.3: Ways to Roll Different Numbers With Two Dice

2	3	4	5	6	7	8	9	10	11	12
1 and 1	1 and 2	1 and 3 2 and 2	1 and 4 2 and 3	1 and 5 2 and 4 3 and 3	1 and 6 2 and 5 3 and 4	2 and 6 3 and 5 4 and 4	3 and 6 4 and 5	4 and 6 5 and 5	5 and 6	6 and 6

Table 2.3 shows the evidence that supports the student's conclusion: there are three ways to roll 6, 7, and 8; two ways to roll 4, 5, 9, and 10; and only one way to roll 2, 3, 11, and 12.

Words and Phrases That Prompt Students to Generate Conclusions

- Generalize
- What conclusions can be drawn
- What inferences can be made
- Create a generalization
- Create a principle
- Create a rule
- Trace the development of
- Form conclusions

Identifying Common Logical Errors

Identifying common logical errors involves analyzing information to determine how true it is. Marzano (2007) and Marzano and Heflebower (2012) reviewed four different categories of errors that are often committed when communicating information or messages: (1) faulty logic, (2) attacks, (3) weak reference, and (4) misinformation. Errors in each of these categories are listed and explained in table 2.4.

Table 2.4: Common Logical Errors

Faulty Logic	**Contradiction:** Presenting conflicting information **Accident:** Failing to recognize that an argument is based on an exception to a rule **False cause:** Confusing a temporal (time) order of events with causality or oversimplifying the reasons behind some event or occurrence **Begging the question:** Making a claim and then arguing for the claim by using statements that are simply the equivalent of the original claim **Evading the issue:** Changing the topic to avoid addressing the issue **Arguing from ignorance:** Arguing that a claim is justified simply because its opposite has not been proven true **Composition/division:** Asserting something about a whole that is really only true of its parts is *composition*; on the flip side, *division* is asserting about all of the parts something that is generally, but not always, true of the whole
Attacks	**Poisoning the well:** Being so completely committed to a position that you explain away absolutely everything that is offered in opposition to your position; this type of attack represents a person's unwillingness to consider anything that may contradict his or her opinion **Arguing against the person:** Rejecting a claim using derogatory facts (real or alleged) about the person who is making the claim **Appealing to force:** Using threats to establish the validity of a claim
Weak Reference	**Sources that reflect biases:** Consistently accepting information that supports what we already believe to be true or consistently rejecting information that goes against what we believe to be true **Sources that lack credibility:** Using a source that is not reputable for a given topic; determining credibility can be subjective, but there are some characteristics that most people agree damage credibility, such as when a source is known to be biased or has little knowledge of the topic **Appealing to authority:** Invoking authority as the last word on an issue **Appealing to the people:** Attempting to justify a claim based on its popularity **Appealing to emotion:** Using a "sob story" as proof for a claim
Misinformation	**Confusing the facts:** Using information that seems to be factual but that has been changed in such a way that it is no longer accurate **Misapplying a concept or generalization:** Misunderstanding or wrongly applying a concept or generalization to support a claim

Source: Marzano, 2007, pp. 78–79.

As shown in table 2.4, there are seven errors involving faulty logic, three errors involving attacks, five errors involving weak reference, and two errors involving misinformation. With a working knowledge of these types of errors, students can analyze their own thinking and that of others.

For example, in ELA, a student uses information and quotes from a blog as evidence and support when putting together an argument for fewer nuclear power plants. After analyzing her argument to look for logical errors, she recognizes that blogs are usually not considered credible sources, and as a result, her argument may contain *sources that lack credibility* (an error of weak reference). To avoid this error, she revises the evidence and support for her argument to only include sources from academic journals and books.

In mathematics, a student uses measurement data to figure out how much plastic tubing he needs to build a model. After completing his final calculations, he realizes that his calculated totals for plastic tubing are significantly different from his estimated totals, prompting him to examine his work for errors. When he rechecks, he recognizes that for two of his measurements, he changed the units from inches to feet without also converting the numerical measurements. This is an example of *confusing the facts*, and it could be remedied by recalculating his totals using the actual factual information, rather than the information that was inadvertently changed.

Words and Phrases That Prompt Students to Identify Common Logical Errors

- Identify errors
- Identify problems
- Identify issues
- Identify misunderstandings
- Assess
- Critique
- Diagnose
- Evaluate
- Edit
- Revise

Presenting and Supporting Claims

Claims are new ideas. The quality of a claim is normally determined by the level and quality of support provided for it. Claims are usually supported by *grounds* and *backing*. Grounds are usually composed of common knowledge (information that is generally acknowledged to be true), expert opinion (statements by individuals who are recognized as experts in their fields), experimental evidence (data generated through experimentation), and factual information (information found in reputable sources such as encyclopedias, dictionaries, or books). Backing is additional information to support grounds (for example, the credentials of an expert whose opinion is used to support a claim).

When students understand the general framework for a well-supported claim, they can more effectively present and support their own claims as well as analyze the claims of others. For example, in ELA, a high school student watches the movie version of a novel she has read and makes the claim that the book is superior to the movie. To support this claim, the student provides the following grounds with related backing:

- **Statements that are generally acknowledged to be true about the situation portrayed in the novel (common knowledge)**—The student observes that although the novel is generally acknowledged to be a tragedy, the movie adds material at the end to create a happy ending. As backing for this support, the student includes a quote from an online synopsis of the novel, stating that it is generally seen to be tragic.
- **Quotes from a book written by a university professor stating that a specific part of the novel is foundational to its underlying message (expert opinion)**—The student observes that the movie skipped the part of the novel deemed "foundational" by the expert. Backing includes information about the professor to support the idea that he is an expert about the novel (such as, "Dr. Simpkins has authored five books about the author of the novel").
- **Results of a survey of her fellow students (experimental evidence)**—The student asks a series of questions to other students who have seen the movie but not read the book and concludes that those students do not have a grasp of the important ideas of the book after watching the movie

only. To provide backing, she includes details about the guidelines she used to conduct her survey, including how many students she interviewed and specific information about their responses (such as what percent of the students gave a certain response to each question).

- **Statistical facts pertaining to the situation described in the book (factual information)—** The student observes that the novel, which is set during the Holocaust, and statistical evidence reveal that not all Germans supported Hitler, the Nazis, and the Holocaust; however, the movie portrays all Germans as enemies of the main character, a Jewish youth. Backing includes information about how and when the statistical evidence was collected.

In mathematics, a student uses different types of grounds when completing geometry proofs. For example, the student relies on the common knowledge that parallel lines do not intersect as part of his reasoning. Although the statement is not usually considered subject to proof (in Euclidean geometry), it is generally acknowledged to be true. He could also state that the sum of any two odd numbers is even and could generate a list of examples as experimental evidence in support of his claim. He might also use the side side side (SSS) postulate to prove that two triangles are congruent. The SSS postulate states that if the sides of two triangles are congruent, as shown in figure 2.1, then the triangles are congruent.

If each of the three sides of a triangle is congruent to each of the three sides of a different triangle, then the two triangles are congruent.

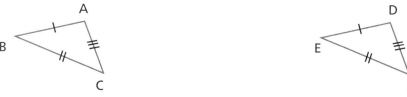

That is, if $\overline{AB} \cong \overline{DE}$, $\overline{BC} \cong \overline{EF}$, and $\overline{AC} \cong \overline{DF}$, then the SSS postulate states that $\Delta ABC \cong \Delta DEF$.

Figure 2.1: SSS postulate (expert opinion or factual information).

If the student proves the SSS postulate himself, then that postulate could be considered factual information. If the student learns from his teacher or textbook that the postulate is true but hasn't proven it himself, it could be considered expert opinion.

Words and Phrases That Prompt Students to Present and Support Claims

- Make and defend
- Predict
- Judge
- Deduce
- What would have to happen
- Develop an argument for
- Under what conditions

Navigating Digital Sources

Navigating digital sources involves using electronic resources to find credible and relevant information. The student should follow certain guidelines when using digital sources. For example, when an ELA student uses the Internet to find the origin of a specific vocabulary word, she needs to be aware of the following guidelines:

- **Look for specific information instead of browsing**—The student searches for her specific vocabulary word, rather than simply browsing online dictionaries.
- **Use the most effective keywords and commands when searching**—The student uses the Google search command "define:" to quickly find what she is looking for.
- **Skim information to decide if it needs to be read closely**—The student finds an essay on word origins in general and skims it to decide that it doesn't have helpful information and shouldn't be read closely.
- **Assess the relevance of each website visited**—The student moves quickly away from websites that only use the vocabulary word in text (rather than giving information about its origin).
- **Assess the credibility of each website visited**—The student realizes that the Oxford English Dictionary is a more credible source than a high schooler's blog, even if both of them claim to be giving the true origin of the word.
- **Confirm information by cross-checking it on multiple websites**—The student finds several explanations of the origin of her word to see if they all agree or if there are areas of disagreement.
- **Be aware that different points of view about a topic may exist**—The student finds two or three very credible sources that differ slightly in their views on the origin of the word. She concludes that the word's origin is a matter of some debate among scholars.

In mathematics, a student uses a database to locate a set of data or statistics for a project. Again, there are guidelines the student should follow. He wants to make sure he has a clear idea of the specific information he is looking for, learn about the database's search system and commands, and verify the accuracy of the information in the database by checking it with what he already knows and with other sources.

Words and Phrases That Prompt Students to Navigate Digital Sources

- What are you looking for
- What is the best way to find
- Skim or read closely
- Assess the relevance of
- Assess the credibility of
- Other sources
- Other points of view

Problem Solving

Problem solving involves accomplishing a goal in spite of obstacles or limiting conditions. If a student is creating a model and doesn't have the materials she needs, lack of materials is an obstacle to the accomplishment of the goal. If the same student has the necessary materials but only has three hours to create the model, then those time restraints are a limiting condition. Marzano and Pickering (1997) and Marzano and Heflebower (2012) present a process that students can use for problem solving:

1. Identify the goal you are trying to accomplish.
2. Identify obstacles or limiting conditions.

3. Determine how each obstacle or limiting condition is preventing the accomplishment of the goal.
4. Identify multiple ways (solutions) to overcome each obstacle or meet each limiting condition.
5. Select the best solutions and apply them.
6. Evaluate whether or not the solutions worked. If they didn't, try different solutions.

In ELA, a student directing an in-class dramatization of a play the class read uses this problem-solving process to accomplish his goal. Obstacles include finding students to play each character, printing a script for each participant, and creating scenery. Limiting conditions include the amount of space available to store props and scenery, money available to pay for printing costs, and the amount of time available for rehearsal. The student has to decide how to deal with these obstacles and limiting conditions (and probably with others not specified here) in order to produce an entertaining and accurate rendition of the dramatic work.

Using the problem-solving process, the student decides to hold auditions to assign roles, ask the school's print shop to produce scripts, forego scenery and use only a few props (created by students in his art class), and schedule rehearsals during lunch periods so that students can quickly eat and still have time to rehearse. After trying these solutions, he realizes that printing scripts through the school's print shop is too expensive, so he sends the script to all the actors electronically and asks each to cover the cost of printing out his or her own script.

In mathematics, a student applies the same problem-solving process to figure out how to buy a car. The student has saved $1000, but she wants a car that costs $5000. She also has a job that would allow her to pay $100 per month toward a car loan. The student identifies her goal as buying a car, with two limiting conditions: only having $1000 and only being able to pay $100 per month. She generates several solutions, such as finding a less expensive car, getting a car loan, or asking her parents for a loan. The student asks her parents but finds them unwilling to lend her the money. She then investigates a car loan, calculating that she would need to find an interest rate of 7 percent and a term of four years to be able to borrow the $4000 she needs.

Words and Phrases That Prompt Students to Problem Solve

- Solve
- How would you overcome
- Adapt
- Develop a strategy to
- Figure out a way to
- How will you reach your goal under these conditions

Decision Making

Decision making involves using criteria to select among alternatives that initially appear to be equal. Marzano and Pickering (1997) and Marzano and Heflebower (2012) described a process that students can use for decision making:

1. Identify the decision that needs to be made.
2. Identify the alternatives that are being considered.
3. Identify the criteria that are important.

4. Determine the extent to which each alternative meets each criterion.
5. Decide which alternative best meets all the criteria.

In ELA, a student needs to choose which novel out of four alternatives she should read and report to the class about. Since the four alternatives have already been defined by her teacher, she generates a list of criteria that are important to her, such as length (not too long), easy-to-understand language, very little violence, and historical setting. The student uses a decision-making matrix like the one in table 2.5 to evaluate each alternative according to these criteria.

Table 2.5: Decision-Making Matrix

Criteria	Alternatives			
0–Does not meet the criterion at all 1–Meets criterion slightly 2–Meets criterion 3–Strongly meets criterion	*Little Women*	*The Adventures of Tom Sawyer*	*A Wrinkle in Time*	*The Dark Is Rising*
Length (not too long)	0	1	2	1
Easy-to-understand language	2	1	2	1
Very little violence	3	1	2	0
Historical setting	2	2	0	1
Total	7	5	6	3

According to the decision matrix in table 2.5, *Little Women* or *A Wrinkle in Time* is probably a good choice for this student.

In mathematics, a student uses the decision-making process to select the best way to represent a set of data for a class presentation. He considers the alternatives of line graph, bar chart, pie chart, and data table. Because he is planning to share his data with his entire class during a presentation and wants them to be able to compare a series of measurements over time, he formulates criteria based on these requirements and then evaluates each alternative according to the criteria.

Words and Phrases That Prompt Students to Make Decisions

- Decide
- Select the best among the following alternatives
- Which among the following would be the best
- What is the best way
- Which of these is most suitable

Experimenting

Experimenting is the process of generating and testing explanations of observed phenomena. Marzano and Pickering (1997) and Marzano and Heflebower (2012) described a process that students can use to conduct experiments:

1. Observe and describe something that occurs.
2. Try to explain the occurrence using information you already know or can find out.
3. Make a prediction based on your explanation.

4. Set up an experiment to test your prediction.
5. Adjust your explanation (if necessary) based on the results of the experiment.

For example, an ELA student reading different versions of the Little Red Riding Hood fable from around the world observes that in each one, the protagonist always wears a red coat, cloak, hat, or cape. He hypothesizes that one way authors communicate information about characters is through what they are wearing. To test this hypothesis, the student examines the clothing of characters in other fables to see if their clothing reveals something about their personalities or beliefs.

In mathematics, a student notices that different regular polygons with the same perimeter have different areas. She wonders how the number of sides of a regular polygon affects the polygon's area and hypothesizes that the more sides a regular polygon has, the greater its area will be. To test her hypothesis, she draws a variety of regular polygons that all have the same perimeter. Then, she compares their areas to see if her explanation is accurate.

Words and Phrases That Prompt Students to Experiment

- Experiment
- Generate and test
- Test the idea that
- What would happen if
- How would you test that
- How would you determine if
- How can this be explained
- Based on the experiment, what can be predicted

Investigating

Investigation involves identifying confusions or contradictions about ideas or events and suggesting ways to resolve those confusions or contradictions. Marzano and Pickering (1997) and Marzano (2007) outlined three different types of investigations:

1. **Definitional investigation** involves identifying the important features and defining characteristics of a typically hard-to-define term or idea (for example, *civil disobedience*, *intelligence*, or *postmodernism*).
2. **Historical investigation** involves explaining the sequence of events and causes of a typically disputed past event or situation (for example, *John F. Kennedy's assassination*, *the initiation of World War I*, or *the discovery of the Americas*).
3. **Projective investigation** involves predicting what will happen in the future or what might have happened in the past if certain conditions will be or were present (for example, *the future of cloning*, *what if the South had won the Civil War*, or *how will genetically modified foods affect human health*).

The same process can be used for all three types of investigations. Marzano and Pickering (1997) and Marzano (2007) described the process as follows:

1. Identify the term or idea (definitional), historical event or situation (historical), or future or hypothetical event (projective) to be investigated.
2. State what is already known or agreed on about the topic.

3. Identify and explain confusions and contradictions related to the topic.
4. Create and defend a resolution to those confusions and contradictions.

For example, an ELA student who has just read *The Red Badge of Courage* decides to conduct a projective investigation using the question, "What if Stephen Crane had lived past age twenty-eight?" She first finds information about other works that Stephen Crane published before he died (six novels, two collections of poetry, and three collections of short stories) and researches major themes and characteristics of his writing. During that process, she learns about how Stephen Crane's work influenced Ernest Hemingway, Robert Frost, Ezra Pound, and Willa Cather. She subsequently concludes that naturalism and realistic fiction using colloquial language might have developed more quickly in American literature if he had lived longer.

In mathematics, a student decides to investigate the concept of negative numbers. He summarizes the basic facts about negative numbers first, and then proceeds to ask questions about negative numbers, such as the following:

- Are negative numbers really numbers? Or are they concepts? I can picture 4 items, but there is no such thing as -4 items. Why are they called numbers when they really represent the lack of something?
- Why does a negative number times a negative number equal a positive number but a negative number plus a negative number equal a negative number? What if a negative number times a negative number equaled a negative number? Would that get rid of imaginary numbers (like the square root of -9)?

The student further researches these questions and issues to create a defensible resolution for them.

Words and Phrases That Prompt Students to Investigate

- Investigate
- Research
- Find out about
- Take a position on
- What are the differing features of
- How did this happen
- Why did this happen
- What would have happened if

Identifying Basic Relationships Between Ideas

Understanding basic relationships between ideas and words is a fundamental language skill that many students have naturally. For example, if a student is told that his homework is due on March 24, he will probably understand that there is a *time* relationship between his homework and March 24. Alternatively, if a student is told that he was given an "incomplete" because he didn't turn his homework in, he will probably understand that there is a *causal* relationship between the incomplete and his not turning homework in. There are two other types of basic relationships that most people naturally identify: *addition* and *contrast*. The four basic types of relationships that normally occur between ideas are summarized in table 2.6 (page 36).

Table 2.6: Basic Relationships Between Ideas

Time	One idea occurs before, during, or after another idea. For example, she walked away **before** he arrived.
Cause	One idea causes another idea. For example, she woke up **because** the alarm buzzed.
Addition	One idea is similar to or adds to another idea. For example, he is blond, **and** he is handsome.
Contrast	One idea does not go with or subtracts from another idea. For example, he is fast **but** doesn't like to play sports.

Source: Adapted from Marzano & Heflebower, 2012, p. 94.

Each of the basic relationships listed in table 2.6 can be subdivided into more specific types of relationships. Visit **marzanoresearch.com/commoncore** for an online-only figure showing these subtypes and the words that signal each subtype. (For a more detailed discussion and examples of basic relationships, see Marzano and Heflebower, 2012.) Although students can usually understand relationships between ideas in everyday speech, learning to consciously analyze relationships between ideas can help students understand those presented in the complex texts recommended in the CCSS.

For example, an ELA student reading Walt Whitman's poem "O Captain! My Captain!" notices that the first stanza contains a strong contrast between the first four lines and last four lines. The first four lines paint a picture of a ship returning to port after a dangerous trip. People shout and cheer and welcome the sailors back home as their brave ship sails into the safe harbor.

> O Captain! my Captain! our fearful trip is done;
> The ship has weather'd every rack, the prize we sought is won;
> The port is near, the bells I hear, the people all exulting,
> While follow eyes the steady keel, the vessel grim and daring:

However, the student notices the word *but* at the beginning of the fifth line, preparing the reader for a contrast as he or she realizes that the captain of the ship has not survived the voyage.

> But O heart! heart! heart!
> O the bleeding drops of red,
> Where on the deck my Captain lies,
> Fallen cold and dead.

Once he notices this contrast, the student recognizes the underlying structure of the rest of the poem (eight-line stanzas with a contrast between the first four lines and the second four lines). After becoming familiar with this pattern, he realizes that in the last stanza, Whitman strays from the structure, breaking the final stanza into two smaller, four-line stanzas (instead of the usual eight-line stanza). Finally, the student infers that one of the main themes of the poem is the conflict caused by the contrasting emotions of the homecoming sailor who is the narrator of the poem. In effect, recognizing and analyzing the basic relationships listed in table 2.6 facilitates an insightful analysis of Whitman's poem.

In mathematics, a student who is aware of the basic types of relationships between ideas connects them to different signs and symbols used in equations. For example, the addition sign (+) denotes an addition relationship between two ideas or numbers. The contrast relationship might be shown using the subtraction sign (-) or the inequality symbols (<, >). The student recognizes the importance of time relationships when learning about basic and compounding interest and notices causal relationships when working with functions, where a specific input value for x leads to a specific output value for y.

Words and Phrases That Prompt Students to Identify Basic Relationships Between Ideas

- Categorize
- Compare and contrast
- Give an example
- Restate
- Differentiate
- Discriminate
- Distinguish
- Summarize
- Sort
- What was the cause of
- What is the relationship between
- Infer
- Create an analogy
- Create a metaphor
- Classify
- Organize
- What was the result of
- Identify a broader category
- Identify categories
- Identify reasons
- Identify different types
- Sequence

Generating and Manipulating Mental Images

When students create mental images for what they learn, they process the information more deeply and are more likely to remember it. Mental images are created in a person's mind, without writing anything down. Sometimes mental images involve using symbols to represent real-world objects, such as when a person pictures an aerial view of a map and a dot moving around on it when listening to directions. One type of mental image that is particularly useful when learning about or investigating a concept is called *thought experiments.* Here, a situation is imagined and different resolutions or possible outcomes are visualized. For example, an ELA student writing a mystery story uses thought experiments to try out different endings. She imagines her final scene, with the detective character confronting three different suspects. In her mind, she pictures what each suspect is wearing, the expression on each person's face as the detective reviews his evidence, the way they move in their chairs, and the gestures they make as they refute the accusations against them. In her mental scene, the student pictures what would happen if one of the suspects was proven guilty by the detective. Then, she "rewinds" the scene and imagines a different suspect being proven guilty. Each time the student mentally plays the scene, she examines how the characters react to different circumstances, allowing her to pick the most compelling ending for her narrative piece.

It is often the case that a teacher needs to guide students through mental imagery to help them understand how to build and manipulate rich mental pictures of the concepts they have learned. In mathematics, a teacher explaining triple-digit addition might begin by having her students use manipulatives to model the addition of hundreds, tens, and ones. After the students have used the manipulatives enough to be comfortable with them, the teacher introduces the idea of picturing and moving the manipulatives in their heads, rather than physically moving them. "Close your eyes and picture the place value blocks in your head," she says. To add 226 + 568, the teacher asks students to picture hundred-squares—squares composed of 100 unit squares. As students picture two hundred-squares and five hundred-squares, the teacher prompts them to add them together to make 700. Students repeat the process with two 10-unit sticks and six 10-unit sticks (equaling 80) and 6 unit squares and 8 unit squares (equaling 14). Finally, the teacher prompts students to picture the seven hundred-squares, the eight ten-unit sticks, and the 14 unit squares. "Picture yourself adding all those pieces together and open your eyes when you have an answer," she says. As students open their eyes, they turn to a partner and compare answers to see if everyone reached the correct answer of 794.

Words and Phrases That Prompt Students to Generate and Manipulate Mental Images

- Symbolize
- Depict
- Represent
- Illustrate
- Draw
- Show
- Use models
- Diagram
- Chart
- Describe the key parts of
- Describe the relationship between

Conative Strategies

Conative skills help students combine what they know and how they feel in order to appropriately address real-world problems. Conative strategies help students interact with others and understand themselves. The following seven strategies can be used by teachers in the classroom to embed the conative processes in the ELA and mathematics practice standards into instruction:

1. Becoming aware of the power of interpretations
2. Cultivating a growth mindset
3. Cultivating resiliency
4. Avoiding negative thinking
5. Taking various perspectives
6. Interacting responsibly
7. Handling controversy and conflict resolution

Here we consider each briefly. As with the cognitive strategies, each conative strategy also includes a list of words and phrases to prompt students.

Becoming Aware of the Power of Interpretations

All human beings automatically and constantly interpret their situations and circumstances. However, only a small percentage of people are aware that their interpretations do not always accurately reflect reality. As students learn to interact and communicate with others, it is important for them to become aware that what they think, feel, believe, and do is often strongly influenced by how they interpret a situation. Marzano and Heflebower (2012) presented a strategy that students can use to become aware of and manage their interpretations:

1. Identify your interpretation of the current situation.
2. Predict what will happen if you continue to react based on your current interpretation.

3. Identify alternative outcomes that are more positive or beneficial.
4. Change your interpretation to obtain a better outcome.

For example, a student working on a group project in ELA realizes that she perceives one of her fellow group members as lazy and unmotivated because the teammate didn't complete the work she was supposed to do for the group's first meeting. After acknowledging that her thoughts about her classmate are dictated by her interpretations, the student realizes they will not be able to work well together unless something changes. She decides to start thinking differently about the classmate and give her the benefit of the doubt. The student later finds out that her classmate's mother was in the hospital right before the group's first meeting, and this changes her interpretation immediately; changes in her behavior soon follow. She is friendlier to her classmate and more helpful with the group work.

In mathematics, a student collecting data for a statistics project realizes that his data collection is being influenced by his desire for the data to support his original hypothesis. Once he becomes aware that he is letting bias affect his interpretations as he collects data, he asks a friend to help him collect data in order to keep his interpretation from biasing the results.

Words and Phrases That Prompt Students to Become Aware of the Power of Interpretations

- Point of view
- Open-minded
- Why do you think
- What makes you believe
- Perspectives
- Alternative interpretations
- Is that how things really are
- Look at it a different way

Cultivating a Growth Mindset

Carol Dweck's (2000) research has shown that people generally approach learning, challenges, and failure with one of two mindsets. A person with a *fixed* mindset believes that each person has a fixed amount of intelligence that doesn't change. A person with a *growth* mindset believes that each person can increase his or her intelligence and abilities. For instance, a person with a fixed mindset might respond to a challenge by saying, "I can't do that because I'm not good at it," whereas a person with a growth mindset might say, "I'll give it my best shot and try to learn how." The different mindsets also predict how people react to failure. A person with a fixed mindset might respond to failure by saying, "I knew I couldn't do that," but a person with a growth mindset might say, "I want to try again! I know I can figure it out if I try." Dweck (2000) also noted that a person can have a fixed mindset in one area and a growth mindset in another area (for example, believing that one is not good at mathematics but responding favorably to challenges in science). The most exciting aspect of Dweck's research was her observation that teachers can help students change from a fixed to a growth mindset by having them identify their current mindset, praising their efforts rather than their ability, and telling them about famous people who overcame obstacles and grew their knowledge and abilities through hard work and determination.

Helping students cultivate growth mindsets usually begins by identifying areas for which they have fixed mindsets. For example, an ELA student initially demonstrates a fixed mindset regarding public speaking, expressing her belief that she has stage fright and will never be able to talk in front of an audience. Her teacher helps her identify that belief as a characteristic of a fixed mindset and tells her about famous people like Elvis Presley, Abraham Lincoln, and Barbra Streisand who experienced stage fright but overcame it to become successful public speakers and performers. The teacher then asks the student to give a very short presentation to two of her peers, friends with whom she is comfortable. The teacher watches and gives her effort-focused feedback, such as, "I liked the way you used your calming strategies, like deep breathing and taking a few steps when you felt nervous. Using those strategies helped you start talking again when you got stuck. Good job!" As the student gains confidence, the teacher asks her to speak to increasingly larger groups of students.

In mathematics, a student believes that, although he is good at addition, subtraction, multiplication, and division, he will never understand fractions and decimals. He refuses to even try problems involving fractions and decimals, saying, "I'm not good at those." The teacher begins by telling him a story about how, when she was in elementary school, she loved fractions right up until fourth grade. "I loved playing with the plastic pie pieces that my second- and third-grade teachers had. Fractions made a lot of sense to me when I thought of them as parts of a pie," she explains. She goes on to say that when she reached fourth grade, however, her teacher didn't have the plastic pie pieces and instead expected students to add and subtract fractions using an algorithm. "They stopped making sense," she says. The teacher then works with the student to help him visualize what really happens when fractions are added, subtracted, multiplied, or divided and helps him make connections to his experience using operations with whole numbers. She praises his effort, saying, "I like the way you drew that problem when you didn't understand it. I saw you figure out the hard part by putting it down on paper. Good work!"

The teacher may also choose to directly teach her students about growth versus fixed mindsets and their influence on how human beings behave. Marzano and Heflebower (2012) listed a variety of techniques to this end. The most important part about making students aware of mindsets is emphasizing the fact that one's mindset can always be changed with awareness and effort.

Words and Phrases That Prompt Students to Cultivate a Growth Mindset

- Effort
- Perseverance
- You stuck with that
- What did you learn by failing the first time
- What will you do differently next time
- How did you grow
- What do you want to learn next

Cultivating Resiliency

Resiliency is the ability to overcome failure, challenge, or adversity. Resiliency is obviously related to and overlaps with the growth mindset. Resilient students respond to difficult situations by redoubling their efforts, rather than making excuses. In ELA, a resilient student responds to a harsh critique of his writing by extensively revising his work based on the feedback given in the critique, believing that his final product will be more effective because of his efforts. In mathematics, a resilient student responds to an inaccurate solution to a problem by re-examining each calculation she made, searching for the error that flawed the solution. When asked about her work, she explains how finding the error on her own deepened her thinking about math and that her improved understanding of the skills involved in the problem will probably help her learn even more during subsequent lessons.

Again, enhancing students' sense of resiliency begins by making them aware of the characteristics of resilient people. Marzano and Heflebower (2012) listed the following characteristics:

> 1. They can tell positive from negative influences, and they can limit the power of those negative influences in their lives.
> 2. They have a clear sense of what they want and do not want for themselves in the future.
> 3. They do not feel resigned to an unsuccessful future, no matter how much adversity they have encountered.
> 4. They have an ability to make and adapt specific plans to reach their short- and long-term goals. (p. 133)

Armed with an understanding of these characteristics, students can examine the resiliency (or lack thereof) of their own behaviors.

Words and Phrases That Prompt Students to Cultivate Resiliency

- Difficulties make you stronger
- How will you overcome this setback
- Determination
- Positive attitude

Avoiding Negative Thinking

Marzano and Heflebower (2012) reviewed two types of negative thinking: *emotional thinking* and *worry*. Emotional thinking involves allowing one's emotions to dictate one's thoughts and actions. For example, a student who feels angry about receiving a poor grade and tells his teacher that she is unreasonable is engaging in emotional thinking. Worry involves persistent negative thinking about various possible outcomes of events. A student who worries that she will fail an upcoming test and that her failure will keep her from getting into the college she wants to attend might allow her anxiety to keep her awake all night right before the test. As a result, she might perform poorly on the test because she was worried about it—not because she wasn't prepared for it.

In ELA, a student engaged in emotional thinking might feel embarrassed by a wrong answer he gave during a class discussion. In his embarrassment, the student decides that he is not going to participate in class discussions any more. Not only will his participation grade suffer, but he will also miss out on opportunities to gain a deeper understanding of the books his class is studying through dialogue with other students and the teacher.

In mathematics, a student encumbered by worry might be so concerned about finishing a quiz within the time allotted that she rushes through it, not taking time to check her answers. Although she finishes in plenty of time, she might still receive a poor grade because her anxiety kept her from using effective mathematical techniques, such as double-checking answers.

As before, avoiding negative thinking starts with understanding its characteristics and one's propensity to exhibit those characteristics. A teacher begins by presenting students with information about emotional thinking and worry. Next, the teacher asks students to examine their own propensity to either one of these two types of thought. To this end, Marzano and Heflebower (2012) offered the following survey questions regarding worry.

Do you often:

- Find yourself thinking about bad things that might happen in the future?
- Feel overwhelmed?
- Feel unable to control your anxious feelings?
- Worry about disappointing or not pleasing others?
- Feel trapped in or avoid social situations where it might be difficult to escape if you wanted to?
- Experience racing or disturbing thoughts that you're unable to get out of your mind?
- Habitually do things like check the clock, check the door locks, or wash your hands even though you know it isn't necessary?
- Feel that you must be perfect?
- Feel that anxiety interferes with your daily life?
- Fear being out of control?
- Find yourself frequently using words such as *can't*, *should*, and *have to*?
- Push yourself to do more, even when you're physically and mentally exhausted? (p. 148)

Once students become aware of their own tendencies for negative thinking and the situations in which they tend to exhibit such thinking, they can be provided with simple strategies for alleviating negative thinking, such as monitoring their inner dialogue with an eye toward keeping it positive and being well-prepared for activities that typically generate negative thinking, like tests.

Words and Phrases That Prompt Students to Avoid Negative Thinking

- Is that what you feel or what you think
- Take a few minutes to settle down
- Take a few minutes to think
- Objective
- How do you feel
- What is the worst that could happen
- How likely is that to happen

Taking Various Perspectives

Taking various perspectives involves identifying the reasoning behind multiple (and often conflicting) perspectives on an issue. Marzano and Pickering (1997) and Marzano and Heflebower (2012) presented guidelines that can help students identify and defend their own and others' perspectives. Those guidelines are:

1. Identify and clearly articulate your perspective.
2. Explain the reasoning that supports your perspective.
3. Identify a different or opposing perspective.
4. Explain the reasoning that supports the different or opposing perspective.

For example, two ELA students reading *Great Expectations* have entirely different perspectives about the character of Estella. One student sees her as cruel, cold, and calculating. Another sees her as a victim of Miss Havisham's machinations, a girl who is unable to recognize that she loves and respects Pip. Although the two students disagree, their teacher asks them to try to explain the reasoning behind the other's perspective. One determines that although she has a negative perspective of Estella, the character can also be seen in a positive light, especially when she explains that she doesn't want to deceive and entrap Pip (as she has done to so many other men). The student with an initially positive perspective about Estella recognizes that Dickens portrays her as a woman who leads men on and then drops them when she no longer has a use for them. Even when she does marry, she only does it for money, and she is hard-hearted and cruel to Miss Havisham, her guardian since childhood. Although neither student changes her perspective, each gains a deeper understanding of the novel as a result of considering different perspectives.

In mathematics, an elementary student learning to add three-digit numbers always uses an algorithm to perform the operation. Another student uses a place value approach instead, adding the hundreds, the tens, the ones, and then adding those sums together. If the student who usually uses the algorithm learns the other student's approach and tries to explain the benefits of it, he might discover that it is a good way to check his work using the algorithm, thus increasing his overall accuracy.

Words and Phrases That Prompt Students to Take Various Perspectives

- What is another way to look at
- How might you think differently
- What reasons do you have for thinking that
- Why might someone disagree

Interacting Responsibly

Responsible interaction involves being accountable for the outcome of an interaction. Students who interact responsibly realize that their words and actions influence others and use assertive behavior and effective communication skills to maintain a positive tone. Assertive behavior includes recognizing one's legitimate needs and expressing them without harming or hurting others. Effective communication includes active listening, paraphrasing, questioning to achieve clarity, and responding nonverbally to a speaker's message.

For example, an ELA student realizes that a fellow student is struggling to express his ideas during a group discussion. Instead of trying to gain the floor and say his own ideas, the student asks the speaker questions to help him clarify areas of confusion or misunderstanding. The student also repeats back, in his own words, the substance of what his fellow student has just said (paraphrasing) or nods his head and smiles to encourage the speaker to keep speaking. When the listening student is given an opportunity to state his ideas, he connects them to his fellow students' ideas, allowing the group to come to a deeper understanding than any single person's ideas would allow.

In mathematics, students are sharing supplies to build models for various mathematical concepts. A student who has planned and collected materials for his model sees another student taking materials from his work station. Instead of reacting aggressively, the student calmly approaches the offending peer and asks him to stop taking materials from his work station. The student assertively explains why he needs the materials back. He also offers to listen to his peer's ideas and help him identify alternative materials that he could use to construct the model. Alternatively, both students might approach the teacher together to find out if extra materials could be obtained.

Words and Phrases That Prompt Students to Interact Responsibly

- What can you do to keep this situation positive
- What are your legitimate needs
- How can you improve the situation
- What did he/she just say
- What questions might you ask to clarify

Handling Controversy and Conflict Resolution

Controversy occurs when two people with incompatible beliefs disagree. *Conflict* occurs when one person is getting in the way of another's goals. For example, if two group members have different ideas about the best way to accomplish a task, they are engaged in controversy. If two different groups both need to use the same book for research, they are engaged in conflict. Teachers can teach their students about the differences between controversy and conflict. For example, a teacher might point out to her students that although controversy and conflict are inevitable, they have choices about how they react to them. Controversy is usually beneficial (if handled appropriately) because it leads to more and better ideas. Conflict, in contrast, should be resolved as soon as possible. David Johnson and Roger Johnson (2005) suggested that conflicts be resolved through negotiation and offered a six-step process for those negotiations:

1. **State the goal**—Each party states what they want or need.
2. **State feelings**—Each party explains how they feel about the conflict situation.
3. **State the reasons for wants and feelings**—Each party explains why they want or need what they do and why they feel the way they do.
4. **Reverse perspectives**—Each party examines the issue from the other party's point of view.
5. **Create three potential agreements**—The parties work together to generate three possible outcomes so that the one most advantageous to both parties can be selected.
6. **Settle**—The parties select one agreement and agree to abide by it.

Both controversy and conflict are inevitable in daily life, and students who understand how to approach controversy and conflict will have more successful interactions with others.

For example, a student who thinks that his ELA group should do a presentation for their final product experiences controversy when another student prefers to create a written report. Both students explain why they think their idea is best: the advocate for a presentation prefers speaking to writing, and the advocate for a report prefers writing to speaking. The group decides to combine both ideas and do a presentation with an accompanying handout. The group also allows members who prefer to write to prepare the handout and PowerPoint presentation while those who prefer to speak lead the classroom discussion during the presentation.

In mathematics, two students experience conflict when each needs to use the school's statistical analysis program, which is only installed on one computer. The two students enter into negotiations to try to resolve the conflict, comparing schedules and computing needs to work out a timeline that will allow both students to complete their work before their project deadlines.

Words and Phrases That Prompt Students to Resolve Controversy and Conflict

- What is getting in your way
- Why do you think
- Opposite perspective
- What are your reasons for
- Is there a way to achieve everyone's goals

In summary, the ten cognitive and seven conative strategies presented here can be used by teachers to infuse 21st century thinking and reasoning skills that correlate directly to the CCSS into classroom instruction. Each of the skills can be applied in ELA and mathematics, and teachers can prompt students to use each of the cognitive and conative skills by using the specific words and phrases listed in this chapter. To monitor students' progress with the knowledge and skills articulated in the practice standards addressed in this chapter and the content standards addressed in chapter 1, teachers can use proficiency scales. We now address how those scales can be developed as well as the process used to develop the proficiency scales featured in part II of this book.

3

Measuring Student Performance on the Common Core State Standards

Forty-five states and the District of Columbia have adopted the CCSS as of the writing of this book. According to Kendall (2011), this widespread adoption means that "the Common Core will dominate dialogue in the United States; the number of states that have signed on represents a critical mass. It will be difficult to work as a teaching professional and be part of the dialogue of education without sharing the context of the Common Core" (p. 55). Most of the teachers in the United States will be expected to ensure that their students are proficient with the CCSS. The transition from previous state standards to the CCSS may not be easy for all teachers. Rothman (2011) predicted that "the adoption of the Common Core State Standards, while hugely significant, pales in scope to what must be done to implement them" (p. 119).

The CCSS describe what students should know or be able to do as a result of instruction in school. As discussed in the introduction, the authors of the CCSS strove to resolve many of the problems with previous standards efforts, including multidimensionality. Each standard in the CCSS was designed to focus on a single dimension of content, rather than combining many dimensions into one standard. Porter, McMaken, Hwang, and Yang (2011b) measured whether or not the CCSS achieved a greater level of focus than previous state standards and found that, when standards from all the states were aggregated into one group of standards, "the aggregated state standards are less focused than is the Common Core" (p. 108). However, when Porter and his colleagues compared the Common Core to sets of standards from individual states, they found that "the Common Core has more focus than some states' standards and less focus than other states' standards" (p. 108). Although more research will shed further light on this issue, it seems that the Common Core is generally more focused than most previous sets of standards but could have been even more focused. Because of this, it is important for teachers to "take the time to analyze each standard and identify its essential concepts and skills" (Bell, 2011, p. 113). For example, mathematics standard 4.OA.A.3 says:

> Solve multistep word problems posed with whole numbers and having whole-number answers using the four operations, including problems in which remainders must be interpreted. Represent these problems using equations with a letter standing for the unknown quantity. Assess the reasonableness of answers using mental computation and estimation strategies including rounding. (NGA & CCSSO, 2010d, p. 29)

This single standard includes three sentences and at least eight different elements of knowledge and skill, as shown in table 3.1.

Table 3.1: Elements of Knowledge and Skills in Mathematics Standard 4.OA.A.3

Knowledge	Skills
Understand the role of letters in equations	Solve multistep word problems
Assess the reasonableness of answers	Add, subtract, multiply, and divide whole numbers
Interpret remainders	Represent multistep word problems with equations
	Use mental computation
	Use estimation strategies (such as rounding)

Once teachers have identified the essential concepts and skills in the standards, they can focus their instruction around those specific elements of knowledge and skill. One important aspect of implementing the CCSS is to translate them into proficiency scales, which can then be used to measure and track students' progress.

Proficiency Scales for the CCSS

Proficiency scales make the CCSS more manageable. Teachers can use the concepts and skills they have identified from the standards to create these scales. Here we explain how to articulate target, simpler, and more complex goals to fit each level of a four-point proficiency scale.

Breaking Down Learning Goals

Marzano (2009) explained that a learning goal is a "statement of what students will know or be able to do" (p. 13). He warned teachers not to confuse learning goals with activities or assignments (things students will be asked to do to work on the learning goal), and he encouraged teachers to think in terms of two types of learning goals: declarative (knowledge that students will *understand*) and procedural (procedures or processes that students will be able to *perform*). Marzano (2009) provided sentence stems for each type of learning goal.

- **Declarative:** Students will understand ______________________.
- **Procedural:** Students will be able to ______________________.

Although the verb *understand* is appropriate when designing learning goals for declarative knowledge, some may find that it is not specific enough. In other words, *understand* does not describe what students will do to demonstrate their understanding of the knowledge involved in the learning goal. Because of this, we often use other verbs, such as *describe* or *explain* when writing learning goals for declarative knowledge. Occasionally, the phrase *will be able to* is also used with declarative learning goals, as in "students will be able to explain the defining characteristics of fables, fairy tales, and myths." These declarative statements still describe knowledge that students will understand, as opposed to what students will be able to perform. Once teachers are familiar with the distinction between declarative and procedural knowledge, the use of alternative verbs is entirely appropriate.

Once specific knowledge and skill elements have been identified from the CCSS (as shown in table 3.1), teachers need to differentiate the elements by creating learning goals for each at different levels of difficulty. A good way to think of this is in terms of a *target* learning goal, a *simpler* learning goal, and a *complex* learning goal. For example, a teacher might create the following target learning goal from the skill element "interpret remainders" in table 3.1.

- **Target:** The student will solve division word problems in which remainders must be interpreted.

The teacher would then create a simpler and more complex learning goal for the same skill.

- **Simpler:** The student will recognize or recall specific vocabulary such as *dividend*, *divisor*, and *remainder* and will identify remainders when solving division number problems (non-word problems).
- **Complex:** The student will investigate how remainders are expressed (for example, with fractions or decimal notation) or otherwise dealt with (for example, dropping, rounding, or sharing) in the real world.

Notice that the simpler learning goal involves recognizing or recalling vocabulary and performing basic processes related to the target learning goal. The complex learning goal involves more complex processes, such as investigation and real-world application.

Creating Proficiency Scales

Once a teacher has identified essential knowledge and skill elements from the CCSS and created target, simpler, and complex learning goals for them, he or she can insert those learning goals into a proficiency scale. A proficiency scale presents knowledge or skills as a continuum of simpler, target, and complex goals that students sequentially work toward. Table 3.2 presents a generic proficiency scale.

Table 3.2: Generic Proficiency Scale

Score 4.0	Complex learning goal	
	Score 3.5	*In addition to score 3.0 performance, partial success at score 4.0 content*
Score 3.0	Target learning goal	
	Score 2.5	*No major errors or omissions regarding score 2.0 content, and partial success at score 3.0 content*
Score 2.0	Simpler learning goal	
	Score 1.5	*Partial success at score 2.0 content, and major errors or omissions regarding score 3.0 content*
Score 1.0	With help, partial success at score 2.0 content and score 3.0 content	
	Score 0.5	*With help, partial success at score 2.0 content but not at score 3.0 content*
Score 0.0	Even with help, no success	

Source: Adapted from Marzano, 2009, p. 67.

The generic proficiency scale shown in table 3.2 can be customized by inserting specific target, simpler, and complex learning goals at the 2.0, 3.0, and 4.0 levels. For example, the target, simpler, and complex learning goals related to interpreting remainders that were presented previously can be placed in the generic scale to create the topic-specific scale shown in table 3.3 (page 50).

Table 3.3: Proficiency Scale for Interpreting Remainders

Score 4.0	The student will investigate how remainders are expressed (for example, with fractions or decimal notation) or otherwise dealt with (for example, dropping, rounding, or sharing) in the real world.	
	Score 3.5	*In addition to score 3.0 performance, partial success at score 4.0 content*
Score 3.0	The student will: • Solve division word problems in which remainders must be interpreted	
	Score 2.5	*No major errors or omissions regarding score 2.0 content, and partial success at score 3.0 content*
Score 2.0	The student will recognize or recall specific vocabulary, such as: • *Dividend, divisor, remainder* The student will perform basic processes, such as: • Identify remainders when solving division number problems (non-word problems)	
	Score 1.5	*Partial success at score 2.0 content, and major errors or omissions regarding score 3.0 content*
Score 1.0	With help, partial success at score 2.0 content and score 3.0 content	
	Score 0.5	*With help, partial success at score 2.0 content but not at score 3.0 content*
Score 0.0	Even with help, no success	

As shown in table 3.3, the target learning goal has been inserted at the 3.0 level of the scale, the simpler learning goal has been placed at the 2.0 level of the scale, and the complex learning goal is used for the 4.0 level of the scale. The scale contains two additional whole-point scores (1.0 and 0.0) and four half-point scores (0.5, 1.5, 2.5, 3.5). The descriptors for these scores do not change from scale to scale. That is, the only content that changes from one scale to the next is the 2.0, 3.0, and 4.0 content. The half-point scores are used to indicate that a student has moved beyond one whole-point score on the scale but is not yet demonstrating proficiency at the next whole-point score. For example, a score of 3.5 indicates that a student correctly answered or performed 2.0 and 3.0 items and tasks, but only earned partial credit on score 4.0 items or tasks. A score of 2.5 indicates that a student has correctly answered *all* the items or correctly performed *all* the tasks regarding the 2.0 content, but has only correctly answered *some* of the items or correctly performed *some* of the tasks regarding the 3.0 content. A score of 1.5 indicates that a student has earned partial credit on items or tasks involving 2.0 content but missed all other types of items. A score of 1.0 indicates that a student missed all the items and tasks on an assessment when working on it independently but was able to demonstrate partial proficiency on 2.0 and 3.0 content with help from the teacher. In other words, the first time the student completed the assessment, she was unable to correctly answer any items or complete any tasks. However, when the teacher sat down with the student and used cues, prompts, questions, and other supports, the student was able to answer or complete *some* of the 2.0 and 3.0 items or tasks. A score of 0.5 indicates that in the same situation (no success independently, so the teacher provides support), a student had partial success with 2.0 items and tasks only. A score of 0.0 indicates that even with the teacher's help, the student was not successful with any of the content.

Marzano Research Laboratory Scales for the CCSS

To help educators implement the CCSS, Marzano Research Laboratory (MRL) convened a group of researchers and teachers to identify the essential knowledge and skills in the CCSS, create learning goals for those knowledge and skill elements, and organize the learning goals into measurement topics and proficiency scales for the CCSS. To create these scales, the work group initially analyzed the ELA and mathematics content standards to identify specific measurement topics for the CCSS.

Designing a System of Measurement Topics

As described in chapter 1, the ELA and mathematics CCSS have somewhat different organization structures. While we adhere to the basic structure of both sets of standards in this book, we also provide a new organizational structure, which we refer to as a *measurement topic*. A measurement topic refers to a category of knowledge or skills that usually extends across several grade levels. The measurement topics were created using an approach similar to the one used to create the categories for the key words and phrases from the practice standards: we identified the overarching topics or themes that were addressed by multiple standards across multiple grade levels. For example, in ELA the second standard for Reading Literature (RL) and Reading Informational Text (RI) at every grade level addresses the topic of themes and central ideas. Therefore, we included the second RL and RI standard at each grade level in the Themes and Central Ideas measurement topic. In mathematics, there is a standard at every grade level (except 6 and 8) that addresses the topic of shapes. Therefore, we grouped these standards together under the measurement topic Shapes.

Organizing the CCSS into measurement topics allows teachers to easily see the progression of knowledge from one grade level to the next. Within each measurement topic at each grade level, we present scales like the one depicted in table 3.3. These scales include the content of the ELA and mathematics CCSS slightly reorganized to highlight the different levels of difficulty within the content articulated in a single standard. The score 3.0 level—the target learning goal—is usually taken directly from the standards. As we explain at the end of this chapter, the 4.0 level takes the standard in focus to a deeper level and is created by each individual teacher. The 2.0 level of each scale identifies specific vocabulary and basic processes related to the measurement topic elements at that grade level. This is not to say the vocabulary terms identified in the scales in part II of this book are the only terms needed for success. Rather, teachers should regard the vocabulary terms as a starting point from which we encourage schools and districts to further identify additional vocabulary terms that they believe are important for their students' success with each measurement topic.

As seen in table 3.1 (page 48), a single standard can list multiple types of information and skill. The scales for each measurement topic are designed to indicate which types of information and skill are easier and which types are more complex. To identify measurement topics and elements within those topics, MRL's work group used the following two guidelines: (1) limit the number of measurement topics and (2) limit the number of elements within each measurement topic.

Limiting the Number of Measurement Topics

As described in chapter 1, one of the goals when creating the CCSS was to make them fewer in number than previous efforts. While that goal has been achieved to a certain extent, the ELA and mathematics CCSS still represent an overwhelming task to the classroom teacher. Consequently, we have tried to limit the number of measurement topics, focusing on those that teachers would most likely want to address multiple times over the course of a year. In other words, we worked to group related standards together as much as possible in order to create a parsimonious model of measurement topics. In some cases, if a standard had substandards (denoted by a, b, c, and so on), we chose to include only the substandards and not the overarching standard. In other cases, we included the overarching standard but not the substandards. Table 3.4 (page 52) provides a list of the measurement topics we identified in ELA and mathematics. The boldface words are the CCSS strands in ELA and the CCSS domains in mathematics.

Table 3.4: Measurement Topics in ELA and Mathematics

English Language Arts	Mathematics
Reading: Questioning, Inference, and Interpretation; Themes and Central Ideas; Story Elements; Connections; Word Impact and Use; Academic Vocabulary; Text Structures and Features; Point of View / Purpose; Visual/Auditory Media and Information Sources; Argument and Reasoning; Literary Comparisons and Source Material; Rhetorical Criticism; Fluency	**Number and Quantity:** Number Names, Counting, Compare Numbers, Place Value, Foundations of Fractions, Fractions, Adding and Subtracting Fractions, Multiplying and Dividing Fractions, Decimal Concepts, Ratios and Unit Rates, Rational and Irrational Numbers, Exponents and Roots, Quantities, Operations With Complex Numbers, Polynomial Identities and Equations
Reading Foundations: Print Concepts, Phonological Awareness, Phonics and Word Analysis	**Operations and Algebra:** Addition and Subtraction, Multiplication and Division, Properties of Operations, Expressions and Equations, Factors and Multiples, Patterns, Equations and Inequalities, Dependent and Independent Variables, Slope, Systems of Equations, Structure of Expressions, Equivalent Expressions, Arithmetic Operations on Polynomials, Zeroes and Factors of Polynomials, Polynomial Identities, Rational Expressions, Creating Equations, Reasoning to Solve Equations, Solving Quadratic Equations, Graphs of Equations and Inequalities
Writing: Argumentative; Informative/Explanatory; Narrative; Task, Purpose, and Audience; Revise and Edit; Technology; Research; Access and Organize Information	**Functions:** Functions, Interpret Functions, Graph Functions, Properties of Functions, Model Relationships, Building New Functions, Linear and Exponential Models, Interpret Linear and Exponential Functions, Trigonometric Functions, Periodic Phenomena, Trigonometric Identities
Speaking and Listening: Collaborative Discussions, Evaluate Presented Information, Speech Writing, Presentation and Delivery	**Geometry:** Shapes, Compose and Decompose Shapes, Lines and Symmetry, Coordinate System, Area, Perimeter, Surface Area, Volume, Scale Drawings, Angles, Pythagorean Theorem, Congruence and Similarity, Transformations, Geometric Theorems, Geometric Constructions, Dilations, Theorems Involving Similarity, Trigonometric Ratios, Geometric Trigonometry, Circle Theorems, Arc Length and Sectors, Conic Sections, Geometric Modeling
Language: Grammar, Sentences, Capitalization and Punctuation, Spelling, Language Conventions, Context Clues, Word Origins and Roots, Reference Materials, Word Relationships	**Measurement, Data, Statistics, and Probability:** Measurement, Represent and Interpret Data, Time, Money, Data Distributions, Random Sampling, Probability, Multivariable Data Distributions, Linear Models, Rules of Probability

As shown in table 3.4, there are thirty-seven measurement topics in ELA: thirteen related to reading, three related to reading foundations, eight related to writing, four related to speaking and listening, and nine related to language. In mathematics, there are seventy-nine different topics: fifteen related to number and quantity, twenty related to operations and algebra, eleven related to functions, twenty-three related to geometry, and ten related to measurement, data, statistics, and probability. This is not to say that each measurement topic is addressed at each grade level. Rather, some measurement topics apply only to one or two grade levels, especially in mathematics. For example, the measurement topic Rules of Probability contains only one scale for high school–level math. Table 3.5 shows how many measurement topics are specific to each grade level.

Table 3.5: Number of Measurement Topics by Grade Level

	ELA	Mathematics
K	34	9
1	34	9
2	34	9
3	35	14
4	35	17
5	35	12
6	33	13
7	33	14
8	33	13
9–10	32	**HS Number and Quantity:** 5
11–12	32	**HS Algebra:** 12
		HS Functions: 11
		HS Geometry: 15
		HS Measurement, Data, Statistics, and Probability: 6

Limiting the Number of Elements Within Each Measurement Topic

As explained previously, it is important to maintain a manageable number of measurement topics in a standards-based system. An important consideration, then, in creating measurement topics is *covariance*. Covariance has been discussed in more technical terms in other works (Marzano, 2006; Marzano & Haystead, 2008), but here we provide a brief explanation of the concept. Essentially, when used in regard to the elements of measurement topics, covariance refers to how closely related elements are within a measurement topic. As an example of a set of covarying elements in a measurement topic, consider the Writing measurement topic of Access and Organize Information at third grade. There are three bulleted 3.0 elements:

- Recall information from experiences or gather information from grade-appropriate print and digital sources (W.3.8)
- Take brief notes on sources and sort evidence into categories (W.3.8)
- Use text features and search tools (for example, keywords, sidebars, hyperlinks) to locate information relevant to a given grade-appropriate topic (RI.3.5)

The main focus of this measurement topic involves effectively interacting with information. Each of the three bulleted elements describes a specific way that students can demonstrate their ability to effectively interact with information, and a student demonstrating proficiency with, for example, using text features and search tools to locate information relevant to his topic, might simultaneously be demonstrating his skill with gathering information from grade-appropriate print and digital sources. In the CCSS, these two dimensions are placed in separate strands (Reading Informational Text and Writing), but our analysis showed that these covarying elements should be grouped together under one measurement topic. Therefore, they appear together in Access and Organize Information.

In addition to making sure that elements within a measurement topic covary, it is also important to keep the number of elements (that is, the number of bullets in the 3.0 section of each scale) for each measurement topic small. If there are too many elements within each measurement topic, it can counteract the benefits of keeping the number of measurement topics small. Tables 3.6 and 3.7 depict how many elements appear at each grade level for each measurement topic.

Table 3.6: Number of Elements Per Measurement Topic Per Grade Level for ELA

	11–12	9–10	8	7	6	5	4	3	2	1	K	Total by Measurement Topic
Reading												
Questioning, Inference, and Interpretation	1	1	1	1	1	1	1	1	1	1	1	11
Themes and Central Ideas	2	2	2	2	2	2	2	2	2	2	3	23
Story Elements	1	1	1	1	1	1	1	1	1	1	1	11
Connections	1	1	1	1	1	1	1	1	1	1	1	11
Word Impact and Use	3	3	3	4	3	2	3	2	2	2	2	29
Academic Vocabulary	3	3	3	3	3	1	1	1	2	3	2	25
Text Structures and Features	2	2	2	2	2	2	3	3	1	1	2	22
Point of View / Purpose	2	2	2	2	2	2	2	1	2	1	1	19
Visual/Auditory Media and Information Sources	2	1	2	2	2	2	2	2	2	3	2	22
Argument and Reasoning	1	2	2	1	1	1	1	1	1	1	1	13
Literary Comparisons and Source Material	1	1	1	1	1	1	1	1	1	1	1	11
Rhetorical Criticism	1	1	1	1	1	1	1	1	1	1	1	11
Fluency	1	1	1	1	1	3	3	3	3	3	2	22
Reading Foundations												
Print Concepts	n/a	n/a	n/a	n/a	n/a	n/a	n/a	n/a	n/a	2	5	7
Phonological Awareness	n/a	n/a	n/a	n/a	n/a	n/a	n/a	n/a	n/a	3	4	7
Phonics and Word Analysis	n/a	n/a	n/a	n/a	n/a	1	1	2	3	3	2	12
Writing												
Argumentative	5	5	5	5	5	4	4	4	5	4	3	49
Informative/Explanatory	6	6	6	6	6	5	5	4	3	3	2	52
Narrative	5	5	5	5	5	5	5	4	4	4	3	50
Task, Purpose, and Audience	1	1	1	1	1	1	1	1	n/a	n/a	n/a	8
Revise and Edit	5	5	5	5	5	5	3	3	3	3	3	45
Technology	1	2	3	3	3	3	3	2	1	1	1	23
Research	3	3	1	1	1	1	1	1	1	1	1	15
Access and Organize Information	3	3	3	3	3	2	2	3	2	2	1	27

	11–12	9–10	8	7	6	5	4	3	2	1	K	Total by Measurement Topic
Speaking and Listening												
Collaborative Discussions	3	3	3	3	3	3	3	3	2	2	1	29
Evaluate Presented Information	2	2	3	2	2	2	2	2	2	2	2	23
Speech Writing	3	1	1	1	1	1	1	1	1	1	1	13
Presentation and Delivery	2	2	3	3	3	2	2	3	3	3	2	28
Language												
Grammar	2	2	4	3	5	5	5	8	5	8	3	50
Sentences	n/a	n/a	n/a	n/a	n/a	1	1	1	1	1	2	7
Capitalization and Punctuation	1	2	2	1	1	4	3	4	3	3	2	26
Spelling	1	1	1	1	1	1	2	3	2	2	2	17
Language Conventions	1	1	1	1	2	1	2	2	1	n/a	n/a	12
Context Clues	1	1	1	1	1	2	2	2	2	2	1	16
Word Origins and Roots	1	1	1	1	1	1	1	4	4	2	1	18
Reference Materials	1	1	1	1	1	1	1	1	1	n/a	n/a	9
Word Relationships	n/a	n/a	1	1	1	1	1	1	1	2	3	12
Total	**68**	**68**	**73**	**70**	**72**	**72**	**73**	**79**	**70**	**75**	**65**	**785**

Table 3.7: Number of Elements Per Measurement Topic Per Grade Level for Mathematics

	HS	8	7	6	5	4	3	2	1	K	Total by Measurement Topic
Number and Quantity											
Number Names	n/a	n/a	n/a	n/a	n/a	n/a	n/a	n/a	2	2	4
Counting	n/a	n/a	n/a	n/a	n/a	n/a	n/a	n/a	n/a	2	2
Compare Numbers	n/a	n/a	n/a	n/a	n/a	n/a	n/a	n/a	n/a	1	1
Place Value	n/a	n/a	n/a	n/a	n/a	2	1	2	2	3	10
Foundations of Fractions	n/a	n/a	n/a	n/a	n/a	n/a	1	n/a	n/a	n/a	1
Fractions	n/a	n/a	n/a	n/a	n/a	1	3	n/a	n/a	n/a	4
Adding and Subtracting Fractions	n/a	n/a	n/a	n/a	2	3	n/a	n/a	n/a	n/a	5
Multiplying and Dividing Fractions	n/a	n/a	n/a	1	2	1	n/a	n/a	n/a	n/a	4
Decimal Concepts	n/a	n/a	n/a	n/a	3	1	n/a	n/a	n/a	n/a	4
Ratios and Unit Rates	n/a	n/a	3	1	n/a	n/a	n/a	n/a	n/a	n/a	4
Rational and Irrational Numbers	3	1	n/a	3	n/a	n/a	n/a	n/a	n/a	n/a	7
Exponents and Roots	1	3	n/a	n/a	n/a	n/a	n/a	n/a	n/a	n/a	4
Quantities	2	n/a	n/a	n/a	n/a	n/a	n/a	n/a	n/a	n/a	2
Operations With Complex Numbers	2	n/a	n/a	n/a	n/a	n/a	n/a	n/a	n/a	n/a	2
Polynomial Identities and Equations	1	n/a	n/a	n/a	n/a	n/a	n/a	n/a	n/a	n/a	1

continued →

	HS	8	7	6	5	4	3	2	1	K	Total by Measurement Topic
Operations and Algebra											
Addition and Subtraction	n/a	n/a	2	1	1	1	1	4	5	3	18
Multiplication and Division	n/a	n/a	3	1	2	3	4	1	n/a	n/a	14
Properties of Operations	n/a	n/a	n/a	n/a	n/a	n/a	2	n/a	2	n/a	4
Expressions and Equations	n/a	n/a	2	2	2	1	2	n/a	n/a	n/a	9
Factors and Multiples	n/a	n/a	n/a	n/a	n/a	2	n/a	n/a	n/a	n/a	2
Patterns	n/a	n/a	n/a	n/a	2	1	n/a	n/a	n/a	n/a	3
Equations and Inequalities	2	1	4	2	n/a	n/a	n/a	n/a	n/a	n/a	9
Dependent and Independent Variables	n/a	n/a	n/a	1	n/a	n/a	n/a	n/a	n/a	n/a	1
Slope	n/a	3	n/a	n/a	n/a	n/a	n/a	n/a	n/a	n/a	3
Systems of Equations	2	2	n/a	n/a	n/a	n/a	n/a	n/a	n/a	n/a	4
Structure of Expressions	2	n/a	n/a	n/a	n/a	n/a	n/a	n/a	n/a	n/a	2
Equivalent Expressions	3	n/a	n/a	n/a	n/a	n/a	n/a	n/a	n/a	n/a	3
Arithmetic Operations on Polynomials	1	n/a	n/a	n/a	n/a	n/a	n/a	n/a	n/a	n/a	1
Zeroes and Factors of Polynomials	2	n/a	n/a	n/a	n/a	n/a	n/a	n/a	n/a	n/a	2
Polynomial Identities	1	n/a	n/a	n/a	n/a	n/a	n/a	n/a	n/a	n/a	1
Rational Expressions	1	n/a	n/a	n/a	n/a	n/a	n/a	n/a	n/a	n/a	1
Creating Equations	4	n/a	n/a	n/a	n/a	n/a	n/a	n/a	n/a	n/a	4
Reasoning to Solve Equations	2	n/a	n/a	n/a	n/a	n/a	n/a	n/a	n/a	n/a	2
Solving Quadratic Equations	2	n/a	n/a	n/a	n/a	n/a	n/a	n/a	n/a	n/a	2
Graphs of Equations and Inequalities	3	n/a	n/a	n/a	n/a	n/a	n/a	n/a	n/a	n/a	3
Functions											
Functions	3	1	n/a	n/a	n/a	n/a	n/a	n/a	n/a	n/a	4
Interpret Functions	5	2	n/a	n/a	n/a	n/a	n/a	n/a	n/a	n/a	7
Graph Functions	5	n/a	n/a	n/a	n/a	n/a	n/a	n/a	n/a	n/a	5
Properties of Functions	3	n/a	n/a	n/a	n/a	n/a	n/a	n/a	n/a	n/a	3
Model Relationships	2	n/a	n/a	n/a	n/a	n/a	n/a	n/a	n/a	n/a	2
Building New Functions	1	n/a	n/a	n/a	n/a	n/a	n/a	n/a	n/a	n/a	1
Linear and Exponential Models	3	n/a	n/a	n/a	n/a	n/a	n/a	n/a	n/a	n/a	3
Interpret Linear and Exponential Functions	1	n/a	n/a	n/a	n/a	n/a	n/a	n/a	n/a	n/a	1
Trigonometric Functions	1	n/a	n/a	n/a	n/a	n/a	n/a	n/a	n/a	n/a	1
Periodic Phenomena	1	n/a	n/a	n/a	n/a	n/a	n/a	n/a	n/a	n/a	1
Trigonometric Identities	1	n/a	n/a	n/a	n/a	n/a	n/a	n/a	n/a	n/a	1

	HS	8	7	6	5	4	3	2	1	K	Total by Measurement Topic
Geometry											
Shapes	1	n/a	1	n/a	1	2	1	1	1	1	9
Compose and Decompose Shapes	n/a	n/a	n/a	n/a	n/a	n/a	1	3	2	1	7
Lines and Symmetry	n/a	n/a	n/a	n/a	n/a	2	n/a	n/a	n/a	n/a	2
Coordinate System	3	n/a	n/a	2	2	n/a	n/a	n/a	n/a	n/a	7
Area	n/a	n/a	2	1	n/a	1	3	n/a	n/a	n/a	7
Perimeter	n/a	n/a	n/a	n/a	n/a	1	3	n/a	n/a	n/a	4
Surface Area	n/a	n/a	1	2	n/a	n/a	n/a	n/a	n/a	n/a	3
Volume	1	1	1	1	2	n/a	n/a	n/a	n/a	n/a	6
Scale Drawings	n/a	n/a	2	n/a	n/a	n/a	n/a	n/a	n/a	n/a	2
Angles	n/a	1	1	n/a	n/a	1	n/a	n/a	n/a	n/a	3
Pythagorean Theorem	n/a	2	n/a	n/a	n/a	n/a	n/a	n/a	n/a	n/a	2
Congruence and Similarity	4	1	n/a	n/a	n/a	n/a	n/a	n/a	n/a	n/a	5
Transformations	4	1	n/a	n/a	n/a	n/a	n/a	n/a	n/a	n/a	5
Geometric Theorems	3	n/a	n/a	n/a	n/a	n/a	n/a	n/a	n/a	n/a	3
Geometric Constructions	1	n/a	n/a	n/a	n/a	n/a	n/a	n/a	n/a	n/a	1
Dilations	2	n/a	n/a	n/a	n/a	n/a	n/a	n/a	n/a	n/a	2
Theorems Involving Similarity	2	n/a	n/a	n/a	n/a	n/a	n/a	n/a	n/a	n/a	2
Trigonometric Ratios	1	n/a	n/a	n/a	n/a	n/a	n/a	n/a	n/a	n/a	1
Geometric Trigonometry	2	n/a	n/a	n/a	n/a	n/a	n/a	n/a	n/a	n/a	2
Circle Theorems	2	n/a	n/a	n/a	n/a	n/a	n/a	n/a	n/a	n/a	2
Arc Length and Sectors	2	n/a	n/a	n/a	n/a	n/a	n/a	n/a	n/a	n/a	2
Conic Sections	1	n/a	n/a	n/a	n/a	n/a	n/a	n/a	n/a	n/a	1
Geometric Modeling	2	n/a	n/a	n/a	n/a	n/a	n/a	n/a	n/a	n/a	2
Measurement, Data, Statistics, and Probability											
Measurement	n/a	n/a	n/a	n/a	1	1	1	2	1	1	7
Represent and Interpret Data	n/a	n/a	n/a	n/a	1	1	3	2	1	1	9
Time	n/a	n/a	n/a	n/a	n/a	n/a	1	1	1	n/a	3
Money	n/a	n/a	n/a	n/a	n/a	n/a	n/a	1	n/a	n/a	1
Data Distributions	3	n/a	1	3	n/a	n/a	n/a	n/a	n/a	n/a	7
Random Sampling	4	n/a	3	n/a	n/a	n/a	n/a	n/a	n/a	n/a	7
Probability	4	n/a	3	n/a	n/a	n/a	n/a	n/a	n/a	n/a	7
Multivariable Data Distributions	5	2	n/a	n/a	n/a	n/a	n/a	n/a	n/a	n/a	7
Linear Models	2	n/a	n/a	n/a	n/a	n/a	n/a	n/a	n/a	n/a	2
Rules of Probability	2	n/a	n/a	n/a	n/a	n/a	n/a	n/a	n/a	n/a	2
Total	**111**	**21**	**29**	**21**	**21**	**25**	**27**	**17**	**17**	**15**	**304**

Typically, we recommend no more than three or four elements per grade level. As seen in tables 3.6 and 3.7, this is usually the case, with a few notable exceptions. For example, several ELA topics that address Writing and Language contain more elements. This is because it is typical for different elements of these topics to be taught during different grading periods. For example, consider the measurement topic of Grammar at third grade. It has eight elements, two of which might be taught during the first quarter, two during the second quarter, two during the third quarter, and two during the fourth quarter.

As explained previously, the elements within each measurement topic are designed to be covariant. That is, the bulleted 3.0 elements contain dimensions of knowledge that are closely related or overlap. This means that teachers can teach them at the same time. So, instead of planning a separate unit for each element of each measurement topic, teachers can plan to teach multiple elements during the same unit. Ideally, individual schools or districts would provide guidance to their teachers about which elements should be taught when.

Sequencing Content

A well-articulated set of measurement topics allows a school or district to give its teachers clear guidance regarding the order in which content should be taught and how much time should be spent on each topic. To do this, the school or district would identify which elements within a measurement topic should be taught during each grading period of the year. For example, table 3.8 shows an example of how a school or district might distribute measurement topic elements across four grading periods for third-grade mathematics.

Table 3.8 indicates that six measurement topics are addressed during each of four grading periods. Notice that not every element of a measurement topic is addressed each time it appears during a grading period. For example, the measurement topic Fractions contains three score 3.0 elements:

- Generate simple equivalent fractions (for example, $\frac{1}{2} = \frac{2}{4}$; $\frac{4}{6} = \frac{2}{3}$) and explain why they are equivalent
- Express whole numbers as fractions
- Use comparison symbols (<, >, and =) to compare fractions and justify the comparison of two fractions with the same numerator or same denominator

In table 3.8, only two of those elements, the first and second, are addressed during the third grading period. Notice that the first element is also addressed during the fourth grading period but then in conjunction with the third element of this measurement topic. This is because the first and second elements are related and the first and third elements are related. In the scenario shown in table 3.8, students would work on the first and second elements during the third grading period. During the fourth grading period, they would extend their understanding of the first element and use what they had already learned about the first element to learn about the third element.

Other elements are handled differently. For example, the measurement topic Expressions and Equations contains two score 3.0 elements:

- Solve two-step word problems using the four operations with a letter standing for the unknown quantity
- Assess the reasonableness of answers using mental computation and estimation strategies

As shown in table 3.8, the first element is studied by itself during the first grading period. During the second grading period, students use what they already know about the first element to learn about the second element, thus deepening their knowledge of the first element. In the third grading period, students study the second element by itself, deepening the knowledge they gained in the previous grading period.

Table 3.8: Sample Scope and Sequence for Third-Grade Mathematics

Measurement Topic	Number of Elements	Grading Period 1	Grading Period 2	Grading Period 3	Grading Period 4
Number and Quantity					
Place Value	1	1st element		1st element	
Foundations of Fractions	1			1st element	1st element
Fractions	3			1st element 2nd element	1st element 3rd element
Operations and Algebra					
Addition and Subtraction	1	1st element			
Multiplication and Division	4	1st element 4th element	2nd element 3rd element		
Properties of Operations	2	1st element 2nd element			
Expressions and Equations	2	1st element	1st element 2nd element	2nd element	
Geometry					
Shapes	1		1st element		
Compose and Decompose Shapes	1			1st element	
Area	3		1st element 2nd element		3rd element
Perimeter	3		1st element 2nd element	1st element 2nd element	3rd element
Measurement, Data, Statistics, and Probability					
Measurement	1				1st element
Represent and Interpret Data	3	1st element 2nd element	1st element 3rd element		
Time	1				1st element
Number of Topics Addressed		6	6	6	6

Developing Complex (4.0) Learning Targets

For the scales in this book, complex (4.0) learning targets are not included. Instead, we use the text, "In addition to score 3.0 performance, the student demonstrates in-depth inferences and applications that go beyond what was taught," for the 4.0 level of each scale in part II. This is because we believe that teachers can and should develop complex (4.0) learning targets for and along with their students. Using the resources provided in chapter 2 and in this chapter, this is easily done. Specifically, in chapter 2 we presented the various cognitive and conative strategies that were derived from the practice standards in the ELA and mathematics CCSS. These processes can be used to develop complex (4.0) learning targets. To illustrate, consider the scale for Word Relationships at grade 5 in table 3.9.

Table 3.9: Grade 5 Scale for Word Relationships

Score 4.0	In addition to score 3.0 performance, the student demonstrates in-depth inferences and applications that go beyond what was taught.	
	Score 3.5	*In addition to score 3.0 performance, partial success at score 4.0 content*
Score 3.0	The student will: • Use the relationship between particular grade-appropriate words (for example, synonyms, antonyms, homographs) to better understand each of the words (L.5.5c)	
	Score 2.5	*No major errors or omissions regarding score 2.0 content, and partial success at score 3.0 content*
Score 2.0	The student will recognize or recall specific vocabulary, such as: • *Antonym, homograph, relationship, synonym, word* The student will perform basic processes, such as: • Identify the relationship between particular grade-appropriate words (for example, synonyms, antonyms, homographs)	
	Score 1.5	*Partial success at score 2.0 content, and major errors or omissions regarding score 3.0 content*
Score 1.0	With help, partial success at score 2.0 content and score 3.0 content	
	Score 0.5	*With help, partial success at score 2.0 content but not at score 3.0 content*
Score 0.0	Even with help, no success	

Elements for scores 3.0 and 2.0 only have been identified in this scale (as they have been in all our scales). To create a complex (4.0) learning target for this scale, a teacher examines the ten cognitive and seven conative strategies from chapter 2 and selects one or more that best fit the score 3.0 content identified in the scale. In this case, the teacher selects the cognitive strategy of identifying basic relationships between ideas. Using that cognitive strategy, the teacher creates the following complex (4.0) learning target for the scale:

The student will compare and contrast the basic relationships expressed by synonyms, antonyms, and homographs.

To support teachers as they match the cognitive and conative strategies in chapter 2 to the different measurement topics, tables 3.10 and 3.11 (page 63) identify the cognitive and conative strategies that we believe best match each measurement topic in the scales. Teachers can use these tables to help create complex learning targets for each proficiency scale in part II (page 81).

Specific cognitive and conative strategies are best suited to particular measurement topics. For example, the measurement topic Area (found under Geometry in the mathematics scales) is a good match for five cognitive skills: generating conclusions, problem solving, experimenting, identifying basic relationships between ideas, and generating and manipulating mental images.

Table 3.10: Cognitive and Conative Strategies Matched to ELA Scale Measurement Topics

	COGNITIVE										CONATIVE						
	Generating conclusions	Identifying common logical errors	Presenting and supporting claims	Navigating digital sources	Problem solving	Decision making	Experimenting	Investigating	Identifying basic relationships between ideas	Generating and manipulating mental images	Becoming aware of the power of interpretations	Cultivating a growth mindset	Cultivating resiliency	Avoiding negative thinking	Taking various perspectives	Interacting responsibly	Handling controversy and conflict resolution
Reading																	
Questioning, Inference, and Interpretation	X	X	X					X	X		X				X		
Themes and Central Ideas	X		X						X								
Story Elements	X		X							X					X		
Connections	X		X					X	X	X							
Word Impact and Use	X		X					X	X	X					X		
Academic Vocabulary				X				X	X	X							
Text Structures and Features	X		X						X								
Point of View / Purpose	X	X	X					X							X		
Visual/Auditory Media and Information Sources	X	X	X	X				X	X	X	X				X		
Argument and Reasoning	X	X	X						X								
Literary Comparisons and Source Material	X			X					X						X		
Rhetorical Criticism	X	X	X						X						X		
Fluency	X								X	X							
Reading Foundations																	
Print Concepts	X							X	X								
Phonological Awareness	X							X	X								
Phonics and Word Analysis	X							X	X								
Writing																	
Argumentative	X	X	X						X		X				X		X
Informative/Explanatory	X	X	X	X				X	X								
Narrative	X				X	X			X	X	X				X		X
Task, Purpose, and Audience			X			X				X	X				X		
Revise and Edit		X	X	X	X	X						X	X	X			
Technology	X	X	X	X	X												

continued →

	COGNITIVE										**CONATIVE**						
	Generating conclusions	**Identifying common logical errors**	**Presenting and supporting claims**	**Navigating digital sources**	**Problem solving**	**Decision making**	**Experimenting**	**Investigating**	**Identifying basic relationships between ideas**	**Generating and manipulating mental images**	**Becoming aware of the power of interpretations**	**Cultivating a growth mindset**	**Cultivating resiliency**	**Avoiding negative thinking**	**Taking various perspectives**	**Interacting responsibly**	**Handling controversy and conflict resolution**
Writing																	
Research		X		X					X		X				X		
Access and Organize Information				X		X		X	X								
Speaking and Listening																	
Collaborative Discussions	X	X	X						X		X				X	X	X
Evaluate Presented Information	X	X	X	X					X		X				X		
Speech Writing	X		X						X	X	X				X		
Presentation and Delivery		X		X					X	X	X				X		
Language																	
Grammar									X								
Sentences	X		X						X	X							X
Capitalization and Punctuation									X								
Spelling				X					X								
Language Conventions			X													X	X
Context Clues	X			X					X	X							
Word Origins and Roots				X				X	X	X							
Reference Materials				X													
Word Relationships	X								X	X							

Table 3.11: Cognitive and Conative Strategies Matched to Mathematics Scale Measurement Topics

	COGNITIVE										CONATIVE						
	Generating conclusions	Identifying common logical errors	Presenting and supporting claims	Navigating digital sources	Problem solving	Decision making	Experimenting	Investigating	Identifying basic relationships between ideas	Generating and manipulating mental images	Becoming aware of the power of interpretations	Cultivating a growth mindset	Cultivating resiliency	Avoiding negative thinking	Taking various perspectives	Interacting responsibly	Handling controversy and conflict resolution
Number and Quantity																	
Number Names									X	X							
Counting	X								X								
Compare Numbers	X								X								
Place Value	X		X						X	X							
Foundations of Fractions	X				X				X	X							
Fractions	X		X		X				X	X							
Adding and Subtracting Fractions	X		X		X				X	X							
Multiplying and Dividing Fractions	X		X		X				X	X							
Decimal Concepts	X		X		X				X	X							
Ratios and Unit Rates	X		X		X				X								
Rational and Irrational Numbers	X		X		X			X	X								
Exponents and Roots	X		X		X				X								
Quantities	X		X		X				X	X					X		
Operations With Complex Numbers	X		X		X				X	X							
Polynomial Identities and Equations	X				X				X								
Operations and Algebra																	
Addition and Subtraction	X				X				X	X							
Multiplication and Division	X				X				X	X	X						
Properties of Operations	X				X				X	X							
Expressions and Equations	X				X				X	X							
Factors and Multiples	X				X				X								
Patterns	X								X	X							
Equations and Inequalities	X				X		X		X	X							
Dependent and Independent Variables	X								X	X							

continued →

	COGNITIVE										CONATIVE						
	Generating conclusions	Identifying common logical errors	Presenting and supporting claims	Navigating digital sources	Problem solving	Decision making	Experimenting	Investigating	Identifying basic relationships between ideas	Generating and manipulating mental images	Becoming aware of the power of interpretations	Cultivating a growth mindset	Cultivating resiliency	Avoiding negative thinking	Taking various perspectives	Interacting responsibly	Handling controversy and conflict resolution
Operations and Algebra																	
Slope	X				X				X	X							
Systems of Equations	X				X				X	X							
Structure of Expressions	X		X		X				X	X							
Equivalent Expressions	X		X		X				X	X							
Arithmetic Operations on Polynomials	X				X				X	X							
Zeroes and Factors of Polynomials	X		X		X				X	X							
Polynomial Identities	X		X		X				X	X							
Rational Expressions	X				X				X	X							
Creating Equations	X				X				X	X	X						
Reasoning to Solve Equations	X	X	X		X												
Solving Quadratic Equations	X				X				X	X							
Graphs of Equations and Inequalities	X				X				X	X							
Functions																	
Functions	X				X				X	X							
Interpret Functions	X				X				X	X							
Graph Functions	X				X				X	X							
Properties of Functions	X				X				X	X							
Model Relationships	X				X				X	X							
Building New Functions	X				X				X	X							
Linear and Exponential Models	X				X			X	X	X							
Interpret Linear and Exponential Functions	X				X				X	X							
Trigonometric Functions	X		X		X				X	X							
Periodic Phenomena	X				X	X		X	X	X							
Trigonometric Identities	X		X		X				X	X							

	COGNITIVE										CONATIVE						
	Generating conclusions	Identifying common logical errors	Presenting and supporting claims	Navigating digital sources	Problem solving	Decision making	Experimenting	Investigating	Identifying basic relationships between ideas	Generating and manipulating mental images	Becoming aware of the power of interpretations	Cultivating a growth mindset	Cultivating resiliency	Avoiding negative thinking	Taking various perspectives	Interacting responsibly	Handling controversy and conflict resolution
Geometry																	
Shapes	X				X			X	X	X							
Compose and Decompose Shapes	X				X	X		X	X	X							
Lines and Symmetry	X		X		X		X		X	X							
Coordinate System	X				X		X	X	X	X							
Area	X				X		X		X	X							
Perimeter	X				X				X	X							
Surface Area	X				X				X	X							
Volume	X		X		X		X		X	X							
Scale Drawings	X				X				X	X							
Angles	X				X			X	X	X							
Pythagorean Theorem	X				X			X	X	X							
Congruence and Similarity	X		X		X	X		X	X	X							
Transformations	X		X		X			X	X	X							
Geometric Theorems	X		X		X				X	X							
Geometric Constructions					X		X			X							
Dilations	X		X				X		X	X							
Theorems Involving Similarity	X		X		X				X	X							
Trigonometric Ratios	X				X				X	X							
Geometric Trigonometry	X				X			X	X	X							
Circle Theorems	X		X		X			X	X	X							
Arc Length and Sectors	X		X		X			X	X	X							
Conic Sections					X			X	X								
Geometric Modeling	X				X			X	X	X							

continued ➛

	COGNITIVE										**CONATIVE**						
	Generating conclusions	Identifying common logical errors	Presenting and supporting claims	Navigating digital sources	Problem solving	Decision making	Experimenting	Investigating	Identifying basic relationships between ideas	Generating and manipulating mental images	Becoming aware of the power of interpretations	Cultivating a growth mindset	Cultivating resiliency	Avoiding negative thinking	Taking various perspectives	Interacting responsibly	Handling controversy and conflict resolution
Measurement, Data, Statistics, and Probability																	
Measurement	X				X			X	X	X							
Represent and Interpret Data	X				X	X		X	X	X							
Time	X				X				X	X							
Money	X				X				X	X							
Data Distributions	X				X	X			X	X					X		
Random Sampling	X		X			X	X	X	X	X					X		
Probability	X		X		X	X	X	X	X	X	X				X		
Multivariable Data Distributions	X							X	X	X							
Linear Models	X				X				X		X						
Rules of Probability	X		X					X	X	X							

A third-grade teacher who has been teaching his students to use a problem-solving process like the one described in chapter 2 (page 31) creates a complex (4.0) learning target by first selecting a word or phrase that typically prompts students to solve problems. Words and phrases that prompt students to perform each of the cognitive and conative strategies outlined in this book are presented in the feature boxes in chapter 2. The words and phrases for problem solving include:

- Solve
- How would you overcome
- Adapt
- Develop a strategy to
- Figure out a way to
- How will you reach your goal under these conditions

The teacher decides to use "develop a strategy to" as the stem for his complex (4.0) learning target. He then combines that stem with content from one of the 3.0 elements from the scale for Area at grade 3. Table 3.12 shows the 3.0 portion of that scale.

Table 3.12: Score 3.0 Grade 3 Scale for Area

Score 3.0	The student will: • Solve real-world problems involving rectangular and rectilinear area (3.MD.C.7b; 3.MD.C.7d) • Use tiling to demonstrate the distributive property by showing that the area of a rectangle with side lengths a and $b + c$ is the sum of $a \times b$ and $a \times c$ (3.MD.C.7c) • Calculate areas of rectilinear figures by decomposing them into nonoverlapping rectangles and adding the area (3.MD.C.7d)

One of the elements at the 3.0 level for the measurement topic Area is "calculate areas of rectilinear figures by decomposing them into nonoverlapping rectangles and adding the area." The teacher combines this content and the sentence stem from the cognitive strategy of problem solving to write the following complex (4.0) learning target:

> *The student will develop an alternative strategy to calculate areas of rectilinear figures (other than decomposing them into nonoverlapping rectangles and adding the area).*

This more complex learning target can then be inserted into the 4.0 level of the grade 3 scale for Area.

The process of creating scales outlined in this chapter should allow a teacher to create scales that he or she can use to measure student performance on the CCSS. However, the process can be time consuming. For this reason, we have included the set of scales for the CCSS that was designed (using the process described in this chapter) by teachers and researchers at Marzano Research Laboratory. This set of scales is presented in part II of this book (page 81), which is composed of two sections: proficiency scales for the ELA CCSS and proficiency scales for the mathematics CCSS. Each section has its own table of contents for ease of use.

In addition to providing MRL's scales for the CCSS in part II of this book, they are also available in searchable form online at **marzanoresearch.com/commoncore** along with performance tasks. Performance tasks are activities that teachers can use to assess students' current levels of performance on the scale for a measurement topic. In the next chapter we address the topics of assessment and grading and offer practical strategies that teachers can use to measure and report on their students' progress with the CCSS.

4

Using the Common Core State Standards for Assessment and Grading

Identifying specific learning goals from the CCSS, organizing those learning goals into a limited number of measurement topics, and using proficiency scales to articulate different levels of performance for each measurement topic are a teacher's first steps toward effectively measuring students' performance on the CCSS. However, high-quality assessments and grading and reporting systems are also necessary to gauge students' levels of performance and knowledge gain on the CCSS and communicate with students and parents about their progress.

Assessing the CCSS

Formal assessments for the CCSS are being produced by the two consortia mentioned in the introduction—the Partnership for Assessment of Readiness for College and Careers and the Smarter Balanced Assessment Consortium. The goals of these formal assessments are to "yield timely data to support and inform instruction, provide accurate information about what students know and can do, and measure achievement against standards that reflect the skills and knowledge required for success in college and the workforce" (K–12 Center at ETS, 2012, p. 15).

The two consortia share some key characteristics. For accountability purposes, each consortium will create two end-of-year assessments: a computer-administered test and a performance task (also called a performance-based assessment). These assessments will be given as close to the end of the school year as possible. The computer-administered tests allow for the use of simulations and more complex multistep items than paper-and-pencil tests normally contain. The performance tasks will be designed to assess Common Core standards that are difficult to evaluate using computer-based platforms. For example, PARCC stated that their performance-based assessments will

> be comprised of two types of tasks [for ELA], one research simulation task based on informational texts and one literature task based on pieces of literary text. . . . The two types of tasks in mathematics will require students to express their mathematical reasoning and to apply key mathematical skills, concepts, and processes to solve complex problems of the

> types encountered in everyday life, work, and decision making. (K–12 Center at ETS, 2012, pp. 17–18)

Smarter Balanced's performance tasks will "involve student-initiated planning, management of information and ideas, interaction with other materials, and production of an extended response such as an oral presentation, exhibit, product development, or an extended written piece" (K–12 Center at ETS, 2012, p. 25).

In addition to the end-of-year assessments, each consortium also plans to design other tests that teachers can administer throughout the school year. These tests will not be required; rather they will be available for teachers to use for diagnostic and progress-monitoring purposes.

Although the consortia have much in common, there are some key differences between the two. Smarter Balanced is using a computer-adaptive testing model for its end-of-year computer-administered assessment. Computer-adaptive testing customizes items to individual students' performance levels as they take the test. This prevents advanced students from having to answer questions that seem too easy and struggling students from having to guess at questions that seem overly difficult. PARCC, although not using computer-adaptive testing, plans to include an additional teacher-administered speaking and listening assessment. Teachers will be required to administer this assessment during the school year, but it will not be used to determine a student's summative end-of-year score.

Items on the new assessments may look different from those found on previous state assessments. Figures 4.1 and 4.2 show examples of item types that might be used on the assessments designed by PARCC or Smarter Balanced.

Delineate and evaluate the argument that Thomas Paine makes in *Common Sense*. Assess the reasoning present in his analysis, including the premises and purposes of his essay.

Source: NGA & CCSSO, 2010c, p. 171.

Figure 4.1: Sample ELA assessment item.

Phil and Cathy want to raise money for charity. They decide to make and sell wooden toys. They could make them in two sizes: small and large.

Phil will carve them from wood. A small toy takes 2 hours to carve and a large toy takes 3 hours to carve. Phil only has a total of 24 hours available for carving. Cathy will decorate them. She only has time to decorate 10 toys.

The small toy will make $8 for charity. The large toy will make $10 for charity. They want to make as much money for charity as they can.

How many small and large toys should they make?

How much money will they then make for charity?

Source: Schoenfeld & Burkhardt, 2012, p. 60.

Figure 4.2: Sample mathematics assessment item.

Both consortia also have a number of sample tasks and test items available on their websites.

In addition to using practice items from the PARCC and Smarter Balanced consortia, teachers can design their own classroom assessments. There are three major types of classroom assessments that can be used by teachers with the help of a proficiency scale: obtrusive, unobtrusive, and student-generated. We discuss each type briefly here, but for a detailed discussion of these three types of assessments, see *Formative Assessment and Standards-Based Grading* (Marzano, 2010).

Obtrusive Assessments

Obtrusive assessments interrupt the flow of instruction in the classroom. For example, a paper-and-pencil test, a demonstration, an oral report, or any other activity for which instruction stops while the assessment takes place is considered obtrusive. Obtrusive assessments often make use of selected-response items (multiple choice, matching, true/false, fill in the blank), constructed-response items (short answer, essay), oral-response items (oral report, probing discussion), and demonstrations (presentations, displays) to measure students' levels of performance. For example, a fourth-grade teacher uses a constructed-response item to measure whether or not a student has achieved proficiency with the 2.0 content for the measurement topic of Perimeter. Score 2.0 for this scale says, "The student will perform basic processes, such as: apply the formula for perimeter in mathematical problems." The teacher uses the short-answer item in figure 4.3 to determine if a student has achieved the 2.0 level of performance for that measurement topic.

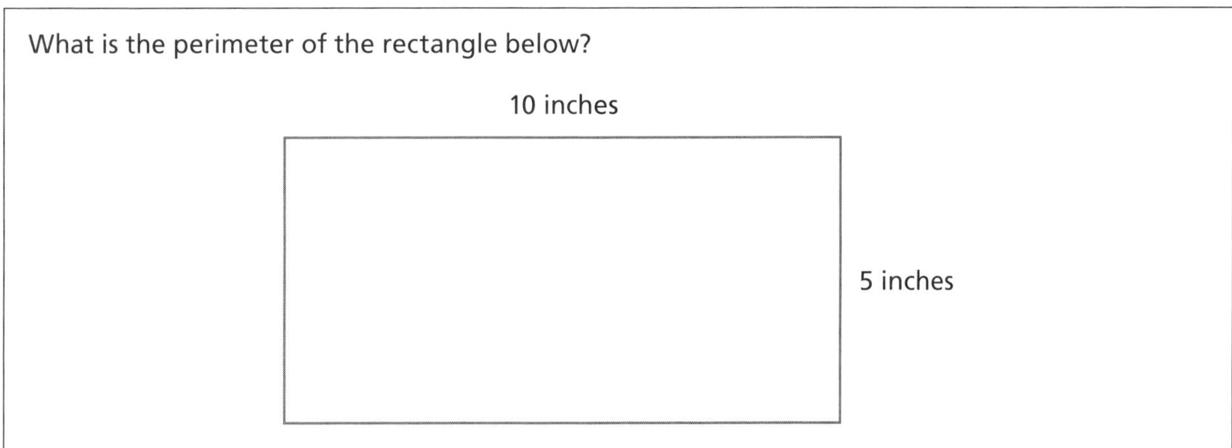

Figure 4.3: Short-answer item for 2.0 content.

Alternatively, the teacher could have used a multiple-choice item like the following to assess students on the same 2.0 content for Perimeter:

How would you determine the perimeter of a rectangle 10 inches long and 5 inches wide?

1. Add the measurements of the four sides together—5 + 5 + 10 + 10.
2. Add the measurements of the length and the width—5 + 10.
3. Multiply the measurements of the length and the width—5 × 10.
4. Divide the length by the width—10 ÷ 5.

It is important to remember that score 2.0 content is simpler than the target learning goal; hence, objectively scored items are often appropriate for assessing this level of the scale.

Unobtrusive Assessments

An unobtrusive assessment does not interrupt the flow of instruction in the classroom. For example, a teacher observes a student using a procedure at the 3.0 level and records a score for that student in the gradebook without alerting the student to the fact that he was being assessed. Unobtrusive assessments can happen anytime and anywhere, and are usually best used to measure students' ability with a skill, process, or procedure. For example, an eighth-grade teacher whose students are working on the measurement topic of Revise and Edit observes one of her students as he revises an essay after receiving peer feedback. She listens to his conversation with his editing partner and notices that he is revising and editing his essay based on the feedback from his peer and is also working with his partner to try a new organizational approach so that his readers (his audience) can follow his argument more effectively. In response to this observation, the teacher records a score of 3.0 for that student for the measurement topic of Revise and Edit since the 3.0 target for that topic at grade 8 is "The student will develop and strengthen grade-appropriate writing for a specific purpose and audience by: planning, revising, editing, rewriting, or trying a new approach."

Student-Generated Assessments

As their name implies, student-generated assessments are tasks designed by students to demonstrate performance at a specific level of the scale. Student-designed assessments are usually designed to prove that a student has moved from one level of the scale to the next level. For example, a freshman high school English teacher offers his students the opportunity to create student-generated assessments to demonstrate their proficiency for the measurement topic of Word Origins and Roots. A student who has already demonstrated proficiency at the 2.0 level ("recognize patterns of word changes that indicate different meanings or parts of speech") demonstrates that she has improved to the 3.0 level—"correctly use grade-appropriate patterns of word changes that indicate different meanings or parts of speech (for example, *analyze*, *analysis*, *analytical*; *advocate*, *advocacy*)"—by writing a narrative in which each character uses a word in ways that indicate that word's different meanings or parts of speech. After composing the story, the student turns it in to the teacher, and the teacher evaluates the student's performance against the 3.0 learning target. If the teacher feels that the product meets the learning target, he assigns that student a score of 3.0.

Creating Common Assessments for the CCSS

Common assessments are staples within most schools and districts across the United States and can be designed using the proficiency scales in part II of this book (page 81). Common assessments are primarily for the purpose of ensuring instructional consistency across classrooms and collecting formal data to be discussed in professional learning community meetings. These data are used to inform instructional practice. The following steps should be employed to develop a high-quality common assessment:

1. **Identify the measurement topic to be assessed**—The content related to the measurement topic is found on the proficiency scale that will serve as the foundation for the assessment. The question to be answered in this step is, "Where do we want students to be at the end of the learning process in relation to this measurement topic?"

2. **Determine the number and type of assessment items for each level of the scale (an assessment blueprint)**—It is important that an adequate number of assessment items are developed for each level on the scale to ensure that the data are trustworthy—typically, at least three to five items per level are needed (an exception is the 4.0 level, which may only require one or two complex items). Also, when discussing potential item types, it is critical to

consider the content being assessed in order to ensure a strong match between the assessment item and the content. For example, if a writing standard is being assessed, a performance assessment is a stronger match to the content than an objectively scored assessment. On the other hand, if a math computation standard is being assessed, multiple-choice, short-answer, or other objectively scored items may work quite well.

3. **Write the assessment items**—Make sure that the language used for the assessment items matches the language on the proficiency scale. This will ensure that the items truly measure students' proficiency with the skills and knowledge represented on the scale. Be sure to write a variety of assessment items for each of the score levels on the scale. Typically, there are fewer score 4.0 items on an assessment than there are for scores 2.0 and 3.0. As stated earlier, it is not uncommon to have only one or two 4.0 items.
4. **Administer the common assessment, score it, and discuss the results**—Following test administration, the assessment is scored. Items can be coded as correct (C), partially correct (PC), or incorrect (I). Based on responses to the items, each student is assigned a score that correlates to a level on the proficiency scale. Assessment results can be used as the basis for discussion in a professional learning community meeting. The results can also be used to plan future instruction for individual students, small groups of students, or the whole class.
5. **Revise the assessment based on the data**—There are times when it becomes clear through data examination that an item is not high quality. For example, if an item has no or very few correct responses, or if a score 2.0 item is consistently answered incorrectly while a score 3.0 item related to the same skill or concept is consistently answered correctly by the same students, item revision may be necessary.

Table 4.1 shows an assessment blueprint and one student's performance on a common assessment. As noted previously, *C* indicates the student answered the item correctly, while *I* means incorrect, and *PC* means partially correct.

Table 4.1: Student Performance on a Common Assessment

Item Number	Student Response Code	Score Level
	Section 1	
1	C	2.0
2	C	2.0
3	C	2.0
4	I	2.0
5	C	2.0
6	C	2.0
	Section 2	
7	C	3.0
8	PC	3.0
9	I	3.0
10	PC	3.0
	Section 3	
11	I	4.0
12	I	4.0

Notice that in table 4.1 (page 73), almost all of the score 2.0 items were answered correctly, some of the 3.0 items were answered correctly, and none of the 4.0 items were answered correctly. Therefore, this student would most likely be assigned a score of 2.5 for this assessment.

Tracking Student Progress on the CCSS

A teacher can use a chart like the one in table 4.2 to track students' progress over time on multiple learning goals. In this particular record-keeping chart, the teacher is keeping track of students' scores on four different measurement topics: A through D. Scores on assessments for a given measurement topic are entered starting at the top left of each cell. When the teacher runs out of room on the left side of the cell, she simply begins a new column on the right side. The box in the lower right corner of each cell is where the teacher records a summative score for each measurement topic. A circle around a score indicates that the teacher gave the student an opportunity to raise his or her score from the previous assessment. A square around a score indicates that the student is judged to have reached a specific score level and would therefore not be expected to receive lower scores in the future. If that student did receive a lower score, the teacher might give the student a chance to raise that score. *Inc.* represents an incomplete assignment.

Table 4.2: Teacher Tracking Chart

	Measurement Topic A		Measurement Topic B		Measurement Topic C		Measurement Topic D	
Allie	2.0 2.5 2.5		2.0 2.0 1.5	2.5	1.0 1.5 2.5		2.5 2.5 2.0	
Tyrone	3.0 3.5 2.5	3.0	2.0 Inc. 3.0		1.5 1.5 2.0		0.5 1.5 2.5	
Serena	2.5 2.5 3.0		2.0 1.5 2.0		2.5 3.0 2.0	3.0	2.5 1.0 2.0	3.0
Clayton	2.0 1.5 2.5	3.0	2.5 2.5 3.0		3.0 3.5 4.0		3.0 3.0 Inc.	
Noah	1.5 2.0 1.0	2.0	1.5 2.0 2.5		0.5 1.0 1.5	1.5	3.5 3.5 3.5	

To understand the order in which scores are entered, consider Noah's scores for measurement topic C. He has four of them. The first score he received was a 0.5. The second was a 1.0, and the third was 1.5. To enter his fourth score of 1.5, the teacher started a second column of scores to the right of the first column.

To understand the use of squares and circles around individual scores, consider Allie's scores for measurement topic B. They are 2.0, 2.0, 1.5, and 2.5. After the second score was earned, the teacher decided that Allie had reached the 2.0 level for that measurement topic, as indicated by the square. However, Allie's third score was a 1.5, lower than her previous scores of 2.0. When the teacher gave Allie a chance to raise this score, as indicated by the circle around the 1.5, Allie raised her score to 2.5 for measurement topic B. Teachers often use student-generated assessments when giving students the opportunity to raise their scores.

Additionally, Tyrone and Clayton have incomplete scores on measurement topics B and D, respectively. These students either missed or did not complete an assessment, but instead of recording a score of 0.0, the teacher simply noted that the assessments were incomplete for these students. This allows the teacher to only record scores that are actual estimates of a student's status for a particular measurement topic. As shown in the generic scale in table 3.2 (page 49), it is possible for a student to be assigned a score of 0.0 (indicating no success, even with help) on an assessment. Using *Inc.* to mark incomplete scores allows teachers to reserve a single meaning for grades of 0.0.

At the end of a unit or grading period, the teacher examines the pattern of scores for each student on each measurement topic and assigns that student a summative score. This summative score is recorded in the box in the lower right corner of each cell of the tracking chart in table 4.2. As Marzano (2010) explained, teachers should not simply average a student's scores over the course of a unit. Instead, the teacher should use the scores recorded to arrive at the best estimate possible of the student's current knowledge status on each measurement topic. For example, in table 4.2, Allie's last score for measurement topic D was a 2.0. However, the teacher had previously judged her to be at the 2.5 level for that topic. Therefore, the teacher might assign Allie a summative score of 2.5 for measurement topic D. Students can track their progress on individual measurement topics using a chart like the one in figure 4.4 (page 76).

As shown in figure 4.4, Allie's teacher recorded six scores for her on the measurement topic of Expressions and Equations. A date is recorded for each score: 2.0 on February 2, 2.5 on February 11, 2.5 on February 15, and so on. To create charts like these, a teacher might have students keep a separate chart for each of the class's learning goals in a folder or notebook. As the teacher assigns scores, students record them on the tracking chart and plot their progress on the line graph. This allows students to keep track of what they need to do to accomplish their goals for a unit.

Grading and Reporting With the CCSS

Most districts require teachers to report students' progress to parents via report card on a regular basis throughout the school year. To do this, teachers can use students' summative scores across several measurement topics to assign an overall grade to that student in a specific subject area. Although Marzano (2010) cautioned against averaging scores within a particular measurement topic to obtain a summative score, it is appropriate to average scores *across several measurement topics* to obtain an overall grade for a particular subject area. Stated differently, while it is inappropriate to average a student's scores within a measurement topic, it is legitimate to average scores across two or more measurement topics. For example, assume that a student obtained the following five summative scores on five different measurement topics studied during a mathematics unit: 3.0, 2.5, 3.5, 3.0, and 4.0. The average of those five summative scores, 3.2, could be a good representation of that student's final status for the math unit, if all of the measurement topics were given equal weight. Alternatively, a teacher might decide that specific topics are more important to mastery of the content. In that case, the teacher could create a weighted average. For the five scores previously enumerated, the teacher might decide that the first and last measurement topics were twice as important as the others. Therefore, he or she would include them twice when calculating the average. (For a more detailed discussion of standards-based grading, see Marzano, 2010.)

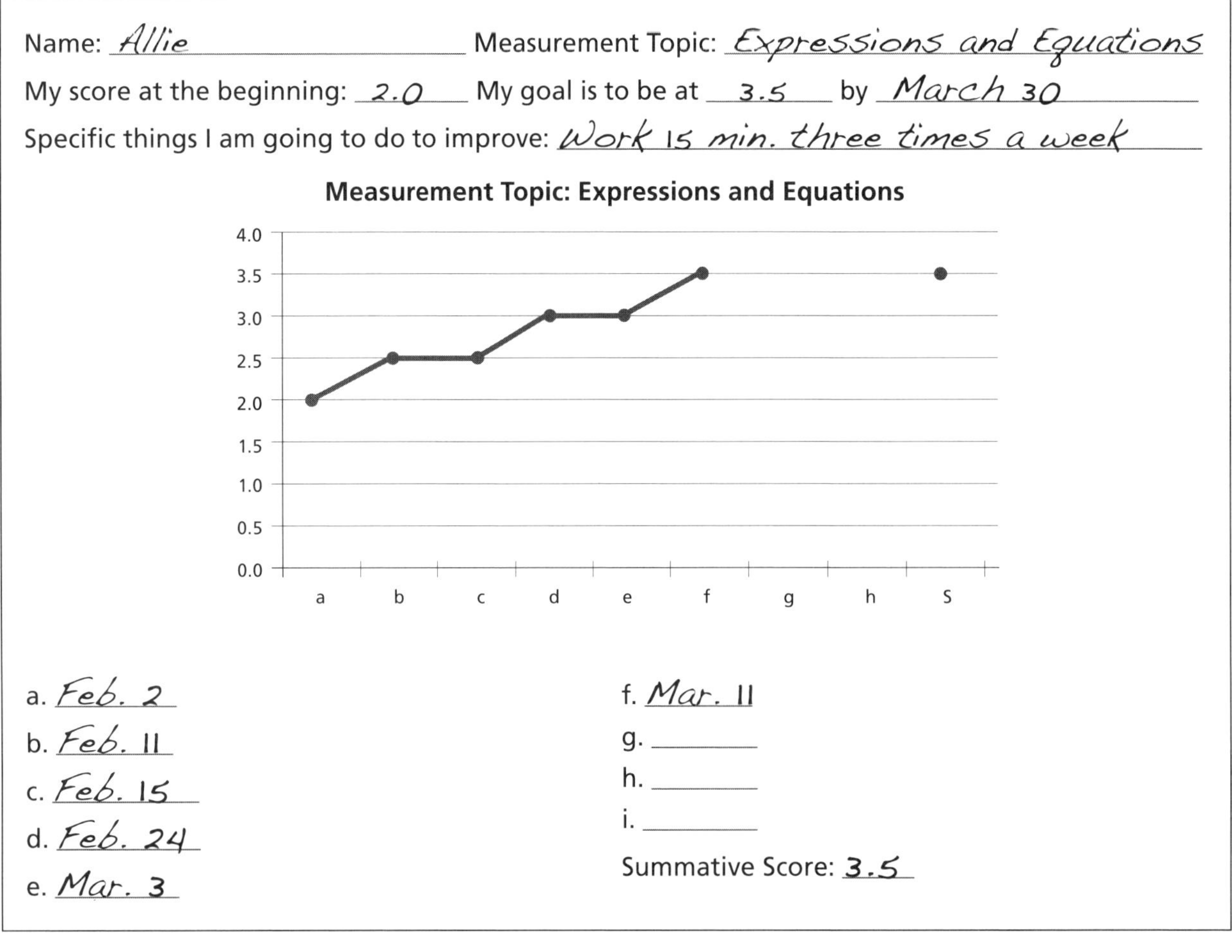

Name: Allie Measurement Topic: Expressions and Equations

My score at the beginning: 2.0 My goal is to be at 3.5 by March 30

Specific things I am going to do to improve: Work 15 min. three times a week

a. Feb. 2

b. Feb. 11

c. Feb. 15

d. Feb. 24

e. Mar. 3

f. Mar. 11

g. ________

h. ________

i. ________

Summative Score: 3.5

Source: Adapted from Marzano, 2010.

Figure 4.4: Student tracking chart.

Many districts and schools use traditional letter grades to report final grades. Teachers can use the conversion scale in table 4.3 to translate numeric grades calculated using a four-point scale into traditional letter grades.

Table 4.3: Conversion Scale to Traditional Grades

Average Scale Score Across Multiple Measurement Topics	Traditional Grades
3.75–4.00	A+
3.26–3.74	A
3.00–3.25	A-
2.84–2.99	B+
2.67–2.83	B
2.50–2.66	B-
2.34–2.49	C+
2.17–2.33	C
2.00–2.16	C-
1.76–1.99	D+

Average Scale Score Across Multiple Measurement Topics	Traditional Grades
1.26–1.75	D
1.00–1.25	D-
Below 1.00	F

Source: Marzano, 2010, p. 106.

Although traditional letter grades are still used in some schools, the standards-based education movement has led many to place an increased emphasis on showing students' growth over a grading period. To that end, a report card such as the one shown in figure 4.5 can be very useful. The darker shading represents a student's score on a measurement topic at the beginning of the unit, and the lighter shading represents the student's score on a measurement topic at the end of the unit.

Name: Allie Fairchild			**Grade Level:** 4		
Address: 123 Hawthorne Street, Someplace, NY 12345			**Teacher:** Ms. Maple		
	Summative Score	**Letter Grade**		**Summative Score**	**Letter Grade**
Language Arts	2.50	B-	**Science**	2.67	B
Mathematics	3.25	A-	**Social Studies**	2.25	C
Identifying Basic Relationships Between Ideas	2.88	B+	**Generating and Manipulating Mental Images**	2.38	C+

	Summative Score	**0.0**	**0.5**	**1.0**	**1.5**	**2.0**	**2.5**	**3.0**	**3.5**	**4.0**
English Language Arts										
Reading										
Questioning, Inference, and Interpretation	3.0									
Themes and Central Ideas	2.0									
Argument and Reasoning	2.5									
Writing										
Argumentative	2.0									
Task, Purpose, and Audience	2.5									
Research	3.5									
Speaking and Listening										
Speech Writing	2.5									
Presentation and Delivery	2.0									
Language										
Grammar	3.0									
Language Conventions	2.0									
Cognitive Skills in Reading										
Identifying Basic Relationships Between Ideas	3.0									
Generating and Manipulating Mental Images	1.5									

Figure 4.5: Report card for academic and cognitive skills.

continued →

	Summative Score	0.0	0.5	1.0	1.5	2.0	2.5	3.0	3.5	4.0
Mathematics										
Number and Quantity										
Fractions	4.0									
Adding and Subtracting Fractions	2.5									
Operations and Algebra										
Multiplication and Division	3.0									
Expressions and Equations	3.5									
Cognitive Skills in Mathematics										
Identifying Basic Relationships Between Ideas	3.0									
Generating and Manipulating Mental Images	2.5									
Science										
Earth Materials and Systems	2.5									
Natural Resources	3.0									
Role of Water	2.5									
Cognitive Skills in Science										
Identifying Basic Relationships Between Ideas	2.5									
Generating and Manipulating Mental Images	3.0									
Social Studies										
Cultural Relationships	2.5									
Physical Environments and Immigration	2.0									
Cognitive Skills in Social Studies										
Identifying Basic Relationships Between Ideas	3.0									
Generating and Manipulating Mental Images	2.5									

Source: Adapted from Marzano & Waters, 2009.

As seen in figure 4.5, traditional numeric and letter grades are reported at the top of the report card. These are generated using the strategies discussed previously in this chapter. However, this report card also allows a teacher to report students' summative scores for individual measurement topics in each subject area. The lighter and darker shading scheme allows teachers to report students' knowledge gain in addition to their final status. For example, the student began with a score of 0.5 for the measurement topic Argumentative Writing. By the end of the unit, however, she had achieved a summative score of 2.0. Therefore, the student's knowledge gain is 1.5.

Also notice that, in each subject area, the teacher has assigned the student summative scores for cognitive skills addressed during the grading period. In the example in figure 4.5, the teachers responsible for each subject area have agreed to focus on the same two cognitive skills during the grading period.

They could just as easily have picked one cognitive and one conative skill or two conative skills. These cognitive skills scores are reported separately for each subject and are aggregated across the subjects to arrive at the overall grade reported at the top of the report card. For example, for identifying basic relationships between ideas, the student received a 3.0 in ELA, a 3.0 in math, a 2.5 in science, and a 3.0 in social studies. The average of those four scores is 2.88, which is reported at the top of the report card. Scales for the various cognitive and conative skills can be found in *Teaching and Assessing 21st Century Skills* (Marzano & Heflebower, 2012).

In conclusion, the measurement topics and their related scales provide a foundation for assessing and grading students in far more meaningful ways than have been used in the past. For assessment, teachers now have options that go beyond the traditional obtrusive test, some of which are generated by the students themselves. Additionally, a grade on a report card can now be broken down into what students know and how far they have progressed relative to specific topics. These methods of scoring and reporting students' progress on the Common Core State Standards can provide a more accurate picture of student performance than was possible with previous sets of standards. Part II of this book is designed to facilitate this type of scoring and reporting by providing measurement topics and scales that teachers can use to implement the CCSS in their classrooms.

Part II

Scoring the Common Core State Standards

Proficiency Scales for the ELA Common Core State Standards

MRL's scales for the Common Core State Standards were designed to include all of the ELA standards from the CCSS. Here we include several notes about MRL's scales for the ELA CCSS that may interest teachers and readers.

- In some cases, the CCSS present substandards for an overarching standard. For example, the overarching Writing standard W.6.1 has five substandards, labeled using a, b, c, d, and e. In cases like this, MRL used one of two approaches: we either included (1) both the overarching standard and the substandards (if the overarching standard contains additional information) or (2) the substandards but not the overarching standard (if the overarching standard does not contain additional information).
- MRL created a single set of Reading measurement topics that includes standards from Reading Literature and Reading Informational Text.
- Writing standards 9 and 10 are not included in MRL's scales because our analysis found them to be more focused on instructional guidance rather than specific ELA content. In other words, Writing standards 9 and 10 give teachers guidance about how to structure lessons and combine content rather than specifying what students should know or be able to do as a result of instruction.

Some scales use the phrases *in context* and *in isolation* to define different levels of expectation. *In context* means that a student independently demonstrates the knowledge or skill while reading, writing, speaking, or listening. *In isolation* means that the student demonstrates an individual aspect of knowledge or skill isolated from other reading, writing, speaking, or listening skills (for example, on a worksheet or individual assessment item).

The numbering system used to cite the Common Core standards used in each scale identifies ELA standards by strand initials, then grade level, and finally, standard number. The strand initials are as follows:

- Reading Literature = RL
- Reading Informational Text = RI
- Reading Foundations = RF
- Writing = W
- Speaking and Listening = SL
- Language = L

For example, in writing (W), the first kindergarten standard (1) would be numbered W.K.1.

Teachers and readers should note that for each measurement topic, the scale for the highest grade level in the topic shows all the scores (including half-point scores). For all other grade levels, the scale shows scores 3.0 and 2.0 only, because the descriptors for the other scores do not change from grade level to grade level.

Reading

Questioning, Inference, and Interpretation

<table>
<tr><th colspan="3">Grades 11–12</th></tr>
<tr><td>Score 4.0</td><td colspan="2">In addition to score 3.0 performance, the student demonstrates in-depth inferences and applications that go beyond what was taught.</td></tr>
<tr><td></td><td>Score 3.5</td><td>In addition to score 3.0 performance, partial success at score 4.0 content</td></tr>
<tr><td>Score 3.0</td><td colspan="2">The student will:
• Cite textual evidence to support analysis of what a grade-appropriate text says explicitly as well as to support inferences drawn from the text, including determining where the text leaves matters uncertain (RL.11–12.1; RI.11–12.1)</td></tr>
<tr><td></td><td>Score 2.5</td><td>No major errors or omissions regarding score 2.0 content, and partial success at score 3.0 content</td></tr>
<tr><td>Score 2.0</td><td colspan="2">The student will recognize or recall specific vocabulary, such as:
• Analysis, cite, explicit, inference, logical, support, text, textual evidence, uncertain
The student will perform basic processes, such as:
• Describe what a grade-appropriate text says explicitly and draw logical inferences</td></tr>
<tr><td></td><td>Score 1.5</td><td>Partial success at score 2.0 content, and major errors or omissions regarding score 3.0 content</td></tr>
<tr><td>Score 1.0</td><td colspan="2">With help, partial success at score 2.0 content and score 3.0 content</td></tr>
<tr><td></td><td>Score 0.5</td><td>With help, partial success at score 2.0 content but not at score 3.0 content</td></tr>
<tr><td>Score 0.0</td><td colspan="2">Even with help, no success</td></tr>
<tr><th colspan="3">Grades 9–10</th></tr>
<tr><td>Score 3.0</td><td colspan="2">The student will:
• Cite textual evidence to support analysis of what a grade-appropriate text says explicitly, as well as to support inferences drawn from the text (RL.9–10.1; RI.9–10.1)</td></tr>
<tr><td>Score 2.0</td><td colspan="2">The student will recognize or recall specific vocabulary, such as:
• Analysis, cite, explicit, inference, logical, support, text, textual evidence
The student will perform basic processes, such as:
• Describe what a grade-appropriate text says explicitly and draw logical inferences</td></tr>
<tr><th colspan="3">Grade 8</th></tr>
<tr><td>Score 3.0</td><td colspan="2">The student will:
• Cite textual evidence that supports an analysis of what a grade-appropriate text says explicitly, as well as to support inferences drawn from the text (RL.8.1; RI.8.1)</td></tr>
<tr><td>Score 2.0</td><td colspan="2">The student will recognize or recall specific vocabulary, such as:
• Analysis, cite, explicit, inference, logical, support, text, textual evidence
The student will perform basic processes, such as:
• Describe what a grade-appropriate text says explicitly and draw logical inferences</td></tr>
<tr><th colspan="3">Grade 7</th></tr>
<tr><td>Score 3.0</td><td colspan="2">The student will:
• Cite textual evidence to support analysis of what a grade-appropriate text says explicitly, as well as to support inferences drawn from the text (RL.7.1; RI.7.1)</td></tr>
</table>

Score 2.0	The student will recognize or recall specific vocabulary, such as: • *Analysis, cite, explicit, inference, logical, support, text, textual evidence* The student will perform basic processes, such as: • Describe what a grade-appropriate text says explicitly and draw logical inferences
	Grade 6
Score 3.0	The student will: • Cite textual evidence to support analysis of what a grade-appropriate text says explicitly, as well as to support inferences drawn from the text (RL.6.1; RI.6.1)
Score 2.0	The student will recognize or recall specific vocabulary, such as: • *Analysis, cite, explicit, inference, logical, support, text, textual evidence* The student will perform basic processes, such as: • Describe what a grade-appropriate text says explicitly and draw logical inferences
	Grade 5
Score 3.0	The student will: • Quote accurately from a grade-appropriate text when explaining what the text says explicitly and when drawing inferences from the text (RL.5.1; RI.5.1)
Score 2.0	The student will recognize or recall specific vocabulary, such as: • *Explicit, inference, logical, quote, text* The student will perform basic processes, such as: • Describe what a grade-appropriate text says explicitly and draw logical inferences
	Grade 4
Score 3.0	The student will: • Refer to details and examples in a grade-appropriate text when explaining what the text says explicitly and when drawing inferences from the text (RL.4.1; RI.4.1)
Score 2.0	The student will recognize or recall specific vocabulary, such as: • *Detail, example, explicit, inference, logical, refer, text* The student will perform basic processes, such as: • Describe what a grade-appropriate text says explicitly and draw logical inferences
	Grade 3
Score 3.0	The student will: • Ask and answer questions to demonstrate understanding of a grade-appropriate text, referring explicitly to the text as the basis for the answers (RL.3.1; RI.3.1)
Score 2.0	The student will recognize or recall specific vocabulary, such as: • *Answer, ask, basis, detail, explicit, question, refer, text* The student will perform basic processes, such as: • Answer teacher-provided questions to demonstrate understanding of key details in a grade-appropriate text referring explicitly to the text as the basis for the answers
	Grade 2
Score 3.0	The student will: • Ask and answer such questions as Who?, What?, Where?, When?, Why?, and How? to demonstrate understanding of key details in a grade-appropriate text (RL.2.1; RI.2.1)

Score 2.0	The student will recognize or recall specific vocabulary, such as: • *Answer, ask, detail, how, question, text, what, when, where, who, why* The student will perform basic processes, such as: • Answer teacher-provided questions such as Who?, What?, Where?, When?, Why?, and How? to demonstrate understanding of key details in a grade-appropriate text
Grade 1	
Score 3.0	The student will: • Ask and answer questions about key details in a grade-appropriate text (RL.1.1; RI.1.1)
Score 2.0	The student will recognize or recall specific vocabulary, such as: • *Answer, ask, detail, question, text* The student will perform basic processes, such as: • Answer teacher-provided questions about key details in a grade-appropriate text
Kindergarten	
Score 3.0	The student will: • Ask and answer questions about key details in a grade-appropriate text (RL.K.1; RI.K.1)
Score 2.0	The student will recognize or recall specific vocabulary, such as: • *Answer, ask, detail, question, text* The student will perform basic processes, such as: • Answer teacher-provided questions about key details in a grade-appropriate text

Themes and Central Ideas

Grades 11–12		
Score 4.0	In addition to score 3.0 performance, the student demonstrates in-depth inferences and applications that go beyond what was taught.	
	Score 3.5	*In addition to score 3.0 performance, partial success at score 4.0 content*
Score 3.0	The student will: • Analyze the development of two or more themes or central ideas over the course of a grade-appropriate text, including how they interact and build on one another (RL.11–12.2; RI.11–12.2) • Provide an objective summary of a grade-appropriate text (RL.11–12.2; RI.11–12.2)	
	Score 2.5	*No major errors or omissions regarding score 2.0 content, and partial success at score 3.0 content*
Score 2.0	The student will recognize or recall specific vocabulary, such as: • *Analyze, central idea, development, interact, objective, summarize, summary, text, theme* The student will perform basic processes, such as: • Determine two or more themes or central ideas of a grade-appropriate text (RL.11–12.2; RI.11–12.2) • Summarize a grade-appropriate text using a teacher-provided graphic organizer	
	Score 1.5	*Partial success at score 2.0 content, and major errors or omissions regarding score 3.0 content*
Score 1.0	With help, partial success at score 2.0 content and score 3.0 content	
	Score 0.5	*With help, partial success at score 2.0 content but not at score 3.0 content*
Score 0.0	Even with help, no success	

<table>
<tr><th colspan="2">Grades 9–10</th></tr>
<tr><td>Score 3.0</td><td>The student will:
• Analyze the development of a theme or central idea over the course of a grade-appropriate text, including how it emerges and is shaped and refined by specific details (RL.9–10.2; RI.9–10.2)
• Provide an objective summary of a grade-appropriate text (RL.9–10.2; RI.9–10.2)</td></tr>
<tr><td>Score 2.0</td><td>The student will recognize or recall specific vocabulary, such as:
• Analyze, central idea, detail, development, emerge, objective, refine, shape, summarize, summary, text, theme
The student will perform basic processes, such as:
• Determine a theme or central idea of a grade-appropriate text (RL.9–10.2; RI.9–10.2)
• Summarize a grade-appropriate text using a teacher-provided graphic organizer</td></tr>
<tr><th colspan="2">Grade 8</th></tr>
<tr><td>Score 3.0</td><td>The student will:
• Analyze the development of a theme or central idea over the course of a grade-appropriate text, including its relationship to characters, setting, plot, and supporting details (RL.8.2; RI.8.2)
• Provide an objective summary of a grade-appropriate text (RL.8.2; RI.8.2)</td></tr>
<tr><td>Score 2.0</td><td>The student will recognize or recall specific vocabulary, such as:
• Analyze, central idea, character, development, objective, plot, relationship, setting, summarize, summary, supporting detail, text, theme
The student will perform basic processes, such as:
• Determine a theme or central idea of a grade-appropriate text (RL.8.2; RI.8.2)
• Summarize a grade-appropriate text using a teacher-provided graphic organizer</td></tr>
<tr><th colspan="2">Grade 7</th></tr>
<tr><td>Score 3.0</td><td>The student will:
• Analyze the development of a theme or central idea over the course of a grade-appropriate text (RL.7.2; RI.7.2)
• Provide an objective summary of a grade-appropriate text (RL.7.2; RI.7.2)</td></tr>
<tr><td>Score 2.0</td><td>The student will recognize or recall specific vocabulary, such as:
• Analyze, central idea, development, objective, summarize, summary, text, theme
The student will perform basic processes, such as:
• Determine a theme or central idea of a grade-appropriate text (RL.7.2; RI.7.2)
• Summarize a grade-appropriate text using a teacher-provided graphic organizer</td></tr>
<tr><th colspan="2">Grade 6</th></tr>
<tr><td>Score 3.0</td><td>The student will:
• Describe how a theme or central idea of a grade-appropriate text is conveyed through particular details (RL.6.2; RI.6.2)
• Provide a summary of a grade-appropriate text distinct from personal opinions and judgments (RL.6.2; RI.6.2)</td></tr>
<tr><td>Score 2.0</td><td>The student will recognize or recall specific vocabulary, such as:
• Central idea, convey, detail, distinct, judgment, opinion, personal, summarize, summary, text, theme
The student will perform basic processes, such as:
• Determine a theme or central idea of a grade-appropriate text (RL.6.2; RI.6.2)
• Identify particular details that convey a teacher-provided theme or central idea of a grade-appropriate text
• Summarize a grade-appropriate text using a teacher-provided graphic organizer</td></tr>
</table>

<table>
<tr><th colspan="2">Grade 5</th></tr>
<tr><td>Score 3.0</td><td>The student will:
• Describe a theme or central idea of a grade-appropriate text from details in the text, including how characters in a story or drama respond to challenges, how the speaker in a poem reflects on a topic, or how key details support the central idea (RL.5.2; RI.5.2)
• Summarize a grade-appropriate text (RL.5.2; RI.5.2)</td></tr>
<tr><td>Score 2.0</td><td>The student will recognize or recall specific vocabulary, such as:
• Central idea, challenge, character, detail, drama, poem, reflect, respond, speaker, story, summarize, support, text, theme, topic
The student will perform basic processes, such as:
• Determine a theme or central idea of a grade-appropriate text (RL.5.2; RI.5.2)
• Identify details that support a teacher-provided theme or central idea of a grade-appropriate text
• Summarize a grade-appropriate text using a teacher-provided graphic organizer</td></tr>
<tr><th colspan="2">Grade 4</th></tr>
<tr><td>Score 3.0</td><td>The student will:
• Describe the theme or central idea of a grade-appropriate text from details in the text (RL.4.2; RI.4.2)
• Summarize a grade-appropriate text (RL.4.2; RI.4.2)</td></tr>
<tr><td>Score 2.0</td><td>The student will recognize or recall specific vocabulary, such as:
• Central idea, detail, summarize, support, text, theme
The student will perform basic processes, such as:
• Determine the theme of a grade-appropriate text (RL.4.2; RI.4.2)
• Identify details that support a teacher-provided theme or central idea of a grade-appropriate text
• Summarize a grade-appropriate text using a teacher-provided graphic organizer</td></tr>
<tr><th colspan="2">Grade 3</th></tr>
<tr><td>Score 3.0</td><td>The student will:
• Explain how the central message, lesson, or moral of fables, folktales, and myths from diverse cultures is conveyed through key details in a grade-appropriate text (RL.3.2)
• Explain how key details support the central idea of a grade-appropriate text (RI.3.2)</td></tr>
<tr><td>Score 2.0</td><td>The student will recognize or recall specific vocabulary, such as:
• Central idea, convey, culture, detail, diverse, fable, folktale, lesson, message, moral, myth, support, text
The student will perform basic processes, such as:
• Determine the central message, lesson, or moral of grade-appropriate fables, folktales, and myths from diverse cultures (RL.3.2)
• Identify key details that support a teacher-provided central idea of a grade-appropriate text (RI.3.2)</td></tr>
<tr><th colspan="2">Grade 2</th></tr>
<tr><td>Score 3.0</td><td>The student will:
• Determine the central message, lesson, or moral of stories from diverse cultures, including fables and folktales (RL.2.2)
• Describe the central idea of a multiparagraph grade-appropriate text, as well as the focus of specific paragraphs within the text (RI.2.2)</td></tr>
</table>

Score 2.0	The student will recognize or recall specific vocabulary, such as: • *Central idea, culture, diverse, fable, focus, folktale, lesson, message, moral, paragraph, story, text* The student will perform basic processes, such as: • Recount grade-appropriate stories, including fables and folktales from diverse cultures (RL.2.2) • Identify the central idea of a multiparagraph grade-appropriate text (RI.2.2) • Recognize or recall the central message, lesson, or moral of grade-appropriate stories, including fables and folktales
Grade 1	
Score 3.0	The student will: • Determine the central message or lesson of grade-appropriate stories (RL.1.2) • Identify the topic, central idea, and key details of a grade-appropriate text (RI.1.2)
Score 2.0	The student will recognize or recall specific vocabulary, such as: • *Central idea, detail, lesson, message, retell, story, text, topic* The student will perform basic processes, such as: • Retell grade-appropriate stories, including key details (RL.1.2) • Retell key details of a grade-appropriate text (RI.1.2) • Recognize or recall the central message or lesson of grade-appropriate stories
Kindergarten	
Score 3.0	The student will: • Retell grade-appropriate familiar stories, including key details (RL.K.2) • Identify the central idea and key details of a grade-appropriate text (RI.K.2) • Retell key details of a grade-appropriate text (RI.K.2)
Score 2.0	The student will recognize or recall specific vocabulary, such as: • *Central idea, detail, retell, story, text* The student will perform basic processes, such as: • Retell grade-appropriate familiar stories using cues (for example, pictures from the story) • Recognize the central idea of a grade-appropriate text

Story Elements

Grades 11–12		
Score 4.0	In addition to score 3.0 performance, the student demonstrates in-depth inferences and applications that go beyond what was taught.	
	Score 3.5	*In addition to score 3.0 performance, partial success at score 4.0 content*
Score 3.0	The student will: • Analyze the impact of the author's choices regarding how to develop and relate elements of a grade-appropriate story or drama (for example, where a story is set, how the action is ordered, how the characters are introduced and developed) (RL.11–12.3)	
	Score 2.5	*No major errors or omissions regarding score 2.0 content, and partial success at score 3.0 content*
Score 2.0	The student will recognize or recall specific vocabulary, such as: • *Action, analyze, author, character, develop, drama, element, impact, introduce, relate, setting, story, text* The student will perform basic processes, such as: • Describe the elements and author's choices in a grade-appropriate text	

	Score 1.5	*Partial success at score 2.0 content, and major errors or omissions regarding score 3.0 content*
Score 1.0	With help, partial success at score 2.0 content and score 3.0 content	
	Score 0.5	*With help, partial success at score 2.0 content but not at score 3.0 content*
Score 0.0	Even with help, no success	
	Grades 9–10	
Score 3.0	The student will: • Analyze how complex characters (for example, those with multiple or conflicting motivations) develop over the course of a grade-appropriate text, interact with other characters, and advance the plot or develop the theme (RL.9–10.3)	
Score 2.0	The student will recognize or recall specific vocabulary, such as: • *Analyze*, *character*, *complex*, *conflict*, *develop*, *interact*, *motivation*, *plot*, *text*, *theme* The student will perform basic processes, such as: • Describe the characters in a grade-appropriate text	
	Grade 8	
Score 3.0	The student will: • Analyze how particular lines of dialogue or incidents in a grade-appropriate story or drama propel the action, reveal aspects of a character, or provoke a decision (RL.8.3)	
Score 2.0	The student will recognize or recall specific vocabulary, such as: • *Action*, *analyze*, *character*, *decision*, *dialogue*, *drama*, *impact*, *incident*, *propel*, *provoke*, *reveal*, *story* The student will perform basic processes, such as: • Identify lines of dialogue or incidents that have an impact on a grade-appropriate story	
	Grade 7	
Score 3.0	The student will: • Analyze how particular elements of a grade-appropriate story or drama interact (for example, how setting shapes the characters or plot) (RL.7.3)	
Score 2.0	The student will recognize or recall specific vocabulary, such as: • *Analyze*, *character*, *drama*, *element*, *interact*, *plot*, *sequence of events*, *setting*, *shape*, *story* The student will perform basic processes, such as: • Identify the basic elements of a grade-appropriate story or drama (for example, main characters, setting, sequence of events)	
	Grade 6	
Score 3.0	The student will: • Describe how a particular grade-appropriate story's or drama's plot unfolds in a series of episodes as well as how the characters respond or change as the plot moves toward a resolution (RL.6.3)	
Score 2.0	The student will recognize or recall specific vocabulary, such as: • *Character*, *drama*, *episode*, *plot*, *resolution*, *respond*, *series*, *story*, *trait* The student will perform basic processes, such as: • Describe the plot of a grade-appropriate story or drama • Identify character traits of major characters in a grade-appropriate story or drama	
	Grade 5	
Score 3.0	The student will: • Compare and contrast two or more characters, settings, or events in a grade-appropriate story or drama, drawing on specific details in the text (for example, how characters interact) (RL.5.3)	

Score 2.0	The student will recognize or recall specific vocabulary, such as: • *Character, compare, contrast, detail, drama, event, interact, setting, story, support, text* The student will perform basic processes, such as: • Describe the characters, settings, and events in a grade-appropriate story or drama • Identify details that support the description of a character, setting, or event in a grade-appropriate story or drama
Grade 4	
Score 3.0	The student will: • Describe in depth a character, setting, or event in a grade-appropriate story or drama, drawing on specific details in the text (for example, a character's thoughts, words, or actions) (RL.4.3)
Score 2.0	The student will recognize or recall specific vocabulary, such as: • *Action, character, detail, drama, event, setting, story, support, text, thought* The student will perform basic processes, such as: • Recognize or recall specific characters, settings, or events from a grade-appropriate story or drama • Identify details that support the description of a character, setting, or event in a grade-appropriate story or drama
Grade 3	
Score 3.0	The student will: • Describe the characters in a grade-appropriate story (for example, their traits, motivations, or feelings) and explain how their actions contribute to the sequence of events (RL.3.3)
Score 2.0	The student will recognize or recall specific vocabulary, such as: • *Action, character, contribute, feeling, motivation, sequence of events, story, trait* The student will perform basic processes, such as: • Recognize or recall the character's traits, motivations, and/or feelings from a grade-appropriate story
Grade 2	
Score 3.0	The student will: • Describe how characters in a grade-appropriate story respond to major events and challenges (RL.2.3)
Score 2.0	The student will recognize or recall specific vocabulary, such as: • *Challenge, character, event, respond, story* The student will perform basic processes, such as: • Recognize or recall how characters in a grade-appropriate story respond to major events and challenges
Grade 1	
Score 3.0	The student will: • Describe the characters, setting, and major events of a grade-appropriate story (RL.1.3)
Score 2.0	The student will recognize or recall specific vocabulary, such as: • *Character, event, setting, story* The student will perform basic processes, such as: • Recognize or recall characters, settings, and major events in a grade-appropriate story
Kindergarten	
Score 3.0	The student will: • Describe characters, settings, and major events in a grade-appropriate story (RL.K.3)

Score 2.0	The student will recognize or recall specific vocabulary, such as: • *Character, event, setting, story* The student will perform basic processes, such as: • Recognize characters, settings, and major events in a grade-appropriate story	

Connections

	Grades 11–12	
Score 4.0	In addition to score 3.0 performance, the student demonstrates in-depth inferences and applications that go beyond what was taught.	
	Score 3.5	*In addition to score 3.0 performance, partial success at score 4.0 content*
Score 3.0	The student will: • Analyze a complex set of ideas or sequence of events and explain how specific individuals, ideas, or events interact over the course of a grade-appropriate text (RI.11–12.3)	
	Score 2.5	*No major errors or omissions regarding score 2.0 content, and partial success at score 3.0 content*
Score 2.0	The student will recognize or recall specific vocabulary, such as: • *Analyze, complex, event, idea, individual, interact, sequence of events, text* The student will perform basic processes, such as: • Describe a complex set of ideas or sequence of events in a grade-appropriate text	
	Score 1.5	*Partial success at score 2.0 content, and major errors or omissions regarding score 3.0 content*
Score 1.0	With help, partial success at score 2.0 content and score 3.0 content	
	Score 0.5	*With help, partial success at score 2.0 content but not at score 3.0 content*
Score 0.0	Even with help, no success	
	Grades 9–10	
Score 3.0	The student will: • Analyze how the author unfolds an analysis or series of ideas or events in a grade-appropriate text, including the order in which the points are made, how they are introduced and developed, and the connections that are drawn between them (RI.9–10.3)	
Score 2.0	The student will recognize or recall specific vocabulary, such as: • *Analysis, analyze, author, connection, develop, event, idea, introduce, point, series* The student will perform basic processes, such as: • Describe how the author unfolds the analysis or series of ideas or events in a grade-appropriate text	
	Grade 8	
Score 3.0	The student will: • Analyze how a grade-appropriate text makes connections among and distinctions between individuals, ideas, or events (for example, through comparisons, analogies, or categories) (RI.8.3)	
Score 2.0	The student will recognize or recall specific vocabulary, such as: • *Analogy, analyze, category, comparison, connection, distinction, event, idea, individual, text* The student will perform basic processes, such as: • Describe the connections between individuals, ideas, or events in a grade-appropriate text	

Grade 7	
Score 3.0	The student will: • Analyze the interactions between individuals, events, and ideas in a grade-appropriate text (for example, how ideas influence individuals or events or how individuals influence ideas or events) (RI.7.3)
Score 2.0	The student will recognize or recall specific vocabulary, such as: • *Analyze*, *event*, *idea*, *individual*, *influence*, *interaction*, *text* The student will perform basic processes, such as: • Describe the interactions between the individuals, events, and ideas in a grade-appropriate text
Grade 6	
Score 3.0	The student will: • Analyze in detail how a key individual, event, or idea is introduced, illustrated, and elaborated in a grade-appropriate text (for example, through examples or anecdotes) (RI.6.3)
Score 2.0	The student will recognize or recall specific vocabulary, such as: • *Analyze*, *anecdote*, *detail*, *elaborate*, *event*, *example*, *idea*, *illustrate*, *individual*, *introduce*, *text* The student will perform basic processes, such as: • Describe the introduction, illustration, or elaboration of a key individual, event, or idea in a grade-appropriate text
Grade 5	
Score 3.0	The student will: • Explain the relationships or interactions between two or more individuals, events, ideas, or concepts in a historical, scientific, or technical grade-appropriate text based on specific information in the text (RI.5.3)
Score 2.0	The student will recognize or recall specific vocabulary, such as: • *Concept*, *detail*, *event*, *historical*, *idea*, *individual*, *information*, *interaction*, *relationship*, *scientific*, *technical*, *text* The student will perform basic processes, such as: • Recognize or recall details of the relationships or interactions between two individuals, events, ideas, or concepts in a grade-appropriate text
Grade 4	
Score 3.0	The student will: • Explain events, procedures, ideas, or concepts in a historical, scientific, or technical grade-appropriate text, including what happened and why, based on specific information in the text (RI.4.3)
Score 2.0	The student will recognize or recall specific vocabulary, such as: • *Concept*, *detail*, *event*, *historical*, *idea*, *information*, *procedure*, *scientific*, *technical*, *text* The student will perform basic processes, such as: • Recognize or recall events, procedures, ideas, or concepts in a grade-appropriate text • Map events, procedures, ideas, or concepts in a grade-appropriate text using a teacher-provided template or graphic organizer
Grade 3	
Score 3.0	The student will: • Describe the relationship between a series of historical events, scientific ideas or concepts, or steps in technical procedures in a grade-appropriate text, using language that pertains to time, sequence, and cause/effect (RI.3.3)

Score 2.0	The student will recognize or recall specific vocabulary, such as: • *Cause/effect, concept, connection, event, historical, idea, procedure, relationship, sequence, series, scientific, technical, text, time* The student will perform basic processes, such as: • Recognize or recall events, ideas, concepts, or steps in a grade-appropriate text as they relate to time or sequence • Map connections between a series of events, ideas, concepts, or steps in a grade-appropriate text using a teacher-provided template or graphic organizer
	Grade 2
Score 3.0	The student will: • Describe the connection between a series of historical events, scientific ideas or concepts, or steps in technical procedures in a grade-appropriate text (RI.2.3)
Score 2.0	The student will recognize or recall specific vocabulary, such as: • *Concept, connection, event, idea, procedure, series, text* The student will perform basic processes, such as: • Recognize or recall events, ideas, concepts, or steps in a grade-appropriate text • Map connections between a series of events, ideas, or steps in a grade-appropriate text using a teacher-provided template or graphic organizer
	Grade 1
Score 3.0	The student will: • Describe the connection between two individuals, events, ideas, or pieces of information in a grade-appropriate text (RI.1.3)
Score 2.0	The student will recognize or recall specific vocabulary, such as: • *Connection, event, idea, individual, information, text* The student will perform basic processes, such as: • Recognize or recall how individuals, events, ideas, and pieces of information in a grade-appropriate text are connected
	Kindergarten
Score 3.0	The student will: • Describe the connection between two individuals, events, ideas, or pieces of information in a grade-appropriate text (RI.K.3)
Score 2.0	The student will recognize or recall specific vocabulary, such as: • *Connection, event, idea, individual, information, text* The student will perform basic processes, such as: • Recognize or recall individuals, events, ideas, or pieces of information that are connected in a grade-appropriate text

Word Impact and Use

	Grades 11–12	
Score 4.0	In addition to score 3.0 performance, the student demonstrates in-depth inferences and applications that go beyond what was taught.	
	Score 3.5	*In addition to score 3.0 performance, partial success at score 4.0 content*

<table>
<tr><td>Score 3.0</td><td colspan="2">The student will:
• Analyze the impact of specific word choices on meaning and tone in a grade-appropriate text, including words with multiple meanings or language that is particularly fresh, engaging, or beautiful (RL.11–12.4)
• Analyze the role of figures of speech (for example, hyperbole, paradox) in a grade-appropriate text (L.11–12.5a)
• Analyze nuances in the meanings of words with similar denotations in a grade-appropriate text (L.11–12.5b)</td></tr>
<tr><td></td><td>Score 2.5</td><td>No major errors or omissions regarding score 2.0 content, and partial success at score 3.0 content</td></tr>
<tr><td>Score 2.0</td><td colspan="2">The student will recognize or recall specific vocabulary, such as:
• Analyze, connotative, denotation, engaging, figurative, figure of speech, hyperbole, impact, interpret, language, meaning, nuance, paradox, role, similar, text, tone
The student will perform basic processes, such as:
• Identify specific words that impact meaning and tone in a grade-appropriate text
• Interpret figures of speech in context in a grade-appropriate text (L.11–12.5a)
• Determine the meaning of words and phrases as they are used in a grade-appropriate text, including figurative and connotative meanings (RL.11–12.4; RI.11–12.4)</td></tr>
<tr><td></td><td>Score 1.5</td><td>Partial success at score 2.0 content, and major errors or omissions regarding score 3.0 content</td></tr>
<tr><td>Score 1.0</td><td colspan="2">With help, partial success at score 2.0 content and score 3.0 content</td></tr>
<tr><td></td><td>Score 0.5</td><td>With help, partial success at score 2.0 content but not at score 3.0 content</td></tr>
<tr><td>Score 0.0</td><td colspan="2">Even with help, no success</td></tr>
<tr><td colspan="3">Grades 9–10</td></tr>
<tr><td>Score 3.0</td><td colspan="2">The student will:
• Analyze the cumulative impact of specific word choices on meaning and tone in a grade-appropriate text (for example, how the language evokes a sense of time and place; how it sets a formal or informal tone) (RL.9–10.4; RI.9–10.4)
• Analyze the role of figures of speech (for example, euphemism, oxymoron) in a grade-appropriate text (L.9–10.5a)
• Analyze nuances in the meaning of words with similar denotations in a grade-appropriate text (L.9–10.5b)</td></tr>
<tr><td>Score 2.0</td><td colspan="2">The student will recognize or recall specific vocabulary, such as:
• Analyze, connotative, cumulative, denotation, euphemism, evoke, figurative, figure of speech, formal tone, impact, informal tone, interpret, language, meaning, nuance, oxymoron, place, role, similar, text, time, tone
The student will perform basic processes, such as:
• Identify specific words that impact meaning and tone in a grade-appropriate text
• Interpret figures of speech (for example, euphemism, oxymoron) in context in a grade-appropriate text (L.9–10.5a)
• Determine the meaning of words and phrases as they are used in a grade-appropriate text, including figurative and connotative meanings (RL.9–10.4; RI.9–10.4)</td></tr>
<tr><td colspan="3">Grade 8</td></tr>
<tr><td>Score 3.0</td><td colspan="2">The student will:
• Analyze the impact of specific word choices on meaning and tone in a grade-appropriate text, including analogies or allusions to other texts (RL.8.4; RI.8.4)
• Interpret figures of speech (for example, verbal irony, puns) in context in a grade-appropriate text (L.8.5a)
• Distinguish among the connotations (associations) of words with similar denotations (definitions) (for example, bullheaded, willful, firm, persistent, resolute) in a grade-appropriate text (L.8.5c)</td></tr>
</table>

<table>
<tr><td>Score 2.0</td><td>The student will recognize or recall specific vocabulary, such as:<ul><li>Allusion, analogy, analyze, association, connotation, connotative, definition, denotation, distinguish, figurative, figure of speech, impact, interpret, meaning, pun, similar, text, tone, verbal irony</li></ul>The student will perform basic processes, such as:<ul><li>Identify specific words that impact meaning and tone in a grade-appropriate text</li><li>Identify analogies or allusions to other texts in a grade-appropriate text</li><li>Identify figures of speech in a grade-appropriate text</li><li>Determine the meaning of words and phrases as they are used in a grade-appropriate text, including figurative and connotative meanings (RL.8.4; RI.8.4)</li></ul></td></tr>
<tr><td colspan="2">Grade 7</td></tr>
<tr><td>Score 3.0</td><td>The student will:<ul><li>Analyze the impact of rhymes and other repetitions of sounds (for example, alliteration) on a specific verse or stanza of a grade-appropriate poem or section of a grade-appropriate story or drama (RL.7.4)</li><li>Analyze the impact of a specific word choice on meaning and tone in a grade-appropriate text (RI.7.4)</li><li>Interpret figures of speech (for example, literary, biblical, and mythological allusions) in a grade-appropriate text (L.7.5a)</li><li>Distinguish among the connotations (associations) of words with similar denotations (definitions) (for example, refined, respectful, polite, diplomatic, condescending) in a grade-appropriate text (L.7.5c)</li></ul></td></tr>
<tr><td>Score 2.0</td><td>The student will recognize or recall specific vocabulary, such as:<ul><li>Alliteration, allusion, analyze, association, biblical, connotation, connotative, definition, denotation, distinguish, drama, figurative, figure of speech, impact, interpret, literary, meaning, mythological, poem, repetition, rhyme, similar, sound, stanza, story, text, tone, verse</li></ul>The student will perform basic processes, such as:<ul><li>Identify examples of rhymes and other repetitions of sound in a grade-appropriate poem, story, or drama</li><li>Identify specific words that impact the meaning and tone of a grade-appropriate text</li><li>Identify figures of speech in a grade-appropriate text</li><li>Describe the background of teacher-provided figures of speech (for example, literary, biblical, and mythological allusions)</li><li>Determine the meaning of words and phrases as they are used in a grade-appropriate text, including figurative and connotative meanings (RL.7.4; RI.7.4)</li></ul></td></tr>
<tr><td colspan="2">Grade 6</td></tr>
<tr><td>Score 3.0</td><td>The student will:<ul><li>Analyze the impact of a specific word choice on meaning and tone in a grade-appropriate text (RL.6.4)</li><li>Interpret figures of speech (for example, personification) in context in a grade-appropriate text (L.6.5a)</li><li>Distinguish among the connotations (associations) of words with similar denotations (definitions) (for example, stingy, scrimping, economical, unwasteful, thrifty) in a grade-appropriate text (L.6.5c)</li></ul></td></tr>
<tr><td>Score 2.0</td><td>The student will recognize or recall specific vocabulary, such as:<ul><li>Analyze, association, connotation, connotative, definition, denotation, distinguish, figurative, figure of speech, impact, interpret, meaning, personification, similar, text, tone</li></ul>The student will perform basic processes, such as:<ul><li>Identify specific words that have an impact on meaning and tone in a grade-appropriate text</li><li>Identify examples of figures of speech in a grade-appropriate text</li><li>Determine the meaning of words and phrases as they are used in a grade-appropriate text, including figurative and connotative meanings (RL.6.4; RI.6.4)</li></ul></td></tr>
</table>

Grade 5	
Score 3.0	The student will: • Interpret figurative language, including similes and metaphors, in context in a grade-appropriate text (L.5.5a) • Interpret idioms, adages, and proverbs in a grade-appropriate text (L.5.5b)
Score 2.0	The student will recognize or recall specific vocabulary, such as: • *Adage*, *figurative*, *language*, *idiom*, *interpret*, *metaphor*, *proverb*, *simile*, *text* The student will perform basic processes, such as: • Identify words and phrases used figuratively in a grade-appropriate text, including metaphors and similes (RL.5.4) • Identify examples of idioms, adages, and proverbs in a grade-appropriate text
Grade 4	
Score 3.0	The student will: • Interpret the meaning of words and phrases in a grade-appropriate text that allude to significant characters found in mythology (for example, *Herculean*) (RL.4.4) • Explain the meaning of simple similes and metaphors (for example, *as pretty as a picture*) in context in a grade-appropriate text (L.4.5a) • Explain the meaning of common idioms, adages, and proverbs in a grade-appropriate text (L.4.5b)
Score 2.0	The student will recognize or recall specific vocabulary, such as: • *Adage*, *allude*, *allusion*, *character*, *idiom*, *interpret*, *meaning*, *metaphor*, *mythology*, *proverb*, *simile*, *text* The student will perform basic processes, such as: • Determine the meaning of words and phrases as they are used in a grade-appropriate text (RL.4.4) • Identify words and phrases in a grade-appropriate text that allude to significant characters found in mythology • Describe the background of teacher-provided allusions (for example, *Hercules was capable of great feats of strength*) • Recognize or recall examples of simple similes and metaphors • Identify common idioms, adages, and proverbs in a grade-appropriate text
Grade 3	
Score 3.0	The student will: • Distinguish the literal and nonliteral meanings of words and phrases in context (for example, *take steps*) in a grade-appropriate text (L.3.5a) • Distinguish shades of meaning among related words that describe states of mind or degrees of certainty (for example, *knew*, *believed*, *suspected*, *heard*, *wondered*) in a grade-appropriate text (L.3.5c)
Score 2.0	The student will recognize or recall specific vocabulary, such as: • *Degree of certainty*, *distinguish*, *literal*, *meaning*, *nonliteral*, *related*, *shade of meaning*, *state of mind*, *text* The student will perform basic processes, such as: • Determine the meaning of literal and nonliteral words and phrases in isolation (RL.3.4) • Determine the meaning of words that describe states of mind or degrees of certainty
Grade 2	
Score 3.0	The student will: • Describe how words and phrases (for example, those with regular beats, alliteration, rhymes, and repeated lines) supply rhythm and meaning in a grade-appropriate story, poem, or song (RL.2.4) • Distinguish shades of meaning among closely related verbs (for example, *toss*, *throw*, *pitch*) and closely related adjectives (for example, *thin*, *slender*, *skinny*, *scrawny*) in a grade-appropriate text (L.2.5b)

Score 2.0	The student will recognize or recall specific vocabulary, such as: • *Adjective, alliteration, beat, distinguish, meaning, poem, related, rhyme, rhythm, shade of meaning, song, story, text, verb* The student will perform basic processes, such as: • Identify examples of regular beats, alliteration, rhymes, and repeated lines in grade-appropriate stories, poems, or songs • Determine the meanings of closely related verbs and adjectives in isolation
Grade 1	
Score 3.0	The student will: • Describe how words and phrases in grade-appropriate stories or poems suggest feelings or appeal to the senses (RL.1.4) • Distinguish shades of meaning among verbs differing in manner (for example, *look*, *peek*, *glance*, *stare*, *glare*, *scowl*) and adjectives differing in intensity (for example, *large*, *gigantic*) by defining or choosing them or by acting out the meanings (L.1.5d)
Score 2.0	The student will recognize or recall specific vocabulary, such as: • *Adjective, appeal, define, distinguish, feeling, meaning, poem, senses, shade of meaning, story, text, verb* The student will perform basic processes, such as: • Identify words and phrases in grade-appropriate stories or poems that suggest feelings or appeal to the senses (RL.1.4) • Determine the meaning of verbs differing in manner and adjectives differing in intensity in isolation
Kindergarten	
Score 3.0	The student will: • Ask and answer questions about unknown words in a grade-appropriate text (RL.K.4) • Distinguish shades of meaning among verbs describing the same general action (for example, *walk*, *march*, *strut*, *prance*) (L.K.5d)
Score 2.0	The student will recognize or recall specific vocabulary, such as: • *Action, answer, ask, meaning, question, shade of meaning, text, verb* The student will perform basic processes, such as: • Answer teacher-provided questions about unknown words in a grade-appropriate text • Determine the meaning of verbs describing the same general action in isolation

Academic Vocabulary

Grades 11–12		
Score 4.0	In addition to score 3.0 performance, the student demonstrates in-depth inferences and applications that go beyond what was taught.	
	Score 3.5	*In addition to score 3.0 performance, partial success at score 4.0 content*
Score 3.0	The student will: • Analyze how an author uses and refines the meaning of a key term or terms over the course of a grade-appropriate text (for example, how Madison defines *faction* in *Federalist* No. 10) (RI.11–12.4) • Verify the preliminary determination of the meaning of a grade-appropriate word or phrase (for example, by checking the inferred meaning in context or in a dictionary) (L.11–12.4d) • Demonstrate independence in gathering vocabulary knowledge when considering a word or phrase important to comprehension or expression (L.11–12.6)	

	Score 2.5	*No major errors or omissions regarding score 2.0 content, and partial success at score 3.0 content*
Score 2.0	The student will recognize or recall specific vocabulary, such as: • *Academic, analyze, author, comprehension, context, determination, dictionary, domain-specific, expression, inferred meaning, meaning, phrase, preliminary, refine, technical meaning, term, text, verify, vocabulary, word* The student will perform basic processes, such as: • Determine the meaning of words and phrases as they are used in a grade-appropriate text, including technical meanings (RI.11–12.4) • Acquire and use accurately general academic and domain-specific words and phrases, sufficient for reading, writing, speaking, and listening at grade level (L.11–12.6)	
	Score 1.5	*Partial success at score 2.0 content, and major errors or omissions regarding score 3.0 content*
Score 1.0	With help, partial success at score 2.0 content and score 3.0 content	
	Score 0.5	*With help, partial success at score 2.0 content but not at score 3.0 content*
Score 0.0	Even with help, no success	
	Grades 9–10	
Score 3.0	The student will: • Determine the meaning of words and phrases as they are used in a grade-appropriate text, including technical meanings (RI.9–10.4) • Verify the preliminary determination of the meaning of a grade-appropriate word or phrase (for example, by checking the inferred meaning in context or in a dictionary) (L.9–10.4d) • Demonstrate independence in gathering vocabulary knowledge when considering a word or phrase important to comprehension or expression (L.9–10.6)	
Score 2.0	The student will recognize or recall specific vocabulary, such as: • *Academic, comprehension, context, determination, dictionary, domain-specific, expression, inferred meaning, meaning, phrase, preliminary, technical meaning, text, verify, vocabulary, word* The student will perform basic processes, such as: • Acquire and use accurately general academic and domain-specific words and phrases, sufficient for reading, writing, speaking, and listening at grade level (L.9–10.6)	
	Grade 8	
Score 3.0	The student will: • Determine the meaning of words and phrases as they are used in a grade-appropriate text, including technical meanings (RI.8.4) • Verify the preliminary determination of the meaning of a grade-appropriate word or phrase (for example, by checking the inferred meaning in context or in a dictionary) (L.8.4d) • Gather vocabulary knowledge when considering a word or phrase important to comprehension or expression (L.8.6)	
Score 2.0	The student will recognize or recall specific vocabulary, such as: • *Academic, comprehension, context, determination, dictionary, domain-specific, expression, inferred meaning, meaning, phrase, preliminary, technical meaning, text, verify, vocabulary, word* The student will perform basic processes, such as: • Acquire and use accurately grade-appropriate general academic and domain-specific words and phrases (L.8.6)	

Grade 7	
Score 3.0	The student will: • Determine the meaning of words and phrases as they are used in a grade-appropriate text, including technical meanings (RI.7.4) • Verify the preliminary determination of the meaning of a grade-appropriate word or phrase (for example, by checking the inferred meaning in context or in a dictionary) (L.7.4d) • Gather vocabulary knowledge when considering a word or phrase important to comprehension or expression (L.7.6)
Score 2.0	The student will recognize or recall specific vocabulary, such as: • *Academic*, *comprehension*, *context*, *determination*, *dictionary*, *domain-specific*, *expression*, *inferred meaning*, *meaning*, *phrase*, *preliminary*, *technical meaning*, *text*, *verify*, *vocabulary*, *word* The student will perform basic processes, such as: • Acquire and use accurately grade-appropriate general academic and domain-specific words and phrases (L.7.6)
Grade 6	
Score 3.0	The student will: • Determine the meaning of words and phrases as they are used in a grade-appropriate text, including technical meanings (RI.6.4) • Verify the preliminary determination of the meaning of a grade-appropriate word or phrase (for example, by checking the inferred meaning in context or in a dictionary) (L.6.4d) • Gather vocabulary knowledge when considering a word or phrase important to comprehension or expression (L.6.6)
Score 2.0	The student will recognize or recall specific vocabulary, such as: • *Academic*, *comprehension*, *context*, *determination*, *dictionary*, *domain-specific*, *expression*, *inferred meaning*, *meaning*, *phrase*, *preliminary*, *technical meaning*, *text*, *verify*, *vocabulary*, *word* The student will perform basic processes, such as: • Acquire and use accurately grade-appropriate general academic and domain-specific words and phrases (L.6.6)
Grade 5	
Score 3.0	The student will: • Determine the meaning of general academic and domain-specific words and phrases in a text relevant to a grade 5 topic or subject area (RI.5.4)
Score 2.0	The student will recognize or recall specific vocabulary, such as: • *Academic*, *addition*, *contrast*, *domain-specific*, *logical*, *meaning*, *phrase*, *relationship*, *text*, *word* The student will perform basic processes, such as: • Acquire and use accurately grade-appropriate general academic and domain-specific words and phrases, including those that signal contrast, addition, and other logical relationships (for example, *however*, *although*, *nevertheless*, *similarly*, *moreover*, *in addition*) (L.5.6)
Grade 4	
Score 3.0	The student will: • Determine the meaning of general academic and domain-specific words or phrases in a text relevant to a grade 4 topic or subject area (RI.4.4)

<table>
<tr><td>Score 2.0</td><td>The student will recognize or recall specific vocabulary, such as:
• Academic, action, basic, domain-specific, emotion, meaning, phrase, state of being, text, word
The student will perform basic processes, such as:
• Acquire and use grade-appropriate general academic and domain-specific words and phrases, including those that signal precise actions, emotions, or states of being (for example, quizzed, whined, stammered) and that are basic to a particular topic (for example, wildlife, conservation, and endangered when discussing animal preservation) (L.4.6)</td></tr>
<tr><td colspan="2">Grade 3</td></tr>
<tr><td>Score 3.0</td><td>The student will:
• Determine the meaning of general academic and domain-specific words and phrases in a text relevant to a grade 3 topic or subject area (RI.3.4)</td></tr>
<tr><td>Score 2.0</td><td>The student will recognize or recall specific vocabulary, such as:
• Academic, conversational, domain-specific, meaning, phrase, relationship, spatial, temporal, text, word
The student will perform basic processes, such as:
• Acquire and use grade-appropriate conversational, general academic, and domain-specific words and phrases, including those that signal spatial and temporal relationships (for example, After dinner that night we went looking for them) (L.3.6)</td></tr>
<tr><td colspan="2">Grade 2</td></tr>
<tr><td>Score 3.0</td><td>The student will:
• Determine the meaning of words and phrases in a text relevant to a grade 2 topic or subject area (RI.2.4)
• Use grade-appropriate words and phrases acquired through conversations, reading and being read to, and responding to a grade-appropriate text, including using adjectives and adverbs to describe (for example, When other kids are happy that makes me happy) (L.2.6)</td></tr>
<tr><td>Score 2.0</td><td>The student will recognize or recall specific vocabulary, such as:
• Adjective, adverb, conversation, meaning, respond, text, word
The student will perform basic processes, such as:
• Recognize or recall the meaning of grade-appropriate general academic and domain-specific words and phrases</td></tr>
<tr><td colspan="2">Grade 1</td></tr>
<tr><td>Score 3.0</td><td>The student will:
• Ask and answer questions to help determine or clarify the meaning of words and phrases in a grade-appropriate text (RI.1.4)
• Define grade-appropriate words by category and by one or more key attributes (for example, a duck is a bird that swims; a tiger is a large cat with stripes) (L.1.5b)
• Use grade-appropriate words and phrases acquired through conversations, reading, and being read to, including frequently occurring conjunctions to signal simple relationships (L.1.6)</td></tr>
<tr><td>Score 2.0</td><td>The student will recognize or recall specific vocabulary, such as:
• Answer, ask, attribute, category, clarify, conjunction, conversation, define, meaning, question, relationship, text, word
The student will perform basic processes, such as:
• Recognize or recall the meaning of grade-appropriate general academic and domain-specific words and phrases</td></tr>
<tr><td colspan="2">Kindergarten</td></tr>
<tr><td>Score 3.0</td><td>The student will:
• Ask and answer questions about unknown words in a grade-appropriate text (RI.K.4)
• Use grade-appropriate words and phrases acquired through conversations, reading, and being read to (L.K.6)</td></tr>
</table>

Score 2.0	The student will recognize or recall specific vocabulary, such as: • *Answer, ask, conversation, meaning, question, text, word* The student will perform basic processes, such as: • Identify unknown words in a grade-appropriate text • Recognize or recall the meaning of grade-appropriate general academic and domain-specific words and phrases

Text Structures and Features

	Grades 11–12	
Score 4.0	In addition to score 3.0 performance, the student demonstrates in-depth inferences and applications that go beyond what was taught.	
	Score 3.5	*In addition to score 3.0 performance, partial success at score 4.0 content*
Score 3.0	The student will: • Analyze how an author's choices concerning how to structure specific parts of a grade-appropriate text (for example, the choice of where to begin or end a story, the choice to provide a comedic or tragic resolution) contribute to its overall structure and meaning as well as its aesthetic impact (RL.11–12.5) • Analyze and evaluate the effectiveness of the structure an author uses in his or her exposition or argument in a grade-appropriate text, including whether the structure makes points clear, convincing, and engaging (RI.11–12.5)	
	Score 2.5	*No major errors or omissions regarding score 2.0 content, and partial success at score 3.0 content*
Score 2.0	The student will recognize or recall specific vocabulary, such as: • *Aesthetic, analyze, argument, author, comedic, engaging, evaluate, exposition, impact, meaning, point, resolution, structure, text, tragic* The student will perform basic processes, such as: • Describe the structure of grade-appropriate texts • Describe the author's structural choices in a grade-appropriate text	
	Score 1.5	*Partial success at score 2.0 content, and major errors or omissions regarding score 3.0 content*
Score 1.0	With help, partial success at score 2.0 content and score 3.0 content	
	Score 0.5	*With help, partial success at score 2.0 content but not at score 3.0 content*
Score 0.0	Even with help, no success	
	Grades 9–10	
Score 3.0	The student will: • Analyze how an author's choices concerning how to structure a grade-appropriate text, order events within it (for example, parallel plots), and manipulate time (for example, pacing, flashbacks) create such effects as mystery, tension, or surprise (RL.9–10.5) • Analyze in detail how an author's ideas or claims are developed and refined by particular sentences, paragraphs, or larger portions of a grade-appropriate text (for example, a section or chapter) (RI.9–10.5)	
Score 2.0	The student will recognize or recall specific vocabulary, such as: • *Analysis, analyze, author, chapter, claim, detail, develop, event, flashback, idea, manipulate, mystery, pacing, paragraph, parallel, plot, refine, section, sentence, series, structure, surprise, tension, text* The student will perform basic processes, such as: • Describe how an author chooses to structure a grade-appropriate text, order events, and manipulate time • Describe how the author lays out an analysis or series of ideas in a grade-appropriate text	

<table>
<tr><th colspan="2">Grade 8</th></tr>
<tr><td>Score 3.0</td><td>The student will:
• Compare and contrast the structure of two or more grade-appropriate texts and analyze how the differing structure of each text contributes to its meaning and style (RL.8.5)
• Analyze in detail the structure of a specific paragraph in a grade-appropriate text, including the role of particular sentences in developing and refining a key concept (RI.8.5)</td></tr>
<tr><td>Score 2.0</td><td>The student will recognize or recall specific vocabulary, such as:
• Analyze, compare, concept, contrast, detail, develop, meaning, paragraph, refine, role, sentence, structure, style, text
The student will perform basic processes, such as:
• Describe the structure of a grade-appropriate text
• Recognize signal words or phrases associated with text structure (for example, following, compared with, therefore, as a result of) in a grade-appropriate text
• Describe the structure of a specific paragraph in a grade-appropriate text</td></tr>
<tr><th colspan="2">Grade 7</th></tr>
<tr><td>Score 3.0</td><td>The student will:
• Analyze how a grade-appropriate drama's or poem's form or structure (for example, soliloquy, sonnet) contributes to its meaning (RL.7.5)
• Analyze the structure an author uses to organize a grade-appropriate text, including how the major sections contribute to the whole and to the development of the ideas (RI.7.5)</td></tr>
<tr><td>Score 2.0</td><td>The student will recognize or recall specific vocabulary, such as:
• Analyze, author, development, drama, form, idea, meaning, organize, poem, soliloquy, sonnet, structure, text
The student will perform basic processes, such as:
• Describe the form or structure of a grade-appropriate drama or poem
• Describe the structure of a given grade-appropriate text
• Recognize signal words or phrases associated with text structure (for example, following, compared with, therefore, as a result of) in a grade-appropriate text</td></tr>
<tr><th colspan="2">Grade 6</th></tr>
<tr><td>Score 3.0</td><td>The student will:
• Analyze how a particular sentence, chapter, scene, or stanza fits into the overall structure of a grade-appropriate text and contributes to the development of the theme, setting, or plot (RL.6.5)
• Analyze how a particular sentence, paragraph, chapter, or section fits into the overall structure of a grade-appropriate text and contributes to the development of the ideas (RI.6.5)</td></tr>
<tr><td>Score 2.0</td><td>The student will recognize or recall specific vocabulary, such as:
• Analyze, chapter, development, drama, form, idea, organizational pattern, paragraph, plot, scene, sentence, setting, stanza, story, structure, text, theme
The student will perform basic processes, such as:
• Map the plot of a grade-appropriate story or drama
• Describe the overall form, structure, or organizational pattern used in a grade-appropriate text</td></tr>
<tr><th colspan="2">Grade 5</th></tr>
<tr><td>Score 3.0</td><td>The student will:
• Explain how a series of chapters, scenes, or stanzas fits together to provide the overall structure of a particular grade-appropriate story, drama, or poem (RL.5.5)
• Compare and contrast the overall structure (for example, chronology, comparison, cause/effect, problem/solution) of events, ideas, concepts, or information in two or more grade-appropriate texts (RI.5.5)</td></tr>
</table>

Score 2.0	The student will recognize or recall specific vocabulary, such as: • *Cause/effect, chapter, chronology, compare, comparison, concept, contrast, drama, event, idea, information, informative, poem, problem/solution, scene, series, stanza, story, structure, text* The student will perform basic processes, such as: • Identify the parts (chapters, scenes, stanzas) of grade-appropriate stories, dramas, and poems • Map the structure of a grade-appropriate informative text using a teacher-provided graphic organizer
	Grade 4
Score 3.0	The student will: • Explain major differences between poems, drama, and prose (RL.4.5) • Refer to the structural elements of poems (for example, verse, rhythm, meter) and drama (for example, casts of characters, settings, descriptions, dialogue, stage directions) when writing or speaking about a grade-appropriate text (RL.4.5) • Describe the overall structure (for example, chronology, comparison, cause/effect, problem/solution) of events, ideas, concepts, or information in a grade-appropriate text or part of a grade-appropriate text (RI.4.5)
Score 2.0	The student will recognize or recall specific vocabulary, such as: • *Cause/effect, cast of characters, chronology, comparison, concept, description, dialogue, drama, event, idea, information, meter, poem, problem/solution, prose, refer, rhythm, setting, stage direction, structural element, structure, text, verse* The student will perform basic processes, such as: • Recognize or recall grade-appropriate examples of poems, drama, and prose • Recognize or recall characteristics of poems, drama, and prose • Identify grade-appropriate examples of text structure
	Grade 3
Score 3.0	The student will: • Describe how each successive part of a grade-appropriate story, drama, or poem builds on earlier sections (RL.3.5) • Refer to parts of stories, dramas, and poems using terms such as chapter, scene, and stanza when writing or speaking about a grade-appropriate text (RL.3.5) • Describe the logical relationships between particular sentences and paragraphs in a grade-appropriate text (for example, comparison, cause/effect, first/second/third in a sequence) (RI.3.8)
Score 2.0	The student will recognize or recall specific vocabulary, such as: • *Cause/effect, chapter, comparison, drama, logical, paragraph, poem, refer, relationship, scene, sentence, sequence, stanza, story, successive, text* The student will perform basic processes, such as: • Identify the parts of grade-appropriate stories, drama, and poems (for example, chapter, scene, stanza) • Identify words that signal relationships between sentences and paragraphs in a grade-appropriate text
	Grade 2
Score 3.0	The student will: • Describe the overall structure of a grade-appropriate story, including describing how the beginning introduces the story and the ending concludes the action (RL.2.5)
Score 2.0	The student will recognize or recall specific vocabulary, such as: • *Action, beginning, conclude, ending, introduce, story, structure, text* The student will perform basic processes, such as: • Identify grade-appropriate examples of text structures (for example, beginning, ending)

Grade 1	
Score 3.0	The student will: • Explain major differences between books that tell stories and books that give information (RL.1.5)
Score 2.0	The student will recognize or recall specific vocabulary, such as: • *Book, information, story* The student will perform basic processes, such as: • Recognize the differences between books that tell stories and books that give information
Kindergarten	
Score 3.0	The student will: • Identify examples of common types of texts (for example, storybooks, poems) (RL.K.5) • Describe the front cover, back cover, and title page of a book (RI.K.5)
Score 2.0	The student will recognize or recall specific vocabulary, such as: • *Back cover, book, example, front cover, poem, storybook, text, title page* The student will perform basic processes, such as: • Recognize common types of texts (for example, storybooks, poems) • Identify the front cover, back cover, and title page of a book

Point of View / Purpose

Grades 11–12		
Score 4.0	In addition to score 3.0 performance, the student demonstrates in-depth inferences and applications that go beyond what was taught.	
	Score 3.5	*In addition to score 3.0 performance, partial success at score 4.0 content*
Score 3.0	The student will: • Analyze a point of view in a grade-appropriate text where distinguishing what is directly stated from what is really meant is required (for example, satire, sarcasm, irony, or understatement) (RL.11–12.6) • Analyze how the style and content of a grade-appropriate text in which the rhetoric is particularly effective contribute to the power, persuasiveness, or beauty of the text (RI.11–12.6)	
	Score 2.5	*No major errors or omissions regarding score 2.0 content, and partial success at score 3.0 content*
Score 2.0	The student will recognize or recall specific vocabulary, such as: • *Analyze, author, distinguish, irony, persuasive, point of view, purpose, rhetoric, sarcasm, satire, style, understatement* The student will perform basic processes, such as: • Recognize or recall examples of satire, sarcasm, irony, and understatement in a grade-appropriate text • Determine an author's point of view or purpose in a grade-appropriate text (RI.11–12.6)	
	Score 1.5	*Partial success at score 2.0 content, and major errors or omissions regarding score 3.0 content*
Score 1.0	With help, partial success at score 2.0 content and score 3.0 content	
	Score 0.5	*With help, partial success at score 2.0 content but not at score 3.0 content*
Score 0.0	Even with help, no success	

<table>
<tr><th colspan="2">Grades 9–10</th></tr>
<tr><td>Score 3.0</td><td>The student will:
• Analyze a particular point of view or cultural experience reflected in a grade-appropriate work of literature from outside the United States, drawing on a wide reading of world literature (RL.9–10.6)
• Analyze how an author uses rhetoric to advance their point of view or purpose in a grade-appropriate text (RI.9–10.6)</td></tr>
<tr><td>Score 2.0</td><td>The student will recognize or recall specific vocabulary, such as:
• Analyze, author, cultural experience, literature, point of view, purpose, rhetoric
The student will perform basic processes, such as:
• Describe how a particular point of view or cultural experience is reflected in a grade-appropriate work of literature
• Determine the author's point of view or purpose in a grade-appropriate text (RI.9–10.6)</td></tr>
<tr><th colspan="2">Grade 8</th></tr>
<tr><td>Score 3.0</td><td>The student will:
• Analyze how differences in the points of view of characters (for example, created through the use of dramatic irony) create such effects as suspense or humor in a grade-appropriate text (RL.8.6)
• Analyze how an author acknowledges and responds to conflicting evidence or viewpoints in a grade-appropriate text (RI.8.6)</td></tr>
<tr><td>Score 2.0</td><td>The student will recognize or recall specific vocabulary, such as:
• Analyze, author, character, dramatic irony, evidence, humor, narrator, point of view, purpose, suspense, viewpoint
The student will perform basic processes, such as:
• Describe the differences in the points of view of characters and narrators in a grade-appropriate text
• Determine an author's point of view or purpose in a grade-appropriate text (RI.8.6)</td></tr>
<tr><th colspan="2">Grade 7</th></tr>
<tr><td>Score 3.0</td><td>The student will:
• Analyze how an author develops and contrasts the points of view of different characters or narrators in a grade-appropriate text (RL.7.6)
• Analyze how an author distinguishes his or her point of view or purpose in a grade-appropriate text from that of others (RI.7.6)</td></tr>
<tr><td>Score 2.0</td><td>The student will recognize or recall specific vocabulary, such as:
• Analyze, author, character, contrast, develop, distinguish, narrator, point of view, purpose
The student will perform basic processes, such as:
• Describe the point of view of characters or narrators in a given grade-appropriate text
• Determine an author's point of view or purpose in a grade-appropriate text (RI.7.6)</td></tr>
<tr><th colspan="2">Grade 6</th></tr>
<tr><td>Score 3.0</td><td>The student will:
• Explain how an author develops the point of view of the narrator or speaker in a grade-appropriate text (RL.6.6)
• Explain how an author's point of view or purpose is conveyed in a grade-appropriate text (RI.6.6)</td></tr>
<tr><td>Score 2.0</td><td>The student will recognize or recall specific vocabulary, such as:
• Author, convey, develop, narrator, point of view, purpose, speaker
The student will perform basic processes, such as:
• Describe the point of view of the narrator or speaker in a grade-appropriate text
• Describe an author's point of view or purpose in a grade-appropriate text (RI.6.6)</td></tr>
</table>

Grade 5	
Score 3.0	The student will: • Describe how a narrator's or speaker's point of view influences how events are described in a grade-appropriate text (RL.5.6) • Analyze multiple accounts of the same grade-appropriate event or topic, noting important similarities and differences in the point of view they represent (RI.5.6)
Score 2.0	The student will recognize or recall specific vocabulary, such as: • *Account, analyze, author, event, difference, influence, narrator, point of view, similarity, topic* The student will perform basic processes, such as: • Identify indicators that an author is expressing a point of view in a grade-appropriate text • Determine when accounts of an event or topic differ significantly in grade-appropriate texts
Grade 4	
Score 3.0	The student will: • Compare and contrast the point of view from which different grade-appropriate stories are narrated, including the difference between first- and third-person narrations (RL.4.6) • Compare and contrast a firsthand and secondhand account of the same grade-appropriate event or topic; describe the differences in focus and the information provided (RI.4.6)
Score 2.0	The student will recognize or recall specific vocabulary, such as: • *Account, compare, contrast, event, firsthand, first person, focus, information, narrate, narration, point of view, secondhand, story, third person, topic* The student will perform basic processes, such as: • Recognize or recall the differences between first- and third-person narrations in grade-appropriate texts • Describe firsthand and secondhand accounts of the same event
Grade 3	
Score 3.0	The student will: • Distinguish his or her own point of view from that of the narrator, characters, and/or author of a grade-appropriate text (RL.3.6; RI.3.6)
Score 2.0	The student will recognize or recall specific vocabulary, such as: • *Author, character, narrator, point of view* The student will perform basic processes, such as: • Describe the points of view of the narrator, characters, and author in a grade-appropriate text
Grade 2	
Score 3.0	The student will: • Describe differences in the points of view of characters in a grade-appropriate text, including by speaking in a different voice for each character when reading dialogue aloud (RL.2.6) • Describe the author's purpose in writing a grade-appropriate text, including the question or topic that the author wants to answer, explain, or describe (RI.2.6)
Score 2.0	The student will recognize or recall specific vocabulary, such as: • *Answer, author, character, dialogue, point of view, purpose, question, topic* The student will perform basic processes, such as: • Identify what various characters are saying in a grade-appropriate story • Identify the author's purpose in writing a grade-appropriate text

Grade 1	
Score 3.0	The student will: • Describe the narrator and the narrator's role in a grade-appropriate text
Score 2.0	The student will recognize or recall specific vocabulary, such as: • *Narrator, story* The student will perform basic processes, such as: • Identify who is telling the story at various points in a grade-appropriate text (RL.1.6)
Kindergarten	
Score 3.0	The student will: • Describe the role of the author and illustrator in telling a story or presenting ideas and information (RL.K.6; RI.K.6)
Score 2.0	The student will recognize or recall specific vocabulary, such as: • *Author, idea, illustrator, information, role, story* The student will perform basic processes, such as: • Identify the author and illustrator of a grade-appropriate text (RL.K.6; RI.K.6)

Visual/Auditory Media and Information Sources

Grades 11–12		
Score 4.0	In addition to score 3.0 performance, the student demonstrates in-depth inferences and applications that go beyond what was taught.	
	Score 3.5	*In addition to score 3.0 performance, partial success at score 4.0 content*
Score 3.0	The student will: • Analyze multiple interpretations of a grade-appropriate story, drama, or poem (for example, recorded or live production of a play or recorded novel or poetry), evaluating how each version interprets the source text (RL.11–12.7) • Integrate and evaluate multiple sources of information presented in different media or formats (for example, visually, quantitatively) as well as in words in order to address a question or solve a problem (RI.11–12.7)	
	Score 2.5	*No major errors or omissions regarding score 2.0 content, and partial success at score 3.0 content*
Score 2.0	The student will recognize or recall specific vocabulary, such as: • *Analyze, drama, evaluate, format, information, interpretation, live, media, novel, play, poem, poetry, problem, quantitative, question, source, story, text, version, visual* The student will perform basic processes, such as: • Compare and contrast interpretations of a grade-appropriate story, drama, or poem to the source text • Locate information from multiple sources presented in different media or formats, including words	
	Score 1.5	*Partial success at score 2.0 content, and major errors or omissions regarding score 3.0 content*
Score 1.0	With help, partial success at score 2.0 content and score 3.0 content	
	Score 0.5	*With help, partial success at score 2.0 content but not at score 3.0 content*
Score 0.0	Even with help, no success	
Grades 9–10		
Score 3.0	The student will: • Analyze the representation of a subject or a key scene in two different artistic mediums, including what is emphasized or absent in each treatment (for example, a person's life story in both print and multimedia) (RL.9–10.7; RI.9–10.7)	

Score 2.0	The student will recognize or recall specific vocabulary, such as: • *Absent*, *analyze*, *artistic*, *compare*, *contrast*, *emphasize*, *medium*, *multimedia*, *print*, *representation*, *scene*, *subject*, *treatment* The student will perform basic processes, such as: • Compare and contrast the representation of a subject or key scene in two different mediums
	Grade 8
Score 3.0	The student will: • Analyze the extent to which a filmed or live production of a grade-appropriate story or drama stays faithful to or departs from the text or script, evaluating the choices made by the director or actors (RL.8.7) • Evaluate the advantages and disadvantages of using different mediums (for example, print or digital text, video, multimedia) to present a particular topic or idea (RI.8.7)
Score 2.0	The student will recognize or recall specific vocabulary, such as: • *Actor*, *advantage*, *analyze*, *compare*, *contrast*, *depart*, *digital*, *director*, *disadvantage*, *drama*, *evaluate*, *faithful*, *film*, *idea*, *live*, *medium*, *multimedia*, *print*, *production*, *script*, *story*, *text*, *topic*, *version*, *video* The student will perform basic processes, such as: • Compare and contrast a filmed or live version with a grade-appropriate text or script • Recognize or recall the advantages and disadvantages of different mediums
	Grade 7
Score 3.0	The student will: • Analyze the effects of techniques unique to audio, filmed, staged, or multimedia versions of a grade-appropriate story, drama, or poem (for example, lighting, sound, color, or camera focus and angles in a film) (RL.7.7) • Analyze the audio, video, or multimedia version's portrayal of the subject of a grade-appropriate text (for example, how the delivery of a speech affects the impact of the words) (RI.7.7)
Score 2.0	The student will recognize or recall specific vocabulary, such as: • *Analyze*, *audio*, *camera angle*, *camera focus*, *color*, *compare*, *contrast*, *delivery*, *drama*, *film*, *impact*, *lighting*, *multimedia*, *poem*, *portrayal*, *sound*, *staged*, *story*, *subject*, *technique*, *text*, *version*, *video* The student will perform basic processes, such as: • Compare and contrast a written grade-appropriate story, drama, or poem to its audio, filmed, staged, or multimedia version (RL.7.7) • Compare and contrast a grade-appropriate text to an audio, video, or multimedia version of the text (RI.7.7)
	Grade 6
Score 3.0	The student will: • Compare and contrast the experience of reading a grade-appropriate story, drama, or poem to listening to or viewing an audio, video, or live version of the text, including contrasting what they "see" and "hear" when reading the text to what they perceive when they listen or watch (RL.6.7) • Integrate information presented in different media or formats (for example, visually, quantitatively, in words) to develop a coherent understanding of a topic or issue (RI.6.7)
Score 2.0	The student will recognize or recall specific vocabulary, such as: • *Audio*, *coherent*, *compare*, *contrast*, *difference*, *drama*, *format*, *information*, *issue*, *live*, *media*, *poem*, *quantitative*, *similarity*, *story*, *text*, *topic*, *version*, *video*, *visual* The student will perform basic processes, such as: • Identify similarities and differences in a grade-appropriate written text and visual representation of the text • Locate information in different media or formats

<table>
<tr><th colspan="2">Grade 5</th></tr>
<tr><td>Score 3.0</td><td>The student will:
• Analyze how visual and multimedia elements contribute to the meaning, tone, or beauty of a grade-appropriate text (for example, graphic novel, multimedia presentation of fiction, folktale, myth, poem) (RL.5.7)
• Draw on information from multiple print or digital sources, demonstrating the ability to locate an answer to a question quickly or to solve a problem efficiently (RI.5.7)</td></tr>
<tr><td>Score 2.0</td><td>The student will recognize or recall specific vocabulary, such as:
• Analyze, answer, digital, fiction, folktale, graphic novel, information, meaning, multimedia element, multimedia presentation, myth, poem, print, problem, question, source, text, tone, visual element
The student will perform basic processes, such as:
• Identify visual and multimedia elements that have an impact on the meaning, tone, or beauty of a grade-appropriate text
• Locate information in grade-appropriate print or digital sources</td></tr>
<tr><th colspan="2">Grade 4</th></tr>
<tr><td>Score 3.0</td><td>The student will:
• Compare and contrast the text of a grade-appropriate story or drama and a visual or oral presentation of the text, identifying where each version reflects specific descriptions and directions in the text (RL.4.7)
• Explain how information presented visually, orally, or quantitatively (for example, in charts, graphs, diagrams, timelines, animations, or interactive elements on web pages) contributes to an understanding of the grade-appropriate text in which it appears (RI.4.7)</td></tr>
<tr><td>Score 2.0</td><td>The student will recognize or recall specific vocabulary, such as:
• Animation, chart, compare, contrast, description, diagram, difference, direction, drama, graph, information, interactive element, oral, quantitative, similarity, story, text, timeline, version, visual, web page
The student will perform basic processes, such as:
• Recognize or recall similarities and differences between a written version and visual representation of the same grade-appropriate story
• Interpret information presented visually, orally, or quantitatively (for example, in charts, graphs, diagrams, timelines, animations, or interactive elements on web pages) (RI.4.7)</td></tr>
<tr><th colspan="2">Grade 3</th></tr>
<tr><td>Score 3.0</td><td>The student will:
• Explain how specific aspects of a grade-appropriate text's illustrations contribute to what is conveyed by the words in a story (for example, create mood, emphasize aspects of a character or setting) (RL.3.7)
• Use information gained from illustrations (for example, maps, photographs) and the words in a grade-appropriate text to demonstrate understanding of the text (for example, where, when, why, and how key events occur) (RI.3.7)</td></tr>
<tr><td>Score 2.0</td><td>The student will recognize or recall specific vocabulary, such as:
• Aspect, character, convey, event, how, illustration, information, map, mood, photograph, setting, story, text, when, where, why
The student will perform basic processes, such as:
• Describe information from the illustrations of a grade-appropriate text
• Identify aspects of illustrations that contribute to what is conveyed by the words (for example, create mood, emphasize aspects of a character or setting)</td></tr>
</table>

Grade 2	
Score 3.0	The student will: • Use information gained from the illustrations and words in a print or digital grade-appropriate text to demonstrate understanding of its characters, setting, or plot (RL.2.7) • Explain how specific images (for example, a diagram showing how a machine works) contribute to and clarify a grade-appropriate text (RI.2.7)
Score 2.0	The student will recognize or recall specific vocabulary, such as: • *Character, clarify, diagram, digital, illustration, image, information, plot, print, setting, text* The student will perform basic processes, such as: • Describe the information provided by specific images in a grade-appropriate text
Grade 1	
Score 3.0	The student will: • Describe the characters, setting, or events of a grade-appropriate story using illustrations from the story (RL.1.7) • Distinguish between information provided by pictures or other illustrations and information provided by the words in a grade-appropriate text (RI.1.6) • Describe the key ideas of a grade-appropriate text using illustrations from the text (RI.1.7)
Score 2.0	The student will recognize or recall specific vocabulary, such as: • *Character, event, idea, illustration, information, setting, story, text* The student will perform basic processes, such as: • Identify illustrations that describe characters, settings, or events in a grade-appropriate story • Recognize information provided by pictures or illustrations in a grade-appropriate text
Kindergarten	
Score 3.0	The student will: • Describe the relationship between illustrations and a grade-appropriate story in which they appear (for example, what moment in a story an illustration depicts) (RL.K.7) • Describe the relationship between illustrations and a grade-appropriate text in which they appear (for example, what person, place, thing, or idea in the text an illustration depicts) (RI.K.7)
Score 2.0	The student will recognize or recall specific vocabulary, such as: • *Depict, idea, illustration, person, place, relationship, story, text* The student will perform basic processes, such as: • Recognize the relationship between illustrations and the grade-appropriate text or story in which they appear

Argument and Reasoning

Grades 11–12		
Score 4.0	In addition to score 3.0 performance, the student demonstrates in-depth inferences and applications that go beyond what was taught.	
	Score 3.5	*In addition to score 3.0 performance, partial success at score 4.0 content*
Score 3.0	The student will: • Evaluate the reasoning in seminal U.S. texts, including the application of constitutional principles and use of legal reasoning (for example, in U.S. Supreme Court majority opinions and dissents) and the premises, purposes, and arguments in works of public advocacy (for example, *The Federalist*, presidential addresses) (RI.11–12.8)	

<table>
<tr><td></td><td>Score 2.5</td><td>No major errors or omissions regarding score 2.0 content, and partial success at score 3.0 content</td></tr>
<tr><td>Score 2.0</td><td colspan="2">The student will recognize or recall specific vocabulary, such as:
• Address, advocacy, argument, constitutional principles, dissent, evaluate, legal reasoning, majority opinion, premise, purpose, reasoning, seminal
The student will perform basic processes, such as:
• Delineate the reasoning in seminal U.S. texts (RI.11–12.8)</td></tr>
<tr><td></td><td>Score 1.5</td><td>Partial success at score 2.0 content, and major errors or omissions regarding score 3.0 content</td></tr>
<tr><td>Score 1.0</td><td colspan="2">With help, partial success at score 2.0 content and score 3.0 content</td></tr>
<tr><td></td><td>Score 0.5</td><td>With help, partial success at score 2.0 content but not at score 3.0 content</td></tr>
<tr><td>Score 0.0</td><td colspan="2">Even with help, no success</td></tr>
<tr><td colspan="3">Grades 9–10</td></tr>
<tr><td>Score 3.0</td><td colspan="2">The student will:
• Evaluate the argument and specific claims in a grade-appropriate text, assessing whether the reasoning is valid and the evidence is relevant and sufficient (RI.9–10.8)
• Identify false statements and fallacious reasoning in a grade-appropriate text (RI.9–10.8)</td></tr>
<tr><td>Score 2.0</td><td colspan="2">The student will recognize or recall specific vocabulary, such as:
• Argument, claim, evidence, fallacious reasoning, reasoning, relevant, sufficient, text, valid
The student will perform basic processes, such as:
• Delineate the argument and specific claims in a grade-appropriate text (RI.9–10.8)
• Identify examples of false statements and fallacious reasoning in isolation</td></tr>
<tr><td colspan="3">Grade 8</td></tr>
<tr><td>Score 3.0</td><td colspan="2">The student will:
• Evaluate the argument and specific claims in a grade-appropriate text, assessing whether the reasoning is sound and the evidence is relevant and sufficient (RI.8.8)
• Identify irrelevant evidence in a grade-appropriate text (RI.8.8)</td></tr>
<tr><td>Score 2.0</td><td colspan="2">The student will recognize or recall specific vocabulary, such as:
• Argument, assess, claim, evaluate, evidence, irrelevant, reasoning, relevant, sound, sufficient, text
The student will perform basic processes, such as:
• Delineate the argument and specific claims in a grade-appropriate text (RI.8.8)
• Recognize examples of irrelevant evidence in isolation</td></tr>
<tr><td colspan="3">Grade 7</td></tr>
<tr><td>Score 3.0</td><td colspan="2">The student will:
• Evaluate the argument and specific claims in a grade-appropriate text, assessing whether the reasoning is sound and the evidence is relevant and sufficient to support the claims (RI.7.8)</td></tr>
<tr><td>Score 2.0</td><td colspan="2">The student will recognize or recall specific vocabulary, such as:
• Argument, assess, claim, evaluate, evidence, opinion, reasoning, relevant, sound, sufficient, support, text
The student will perform basic processes, such as:
• Trace the arguments and reasoning in a grade-appropriate text (RI.7.8)
• Identify examples of opinion in a grade-appropriate text and the words that signal an opinion</td></tr>
<tr><td colspan="3">Grade 6</td></tr>
<tr><td>Score 3.0</td><td colspan="2">The student will:
• Evaluate the argument and specific claims in a grade-appropriate text, distinguishing claims that are supported by reasons and evidence from claims that are not (RI.6.8)</td></tr>
</table>

Score 2.0	The student will recognize or recall specific vocabulary, such as: • *Argument*, *claim*, *distinguish*, *evidence*, *opinion*, *reason*, *support*, *text* The student will perform basic processes, such as: • Trace the arguments and specific claims used to support the argument in a grade-appropriate text (RI.6.8) • Identify examples of opinion in a grade-appropriate text and the words that signal an opinion
Grade 5	
Score 3.0	The student will: • Explain how an author uses reasons and evidence to support particular points in a grade-appropriate text (RI.5.8)
Score 2.0	The student will recognize or recall specific vocabulary, such as: • *Author*, *evidence*, *point*, *reason*, *support*, *text* The student will perform basic processes, such as: • Identify which reasons and evidence support which points in a grade-appropriate text (RI.5.8)
Grade 4	
Score 3.0	The student will: • Explain how an author uses reasons and evidence to support particular points in a grade-appropriate text (RI.4.8)
Score 2.0	The student will recognize or recall specific vocabulary, such as: • *Author*, *evidence*, *point*, *reason*, *support*, *text* The student will perform basic processes, such as: • Identify the reasons and evidence used to support particular points in a grade-appropriate text
Grade 3	
Score 3.0	The student will: • Describe how reasons support specific points the author makes in a grade-appropriate text
Score 2.0	The student will recognize or recall specific vocabulary, such as: • *Author*, *point*, *reason*, *support*, *text* The student will perform basic processes, such as: • Identify reasons the author gives to support specific points in a grade-appropriate text
Grade 2	
Score 3.0	The student will: • Describe how reasons support specific points the author makes in a grade-appropriate text (RI.2.8)
Score 2.0	The student will recognize or recall specific vocabulary, such as: • *Author*, *point*, *reason*, *support*, *text* The student will perform basic processes, such as: • Identify the reasons the author gives to support specific points in a grade-appropriate text
Grade 1	
Score 3.0	The student will: • Identify the reasons an author gives to support points in a grade-appropriate text (RI.1.8)
Score 2.0	The student will recognize or recall specific vocabulary, such as: • *Author*, *point*, *reason*, *support*, *text* The student will perform basic processes, such as: • Recognize teacher-provided points or arguments that an author makes in a grade-appropriate text

Kindergarten		
Score 3.0	The student will: • Identify the reasons an author gives to support points in a grade-appropriate text (RI.K.8)	
Score 2.0	The student will recognize or recall specific vocabulary, such as: • *Author, detail, point, reason, support, text, topic* The student will perform basic processes, such as: • Recognize details that support a teacher-provided main topic	

Literary Comparisons and Source Material

Grades 11–12		
Score 4.0	In addition to score 3.0 performance, the student demonstrates in-depth inferences and applications that go beyond what was taught.	
	Score 3.5	*In addition to score 3.0 performance, partial success at score 4.0 content*
Score 3.0	The student will: • Describe how two or more foundational works of American literature from the same time period (for example, the 18th, 19th, or 20th century) treat similar themes or topics (RL.11–12.9)	
	Score 2.5	*No major errors or omissions regarding score 2.0 content, and partial success at score 3.0 content*
Score 2.0	The student will recognize or recall specific vocabulary, such as: • *American, 18th century, foundational, literature, 19th century, similar, theme, time period, topic, 20th century* The student will perform basic processes, such as: • Recognize or recall accurate statements about similar themes or topics in foundational works of American literature from the 18th, 19th, and early 20th centuries	
	Score 1.5	*Partial success at score 2.0 content, and major errors or omissions regarding score 3.0 content*
Score 1.0	With help, partial success at score 2.0 content and score 3.0 content	
	Score 0.5	*With help, partial success at score 2.0 content but not at score 3.0 content*
Score 0.0	Even with help, no success	
Grades 9–10		
Score 3.0	The student will: • Analyze how an author draws on and transforms source material in a specific grade-appropriate work (for example, how Shakespeare treats a theme or topic from Ovid or the Bible or how a later author draws on a play by Shakespeare) (RL.9–10.9)	
Score 2.0	The student will recognize or recall specific vocabulary, such as: • *Analyze, author, source, theme, topic, transform* The student will perform basic processes, such as: • Identify examples of the use of source materials in a specific grade-appropriate work	
Grade 8		
Score 3.0	The student will: • Analyze how a modern work of fiction draws on themes, patterns of events, or character types from myths, traditional stories, or religious works such as the Bible, including describing how the material is rendered new (RL.8.9)	

Score 2.0	The student will recognize or recall specific vocabulary, such as: • *Analyze*, *character*, *fiction*, *modern*, *myth*, *religious*, *render*, *story*, *theme*, *traditional* The student will perform basic processes, such as: • Identify examples of themes, patterns of events, or character types from myths, traditional stories, or religious works in modern works of fiction
	Grade 7
Score 3.0	The student will: • Compare and contrast a fictional portrayal of a time, place, or character and a historical account of the same period as a means of understanding how authors of fiction use or alter history (RL.7.9)
Score 2.0	The student will recognize or recall specific vocabulary, such as: • *Account*, *alter*, *author*, *character*, *compare*, *contrast*, *fiction*, *fictional*, *historical*, *period*, *place*, *portrayal*, *time* The student will perform basic processes, such as: • Describe how fictional and historical accounts portray a time, place, or character
	Grade 6
Score 3.0	The student will: • Compare and contrast grade-appropriate texts in different forms or genres (for example, stories and poems; historical novels and fantasy stories) in terms of their approaches to similar themes and topics (RL.6.9)
Score 2.0	The student will recognize or recall specific vocabulary, such as: • *Compare*, *contrast*, *fantasy*, *form*, *genre*, *historical*, *novel*, *poem*, *similar*, *story*, *text*, *theme*, *topic* The student will perform basic processes, such as: • Identify topics or themes in grade-appropriate texts in different genres
	Grade 5
Score 3.0	The student will: • Compare and contrast grade-appropriate stories in the same genre (for example, mysteries and adventure stories) on their approaches to similar themes and topics (RL.5.9)
Score 2.0	The student will recognize or recall specific vocabulary, such as: • *Adventure*, *compare*, *contrast*, *genre*, *mystery*, *similar*, *story*, *theme*, *topic* The student will perform basic processes, such as: • Identify themes and topics in two or more grade-appropriate stories from the same genre
	Grade 4
Score 3.0	The student will: • Compare and contrast the treatment of similar themes and topics (for example, opposition of good and evil) and patterns of events (for example, the quest) in grade-appropriate stories, myths, and traditional literature from different cultures (RL.4.9)
Score 2.0	The student will recognize or recall specific vocabulary, such as: • *Compare*, *contrast*, *culture*, *event*, *literature*, *myth*, *pattern*, *quest*, *similar*, *story*, *theme*, *topic*, *traditional*, *treatment* The student will perform basic processes, such as: • Identify examples of themes, topics, and patterns of events in grade-appropriate stories, myths, and traditional literature from different cultures
	Grade 3
Score 3.0	The student will: • Compare and contrast the themes, settings, and plots of grade-appropriate stories written by the same author about the same or similar characters (for example, in books from a series) (RL.3.9)

Score 2.0	The student will recognize or recall specific vocabulary, such as: • *Author, character, compare, contrast, plot, series, setting, similar, story, theme* The student will perform basic processes, such as: • Recognize or recall isolated facts or details about the themes, settings, and plots of grade-appropriate stories written by the same author about the same or similar characters
Grade 2	
Score 3.0	The student will: • Compare and contrast two or more versions of the same grade-appropriate story (for example, Cinderella stories) by different authors or from different cultures (RL.2.9)
Score 2.0	The student will recognize or recall specific vocabulary, such as: • *Author, compare, contrast, culture, story, version* The student will perform basic processes, such as: • Recognize or recall differences between two or more versions of the same grade-appropriate story
Grade 1	
Score 3.0	The student will: • Compare and contrast the adventures and experiences of characters in grade-appropriate stories (RL.1.9)
Score 2.0	The student will recognize or recall specific vocabulary, such as: • *Adventure, character, compare, contrast, experience, story* The student will perform basic processes, such as: • Recognize or recall details about the adventures and experiences of characters in grade-appropriate stories
Kindergarten	
Score 3.0	The student will: • Compare and contrast the adventures and experiences of characters in familiar grade-appropriate stories (RL.K.9)
Score 2.0	The student will recognize or recall specific vocabulary, such as: • *Adventure, character, compare, contrast, experience, story* The student will perform basic processes, such as: • Recognize or recall details of the adventures and experiences of characters in a familiar grade-appropriate story

Rhetorical Criticism

Grades 11–12		
Score 4.0	In addition to score 3.0 performance, the student demonstrates in-depth inferences and applications that go beyond what was taught.	
	Score 3.5	*In addition to score 3.0 performance, partial success at score 4.0 content*
Score 3.0	The student will: • Analyze 17th, 18th, and 19th century foundational U.S. documents of historical and literary significance (for example, the Declaration of Independence, the Preamble to the Constitution, the Bill of Rights, and Lincoln's second inaugural address) for their themes, purposes, and rhetorical features (RI.11–12.9)	
	Score 2.5	*No major errors or omissions regarding score 2.0 content, and partial success at score 3.0 content*

Score 2.0	The student will recognize or recall specific vocabulary, such as: • *Analyze*, *18th century*, *foundational*, *historical*, *literary*, *19th century*, *persuasive technique*, *purpose*, *rhetorical feature*, *17th century*, *significance*, *theme* The student will perform basic processes, such as: • Identify rhetorical features, persuasive techniques, purposes, and/or themes in specified 17th, 18th, and 19th century U.S. documents of historical and literary significance	
	Score 1.5	*Partial success at score 2.0 content, and major errors or omissions regarding score 3.0 content*
Score 1.0	With help, partial success at score 2.0 content and score 3.0 content	
	Score 0.5	*With help, partial success at score 2.0 content but not at score 3.0 content*
Score 0.0	Even with help, no success	
	Grades 9–10	
Score 3.0	The student will: • Analyze the rhetorical features of seminal U.S. documents of historical and literary significance (for example, Washington's Farewell Address, the Gettysburg Address, Roosevelt's Four Freedoms speech, King's "Letter from Birmingham Jail"), including how they address related themes and concepts (RI.9–10.9)	
Score 2.0	The student will recognize or recall specific vocabulary, such as: • *Analyze*, *concept*, *historical*, *literary*, *rhetorical feature*, *seminal*, *significance*, *theme* The student will perform basic processes, such as: • Identify rhetorical features of seminal U.S documents of historical and literary significance • Identify themes and concepts from seminal U.S documents of historical and literary significance	
	Grade 8	
Score 3.0	The student will: • Analyze how or why two or more grade-appropriate texts provide conflicting information on matters of facts or interpretation on the same topic (RI.8.9)	
Score 2.0	The student will recognize or recall specific vocabulary, such as: • *Analyze*, *conflict*, *fact*, *interpretation*, *source*, *text*, *topic* The student will perform basic processes, such as: • Identify where two grade-appropriate texts disagree on matters of facts or interpretation (RI.8.9)	
	Grade 7	
Score 3.0	The student will: • Analyze how two or more authors writing about the same topic shape their presentations of key information by emphasizing different evidence or advancing different interpretations of facts (RI.7.9)	
Score 2.0	The student will recognize or recall specific vocabulary, such as: • *Analyze*, *author*, *evidence*, *fact*, *information*, *interpretation*, *source*, *text*, *topic* The student will perform basic processes, such as: • Describe the way two different authors present the same information in a grade-appropriate text • Identify key information presented by each source for the same topic in a grade-appropriate text	
	Grade 6	
Score 3.0	The student will: • Compare and contrast one author's presentation of events with that of another (for example, a memoir written by and a biography on the same person) (RI.6.9)	

Score 2.0	The student will recognize or recall specific vocabulary, such as: • *Author, biography, compare, contrast, event, memoir, topic* The student will perform basic processes, such as: • Identify key events provided by two authors on the same topic
	Grade 5
Score 3.0	The student will: • Integrate information from several grade-appropriate texts on the same topic in order to write or speak about the subject knowledgeably (RI.5.9)
Score 2.0	The student will recognize or recall specific vocabulary, such as: • *Information, integrate, text, topic* The student will perform basic processes, such as: • Identify important information from several grade-appropriate texts about the same topic
	Grade 4
Score 3.0	The student will: • Integrate information from two grade-appropriate texts on the same topic in order to write or speak about the subject knowledgeably (RI.4.9)
Score 2.0	The student will recognize or recall specific vocabulary, such as: • *Information, integrate, text, topic* The student will perform basic processes, such as: • Identify important information from two grade-appropriate texts about the same topic
	Grade 3
Score 3.0	The student will: • Compare and contrast the most important points and key details presented in two grade-appropriate texts on the same topic (RI.3.9)
Score 2.0	The student will recognize or recall specific vocabulary, such as: • *Compare, contrast, detail, point, text, topic* The student will perform basic processes, such as: • Identify the important points and key details presented in two grade-appropriate texts on the same topic
	Grade 2
Score 3.0	The student will: • Compare and contrast the most important points presented by two grade-appropriate texts on the same topic (RI.2.9)
Score 2.0	The student will recognize or recall specific vocabulary, such as: • *Compare, contrast, point, text, topic* The student will perform basic processes, such as: • Identify the most important points in two grade-appropriate texts on the same topic
	Grade 1
Score 3.0	The student will: • Describe basic similarities in and differences between two grade-appropriate texts on the same topic (for example, in illustrations, descriptions, or procedures) (RI.1.9)

Score 2.0	The student will recognize or recall specific vocabulary, such as: • *Description, illustration, procedure, similarity, text, topic* The student will perform basic processes, such as: • Identify basic similarities in and differences between two grade-appropriate texts on the same topic (for example, in illustrations, descriptions, or procedures) (RI.1.9)	
	Kindergarten	
Score 3.0	The student will: • Identify basic similarities in and differences between two grade-appropriate texts on the same topic (for example, in illustrations, descriptions, or procedures) (RI.K.9)	
Score 2.0	The student will recognize or recall specific vocabulary, such as: • *Description, illustration, procedure, similarity, text, topic* The student will perform basic processes, such as: • Identify features (for example, illustrations, descriptions, or procedures) of a grade-appropriate text	

Fluency

	Grades 11–12	
Score 4.0	In addition to score 3.0 performance, the student demonstrates in-depth inferences and applications that go beyond what was taught.	
	Score 3.5	*In addition to score 3.0 performance, partial success at score 4.0 content*
Score 3.0	The student will: • Read and comprehend grade-appropriate literature and informational text (RL.11–12.10; RI.11–12.10)	
	Score 2.5	*No major errors or omissions regarding score 2.0 content, and partial success at score 3.0 content*
Score 2.0	The student will recognize or recall specific vocabulary, such as: • *Comprehend, informational, literature, text* The student will perform basic processes, such as: • Read grade-appropriate literature and informational text using a teacher-directed comprehension strategy (for example, modeling, predicting, questioning, graphic organizers/scaffolding, reciprocal reading, outlining, and note taking)	
	Score 1.5	*Partial success at score 2.0 content, and major errors or omissions regarding score 3.0 content*
Score 1.0	With help, partial success at score 2.0 content and score 3.0 content	
	Score 0.5	*With help, partial success at score 2.0 content but not at score 3.0 content*
Score 0.0	Even with help, no success	
	Grades 9–10	
Score 3.0	The student will: • Read and comprehend grade-appropriate literature and informational text (RL.9–10.10; RI.9–10.10)	
Score 2.0	The student will recognize or recall specific vocabulary, such as: • *Comprehend, informational, literature, text* The student will perform basic processes, such as: • Read grade-appropriate literature and informational text using a teacher-directed comprehension strategy (for example, modeling, predicting, questioning, graphic organizers/scaffolding, reciprocal reading, outlining, and note taking)	

	Grade 8
Score 3.0	The student will: • Read and comprehend grade-appropriate literature and informational text (RL.8.10; RI.8.10)
Score 2.0	The student will recognize or recall specific vocabulary, such as: • *Comprehend*, *informational*, *literature*, *text* The student will perform basic processes, such as: • Read grade-appropriate literature and informational text using a teacher-directed comprehension strategy (for example, modeling, predicting, questioning, graphic organizers/scaffolding, reciprocal reading, outlining, and note taking)
	Grade 7
Score 3.0	The student will: • Read and comprehend grade-appropriate literature and informational text (RL.7.10; RI.7.10)
Score 2.0	The student will recognize or recall specific vocabulary, such as: • *Comprehend*, *informational*, *literature*, *text* The student will perform basic processes, such as: • Read grade-appropriate literature and informational text using a teacher-directed comprehension strategy (for example, modeling, predicting, questioning, graphic organizers/scaffolding, and reciprocal reading)
	Grade 6
Score 3.0	The student will: • Read and comprehend grade-appropriate literature and informational text (RL.6.10; RI.6.10)
Score 2.0	The student will recognize or recall specific vocabulary, such as: • *Comprehend*, *informational*, *literature*, *text* The student will perform basic processes, such as: • Read grade-appropriate literature and informational text using teacher-directed comprehension strategies (for example, modeling, predicting, questioning, graphic organizers/scaffolding, and reciprocal reading)
	Grade 5
Score 3.0	The student will: • Read and comprehend grade-appropriate literature and informational text (RL.5.10; RI.5.10) • Read grade-appropriate text with purpose and understanding (RF.5.4a) • Read grade-appropriate prose and poetry orally with accuracy, appropriate rate, and expression on successive readings (RF.5.4b)
Score 2.0	The student will recognize or recall specific vocabulary, such as: • *Accuracy*, *expression*, *informational*, *literature*, *orally*, *poetry*, *prose*, *purpose*, *rate*, *text* The student will perform basic processes, such as: • Read grade-appropriate literature and informational text using teacher-directed comprehension strategies (for example, modeling, predicting, questioning, graphic organizers/scaffolding, and reciprocal reading) • Describe the purpose for reading a grade-appropriate text • Read grade-appropriate prose and poetry orally with accuracy, appropriate rate, and expression using teacher-directed fluency strategies (for example, modeling, listening to recordings of others reading, recording and listening to self reading)
	Grade 4
Score 3.0	The student will: • Read and comprehend grade-appropriate literature and informational text (RL.4.10; RI.4.10) • Read grade-appropriate text with purpose and understanding (RF.4.4a) • Read grade-appropriate prose and poetry orally with accuracy, appropriate rate, and expression on successive readings (RF.4.4b)

<table>
<tr><td>Score 2.0</td><td>The student will recognize or recall specific vocabulary, such as:
• Accuracy, expression, informational, literature, orally, poetry, prose, purpose, rate, text
The student will perform basic processes, such as:
• Read grade-appropriate literature and informational text using teacher-directed comprehension strategies (modeling, predicting, questioning, graphic organizers/scaffolding, and reciprocal reading)
• Describe the purpose for reading a grade-appropriate text
• Read grade-appropriate prose and poetry orally with accuracy, appropriate rate, and expression using teacher-directed fluency strategies (for example, modeling, listening to recordings of others reading, recording and listening to self reading)</td></tr>
<tr><td colspan="2">Grade 3</td></tr>
<tr><td>Score 3.0</td><td>The student will:
• Read and comprehend grade-appropriate literature and informational text (RL.3.10; RI.3.10)
• Read grade-appropriate text with purpose and understanding (RF.3.4a)
• Read grade-appropriate prose and poetry orally with accuracy, appropriate rate, and expression on successive readings (RF.3.4b)</td></tr>
<tr><td>Score 2.0</td><td>The student will recognize or recall specific vocabulary, such as:
• Accuracy, expression, informational, literature, orally, poetry, prose, purpose, rate, text
The student will perform basic processes, such as:
• Read grade-appropriate literature and informational text using teacher-directed comprehension strategies (for example, modeling, predicting, questioning, graphic organizers/scaffolding, and reciprocal reading)
• Describe the purpose for reading a grade-appropriate text
• Read grade-appropriate prose and poetry orally with accuracy, appropriate rate, and expression using teacher-directed fluency strategies (for example, modeling, listening to recordings of others reading, recording and listening to self reading)</td></tr>
<tr><td colspan="2">Grade 2</td></tr>
<tr><td>Score 3.0</td><td>The student will:
• Read and comprehend grade-appropriate literature and informational text (RL.2.10; RI.2.10)
• Read grade-appropriate text with purpose and understanding (RF.2.4a)
• Read grade-appropriate text orally with accuracy, appropriate rate, and expression on successive readings (RF.2.4b)</td></tr>
<tr><td>Score 2.0</td><td>The student will recognize or recall specific vocabulary, such as:
• Accuracy, expression, informational, literature, orally, purpose, rate, text
The student will perform basic processes, such as:
• Read grade-appropriate literature and informational text using teacher-directed comprehension strategies (for example, modeling, predicting, questioning, graphic organizers/scaffolding, and reciprocal reading)
• Describe the purpose for reading a grade-appropriate text
• Read grade-appropriate prose and poetry orally with accuracy, appropriate rate, and expression using teacher-directed fluency strategies (for example, modeling, listening to recordings of others reading, recording and listening to self reading)</td></tr>
<tr><td colspan="2">Grade 1</td></tr>
<tr><td>Score 3.0</td><td>The student will:
• Read and comprehend grade-appropriate prose, poetry, and informational text (RL.1.10; RI.1.10)
• Read grade-appropriate text with purpose and understanding (RF.1.4a)
• Read grade-appropriate text orally with accuracy, appropriate rate, and expression on successive readings (RF.1.4b)</td></tr>
</table>

Score 2.0	The student will recognize or recall specific vocabulary, such as: • *Accuracy, expression, informational, literature, orally, poetry, purpose, rate, text* The student will perform basic processes, such as: • Read grade-appropriate literature and informational text using teacher-directed comprehension strategies (for example, modeling, predicting, questioning, graphic organizers/scaffolding, and reciprocal reading) • Identify the purpose for reading a grade-appropriate text • Read grade-appropriate prose and poetry orally with accuracy, appropriate rate, and expression using teacher-directed fluency strategies (for example, modeling, listening to recordings of others reading, recording and listening to self reading)
	Kindergarten
Score 3.0	The student will: • Actively engage in group reading activities with purpose and understanding (RL.K.10; RI.K.10) • Read grade-appropriate text with purpose and understanding (RF.K.4)
Score 2.0	The student will recognize or recall specific vocabulary, such as: • *Engage, purpose, text* The student will perform basic processes, such as: • Participate in group reading activities • Identify the purpose for reading a grade-appropriate text

Reading Foundations

Print Concepts

	Grades 11–12, 9–10, 8, 7, 6, 5, 4, 3, 2	
Score 3.0	Not applicable.	
Score 2.0	Not applicable.	
	Grade 1	
Score 4.0	In addition to score 3.0 performance, the student demonstrates in-depth inferences and applications that go beyond what was taught.	
	Score 3.5	*In addition to score 3.0 performance, partial success at score 4.0 content*
Score 3.0	The student will: • Identify the distinguishing features of a sentence in context (for example, first word, capitalization, ending punctuation) (RF.1.1a) • Print all upper- and lowercase letters (L.1.1a)	
	Score 2.5	*No major errors or omissions regarding score 2.0 content, and partial success at score 3.0 content*
Score 2.0	The student will recognize or recall specific vocabulary, such as: • *Capitalization, feature, letter, lowercase, punctuation, sentence, uppercase* The student will perform basic processes, such as: • Recognize the distinguishing features of a teacher-provided sentence • Recognize or recall the features of a sentence	
	Score 1.5	*Partial success at score 2.0 content, and major errors or omissions regarding score 3.0 content*
Score 1.0	With help, partial success at score 2.0 content and score 3.0 content	
	Score 0.5	*With help, partial success at score 2.0 content but not at score 3.0 content*
Score 0.0	Even with help, no success	
	Kindergarten	
Score 3.0	The student will: • Follow words from left to right, top to bottom, and page by page (RF.K.1a) • Recognize that spoken words are represented in written language by specific sequences of letters (RF.K.1b) • Understand that words are separated by spaces in print (RF.K.1c) • Name all upper- and lowercase letters of the alphabet (RF.K.1d) • Print upper- and lowercase letters (L.K.1a)	
Score 2.0	The student will recognize or recall specific vocabulary, such as: • *Alphabet, book, bottom, left, letter, lowercase, page, print, right, space, top, uppercase, word* The student will perform basic processes, such as: • Orient book or text properly • Identify a word on the page • Identify letters in a word • Recognize all upper- and lowercase letters of the alphabet (RF.K.1d) • Use a teacher-provided model to print upper- and lowercase letters	

Phonological Awareness

Grades 11–12, 9–10, 8, 7, 6, 5, 4, 3, 2		
Score 3.0	Not applicable.	
Score 2.0	Not applicable.	
Grade 1		
Score 4.0	In addition to score 3.0 performance, the student demonstrates in-depth inferences and applications that go beyond what was taught.	
	Score 3.5	*In addition to score 3.0 performance, partial success at score 4.0 content*
Score 3.0	The student will: • Distinguish long from short vowel sounds in spoken single-syllable words (RF.1.2a) • Orally produce single-syllable words by blending sounds (phonemes), including consonant blends (RF.1.2b) • Segment spoken single-syllable words into their complete sequence of individual sounds (phonemes) (RF.1.2d)	
	Score 2.5	*No major errors or omissions regarding score 2.0 content, and partial success at score 3.0 content*
Score 2.0	The student will recognize or recall specific vocabulary, such as: • *Blend, consonant blend, long vowel, segment, sequence, short vowel, single, sound, syllable, word* The student will perform basic processes, such as: • Recognize examples of long and short vowel sounds • Isolate and pronounce initial, medial vowel, and final sounds (phonemes) in spoken single-syllable words (RF.1.2c)	
	Score 1.5	*Partial success at score 2.0 content, and major errors or omissions regarding score 3.0 content*
Score 1.0	With help, partial success at score 2.0 content and score 3.0 content	
	Score 0.5	*With help, partial success at score 2.0 content but not at score 3.0 content*
Score 0.0	Even with help, no success	
Kindergarten		
Score 3.0	The student will: • Produce rhyming words (RF.K.2a) • Blend and segment syllables in spoken words (RF.K.2b) • Blend and segment onsets and rimes of single-syllable spoken words (RF.K.2c) • Add or substitute individual sounds (phonemes) in simple, one-syllable words to make new words (RF.K.2e)	
Score 2.0	The student will recognize or recall specific vocabulary, such as: • *Blend, onset, rhyming, rime, segment, single, sound, syllable, word* The student will perform basic processes, such as: • Recognize rhyming words (RF.K.2a) • Count and pronounce syllables in spoken words (RF.K.2b) • Identify onsets and rimes of single-syllable spoken words • Isolate and pronounce the initial, medial vowel, and final sounds (phonemes) in three-phoneme (consonant-vowel-consonant, or CVC) words (not including CVCs ending with /l/, /r/, or /x/) (RF.K.2d)	

Phonics and Word Analysis

Grades 11–12, 9–10, 8, 7, 6		
Score 3.0	Not applicable.	
Score 2.0	Not applicable.	
Grade 5		
Score 4.0	In addition to score 3.0 performance, the student demonstrates in-depth inferences and applications that go beyond what was taught.	
	Score 3.5	*In addition to score 3.0 performance, partial success at score 4.0 content*
Score 3.0	The student will: • Use combined knowledge of all letter-sound correspondences, syllabication patterns, and morphology (for example, roots and affixes) to accurately read unfamiliar grade-appropriate multisyllabic words in context (RF.5.3a)	
	Score 2.5	*No major errors or omissions regarding score 2.0 content, and partial success at score 3.0 content*
Score 2.0	The student will recognize or recall specific vocabulary, such as: • *Affix, correspondence, letter, multisyllabic, root, sound, syllabication, word* The student will perform basic processes, such as: • Use combined knowledge of all letter-sound correspondences, syllabication patterns, and morphology (for example, roots and affixes) to accurately read unfamiliar grade-appropriate multisyllabic words in isolation	
	Score 1.5	*Partial success at score 2.0 content, and major errors or omissions regarding score 3.0 content*
Score 1.0	With help, partial success at score 2.0 content and score 3.0 content	
	Score 0.5	*With help, partial success at score 2.0 content but not at score 3.0 content*
Score 0.0	Even with help, no success	
Grade 4		
Score 3.0	The student will: • Use combined knowledge of all letter-sound correspondences, syllabication patterns, and morphology (for example, roots and affixes) to accurately read unfamiliar grade-appropriate multisyllabic words in context (RF.4.3a)	
Score 2.0	The student will recognize or recall specific vocabulary, such as: • *Affix, correspondence, letter, multisyllabic, root, sound, syllabication, word* The student will perform basic processes, such as: • Apply grade-level phonics and word analysis skills when decoding words in isolation • Use combined knowledge of all letter-sound correspondences, syllabication patterns, and morphology (for example, roots and affixes) to accurately read unfamiliar grade-appropriate multisyllabic words in isolation	
Grade 3		
Score 3.0	The student will: • Decode multisyllable words (RF.3.3c) • Read grade-appropriate irregularly spelled words (RF.3.3d)	
Score 2.0	The student will recognize or recall specific vocabulary, such as: • *Irregular, multisyllable, word* The student will perform basic processes, such as: • Demonstrate grade-appropriate phonics and word analysis skills in isolation	

<table>
<tr><th colspan="2">Grade 2</th></tr>
<tr><td>Score 3.0</td><td>The student will:<ul><li>Decode regularly spelled two-syllable words with long vowels (RF.2.3c)</li><li>Identify words with inconsistent but common spelling-sound correspondences (RF.2.3e)</li><li>Read grade-appropriate irregularly spelled words (RF.2.3f)</li></ul></td></tr>
<tr><td>Score 2.0</td><td>The student will recognize or recall specific vocabulary, such as:<ul><li>Correspondence, irregular, long vowel, regular, short vowel, sound, syllable, vowel team, word</li></ul>The student will perform basic processes, such as:<ul><li>Distinguish long and short vowels when reading regularly spelled one-syllable words (RF.2.3a)</li><li>Recognize spelling-sound correspondences for additional common vowel teams (RF.2.3b)</li><li>Recognize grade-appropriate irregularly spelled words (RF.2.3f)</li></ul></td></tr>
<tr><th colspan="2">Grade 1</th></tr>
<tr><td>Score 3.0</td><td>The student will:<ul><li>Decode two-syllable words following basic patterns by breaking the words into syllables (RF.1.3e)</li><li>Read grade-appropriate words with inflectional endings (RF.1.3f)</li><li>Read grade-appropriate irregularly spelled words (RF.1.3g)</li></ul></td></tr>
<tr><td>Score 2.0</td><td>The student will recognize or recall specific vocabulary, such as:<ul><li>Irregular, regular, sound, syllable, word</li></ul>The student will perform basic processes, such as:<ul><li>Recognize or recall the spelling-sound correspondences for common consonant digraphs (RF.1.3a)</li><li>Decode regularly spelled one-syllable words (RF.1.3b)</li><li>Recognize or recall final -e and common vowel team conventions for representing long vowel sounds (RF.1.3c)</li><li>Determine the number of syllables in a printed word based on the knowledge that every syllable must have a vowel sound (RF.1.3d)</li><li>Recognize grade-appropriate irregularly spelled words (RF.1.3g)</li></ul></td></tr>
<tr><th colspan="2">Kindergarten</th></tr>
<tr><td>Score 3.0</td><td>The student will:<ul><li>Read common high-frequency words by sight (for example, the, of, to, you, she, my, is, are, do, does) (RF.K.3c)</li><li>Distinguish between similarly spelled words by identifying the sounds of the letters that differ (RF.K.3d)</li></ul></td></tr>
<tr><td>Score 2.0</td><td>The student will recognize or recall specific vocabulary, such as:<ul><li>Consonant, high-frequency, letter, long vowel, short vowel, similar, sound, vowel, word</li></ul>The student will perform basic processes, such as:<ul><li>Produce the primary or many of the most frequent sounds for each consonant (RF.K.3a)</li><li>Associate the long and short sounds with common spellings (graphemes) for the five major vowels (RF.K.3b)</li></ul></td></tr>
</table>

Writing

Argumentative

Grades 11–12		
Score 4.0	In addition to score 3.0 performance, the student demonstrates in-depth inferences and applications that go beyond what was taught.	
	Score 3.5	*In addition to score 3.0 performance, partial success at score 4.0 content*
Score 3.0	The student will write grade-appropriate arguments to support claims in an analysis of substantive topics or texts, using valid reasoning and relevant and sufficient evidence (W.11–12.1): • Introduce precise, knowledgeable claims, establish the significance of the claims, distinguish the claims from alternate or opposing claims, and create an organization that logically sequences claims, counterclaims, reasons, and evidence (W.11–12.1a) • Develop claims and counterclaims fairly and thoroughly, supplying the most relevant evidence for each while pointing out the strengths and limitations of both in a manner that anticipates the audience's knowledge level, concerns, values, and possible biases (W.11–12.1b) • Use words, phrases, and clauses as well as varied syntax to link the major sections of the text, create cohesion, and clarify the relationships between claims and reasons, between reasons and evidence, and between claims and counterclaims (W.11–12.1c) • Establish and maintain a formal style and objective tone while attending to the norms and conventions of the discipline in which they are writing (W.11–12.1d) • Provide a concluding statement or section that follows from and supports the argument presented (W.11–12.1e)	
	Score 2.5	*No major errors or omissions regarding score 2.0 content, and partial success at score 3.0 content*
Score 2.0	The student will recognize or recall specific vocabulary, such as: • *Alternate, anticipate, argument, audience, bias, claim, clarify, clause, cohesion, concluding statement, convention, counterclaim, discipline, evidence, fair, formal style, introduce, limitation, link, logical, norm, objective tone, opposing, organization, phrase, precise, reason, reasoning, relationship, relevant, sequence, significance, strength, support, syntax, thorough, text, topic, valid, value* The student will perform basic processes, such as: • Identify claims and counterclaims from teacher-provided examples • Articulate specified patterns of logical sequence for argumentation • Establish a claim and provide relevant evidence for the claim • Write arguments using a teacher-provided template (which includes all of the 3.0 elements)	
	Score 1.5	*Partial success at score 2.0 content, and major errors or omissions regarding score 3.0 content*
Score 1.0	With help, partial success at score 2.0 content and score 3.0 content	
	Score 0.5	*With help, partial success at score 2.0 content but not at score 3.0 content*
Score 0.0	Even with help, no success	

<table>
<tr><th colspan="2">Grades 9–10</th></tr>
<tr><td>Score 3.0</td><td>The student will write grade-appropriate arguments to support claims in an analysis of substantive topics or texts, using valid reasoning and relevant and sufficient evidence (W.9–10.1):
• Introduce precise claims, distinguish the claims from alternate or opposing claims, and create an organization that establishes clear relationships among claims, counterclaims, reasons, and evidence (W.9–10.1a)
• Develop claims and counterclaims fairly, supplying evidence for each while pointing out the strengths and limitations of both in a manner that anticipates the audience's knowledge level and concerns (W.9–10.1b)
• Use words, phrases, and clauses to link the major sections of the text, create cohesion, and clarify the relationships between claims and reasons, between reasons and evidence, and between claims and counterclaims (W.9–10.1c)
• Establish and maintain a formal style and objective tone while attending to the norms and conventions of the discipline in which they are writing (W.9–10.1d)
• Provide a concluding statement or section that follows from and supports the argument presented (W.9–10.1e)</td></tr>
<tr><td>Score 2.0</td><td>The student will recognize or recall specific vocabulary, such as:
• Alternate, anticipate, argument, audience, claim, clarify, clause, cohesion, concluding statement, convention, counterclaim, discipline, evidence, fair, formal style, introduce, limitation, link, norm, objective tone, opposing, organization, phrase, precise, reason, reasoning, relationship, relevant, strength, support, text, topic, valid
The student will perform basic processes, such as:
• Identify claims and counterclaims from teacher-provided examples
• Establish a claim and provide relevant evidence for the claim
• Write arguments using a teacher-provided template (which includes all of the 3.0 elements)</td></tr>
<tr><th colspan="2">Grade 8</th></tr>
<tr><td>Score 3.0</td><td>The student will write grade-appropriate arguments to support claims with clear reasons and relevant evidence (W.8.1):
• Introduce claims, acknowledge and distinguish the claims from alternate or opposing claims, and organize the reasons and evidence logically (W.8.1a)
• Support claims with logical reasoning and relevant evidence, using accurate, credible sources and demonstrating an understanding of the topic or text (W.8.1b)
• Use words, phrases, and clauses to create cohesion and clarify the relationships between claims, counterclaims, reasons, and evidence (W.8.1c)
• Establish and maintain a formal style (W.8.1d)
• Provide a concluding statement or section that follows from and supports the argument presented (W.8.1e)</td></tr>
<tr><td>Score 2.0</td><td>The student will recognize or recall specific vocabulary, such as:
• Accurate, alternate, argument, claim, clarify, clause, cohesion, concluding statement, counterclaim, credible, evidence, formal style, introduce, logical, opinion, opposing, organize, phrase, position, reason, reasoning, relationship, relevant, source, support, text, topic
The student will perform basic processes, such as:
• Generate an opinion on a topic and relevant reasons/examples to support that opinion
• Generate relevant counterclaims to a position
• Write arguments using a teacher-provided template (which includes all of the 3.0 elements)</td></tr>
</table>

Grade 7	
Score 3.0	The student will write grade-appropriate arguments to support claims with clear reasons and relevant evidence (W.7.1): • Introduce claims, acknowledge alternate or opposing claims, and organize the reasons and evidence logically (W.7.1a) • Support claims with logical reasoning and relevant evidence, using accurate, credible sources and demonstrating an understanding of the topic or text (W.7.1b) • Use words, phrases, and clauses to create cohesion and clarify the relationships among claims, reasons, and evidence (W.7.1c) • Establish and maintain a formal style (W.7.1d) • Provide a concluding statement or section that follows from and supports the argument presented (W.7.1e)
Score 2.0	The student will recognize or recall specific vocabulary, such as: • *Accurate*, *alternate*, *argument*, *claim*, *clarify*, *clause*, *cohesion*, *concluding statement*, *credible*, *evidence*, *formal style*, *introduce*, *logical*, *opposing*, *organize*, *phrase*, *reason*, *reasoning*, *relationship*, *relevant*, *source*, *support*, *text*, *topic* The student will perform basic processes, such as: • Identify the characteristics of a model argument composition • Write arguments using a teacher-provided template (which includes all of the 3.0 elements)
Grade 6	
Score 3.0	The student will write grade-appropriate arguments to support claims with clear reasons and relevant evidence (W.6.1): • Introduce claims and organize the reasons and evidence clearly (W.6.1a) • Support claims with clear reasons and relevant evidence, using credible sources and demonstrating an understanding of the topic or text (W.6.1b) • Use words, phrases, and clauses to clarify the relationships among claims and reasons (W.6.1c) • Establish and maintain a formal style (W.6.1d) • Provide a concluding statement or section that follows from the argument presented (W.6.1e)
Score 2.0	The student will recognize or recall specific vocabulary, such as: • *Argument*, *claim*, *clarify*, *clause*, *concluding statement*, *credible*, *evidence*, *formal style*, *introduce*, *organize*, *phrase*, *reason*, *relationship*, *relevant*, *source*, *support*, *text*, *topic* The student will perform basic processes, such as: • Write arguments using a teacher-provided template (which includes all of the 3.0 elements)
Grade 5	
Score 3.0	The student will write opinion pieces on grade-appropriate topics or texts, supporting a point of view with reasons and information (W.5.1): • Introduce a topic or text clearly, state an opinion, and create an organizational structure in which ideas are logically grouped to support the writer's purpose (W.5.1a) • Provide logically ordered reasons that are supported by facts and details (W.5.1b) • Link opinion and reasons using words, phrases, and clauses (for example, *consequently*, *specifically*) (W.5.1c) • Provide a concluding statement or section related to the opinion presented (W.5.1d)

<table>
<tr><td>Score 2.0</td><td>The student will recognize or recall specific vocabulary, such as:
• Clause, concluding statement, detail, fact, idea, information, introduce, link, logical, opinion, organizational structure, phrase, point of view, purpose, reason, support, text, topic
The student will perform basic processes, such as:
• Write opinion pieces using a teacher-provided template or graphic organizer</td></tr>
<tr><td colspan="2">Grade 4</td></tr>
<tr><td>Score 3.0</td><td>The student will write opinion pieces on grade-appropriate topics or texts, supporting a point of view with reasons and information (W.4.1):
• Introduce a topic or text clearly, state an opinion, and create an organizational structure in which related ideas are grouped to support the writer's purpose (W.4.1a)
• Provide reasons that are supported by facts and details (W.4.1b)
• Link opinion and reasons using words and phrases (for example, for instance, in order to, in addition) (W.4.1c)
• Provide a concluding statement or section related to the opinion presented (W.4.1d)</td></tr>
<tr><td>Score 2.0</td><td>The student will recognize or recall specific vocabulary, such as:
• Concluding statement, detail, fact, idea, information, introduce, link, opinion, organizational structure, point of view, phrase, purpose, reason, support, text, topic
The student will perform basic processes, such as:
• Write opinion pieces using a teacher-provided template or graphic organizer</td></tr>
<tr><td colspan="2">Grade 3</td></tr>
<tr><td>Score 3.0</td><td>The student will write opinion pieces on grade-appropriate topics or texts, supporting a point of view with reasons (W.3.1):
• Introduce the topic or text they are writing about, state an opinion, and create an organizational structure that lists reasons (W.3.1a)
• Provide reasons that support the opinion (W.3.1b)
• Use linking words and phrases (for example, because, therefore, since, for example) to connect opinions and reasons (W.3.1c)
• Provide a concluding statement or section (W.3.1d)</td></tr>
<tr><td>Score 2.0</td><td>The student will recognize or recall specific vocabulary, such as:
• Concluding statement, connect, introduce, linking, opinion, organizational structure, phrase, point of view, reason, support, text, topic
The student will perform basic processes, such as:
• Write opinion pieces using a teacher-provided template or graphic organizer</td></tr>
<tr><td colspan="2">Grade 2</td></tr>
<tr><td>Score 3.0</td><td>The student will demonstrate the features of opinion writing (W.2.1):
• Introduce the topic or book they are writing about
• State an opinion
• Supply reasons that support the opinion
• Use linking words (for example, because, and, also) to connect opinion and reasons
• Provide a concluding statement or section</td></tr>
<tr><td>Score 2.0</td><td>The student will recognize or recall specific vocabulary, such as:
• Concluding statement, connect, introduce, linking, opinion, reason, support, topic
The student will perform basic processes, such as:
• Complete a teacher-provided template to represent opinions</td></tr>
</table>

Grade 1	
Score 3.0	The student will demonstrate the features of opinion writing (W.1.1): • Introduce the topic or name the book they are writing about • State an opinion • Supply a reason for the opinion • Provide a sense of closure
Score 2.0	The student will recognize or recall specific vocabulary, such as: • *Closure, introduce, opinion, reason, topic* The student will perform basic processes, such as: • Complete a teacher-provided template to represent opinions
Kindergarten	
Score 3.0	The student will demonstrate the features of opinion writing (W.K.1): • Use a combination of drawing, dictating, and writing to compose opinion pieces • Tell a reader the topic or name of the book they are writing about • State an opinion or preference about the topic or book
Score 2.0	The student will recognize or recall specific vocabulary, such as: • *Compose, dictate, opinion, preference, topic* The student will perform basic processes, such as: • Complete a teacher-provided template to represent opinions

Informative/Explanatory

Grades 11–12		
Score 4.0	In addition to score 3.0 performance, the student demonstrates in-depth inferences and applications that go beyond what was taught.	
	Score 3.5	*In addition to score 3.0 performance, partial success at score 4.0 content*
Score 3.0	The student will write grade-appropriate informative/explanatory texts to examine and convey complex ideas, concepts, and information clearly and accurately through the effective selection, organization, and analysis of content (W.11–12.2): • Introduce a topic; organize complex ideas, concepts, and information so that each new element builds on that which precedes it to create a unified whole; include formatting (for example, headings), graphics (for example, figures, tables), and multimedia when useful to aiding comprehension (W.11–12.2a) • Develop the topic thoroughly by selecting the most significant and relevant facts, extended definitions, concrete details, quotations, or other information and examples appropriate to the audience's knowledge of the topic (W.11–12.2b) • Use appropriate and varied transitions and syntax to link the major sections of the text, create cohesion, and clarify the relationships among complex ideas and concepts (W.11–12.2c) • Use precise language, domain-specific vocabulary, and techniques such as metaphor, simile, and analogy to manage the complexity of the topic (W.11–12.2d) • Establish and maintain a formal style and objective tone while attending to the norms and conventions of the discipline in which they are writing (W.11–12.2e) • Provide a concluding statement or section that follows from and supports the information or explanation presented (for example, articulating implications or the significance of the topic) (W.11–12.2f)	
	Score 2.5	*No major errors or omissions regarding score 2.0 content, and partial success at score 3.0 content*

<table>
<tr><td>Score 2.0</td><td colspan="2">The student will recognize or recall specific vocabulary, such as:
• Analogy, analysis, articulate, audience, clarify, cohesion, complex, comprehension, concept, concluding statement, concrete, convention, convey, definition, detail, discipline, domain-specific vocabulary, element, example, fact, figure, formal style, formatting, graphic, heading, idea, implication, information, informative/explanatory, introduce, link, metaphor, multimedia, norm, objective tone, organization, organize, precise, quotation, relationship, relevant, revise, selection, significance, significant, simile, support, syntax, table, technique, thesis, topic, transition, unified, varied
The student will perform basic processes, such as:
• Select a topic from a list or teacher-provided prompt
• Create and revise a thesis
• Organize ideas and information
• Write an informative/explanatory composition using a teacher-provided template (which includes all of the 3.0 elements)</td></tr>
<tr><td></td><td>Score 1.5</td><td>Partial success at score 2.0 content, and major errors or omissions regarding score 3.0 content</td></tr>
<tr><td>Score 1.0</td><td colspan="2">With help, partial success at score 2.0 content and score 3.0 content</td></tr>
<tr><td></td><td>Score 0.5</td><td>With help, partial success at score 2.0 content but not at score 3.0 content</td></tr>
<tr><td>Score 0.0</td><td colspan="2">Even with help, no success</td></tr>
<tr><td colspan="3">Grades 9–10</td></tr>
<tr><td>Score 3.0</td><td colspan="2">The student will write grade-appropriate informative/explanatory texts to examine and convey complex ideas, concepts, and information clearly and accurately through the effective selection, organization, and analysis of content (W.9–10.2):
• Introduce a topic; organize complex ideas, concepts, and information to make important connections and distinctions; include formatting (for example, headings), graphics (for example, figures, tables), and multimedia when useful to aiding comprehension (W.9–10.2a)
• Develop the topic with well-chosen, relevant, and sufficient facts, extended definitions, concrete details, quotations, or other information and examples appropriate to the audience's knowledge of the topic (W.9–10.2b)
• Use appropriate and varied transitions to link the major sections of the text, create cohesion, and clarify the relationships among complex ideas and concepts (W.9–10.2c)
• Use precise language and domain-specific vocabulary to manage the complexity of the topic (W.9–10.2d)
• Establish and maintain a formal style and objective tone while attending to the norms and conventions of the discipline in which they are writing (W.9–10.2e)
• Provide a concluding statement or section that follows from and supports the information or explanation presented (for example, articulating implications or the significance of the topic) (W.9–10.2f)</td></tr>
<tr><td>Score 2.0</td><td colspan="2">The student will recognize or recall specific vocabulary, such as:
• Analysis, articulate, audience, clarify, cohesion, complex, comprehension, concept, concluding statement, concrete, connection, convey, convention, definition, detail, discipline, distinction, domain-specific vocabulary, example, fact, figure, formal style, formatting, graphic, heading, idea, implication, information, informative/explanatory, introduce, link, multimedia, norm, objective tone, organization, organize, precise, quotation, relationship, relevant, revise, selection, significance, sufficient, support, table, thesis, topic, transition, varied
The student will perform basic processes, such as:
• Select a topic from a list or teacher-provided prompt
• Create and revise a thesis
• Organize ideas and information
• Write an informative/explanatory composition using a teacher-provided template (which includes all of the 3.0 elements)</td></tr>
</table>

<table>
<tr><th colspan="2">Grade 8</th></tr>
<tr><td>Score 3.0</td><td>The student will write grade-appropriate informative/explanatory texts to examine a topic and convey ideas, concepts, and information through the selection, organization, and analysis of relevant content (W.8.2):<ul><li>Introduce a topic clearly, previewing what is to follow; organize ideas, concepts, and information into broader categories; include formatting (for example, headings), graphics (for example, charts, tables), and multimedia when useful to aiding comprehension (W.8.2a)</li><li>Develop the topic with relevant, well-chosen facts, definitions, concrete details, quotations, or other information and examples (W.8.2b)</li><li>Use appropriate and varied transitions to create cohesion and clarify the relationships among ideas and concepts (W.8.2c)</li><li>Use precise language and domain-specific vocabulary to inform about or explain the topic (W.8.2d)</li><li>Establish and maintain a formal style (W.8.2e)</li><li>Provide a concluding statement or section that follows from and supports the information or explanation presented (W.8.2f)</li></ul></td></tr>
<tr><td>Score 2.0</td><td>The student will recognize or recall specific vocabulary, such as:<ul><li>Analysis, category, chart, clarify, cohesion, comprehension, concept, concluding statement, concrete, convey, definition, detail, domain-specific vocabulary, example, explain, fact, formal style, formatting, graphic, heading, idea, inform, information, informative/explanatory, introduce, multimedia, organization, organize, precise, preview, quotation, relationship, relevant, selection, support, table, topic, transition, varied</li></ul>The student will perform basic processes, such as:<ul><li>Identify the characteristics of a model informative/explanatory piece</li><li>Generate a list of details from relevant information related to a topic</li><li>Write informative/explanatory pieces using a teacher-provided template (which includes all of the 3.0 elements)</li></ul></td></tr>
<tr><th colspan="2">Grade 7</th></tr>
<tr><td>Score 3.0</td><td>The student will write grade-appropriate informative/explanatory texts to examine a topic and convey ideas, concepts, and information through the selection, organization, and analysis of relevant content (W.7.2):<ul><li>Introduce a topic clearly, previewing what is to follow; organize ideas, concepts, and information, using strategies such as definition, classification, comparison/contrast, and cause/effect; include formatting (for example, headings), graphics (for example, charts, tables), and multimedia when useful to aiding comprehension (W.7.2a)</li><li>Develop the topic with relevant facts, definitions, concrete details, quotations, or other information and examples (W.7.2b)</li><li>Use appropriate transitions to create cohesion and clarify the relationships among ideas and concepts (W.7.2c)</li><li>Use precise language and domain-specific vocabulary to inform about or explain the topic (W.7.2d)</li><li>Establish and maintain a formal style (W.7.2e)</li><li>Provide a concluding statement or section that follows from and supports the information or explanation presented (W.7.2f)</li></ul></td></tr>
<tr><td>Score 2.0</td><td>The student will recognize or recall specific vocabulary, such as:<ul><li>Analysis, cause/effect, chart, clarify, classification, cohesion, comparison/contrast, comprehension, concept, concluding statement, concrete, convey, definition, detail, domain-specific vocabulary, example, explain, fact, formal style, formatting, graphic, heading, idea, inform, information, informative/explanatory, introduce, multimedia, organization, organize, precise, preview, quotation, relationship, relevant, selection, strategy, support, table, topic, transition</li></ul>The student will perform basic processes, such as:<ul><li>Identify the characteristics of a model informative/explanatory piece</li><li>Generate a list of details from relevant information related to the topic</li><li>Write informative/explanatory pieces using a teacher-provided template (which includes all of the 3.0 elements)</li></ul></td></tr>
</table>

<table>
<tr><th colspan="2">Grade 6</th></tr>
<tr><td>Score 3.0</td><td>The student will write grade-appropriate informative/explanatory texts to examine a topic and convey ideas, concepts, and information through the selection, organization, and analysis of relevant content (W.6.2):
• Introduce a topic; organize ideas, concepts, and information, using strategies such as definition, classification, comparison/contrast, and cause/effect; include formatting (for example, headings), graphics (for example, charts, tables), and multimedia when useful to aiding comprehension (W.6.2a)
• Develop the topic with relevant facts, definitions, concrete details, quotations, or other information and examples (W.6.2b)
• Use appropriate transitions to clarify the relationships among ideas and concepts (W.6.2c)
• Use precise language and domain-specific vocabulary to inform about or explain the topic (W.6.2d)
• Establish and maintain a formal style (W.6.2e)
• Provide a concluding statement or section that follows from the information or explanation presented (W.6.2f)</td></tr>
<tr><td>Score 2.0</td><td>The student will recognize or recall specific vocabulary, such as:
• Analysis, cause/effect, chart, clarify, classification, comparison/contrast, comprehension, concept, concluding statement, concrete, convey, definition, detail, domain-specific vocabulary, example, explain, fact, formal style, formatting, graphic, heading, idea, inform, information, informative/explanatory, introduce, multimedia, organization, organize, precise, quotation, relationship, relevant, selection, strategy, table, topic, transition
The student will perform basic processes, such as:
• Identify the characteristics of a model informative/explanatory piece
• Generate a list of details from relevant information related to the topic
• Write informative/explanatory pieces using a teacher-provided template (which includes all of the 3.0 elements)</td></tr>
<tr><th colspan="2">Grade 5</th></tr>
<tr><td>Score 3.0</td><td>The student will write grade-appropriate informative/explanatory texts to examine a topic and convey ideas and information clearly (W.5.2):
• Introduce a topic clearly, provide a general observation and focus, and group related information logically; include formatting (for example, headings), illustrations, and multimedia when useful to aiding comprehension (W.5.2a)
• Develop the topic with facts, definitions, concrete details, quotations, or other information and examples related to the topic (W.5.2b)
• Link ideas within and across categories of information using words, phrases, and clauses (for example, in contrast, especially) (W.5.2c)
• Use precise language and domain-specific vocabulary to inform about or explain the topic (W.5.2d)
• Provide a concluding statement or section related to the information or explanation presented (W.5.2e)</td></tr>
<tr><td>Score 2.0</td><td>The student will recognize or recall specific vocabulary, such as:
• Category, clause, comprehension, concluding statement, concrete, convey, definition, detail, domain-specific vocabulary, example, explain, fact, focus, formatting, heading, idea, illustration, inform, information, informative/explanatory, introduce, link, logical, multimedia, observation, phrase, precise, quotation, related, topic
The student will perform basic processes, such as:
• Write informative/explanatory pieces using a teacher-provided template or graphic organizer</td></tr>
</table>

Grade 4	
Score 3.0	The student will write grade-appropriate informative/explanatory texts to examine a topic and convey ideas and information clearly (W.4.2): • Introduce a topic clearly and group related information in paragraphs and sections; include formatting (for example, headings), illustrations, and multimedia when useful to aiding comprehension (W.4.2a) • Develop the topic with facts, definitions, concrete details, quotations, or other information and examples related to the topic (W.4.2b) • Link ideas within categories of information using words and phrases (for example, *another*, *for example*, *also*, *because*) (W.4.2c) • Use precise language and domain-specific vocabulary to inform about or explain the topic (W.4.2d) • Provide a concluding statement or section related to the information or explanation presented (W.4.2e)
Score 2.0	The student will recognize or recall specific vocabulary, such as: • *Category*, *comprehension*, *concluding statement*, *concrete*, *convey*, *definition*, *detail*, *domain-specific vocabulary*, *example*, *explain*, *fact*, *formatting*, *heading*, *idea*, *illustration*, *inform*, *information*, *informative/explanatory*, *introduce*, *link*, *multimedia*, *paragraph*, *phrase*, *precise*, *quotation*, *related*, *topic* The student will perform basic processes, such as: • Write informative/explanatory pieces using a teacher-provided template or graphic organizer
Grade 3	
Score 3.0	The student will write grade-appropriate informative/explanatory texts to examine a topic and convey ideas and information clearly (W.3.2): • Introduce a topic and group related information together; include illustrations when useful to aiding comprehension (W.3.2a) • Develop the topic with facts, definitions, and details (W.3.2b) • Use linking words and phrases (for example, *also*, *another*, *and*, *more*, *but*) to connect ideas within categories of information (W.3.2c) • Provide a concluding statement or section (W.3.2d)
Score 2.0	The student will recognize or recall specific vocabulary, such as: • *Category*, *comprehension*, *concluding statement*, *connect*, *convey*, *definition*, *detail*, *fact*, *idea*, *illustration*, *information*, *informative/explanatory*, *introduce*, *linking*, *phrase*, *related*, *topic* The student will perform basic processes, such as: • Write informative/explanatory pieces using a teacher-provided template or graphic organizer
Grade 2	
Score 3.0	The student will demonstrate grade-appropriate features of informative/explanatory writing (W.2.2): • Introduce a topic • Use facts and definitions to develop points • Provide a concluding statement or section
Score 2.0	The student will recognize or recall specific vocabulary, such as: • *Concluding statement*, *definition*, *fact*, *informative/explanatory*, *introduce*, *point*, *topic* The student will perform basic processes, such as: • Write informative/explanatory pieces using a teacher-provided template or graphic organizer

Grade 1		
Score 3.0	The student will demonstrate grade-appropriate features of informative/explanatory writing (W.1.2): • Name a topic • Supply facts about the topic • Provide a sense of closure	
Score 2.0	The student will recognize or recall specific vocabulary, such as: • *Closure, fact, informative/explanatory, topic* The student will perform basic processes, such as: • Write informative/explanatory pieces using a teacher-provided template or graphic organizer	
Kindergarten		
Score 3.0	The student will demonstrate grade-appropriate features of informative/explanatory writing (W.K.2): • Name a topic • Supply information about the topic	
Score 2.0	The student will recognize or recall specific vocabulary, such as: • *Information, informative/explanatory, topic* The student will perform basic processes, such as: • Complete a teacher-provided template for representing informative/explanatory information	

Narrative

Grades 11–12		
Score 4.0	In addition to score 3.0 performance, the student demonstrates in-depth inferences and applications that go beyond what was taught.	
	Score 3.5	*In addition to score 3.0 performance, partial success at score 4.0 content*
Score 3.0	The student will write grade-appropriate narratives to develop real or imagined experiences or events using effective technique, well-chosen details, and well-structured event sequences (W.11–12.3): • Engage and orient the reader by setting out a problem, situation, or observation and its significance, establishing one or multiple points of view, and introducing a narrator and/or characters; create a smooth progression of experiences or events (W.11–12.3a) • Use narrative techniques, such as dialogue, pacing, description, reflection, and multiple plot lines, to develop experiences, events, and/or characters (W.11–12.3b) • Use a variety of techniques to sequence events so that they build on one another to create a coherent whole and build toward a particular tone and outcome (for example, a sense of mystery, suspense, growth, or resolution) (W.11–12.3c) • Use precise words and phrases, telling details, and sensory language to convey a vivid picture of the experiences, events, setting, and/or characters (W.11–12.3d) • Provide a conclusion that follows from and reflects on what is experienced, observed, or resolved over the course of the narrative (W.11–12.3e)	
	Score 2.5	*No major errors or omissions regarding score 2.0 content, and partial success at score 3.0 content*

<table>
<tr><td>Score 2.0</td><td colspan="2">The student will recognize or recall specific vocabulary, such as:
• Character, coherent, conclusion, convey, description, detail, dialogue, engage, event, experience, growth, mystery, narrative, narrator, observation, organize, orient, outcome, pacing, phrase, plan, plot line, point of view, precise, problem, progression, reflection, resolution, resolve, sensory, sequence, setting, significance, situation, suspense, technique, tone, vivid
The student will perform basic processes, such as:
• Use a teacher-provided template for planning and organizing a narrative
• Describe the use of narrative techniques such as dialogue, pacing, description, reflection, and multiple plot lines, and techniques to sequence events and build toward a particular tone and outcome
• Write narratives using a teacher-provided template or graphic organizer</td></tr>
<tr><td></td><td>Score 1.5</td><td>Partial success at score 2.0 content, and major errors or omissions regarding score 3.0 content</td></tr>
<tr><td>Score 1.0</td><td colspan="2">With help, partial success at score 2.0 content and score 3.0 content</td></tr>
<tr><td></td><td>Score 0.5</td><td>With help, partial success at score 2.0 content but not at score 3.0 content</td></tr>
<tr><td>Score 0.0</td><td colspan="2">Even with help, no success</td></tr>
<tr><td colspan="3">Grades 9–10</td></tr>
<tr><td>Score 3.0</td><td colspan="2">The student will write grade-appropriate narratives to develop real or imagined experiences or events using effective technique, well-chosen details, and well-structured event sequences (W.9–10.3):
• Engage and orient the reader by setting out a problem, situation, or observation, establishing one or multiple points of view, and introducing a narrator and/or characters (W.9–10.3a)
• Use narrative techniques, such as dialogue, pacing, description, reflection, and multiple plot lines to develop experiences, events, and/or characters (W.9–10.3b)
• Use a variety of techniques to sequence events so that they build on one another to create a coherent whole (W.9–10.3c)
• Use precise words and phrases, telling details, and sensory language to convey a vivid picture of the experiences, events, setting, and/or characters (W.9–10.3d)
• Provide a conclusion that follows from and reflects on what is experienced, observed, or resolved over the course of the narrative (W.9–10.3e)</td></tr>
<tr><td>Score 2.0</td><td colspan="2">The student will recognize or recall specific vocabulary, such as:
• Character, coherent, conclusion, convey, description, detail, dialogue, engage, event, experience, narrative, narrator, observation, organize, orient, pacing, phrase, plan, plot line, point of view, precise, problem, reflection, resolve, sensory, sequence, setting, situation, technique, vivid
The student will perform basic processes, such as:
• Use a teacher-provided template for planning and organizing a narrative
• Describe the use of narrative techniques such as dialogue, pacing, description, reflection, and multiple plot lines, and techniques to sequence events
• Write narratives using a teacher-provided template or graphic organizer</td></tr>
<tr><td colspan="3">Grade 8</td></tr>
<tr><td>Score 3.0</td><td colspan="2">The student will write grade-appropriate narratives to develop real or imagined experiences or events using effective technique, relevant descriptive details, and well-structured event sequences (W.8.3):
• Engage and orient the reader by establishing a context and point of view and introducing a narrator and/or characters; organize an event sequence that unfolds naturally and logically (W.8.3a)
• Use narrative techniques, such as dialogue, pacing, description, and reflection, to develop experiences, events, and/or characters (W.8.3b)
• Use a variety of transition words, phrases, and clauses to convey sequence, signal shifts from one time frame or setting to another, and show the relationships among experiences and events (W.8.3c)
• Use precise words and phrases, relevant descriptive details, and sensory language to capture the action and convey experiences and events (W.8.3d)
• Provide a conclusion that follows from and reflects on the narrated experiences or events (W.8.3e)</td></tr>
</table>

<table>
<tr><td>Score 2.0</td><td>The student will recognize or recall specific vocabulary, such as:
• Action, character, clause, conclusion, context, convey, description, detail, dialogue, engage, event, experience, logical, narrative, narrator, organize, orient, pacing, phrase, plan, point of view, precise, reflection, relationship, relevant, sensory, sequence, setting, technique, time frame, transition
The student will perform basic processes, such as:
• Use a teacher-provided template for planning and organizing a narrative
• Describe the use of narrative techniques such as dialogue, pacing, description, and reflection, and the use of transition words, phrases, and clauses
• Write narratives using a teacher-provided template or graphic organizer</td></tr>
<tr><td colspan="2">Grade 7</td></tr>
<tr><td>Score 3.0</td><td>The student will write grade-appropriate narratives to develop real or imagined experiences or events using effective technique, relevant descriptive details, and well-structured event sequences (W.7.3):
• Engage and orient the reader by establishing a context and point of view and introducing a narrator and/or characters; organize an event sequence that unfolds naturally and logically (W.7.3a)
• Use narrative techniques, such as dialogue, pacing, and description, to develop experiences, events, and/or characters (W.7.3b)
• Use a variety of transition words, phrases, and clauses to convey sequence and signal shifts from one time frame or setting to another (W.7.3c)
• Use precise words and phrases, relevant descriptive details, and sensory language to capture the action and convey experiences and events (W.7.3d)
• Provide a conclusion that follows from and reflects on the narrated experiences or events (W.7.3e)</td></tr>
<tr><td>Score 2.0</td><td>The student will recognize or recall specific vocabulary, such as:
• Action, character, clause, conclusion, context, convey, description, detail, dialogue, engage, event, experience, logical, narrative, narrator, organize, orient, pacing, phrase, plan, point of view, precise, relevant, sensory, sequence, setting, technique, time frame, transition
The student will perform basic processes, such as:
• Use a teacher-provided template for planning and organizing a narrative
• Describe the use of narrative techniques such as dialogue, pacing, and description, and the use of transition words, phrases, and clauses
• Write narratives using a teacher-provided template or graphic organizer</td></tr>
<tr><td colspan="2">Grade 6</td></tr>
<tr><td>Score 3.0</td><td>The student will write grade-appropriate narratives to develop real or imagined experiences or events using effective technique, relevant descriptive details, and well-structured event sequences (W.6.3):
• Engage and orient the reader by establishing a context and introducing a narrator and/or characters; organize an event sequence that unfolds naturally and logically (W.6.3a)
• Use narrative techniques, such as dialogue, pacing, and description, to develop experiences, events, and/or characters (W.6.3b)
• Use a variety of transition words, phrases, and clauses to convey sequence and signal shifts from one time frame or setting to another (W.6.3c)
• Use precise words and phrases, relevant descriptive details, and sensory language to convey experiences and events (W.6.3d)
• Provide a conclusion that follows from the narrated experiences or events (W.6.3e)</td></tr>
</table>

Score 2.0	The student will recognize or recall specific vocabulary, such as: • *Character, clause, conclusion, context, convey, description, detail, dialogue, engage, event, experience, logical, narrative, narrator, organize, orient, pacing, phrase, plan, precise, relevant, sensory, sequence, setting, technique, time frame, transition* The student will perform basic processes, such as: • Use a teacher-provided template for planning and organizing a narrative • Describe the use of narrative techniques such as dialogue, pacing, and description, and the use of transition words, phrases, and clauses • Write narratives using a teacher-provided template or graphic organizer
Grade 5	
Score 3.0	The student will write grade-appropriate narratives to develop real or imagined experiences or events using effective technique, descriptive details, and clear event sequences (W.5.3): • Orient the reader by establishing a situation and introducing a narrator and/or characters; organize an event sequence that unfolds naturally (W.5.3a) • Use narrative techniques, such as dialogue, description, and pacing, to develop experiences and events or show the responses of characters to situations (W.5.3b) • Use a variety of transitional words, phrases, and clauses to manage the sequence of events (W.5.3c) • Use concrete words and phrases and sensory details to convey experiences and events precisely (W.5.3d) • Provide a conclusion that follows from the narrated experiences or events (W.5.3e)
Score 2.0	The student will recognize or recall specific vocabulary, such as: • *Character, clause, conclusion, concrete, convey, description, detail, dialogue, event, experience, narrative, narrator, organize, orient, pacing, phrase, precise, response, sensory, sequence, situation, technique, transition* The student will perform basic processes, such as: • Write narrative pieces using a teacher-provided template or graphic organizer • Describe the use of narrative techniques such as dialogue, description, and pacing • Use teacher-provided transitional words, phrases, and clauses
Grade 4	
Score 3.0	The student will write grade-appropriate narratives to develop real or imagined experiences or events using effective technique, descriptive details, and clear event sequences (W.4.3): • Orient the reader by establishing a situation and introducing a narrator and/or characters; organize an event sequence that unfolds naturally (W.4.3a) • Use dialogue and description to develop experiences and events or show the responses of characters to situations (W.4.3b) • Use a variety of transitional words and phrases to manage the sequence of events (W.4.3c) • Use concrete words and phrases and sensory details to convey experiences and events precisely (W.4.3d) • Provide a conclusion that follows from the narrated experiences or events (W.4.3e)
Score 2.0	The student will recognize or recall specific vocabulary, such as: • *Character, conclusion, concrete, convey, description, detail, dialogue, event, experience, narrative, narrator, organize, orient, phrase, precise, response, sensory, sequence, situation, technique, transition* The student will perform basic processes, such as: • Write narrative pieces using a teacher-provided template or graphic organizer • Identify examples of transitional words and phrases

	Grade 3
Score 3.0	The student will write grade-appropriate narratives to develop real or imagined experiences or events using effective technique, descriptive details, and clear event sequences (W.3.3): • Establish a situation and introduce a narrator and/or characters; organize an event sequence that unfolds naturally (W.3.3a) • Use dialogue and descriptions of actions, thoughts, and feelings to develop experiences and events or show the response of characters to situations (W.3.3b) • Use temporal words and phrases to signal event order (W.3.3c) • Provide a sense of closure (W.3.3d)
Score 2.0	The student will recognize or recall specific vocabulary, such as: • *Action*, *character*, *closure*, *description*, *detail*, *dialogue*, *event*, *experience*, *narrative*, *narrator*, *organize*, *phrase*, *response*, *sequence*, *situation*, *technique*, *time order* The student will perform basic processes, such as: • Write narrative pieces using a teacher-provided template or graphic organizer
	Grade 2
Score 3.0	The student will write grade-appropriate narratives that (W.2.3): • Recount a well-elaborated event or short sequence of events • Include details to describe actions, thoughts, and feelings • Use temporal words to signal event order (for example, *first*, *then*, *next*) • Provide a sense of closure
Score 2.0	The student will recognize or recall specific vocabulary, such as: • *Action*, *closure*, *detail*, *elaborate*, *event*, *narrative*, *sequence*, *time order* The student will perform basic processes, such as: • Write narrative pieces using a teacher-provided template or graphic organizer
	Grade 1
Score 3.0	The student will write grade-appropriate narratives that (W.1.3): • Recount two or more appropriately sequenced events • Include details regarding what happened • Use temporal words to signal event order • Provide a sense of closure
Score 2.0	The student will recognize or recall specific vocabulary, such as: • *Closure*, *detail*, *event*, *narrative*, *sequence*, *time order* The student will perform basic processes, such as: • Write narrative pieces using a teacher-provided template or graphic organizer
	Kindergarten
Score 3.0	The student will write grade-appropriate narratives that (W.K.3): • Narrate a single event or several loosely linked events • Tell about events in the order in which they occurred • Provide a reaction to what happened
Score 2.0	The student will recognize or recall specific vocabulary, such as: • *Event*, *narrate*, *narrative*, *order*, *reaction* The student will perform basic processes, such as: • Use a combination of drawing, dictating, and writing to narrate a single event or several loosely linked events

Task, Purpose, and Audience

Grades 11–12		
Score 4.0	In addition to score 3.0 performance, the student demonstrates in-depth inferences and applications that go beyond what was taught.	
	Score 3.5	*In addition to score 3.0 performance, partial success at score 4.0 content*
Score 3.0	The student will: • Produce clear and coherent grade-appropriate writing in which the development, organization, and style are appropriate to task, purpose, and audience (for example, opinion, informative/explanatory, narrative, and research writing) (W.11–12.4)	
	Score 2.5	*No major errors or omissions regarding score 2.0 content, and partial success at score 3.0 content*
Score 2.0	The student will recognize or recall specific vocabulary, such as: • *Audience*, *coherent*, *development*, *informative/explanatory*, *narrative*, *opinion*, *organization*, *purpose*, *research*, *style*, *task* The student will perform basic processes, such as: • Describe the task, purpose, and audience for a given writing task • Describe how to modify samples of writing for a specific task, purpose, and audience • Produce writing appropriate to task, purpose, and audience using a teacher-provided template or graphic organizer	
	Score 1.5	*Partial success at score 2.0 content, and major errors or omissions regarding score 3.0 content*
Score 1.0	With help, partial success at score 2.0 content and score 3.0 content	
	Score 0.5	*With help, partial success at score 2.0 content but not at score 3.0 content*
Score 0.0	Even with help, no success	
Grades 9–10		
Score 3.0	The student will: • Produce clear and coherent grade-appropriate writing in which the development, organization, and style are appropriate to the task, purpose, and audience (for example, opinion, informative/explanatory, narrative, and research writing) (W.9–10.4)	
Score 2.0	The student will recognize or recall specific vocabulary, such as: • *Audience*, *coherent*, *development*, *informative/explanatory*, *narrative*, *opinion*, *organization*, *purpose*, *research*, *style*, *task* The student will perform basic processes, such as: • Describe the task, purpose, and audience for a given writing task • Describe how to modify samples of writing for a specific task, purpose, and audience • Produce writing appropriate to task, purpose, and audience using a teacher-provided template or graphic organizer	
Grade 8		
Score 3.0	The student will: • Produce clear and coherent grade-appropriate writing in which the development, organization, and style are appropriate to task, purpose, and audience (for example, opinion, informative/explanatory, narrative, and research writing) (W.8.4)	

<table>
<tr><td>Score 2.0</td><td>The student will recognize or recall specific vocabulary, such as:<ul><li>Audience, coherent, development, informative/explanatory, narrative, opinion, organization, purpose, research, style, task</li></ul>The student will perform basic processes, such as:<ul><li>Describe the task, purpose, and audience for a given writing task</li><li>Describe how to modify samples of writing for a specific task, purpose, and audience</li><li>Produce writing appropriate to task, purpose, and audience using a teacher-provided template or graphic organizer</li></ul></td></tr>
<tr><td colspan="2">Grade 7</td></tr>
<tr><td>Score 3.0</td><td>The student will:<ul><li>Produce clear and coherent grade-appropriate writing in which the development, organization, and style are appropriate to task, purpose, and audience (for example, opinion, informative/explanatory, narrative, and research writing) (W.7.4)</li></ul></td></tr>
<tr><td>Score 2.0</td><td>The student will recognize or recall specific vocabulary, such as:<ul><li>Audience, coherent, development, informative/explanatory, narrative, opinion, organization, purpose, research, style, task</li></ul>The student will perform basic processes, such as:<ul><li>Describe the task, purpose, and audience for a given writing task</li><li>Describe how to modify samples of writing for a specific task, purpose, and audience</li><li>Produce writing appropriate to task, purpose, and audience using a teacher-provided template or graphic organizer</li></ul></td></tr>
<tr><td colspan="2">Grade 6</td></tr>
<tr><td>Score 3.0</td><td>The student will:<ul><li>Produce clear and coherent grade-appropriate writing in which the development, organization, and style are appropriate to task, purpose, and audience (for example, opinion, informative/explanatory, narrative, and research writing) (W.6.4)</li></ul></td></tr>
<tr><td>Score 2.0</td><td>The student will recognize or recall specific vocabulary, such as:<ul><li>Audience, coherent, development, informative/explanatory, narrative, opinion, organization, purpose, research, style, task</li></ul>The student will perform basic processes, such as:<ul><li>Describe the task, purpose, and audience for a given writing task</li><li>Produce writing appropriate to task, purpose, and audience using a teacher-provided template or graphic organizer</li></ul></td></tr>
<tr><td colspan="2">Grade 5</td></tr>
<tr><td>Score 3.0</td><td>The student will:<ul><li>Produce clear and coherent grade-appropriate writing in which the development and organization are appropriate to task, purpose, and audience (for example, opinion, informative/explanatory, narrative, and research writing) (W.5.4)</li></ul></td></tr>
<tr><td>Score 2.0</td><td>The student will recognize or recall specific vocabulary, such as:<ul><li>Audience, coherent, development, informative/explanatory, narrative, opinion, organization, purpose, research, task</li></ul>The student will perform basic processes, such as:<ul><li>Describe the task, purpose, and audience for a given writing task</li><li>Produce writing appropriate to task, purpose, and audience using a teacher-provided template or graphic organizer</li></ul></td></tr>
</table>

Grade 4	
Score 3.0	The student will: • Produce clear and coherent grade-appropriate writing in which the development and organization are appropriate to task, purpose, and audience (for example, opinion, informative/explanatory, narrative, and research writing) (W.4.4)
Score 2.0	The student will recognize or recall specific vocabulary, such as: • *Coherent, development, informative/explanatory, narrative, opinion, organization, purpose, research, task* The student will perform basic processes, such as: • Identify task, purpose, and audience for writing • Produce writing appropriate to task and purpose using a teacher-provided template or graphic organizer
Grade 3	
Score 3.0	The student will: • Produce grade-appropriate writing in which the development and organization are appropriate to task and purpose (for example, opinion, informative/explanatory, narrative, and research writing) (W.3.4)
Score 2.0	The student will recognize or recall specific vocabulary, such as: • *Development, informative/explanatory, narrative, opinion, organization, purpose, research, task* The student will perform basic processes, such as: • Identify the task and purpose for writing • Produce writing appropriate to task and purpose using a teacher-provided template or graphic organizer
Grades 2, 1, and Kindergarten	
Score 3.0	Not applicable.
Score 2.0	Not applicable.

Revise and Edit

Grades 11–12		
Score 4.0	In addition to score 3.0 performance, the student demonstrates in-depth inferences and applications that go beyond what was taught.	
	Score 3.5	*In addition to score 3.0 performance, partial success at score 4.0 content*
Score 3.0	The student will develop and strengthen grade-appropriate writing for a specific audience and purpose by (W.11–12.5): • Planning • Revising • Editing • Rewriting • Trying a new approach	
	Score 2.5	*No major errors or omissions regarding score 2.0 content, and partial success at score 3.0 content*
Score 2.0	The student will recognize or recall specific vocabulary, such as: • *Audience, edit, plan, purpose, revise, rewrite* The student will perform basic processes, such as: • Plan writing using a teacher-provided planning template or graphic organizer • Revise and edit writing based on teacher and peer feedback	
	Score 1.5	*Partial success at score 2.0 content, and major errors or omissions regarding score 3.0 content*

<table>
<tr><td>Score 1.0</td><td colspan="2">With help, partial success at score 2.0 content and score 3.0 content</td></tr>
<tr><td></td><td>Score 0.5</td><td>With help, partial success at score 2.0 content but not at score 3.0 content</td></tr>
<tr><td>Score 0.0</td><td colspan="2">Even with help, no success</td></tr>
<tr><td colspan="3" align="center">Grades 9–10</td></tr>
<tr><td>Score 3.0</td><td colspan="2">The student will develop and strengthen grade-appropriate writing for a specific audience and purpose by (W.9–10.5):
• Planning
• Revising
• Editing
• Rewriting
• Trying a new approach</td></tr>
<tr><td>Score 2.0</td><td colspan="2">The student will recognize or recall specific vocabulary, such as:
• Audience, edit, plan, purpose, revise, rewrite
The student will perform basic processes, such as:
• Plan writing using a teacher-provided planning template or graphic organizer
• Revise and edit writing based on teacher and peer feedback</td></tr>
<tr><td colspan="3" align="center">Grade 8</td></tr>
<tr><td>Score 3.0</td><td colspan="2">The student will develop and strengthen grade-appropriate writing for a specific purpose and audience by (W.8.5):
• Planning
• Revising
• Editing
• Rewriting
• Trying a new approach</td></tr>
<tr><td>Score 2.0</td><td colspan="2">The student will recognize or recall specific vocabulary, such as:
• Audience, edit, plan, purpose, revise, rewrite
The student will perform basic processes, such as:
• Plan writing using a teacher-provided planning template or graphic organizer
• Revise and edit writing based on teacher and peer feedback</td></tr>
<tr><td colspan="3" align="center">Grade 7</td></tr>
<tr><td>Score 3.0</td><td colspan="2">The student will develop and strengthen grade-appropriate writing for a specific audience and purpose by (W.7.5):
• Planning
• Revising
• Editing
• Rewriting
• Trying a new approach</td></tr>
<tr><td>Score 2.0</td><td colspan="2">The student will recognize or recall specific vocabulary, such as:
• Audience, edit, plan, purpose, revise, rewrite
The student will perform basic processes, such as:
• Plan writing using a teacher-provided planning template or graphic organizer
• Revise and edit writing based on teacher and peer feedback</td></tr>
</table>

	Grade 6
Score 3.0	The student will develop and strengthen grade-appropriate writing by (W.6.5): • Planning • Revising • Editing • Rewriting • Trying a new approach
Score 2.0	The student will recognize or recall specific vocabulary, such as: • *Edit*, *plan*, *revise*, *rewrite* The student will perform basic processes, such as: • Plan writing using a teacher-provided planning template or graphic organizer • Revise and edit writing based on teacher and peer feedback
	Grade 5
Score 3.0	The student will develop and strengthen grade-appropriate writing by (W.5.5): • Planning • Revising • Editing • Rewriting • Trying a new approach
Score 2.0	The student will recognize or recall specific vocabulary, such as: • *Edit*, *plan*, *revise*, *rewrite* The student will perform basic processes, such as: • Plan writing using a teacher-provided planning template or graphic organizer • Revise and edit writing based on teacher and peer feedback
	Grade 4
Score 3.0	The student will develop and strengthen grade-appropriate writing by (W.4.5): • Planning • Revising • Editing
Score 2.0	The student will recognize or recall specific vocabulary, such as: • *Edit*, *plan*, *revise* The student will perform basic processes, such as: • Plan writing using a teacher-provided planning template or graphic organizer • Revise and edit writing based on teacher and peer feedback
	Grade 3
Score 3.0	The student will develop and strengthen grade-appropriate writing by (W.3.5): • Planning • Revising • Editing

<table>
<tr><td>Score 2.0</td><td>The student will recognize or recall specific vocabulary, such as:
• Edit, plan, revise
The student will perform basic processes, such as:
• Plan writing using a teacher-provided planning template or graphic organizer
• Revise and edit writing based on teacher and peer feedback</td></tr>
<tr><td colspan="2">Grade 2</td></tr>
<tr><td>Score 3.0</td><td>The student will develop and strengthen grade-appropriate writing (for example, focus on a topic, strengthen writing as needed) by (W.2.5):
• Planning
• Revising
• Editing</td></tr>
<tr><td>Score 2.0</td><td>The student will recognize or recall specific vocabulary, such as:
• Edit, focus, plan, revise, topic
The student will perform basic processes, such as:
• Plan writing using a teacher-provided planning template or graphic organizer
• Revise and edit writing based on teacher and peer feedback</td></tr>
<tr><td colspan="2">Grade 1</td></tr>
<tr><td>Score 3.0</td><td>The student will develop and strengthen grade-appropriate writing to (for example, focus on a topic, respond to questions and suggestions from peers, and add details to strengthen writing as needed) by (W.1.5):
• Planning
• Revising
• Editing</td></tr>
<tr><td>Score 2.0</td><td>The student will recognize or recall specific vocabulary, such as:
• Edit, focus, plan, revise, topic
The student will perform basic processes, such as:
• Plan writing using a teacher-provided planning template or graphic organizer
• Revise and edit writing based on teacher and peer feedback</td></tr>
<tr><td colspan="2">Kindergarten</td></tr>
<tr><td>Score 3.0</td><td>The student will develop and strengthen grade-appropriate writing (for example, respond to questions and suggestions from peers, add details to strengthen writing) by (W.K.5):
• Planning
• Revising
• Editing</td></tr>
<tr><td>Score 2.0</td><td>The student will recognize or recall specific vocabulary, such as:
• Edit, plan, revise
The student will perform basic processes, such as:
• Plan writing based on specific prompts from the teacher
• Revise writing based on specific prompts from the teacher (W.K.5)</td></tr>
</table>

Technology

Grades 11–12		
Score 4.0	In addition to score 3.0 performance, the student demonstrates in-depth inferences and applications that go beyond what was taught.	
	Score 3.5	*In addition to score 3.0 performance, partial success at score 4.0 content*
Score 3.0	The student will use technology, including the Internet, to: • Produce, publish, and update individual or shared grade-appropriate writing products (W.11–12.6)	
	Score 2.5	*No major errors or omissions regarding score 2.0 content, and partial success at score 3.0 content*
Score 2.0	The student will recognize or recall specific vocabulary, such as: • *Ethical, Internet, publish, technology, update* The student will perform basic processes, such as: • Demonstrate the features of various grade-appropriate technologies (for example, word processor, blog, file sharing) • Describe the ethical use of various grade-appropriate technologies	
	Score 1.5	*Partial success at score 2.0 content, and major errors or omissions regarding score 3.0 content*
Score 1.0	With help, partial success at score 2.0 content and score 3.0 content	
	Score 0.5	*With help, partial success at score 2.0 content but not at score 3.0 content*
Score 0.0	Even with help, no success	
Grades 9–10		
Score 3.0	The student will use technology, including the Internet, to: • Produce, publish, and update individual or shared grade-appropriate writing products (W.9–10.6) • Link to other information and display information flexibly and dynamically (W.9–10.6)	
Score 2.0	The student will recognize or recall specific vocabulary, such as: • *Dynamic, ethical, flexible, information, Internet, link, publish, technology, relevant, source, update* The student will perform basic processes, such as: • Demonstrate the features of various grade-appropriate technologies (for example, word processor, blog, presentation software) • Describe the ethical use of various grade-appropriate technologies	
Grade 8		
Score 3.0	The student will use technology, including the Internet, to: • Produce and publish grade-appropriate writing (W.8.6) • Present the relationships between information and ideas efficiently (W.8.6) • Interact and collaborate with others (W.8.6)	
Score 2.0	The student will recognize or recall specific vocabulary, such as: • *Collaborate, idea, information, interact, Internet, publish, relationship, relevant, source, technology* The student will perform basic processes, such as: • Demonstrate the features of various grade-appropriate technologies (for example, word processor, online work space, presentation software) • Identify relevant information from a variety of grade-appropriate sources	

<table>
<tr><th colspan="2">Grade 7</th></tr>
<tr><td>Score 3.0</td><td>The student will use technology, including the Internet, to:
• Produce and publish grade-appropriate writing (W.7.6)
• Link to and cite sources (W.7.6)
• Interact and collaborate with others (W.7.6)</td></tr>
<tr><td>Score 2.0</td><td>The student will recognize or recall specific vocabulary, such as:
• Cite, collaborate, interact, Internet, link, publish, source, technology
The student will perform basic processes, such as:
• Demonstrate the features of various grade-appropriate technologies (for example, word processor, presentation software, search engine)</td></tr>
<tr><th colspan="2">Grade 6</th></tr>
<tr><td>Score 3.0</td><td>The student will use technology, including the Internet, to:
• Produce and publish grade-appropriate writing (W.6.6)
• Interact and collaborate with others (W.6.6)
• Type a minimum of three pages in a single sitting (W.6.6)</td></tr>
<tr><td>Score 2.0</td><td>The student will recognize or recall specific vocabulary, such as:
• Collaborate, interact, Internet, publish, technology
The student will perform basic processes, such as:
• Demonstrate the features of various grade-appropriate technologies (for example, word processor, web-based meeting/chat session)
• Type two pages in a single sitting</td></tr>
<tr><th colspan="2">Grade 5</th></tr>
<tr><td>Score 3.0</td><td>The student will use technology, including the Internet, to:
• Produce and publish grade-appropriate writing (W.5.6)
• Interact and collaborate with others (W.5.6)
• Type a minimum of two pages in a single sitting (W.5.6)</td></tr>
<tr><td>Score 2.0</td><td>The student will recognize or recall specific vocabulary, such as:
• Collaborate, interact, Internet, publish, technology
The student will perform basic processes, such as:
• Demonstrate the features of various grade-appropriate technologies (for example, word processor, web browser, search engine)
• Type one page in a single sitting</td></tr>
<tr><th colspan="2">Grade 4</th></tr>
<tr><td>Score 3.0</td><td>The student will use technology, including the Internet, to:
• Produce and publish grade-appropriate writing (W.4.6)
• Interact and collaborate with others (W.4.6)
• Type a minimum of one page in a single sitting (W.4.6)</td></tr>
<tr><td>Score 2.0</td><td>The student will recognize or recall specific vocabulary, such as:
• Collaborate, interact, Internet, publish, technology
The student will perform basic processes, such as:
• Demonstrate the features of various grade-appropriate technologies (for example, word processor, email, chat room)
• Demonstrate basic use of a keyboard</td></tr>
</table>

Grade 3	
Score 3.0	The student will use technology to: • Produce and publish grade-appropriate writing (using keyboarding skills) (W.3.6) • Interact and collaborate with others (W.3.6)
Score 2.0	The student will recognize or recall specific vocabulary, such as: • *Collaborate*, *interact*, *keyboarding*, *publish*, *technology* The student will perform basic processes, such as: • Demonstrate the features of various grade-appropriate technologies (for example, word processor, email)
Grade 2	
Score 3.0	The student will: • Use a variety of digital tools to produce and publish grade-appropriate writing independently (W.2.6)
Score 2.0	The student will recognize or recall specific vocabulary, such as: • *Digital*, *independently*, *publish*, *technology*, *tool* The student will perform basic processes, such as: • Demonstrate the features of various grade-appropriate technologies (for example, word processor)
Grade 1	
Score 3.0	The student will: • Use a variety of digital tools to produce and publish grade-appropriate writing in collaboration with peers (W.1.6)
Score 2.0	The student will recognize or recall specific vocabulary, such as: • *Collaboration*, *digital*, *publish*, *technology*, *tool* The student will perform basic processes, such as: • Demonstrate the features of various grade-appropriate technologies (for example, word processor)
Kindergarten	
Score 3.0	The student will: • Use a variety of digital tools to produce and publish grade-appropriate writing (W.K.6)
Score 2.0	The student will recognize or recall specific vocabulary, such as: • *Digital*, *publish*, *technology*, *tool* The student will perform basic processes, such as: • Demonstrate the features of various grade-appropriate technologies (for example, word processor)

Research

Grades 11–12		
Score 4.0	In addition to score 3.0 performance, the student demonstrates in-depth inferences and applications that go beyond what was taught.	
	Score 3.5	*In addition to score 3.0 performance, partial success at score 4.0 content*
Score 3.0	The student will: • Conduct short as well as more sustained grade-appropriate research projects to answer a question (including a self-generated question) or solve a problem (W.11–12.7) • Narrow or broaden the inquiry when appropriate (W.11–12.7) • Synthesize multiple sources on the subject, demonstrating understanding of the subject under investigation (W.11–12.7)	

	Score 2.5	*No major errors or omissions regarding score 2.0 content, and partial success at score 3.0 content*
Score 2.0	The student will recognize or recall specific vocabulary, such as: • *Broaden, citation, information, inquiry, investigation, narrow, notes, organize, problem, question, research, research project, source, synthesize, topic* The student will perform basic processes, such as: • Select a topic • Write and revise a grade-appropriate research question • Strategically read grade-appropriate resources • Take effective notes • Organize and synthesize information collected from more than one source • Demonstrate use of appropriate citations • Write a research composition following a teacher-provided template	
	Score 1.5	*Partial success at score 2.0 content, and major errors or omissions regarding score 3.0 content*
Score 1.0	With help, partial success at score 2.0 content and score 3.0 content	
	Score 0.5	*With help, partial success at score 2.0 content but not at score 3.0 content*
Score 0.0	Even with help, no success	
Grades 9–10		
Score 3.0	The student will: • Conduct short as well as more sustained grade-appropriate research projects to answer a question or solve a problem (W.9–10.7) • Narrow or broaden the inquiry when appropriate (W.9–10.7) • Synthesize multiple sources on the subject, demonstrating an understanding of the subject under investigation (W.9–10.7)	
Score 2.0	The student will recognize or recall specific vocabulary, such as: • *Broaden, citation, information, inquiry, investigation, narrow, notes, organize, problem, question, research, research project, source, synthesize, topic* The student will perform basic processes, such as: • Select a topic • Write and revise a grade-appropriate research question • Strategically read grade-appropriate resources • Take effective notes • Organize and synthesize information collected from more than one source • Write a research composition with appropriate citations utilizing a teacher-provided template	
Grade 8		
Score 3.0	The student will: • Conduct short grade-appropriate research projects to answer a self-generated question, drawing on several sources and generating additional related, focused questions that allow for multiple avenues of exploration (W.8.7)	
Score 2.0	The student will recognize or recall specific vocabulary, such as: • *Avenue of exploration, focused, question, related, research, research project, source* The student will perform basic processes, such as: • Develop a grade-appropriate research question • Demonstrate each step of the research process in isolation using a teacher-provided template (for example, develop research questions, locate appropriate sources, record information related to topic, and/or form questions not answered in current sources)	

<table>
<tr><th colspan="2">Grade 7</th></tr>
<tr><td>Score 3.0</td><td>The student will:
• Conduct short grade-appropriate research projects to answer a question, drawing on several sources and generating additional related, focused questions for further research and investigation (W.7.7)</td></tr>
<tr><td>Score 2.0</td><td>The student will recognize or recall specific vocabulary, such as:
• Focused, investigation, question, related, research, research project, source
The student will perform basic processes, such as:
• Develop a grade-appropriate research question
• Demonstrate each step of the research process in isolation using a teacher-provided template (for example, locate appropriate sources, record information related to topic, and/or form questions not answered in current sources)</td></tr>
<tr><th colspan="2">Grade 6</th></tr>
<tr><td>Score 3.0</td><td>The student will:
• Conduct short grade-appropriate research projects to answer a question, drawing on several sources and refocusing the inquiry when appropriate (W.6.7)</td></tr>
<tr><td>Score 2.0</td><td>The student will recognize or recall specific vocabulary, such as:
• Inquiry, question, refocus, research, research project, source
The student will perform basic processes, such as:
• Develop a grade-appropriate research question
• Demonstrate each step of the research process in isolation using a teacher-provided template (for example, generate appropriate keyword searches, locate appropriate sources, record information related to topic)</td></tr>
<tr><th colspan="2">Grade 5</th></tr>
<tr><td>Score 3.0</td><td>The student will:
• Conduct short grade-appropriate research projects that use several sources to build knowledge through investigation of different aspects of a topic (W.5.7)</td></tr>
<tr><td>Score 2.0</td><td>The student will recognize or recall specific vocabulary, such as:
• Aspect, investigation, knowledge, research, question, research project, source, topic
The student will perform basic processes, such as:
• Use teacher-provided sources to answer grade-appropriate research questions
• Demonstrate each step of the research process in isolation using a teacher-provided template (for example, generate appropriate keyword searches, locate appropriate sources, record information related to topic)</td></tr>
<tr><th colspan="2">Grade 4</th></tr>
<tr><td>Score 3.0</td><td>The student will:
• Conduct short grade-appropriate research projects that build knowledge through investigation of different aspects of a topic (W.4.7)</td></tr>
<tr><td>Score 2.0</td><td>The student will recognize or recall specific vocabulary, such as:
• Aspect, investigation, knowledge, question, research, research project, topic
The student will perform basic processes, such as:
• Use teacher-provided sources to answer grade-appropriate research questions
• Demonstrate each step of the research process in isolation using a teacher-provided template (for example, generate appropriate keyword searches, locate appropriate sources, record information related to topic)</td></tr>
<tr><th colspan="2">Grade 3</th></tr>
<tr><td>Score 3.0</td><td>The student will:
• Conduct short grade-appropriate research projects that build knowledge about a topic (W.3.7)</td></tr>
</table>

Score 2.0	The student will recognize or recall specific vocabulary, such as: • *Knowledge, question, research, research project, topic* The student will perform basic processes, such as: • Use teacher-provided sources to answer grade-appropriate research questions • Demonstrate each step of the research process in isolation using a teacher-provided template (for example, generate appropriate keyword searches, locate appropriate sources, record information related to topic)
	Grade 2
Score 3.0	The student will: • Demonstrate the features of grade-appropriate research writing (for example, read a number of books on a single topic to produce a report; record science observations) (W.2.7)
Score 2.0	The student will recognize or recall specific vocabulary, such as: • *Observation, record, report, research, topic* The student will perform basic processes, such as: • Write grade-appropriate research pieces using a teacher-provided template or graphic organizer
	Grade 1
Score 3.0	The student will: • Write grade-appropriate research products (for example, explore a number of "how-to" books on a given topic and use them to write a sequence of instructions) (W.1.7)
Score 2.0	The student will recognize or recall specific vocabulary, such as: • *Instruction, research, sequence, topic* The student will perform basic processes, such as: • Write grade-appropriate research pieces using a teacher-provided template or graphic organizer
	Kindergarten
Score 3.0	The student will: • Participate in shared grade-appropriate research and writing projects (for example, explore a number of books by a favorite author and express opinions about them) (W.K.7)
Score 2.0	The student will recognize or recall specific vocabulary, such as: • *Author, opinion, research* The student will perform basic processes, such as: • Participate in shared grade-appropriate research and writing projects (for example, explore a number of books by a favorite author and express opinions about them) using explicit teacher direction or a teacher-provided template

Access and Organize Information

	Grades 11–12	
Score 4.0	In addition to score 3.0 performance, the student demonstrates in-depth inferences and applications that go beyond what was taught.	
	Score 3.5	*In addition to score 3.0 performance, partial success at score 4.0 content*
Score 3.0	The student will: • Gather relevant information from multiple authoritative grade-appropriate print and digital sources, using advanced searches effectively (W.11–12.8) • Assess the strengths and limitations of each source in terms of the task, purpose, and audience (W.11–12.8) • Integrate information into the text selectively to maintain the flow of ideas, avoiding plagiarism and overreliance on any one source following a standard format for citation (W.11–12.8)	

<table>
<tr><td></td><td>Score 2.5</td><td>No major errors or omissions regarding score 2.0 content, and partial success at score 3.0 content</td></tr>
<tr><td>Score 2.0</td><td colspan="2">The student will recognize or recall specific vocabulary, such as:
• Audience, authoritative, citation format, credible, digital, flow of ideas, information, integrate, limitation, overreliance, paraphrase, plagiarism, print, purpose, relevant, search, source, task, text
The student will perform basic processes, such as:
• Use a teacher-provided template or process to gather information
• Describe features of credible sources
• Evaluate selected information with a teacher-provided template
• Paraphrase and incorporate information from three or more grade-appropriate sources into written notes, a graphic organizer, or outline using explicit teacher direction or a teacher-provided template</td></tr>
<tr><td></td><td>Score 1.5</td><td>Partial success at score 2.0 content, and major errors or omissions regarding score 3.0 content</td></tr>
<tr><td>Score 1.0</td><td colspan="2">With help, partial success at score 2.0 content and score 3.0 content</td></tr>
<tr><td></td><td>Score 0.5</td><td>With help, partial success at score 2.0 content but not at score 3.0 content</td></tr>
<tr><td>Score 0.0</td><td colspan="2">Even with help, no success</td></tr>
<tr><td colspan="3">Grades 9–10</td></tr>
<tr><td>Score 3.0</td><td colspan="2">The student will:
• Gather relevant information from multiple authoritative grade-appropriate print and digital sources, using advanced searches effectively (W.9–10.8)
• Assess the usefulness of each source in answering a grade-appropriate research question (W.9–10.8)
• Integrate information into the text selectively to maintain the flow of ideas, avoiding plagiarism and following a standard format for citation (W.9–10.8)</td></tr>
<tr><td>Score 2.0</td><td colspan="2">The student will recognize or recall specific vocabulary, such as:
• Authoritative, citation format, digital, flow of ideas, information, integrate, paraphrase, plagiarism, print, question, relevant, research, search, source, text
The student will perform basic processes, such as:
• Use a teacher-provided template or process to gather information
• Describe the characteristics of a useful source
• Paraphrase and incorporate information from three or more grade-appropriate sources into written notes, a graphic organizer, or outline using explicit teacher direction or a teacher-provided template</td></tr>
<tr><td colspan="3">Grade 8</td></tr>
<tr><td>Score 3.0</td><td colspan="2">The student will:
• Gather relevant information from multiple grade-appropriate print and digital sources, using search terms effectively (W.8.8)
• Assess the credibility and accuracy of each source (W.8.8)
• Quote or paraphrase the data and conclusions of others while avoiding plagiarism and following a standard format for citation (W.8.8)</td></tr>
<tr><td>Score 2.0</td><td colspan="2">The student will recognize or recall specific vocabulary, such as:
• Accuracy, citation format, cite, conclusion, credibility, data, digital, information, paraphrase, plagiarism, print, quote, relevant, search, source, term
The student will perform basic processes, such as:
• Use a teacher-provided template to compile and cite grade-appropriate information
• Describe the criteria for credible and accurate sources</td></tr>
</table>

Grade 7	
Score 3.0	The student will: • Gather relevant information from multiple grade-appropriate print and digital sources, using search terms effectively (W.7.8) • Assess the credibility and accuracy of each source (W.7.8) • Quote or paraphrase the data and conclusions of others while avoiding plagiarism and following a standard format for citation (W.7.8)
Score 2.0	The student will recognize or recall specific vocabulary, such as: • *Accuracy*, *citation format*, *cite*, *conclusion*, *credibility*, *data*, *digital*, *information*, *paraphrase*, *plagiarism*, *print*, *quote*, *relevant*, *search*, *source*, *term* The student will perform basic processes, such as: • Use a teacher-provided template or process to compile and cite grade-appropriate information • Describe the criteria for credible and accurate sources
Grade 6	
Score 3.0	The student will: • Gather relevant information from multiple grade-appropriate print and digital sources (W.6.8) • Assess the credibility of each source (W.6.8) • Quote or paraphrase the data and conclusions of others while avoiding plagiarism, and provide basic bibliographic information for sources (W.6.8)
Score 2.0	The student will recognize or recall specific vocabulary, such as: • *Bibliography*, *cite*, *conclusion*, *credibility*, *data*, *digital*, *information*, *paraphrase*, *plagiarism*, *print*, *quote*, *relevant*, *source* The student will perform basic processes, such as: • Use a teacher-provided template or process to compile and cite grade-appropriate information • Describe the criteria for credible sources
Grade 5	
Score 3.0	The student will: • Recall relevant information from experiences or gather relevant information from grade-appropriate print and digital sources (W.5.8) • Summarize or paraphrase information in notes and finished work, and provide a list of sources (W.5.8)
Score 2.0	The student will recognize or recall specific vocabulary, such as: • *Digital*, *experience*, *information*, *notes*, *paraphrase*, *print*, *recall*, *relevant*, *source*, *summarize* The student will perform basic processes, such as: • Gather and record information from grade-appropriate print and digital sources using a teacher-provided template
Grade 4	
Score 3.0	The student will: • Recall relevant information from experiences or gather relevant information from grade-appropriate print and digital sources (W.4.8) • Take notes, categorize information, and provide a list of sources (W.4.8)

Score 2.0	The student will recognize or recall specific vocabulary, such as: • *Categorize*, *digital*, *experience*, *information*, *notes*, *print*, *recall*, *relevant*, *source* The student will perform basic processes, such as: • Gather and record information from grade-appropriate print and digital sources using a teacher-provided template • Categorize information into teacher-provided categories
Grade 3	
Score 3.0	The student will: • Recall information from experiences or gather information from grade-appropriate print and digital sources (W.3.8) • Take brief notes on sources and sort evidence into categories (W.3.8) • Use text features and search tools (for example, keywords, sidebars, hyperlinks) to locate information relevant to a given grade-appropriate topic (RI.3.5)
Score 2.0	The student will recognize or recall specific vocabulary, such as: • *Category*, *digital*, *evidence*, *experience*, *hyperlink*, *information*, *keyword*, *notes*, *print*, *recall*, *relevant*, *search tool*, *sidebar*, *sort*, *source*, *text feature*, *topic* The student will perform basic processes, such as: • Sort evidence into teacher-provided categories • Take notes using a teacher-provided template or graphic organizer • Describe the use of grade-appropriate text features and search tools (for example, keywords, sidebars, hyperlinks)
Grade 2	
Score 3.0	The student will: • Recall information from experiences or gather information from grade-appropriate sources to answer a self-generated question (W.2.8) • Locate key facts or information in a grade-appropriate text efficiently using various text features (for example, captions, bold print, subheadings, glossaries, indexes, electronic menus, icons) (RI.2.5)
Score 2.0	The student will recognize or recall specific vocabulary, such as: • *Answer*, *bold print*, *caption*, *electronic menu*, *experience*, *fact*, *glossary*, *icon*, *index*, *information*, *question*, *recall*, *source*, *subheading*, *text*, *text feature* The student will perform basic processes, such as: • Recall information from experiences or gather information from teacher-provided grade-appropriate sources to answer a self-generated question • Identify text features of grade-appropriate informational texts (for example, captions, bold print, subheadings, glossaries, indexes, electronic menus, icons) (RI.2.5)
Grade 1	
Score 3.0	The student will: • Recall information from experiences or gather information from teacher-provided grade-appropriate sources to answer a teacher-provided question (W.1.8) • Locate key facts or information in a grade-appropriate text using various text features (for example, headings, tables of contents, glossaries, electronic menus, icons) (RI.1.5)

Score 2.0	The student will recognize or recall specific vocabulary, such as: • *Answer, electronic menu, experience, fact, glossary, heading, icon, information, question, recall, source, table of contents, text, text feature* The student will perform basic processes, such as: • Find answers to teacher-provided questions using teacher-provided grade-appropriate resources • Identify various text features of grade-appropriate informational texts (for example, headings, tables of contents, glossaries, electronic menus, icons) (RI.1.5)
Kindergarten	
Score 3.0	The student will: • Recall information from experiences or gather information from teacher-provided grade-appropriate sources to answer a teacher-provided question (W.K.8)
Score 2.0	The student will recognize or recall specific vocabulary, such as: • *Answer, experience, information, question, recall, source* The student will perform basic processes, such as: • Recognize or recall examples of appropriate materials to find information • Find answers to teacher-provided questions using teacher-provided grade-appropriate resources

Speaking and Listening

Collaborative Discussions

<table>
<tr><th colspan="3">Grades 11–12</th></tr>
<tr><td>Score 4.0</td><td colspan="2">In addition to score 3.0 performance, the student demonstrates in-depth inferences and applications that go beyond what was taught.</td></tr>
<tr><td></td><td>Score 3.5</td><td>In addition to score 3.0 performance, partial success at score 4.0 content</td></tr>
<tr><td>Score 3.0</td><td colspan="2">The student will initiate and participate effectively in a range of collaborative discussions (one on one, in groups, and teacher led) with diverse partners on grade-appropriate topics, texts, and issues, building on others' ideas and expressing their own clearly and persuasively (SL.11–12.1):
• Come to discussions prepared, having read and researched material under study; explicitly draw on that preparation by referring to evidence from texts and other research on the topic or issue to stimulate a thoughtful, well-reasoned exchange of ideas (SL.11–12.1a)
• Propel conversations by posing and responding to questions that probe reasoning and evidence; ensure a hearing for a full range of positions on a topic or issue; clarify, verify, or challenge ideas and conclusions; promote divergent and creative perspectives (SL.11–12.1c)
• Respond thoughtfully to diverse perspectives; synthesize comments, claims, and evidence made on all sides of an issue; resolve contradictions when possible; determine what additional information or research is required to deepen the investigation or complete the task (SL.11–12.1d)</td></tr>
<tr><td></td><td>Score 2.5</td><td>No major errors or omissions regarding score 2.0 content, and partial success at score 3.0 content</td></tr>
<tr><td>Score 2.0</td><td colspan="2">The student will recognize or recall specific vocabulary, such as:
• Challenge, claim, clarify, conclusion, contradiction, conversation, creative, deadline, decision, discussion, divergent, diverse, evidence, exchange of ideas, explicit, goal, idea, information, investigation, issue, participation, peer, perspective, persuasive, pose, position, preparation, probe, question, reasoning, refer, research, resolve, respond, role, synthesize, text, topic, verify
The student will perform basic processes, such as:
• Work with peers to promote civil, democratic discussions and decision making, set clear goals and deadlines, and establish individual roles as needed (SL.11–12.1b)
• Participate actively in one-on-one, small-group, or class discussions in a thoughtful and appropriate manner
• Prepare for participation in a discussion</td></tr>
<tr><td></td><td>Score 1.5</td><td>Partial success at score 2.0 content, and major errors or omissions regarding score 3.0 content</td></tr>
<tr><td>Score 1.0</td><td colspan="2">With help, partial success at score 2.0 content and score 3.0 content</td></tr>
<tr><td></td><td>Score 0.5</td><td>With help, partial success at score 2.0 content but not at score 3.0 content</td></tr>
<tr><td>Score 0.0</td><td colspan="2">Even with help, no success</td></tr>
</table>

<table>
<tr><th colspan="2">Grades 9–10</th></tr>
<tr><td>Score 3.0</td><td>The student will initiate and participate effectively in a range of collaborative discussions (one on one, in groups, and teacher led) with diverse partners on grade-appropriate topics, texts, and issues, building on others' ideas and expressing their own clearly and persuasively (SL.9–10.1):
• Come to discussions prepared, having read and researched material under study; explicitly draw on that preparation by referring to evidence from texts and other research on the topic or issue to stimulate a thoughtful, well-reasoned exchange of ideas (SL.9–10.1a)
• Propel conversations by posing and responding to questions that relate the current discussion to broader themes or larger ideas; actively incorporate others into the discussion; clarify, verify, or challenge ideas and conclusions (SL.9–10.1c)
• Respond thoughtfully to diverse perspectives, summarize points of agreement and disagreement, and, when warranted, qualify or justify their own views and understanding and make new connections in light of the evidence and reasoning presented (SL.9–10.1d)</td></tr>
<tr><td>Score 2.0</td><td>The student will recognize or recall specific vocabulary, such as:
• Agreement, alternate, challenge, clarify, conclusion, connection, consensus, conversation, deadline, decision, disagreement, discussion, diverse, evidence, exchange of ideas, explicit, goal, idea, issue, justify, participation, peer, perspective, persuasive, point, pose, preparation, qualify, question, reasoning, refer, research, respond, role, summarize, text, theme, topic, verify, view, vote, warranted
The student will perform basic processes, such as:
• Work with peers to set rules for collegial discussions and decision making (for example, informal consensus, taking votes on key issues, presentation of alternate views), clear goals and deadlines, and individual roles as needed (SL.9–10.1b)
• Participate actively in one-on-one, small-group, or class discussions in a thoughtful and appropriate manner
• Prepare for participation in a discussion</td></tr>
<tr><th colspan="2">Grade 8</th></tr>
<tr><td>Score 3.0</td><td>The student will engage effectively in a range of collaborative discussions (one on one, in groups, and teacher led) with diverse partners on grade-appropriate topics, texts, and issues, building on others' ideas and expressing their own clearly (SL.8.1):
• Come to discussions prepared, having read or researched material under study; explicitly draw on that preparation by referring to evidence on the topic, text, or issue to probe and reflect on ideas under discussion (SL.8.1a)
• Pose questions that connect the ideas of several speakers and respond to others' questions and comments with relevant evidence, observations, and ideas (SL.8.1c)
• Acknowledge new information expressed by others, and, when warranted, qualify or justify their own views in light of the evidence presented (SL.8.1d)</td></tr>
<tr><td>Score 2.0</td><td>The student will recognize or recall specific vocabulary, such as:
• Connect, deadline, decision, discussion, diverse, evidence, explicit, goal, idea, information, issue, justify, observation, pose, preparation, probe, qualify, question, refer, reflect, relevant, research, respond, role, text, topic, view, warranted
The student will perform basic processes, such as:
• Follow rules for collegial discussions and decision making, track progress toward specific goals and deadlines, and define individual roles as needed (SL.8.1b)
• Participate actively in one-on-one, small-group, or class discussions in a thoughtful and appropriate manner
• Prepare for participation in a discussion</td></tr>
</table>

<table>
<tr><th colspan="2">Grade 7</th></tr>
<tr><td>Score 3.0</td><td>The student will engage effectively in a range of collaborative discussions (one on one, in groups, and teacher led) with diverse partners on grade-appropriate topics, texts, and issues, building on others' ideas and expressing their own clearly (SL.7.1):
• Come to discussions prepared, having read or researched material under study; explicitly draw on that preparation by referring to evidence on the topic, text, or issue to probe and reflect on ideas under discussion (SL.7.1a)
• Pose questions that elicit elaboration and respond to others' questions and comments with relevant observations and ideas that bring the discussion back on topic as needed (SL.7.1c)
• Acknowledge new information expressed by others and, when warranted, modify their own views (SL.7.1d)</td></tr>
<tr><td>Score 2.0</td><td>The student will recognize or recall specific vocabulary, such as:
• Deadline, discussion, diverse, elaboration, evidence, explicit, goal, idea, information, issue, modify, observation, pose, probe, preparation, question, refer, reflect, relevant, research, respond, role, text, topic, view, warranted
The student will perform basic processes, such as:
• Follow rules for collegial discussions, track progress toward specific goals and deadlines, and define individual roles as needed (SL.7.1b)
• Participate actively in one-on-one, small-group, or class discussions in a thoughtful and appropriate manner
• Prepare for participation in a discussion</td></tr>
<tr><th colspan="2">Grade 6</th></tr>
<tr><td>Score 3.0</td><td>The student will engage effectively in a range of collaborative discussions (one on one, in groups, and teacher led) with diverse partners on grade-appropriate topics, texts, and issues, building on others' ideas and expressing their own clearly (SL.6.1):
• Come to discussions prepared, having read or studied required material; explicitly draw on that preparation by referring to evidence on the topic, text, or issue to probe and reflect on ideas under discussion (SL.6.1a)
• Pose and respond to specific questions with elaboration and detail by making comments that contribute to the topic, text, or issue under discussion (SL.6.1c)
• Review the key ideas expressed and demonstrate understanding of multiple perspectives through reflection and paraphrasing (SL.6.1d)</td></tr>
<tr><td>Score 2.0</td><td>The student will recognize or recall specific vocabulary, such as:
• Contribute, deadline, diverse, detail, discussion, elaboration, evidence, explicit, goal, idea, issue, paraphrase, perspective, pose, preparation, probe, question, refer, reflect, reflection, respond, role, text, topic
The student will perform basic processes, such as:
• Follow rules for collegial discussions, set specific goals and deadlines, and define individual roles as needed (SL.6.1b)
• Participate actively in one-on-one, small-group, or class discussions in a thoughtful and appropriate manner
• Prepare for participation in a discussion</td></tr>
<tr><th colspan="2">Grade 5</th></tr>
<tr><td>Score 3.0</td><td>The student will engage effectively in a range of collaborative discussions (one on one, in groups, and teacher led) with diverse partners on grade-appropriate topics and texts, building on others' ideas and expressing their own clearly (SL.5.1):
• Come to discussions prepared, having read or studied required material; explicitly draw on that preparation and other information known about the topic to explore ideas under discussion (SL.5.1a)
• Pose and respond to specific questions by making comments that contribute to the discussion and elaborate on the remarks of others (SL.5.1c)
• Review the key ideas expressed and draw conclusions in light of information and knowledge gained from the discussions (SL.5.1d)</td></tr>
</table>

Score 2.0	The student will recognize or recall specific vocabulary, such as: • *Conclusion, contribute, discussion, diverse, elaborate, explicit, idea, information, pose, preparation, question, respond, role, text, topic* The student will perform basic processes, such as: • Follow agreed-on rules for discussions and carry out assigned roles (SL.5.1b) • Participate actively in one-on-one, small-group, or class discussions in a thoughtful and appropriate manner • Prepare for participation in a discussion
Grade 4	
Score 3.0	The student will engage effectively in a range of collaborative discussions (one on one, in groups, and teacher led) with diverse partners on grade-appropriate topics and texts, building on others' ideas and expressing their own clearly (SL.4.1): • Come to discussions prepared, having read or studied required material; explicitly draw on that preparation and other information known about the topic to explore ideas under discussion (SL.4.1a) • Pose and respond to specific questions to clarify or follow up on information, and make comments that contribute to the discussion and link to the remarks of others (SL.4.1c) • Review the key ideas expressed and explain their own ideas and understanding in light of the discussion (SL.4.1d)
Score 2.0	The student will recognize or recall specific vocabulary, such as: • *Clarify, contribute, discussion, diverse, explicit, idea, information, link, pose, preparation, question, respond, role, text, topic* The student will perform basic processes, such as: • Follow agreed-on rules for discussions and carry out assigned roles (SL.4.1b) • Participate actively in one-on-one, small-group, or class discussions in a thoughtful and appropriate manner • Prepare for participation in a discussion
Grade 3	
Score 3.0	The student will engage effectively in a range of collaborative discussions (one on one, in groups, and teacher led) with diverse partners on grade-appropriate topics and texts, building on others' ideas and expressing their own clearly (SL.3.1): • Come to discussions prepared, having read or studied required material; explicitly draw on that preparation and other information known about the topic to explore ideas under discussion (SL.3.1a) • Ask questions to check understanding of information presented, stay on topic, and link their comments to the remarks of others (SL.3.1c) • Explain their own ideas and understanding in light of the discussion (SL.3.1d)
Score 2.0	The student will recognize or recall specific vocabulary, such as: • *Discussion, diverse, explicit, idea, information, link, preparation, question, text, topic* The student will perform basic processes, such as: • Follow agreed-on rules for discussions (for example, gaining the floor in respectful ways, listening to others with care, speaking one at a time about the topics and texts under discussion) (SL.3.1b) • Participate actively in one-on-one, small-group, or class discussions in a thoughtful and appropriate manner • Prepare for participation in a discussion
Grade 2	
Score 3.0	The student will participate in collaborative conversations with diverse partners about grade-appropriate topics and texts with peers and adults in small and larger groups (SL.2.1): • Build on others' talk in conversations by linking their comments to the remarks of others (SL.2.1b) • Ask for clarification and further explanation as needed about the topics and texts under discussion (SL.2.1c)

Score 2.0	The student will recognize or recall specific vocabulary, such as: • *Clarification, conversation, discussion, explanation, link, text, topic* The student will perform basic processes, such as: • Follow agreed-on rules for discussions (for example, gaining the floor in respectful ways, listening to others with care, speaking one at a time about the topics and texts under discussion) (SL.2.1a)
	Grade 1
Score 3.0	The student will participate in collaborative conversations with diverse partners about grade-appropriate topics and texts with peers and adults in small and larger groups (SL.1.1): • Build on others' talk in conversations by responding to the comments of others through multiple exchanges (SL.1.1b) • Ask questions to clear up any confusion about the topics and texts under discussion (SL.1.1c)
Score 2.0	The student will recognize or recall specific vocabulary, such as: • *Confusion, conversation, discussion, exchange, question, text, topic* The student will perform basic processes, such as: • Participate in collaborative conversations with diverse partners about grade-appropriate topics and texts with teacher modeling • Follow agreed-on rules for discussions (for example, listening to others with care, speaking one at a time about the topics and texts under discussion) (SL.1.1a)
	Kindergarten
Score 3.0	The student will participate in collaborative conversations with diverse partners about grade-appropriate topics and texts with peers and adults in small and larger groups (SL.K.1): • Continue a conversation through multiple exchanges (SL.K.1b)
Score 2.0	The student will recognize or recall specific vocabulary, such as: • *Conversation, discussion, exchange, text, topic* The student will perform basic processes, such as: • Participate in collaborative conversations with diverse partners about grade-appropriate topics and texts with peers and adults in groups with teacher modeling • Follow agreed-on rules for discussions (for example, listening to others and taking turns speaking about the topics and texts under discussion) (SL.K.1a)

Evaluate Presented Information

	Grades 11–12	
Score 4.0	In addition to score 3.0 performance, the student demonstrates in-depth inferences and applications that go beyond what was taught.	
	Score 3.5	*In addition to score 3.0 performance, partial success at score 4.0 content*
Score 3.0	The student will: • Evaluate the credibility and accuracy of multiple grade-appropriate sources of information presented in diverse formats and media (for example, visually, quantitatively, orally) and note any discrepancies among the data in order to make informed decisions and solve problems (SL.11–12.2) • Evaluate a speaker's point of view, reasoning, and use of evidence and rhetoric, assessing the stance, premises, links among ideas, word choice, points of emphasis, and tone used (SL.11–12.3)	
	Score 2.5	*No major errors or omissions regarding score 2.0 content, and partial success at score 3.0 content*

Score 2.0	The student will recognize or recall specific vocabulary, such as: • *Accuracy, credibility, data, decision, discrepancy, diverse, emphasis, evidence, format, idea, information, link, media, orally, point, point of view, premise, problem, quantitative, reasoning, rhetoric, source, stance, tone, visual* The student will perform basic processes, such as: • Identify specified language and rhetorical strategies used to inform and persuade • Identify the characteristics of credible and accurate sources of information • Identify a speaker's point of view, reasoning, and use of evidence and rhetoric	
	Score 1.5	*Partial success at score 2.0 content, and major errors or omissions regarding score 3.0 content*
Score 1.0	With help, partial success at score 2.0 content and score 3.0 content	
	Score 0.5	*With help, partial success at score 2.0 content but not at score 3.0 content*
Score 0.0	Even with help, no success	
	Grades 9–10	
Score 3.0	The student will: • Integrate information from and evaluate the credibility and accuracy of multiple grade-appropriate sources of information presented in diverse media or formats (for example, visually, quantitatively, orally) (SL.9–10.2) • Evaluate a speaker's point of view, reasoning, and use of evidence and rhetoric, identifying any fallacious reasoning or exaggerated or distorted evidence (SL.9–10.3)	
Score 2.0	The student will recognize or recall specific vocabulary, such as: • *Accuracy, credibility, distort, diverse, evidence, exaggerate, fallacious reasoning, format, information, media, orally, point of view, quantitative, reasoning, rhetoric, source, visual* The student will perform basic processes, such as: • Identify the characteristics of credible and accurate sources of information • Identify evidence used by a speaker to support his or her message • Identify a speaker's point of view, reasoning, and use of evidence and rhetoric	
	Grade 8	
Score 3.0	The student will: • Analyze the purpose of information presented in diverse grade-appropriate media and formats (for example, visually, quantitatively, orally) (SL.8.2) • Evaluate the motives (for example, social, commercial, political) behind information presented in diverse grade-appropriate media and formats (SL.8.2) • Evaluate the speaker's argument, the soundness of the reasoning, and relevance and sufficiency of the evidence and identify when irrelevant evidence is introduced (SL.8.3)	
Score 2.0	The student will recognize or recall specific vocabulary, such as: • *Argument, claim, commercial, diverse, evidence, format, information, irrelevant, media, motive, orally, political, quantitative, reasoning, relevance, social, soundness, sufficiency, visual* The student will perform basic processes, such as: • Identify the purposes and motives behind information presented in diverse grade-appropriate media and formats (for example, visually, quantitatively, orally) • Describe a speaker's argument and specific claims (SL.8.3)	
	Grade 7	
Score 3.0	The student will: • Explain how the main ideas and supporting details presented in diverse grade-appropriate media and formats (for example, visually, quantitatively, orally) clarify a topic, text, or issue under study (SL.7.2) • Evaluate a speaker's argument and specific claims, the soundness of the reasoning, and the relevance and sufficiency of the evidence (SL.7.3)	

Score 2.0	The student will recognize or recall specific vocabulary, such as: • *Argument, claim, clarify, diverse, evidence, format, issue, main idea, media, orally, quantitative, reasoning, relevance, soundness, sufficiency, supporting detail, text, topic, visual* The student will perform basic processes, such as: • Identify the main ideas and supporting details presented in diverse grade-appropriate media and formats (for example, visually, quantitatively, orally) (SL.7.2) • Describe a speaker's argument and specific claims (SL.7.3)
	Grade 6
Score 3.0	The student will: • Explain how information presented in diverse grade-appropriate media and formats (for example, visually, quantitatively, orally) contributes to a topic, text, or issue under study (SL.6.2) • Distinguish claims made by a speaker that are supported by reasons and evidence from claims that are not (SL.6.3)
Score 2.0	The student will recognize or recall specific vocabulary, such as: • *Claim, distinguish, diverse, evidence, format, information, issue, media, orally, quantitative, reason, support, text, topic, visual* The student will perform basic processes, such as: • Interpret information presented in diverse grade-appropriate media and formats (for example, visually, quantitatively, orally) (SL.6.2) • Identify a speaker's claims and specific evidence (SL.6.3)
	Grade 5
Score 3.0	The student will: • Summarize a written grade-appropriate text read aloud or information presented in diverse grade-appropriate media and formats, including visually, quantitatively, and orally (SL.5.2) • Explain how each claim made by a speaker is supported by reasons and evidence (SL.5.3)
Score 2.0	The student will recognize or recall specific vocabulary, such as: • *Claim, diverse, evidence, format, information, media, orally, point, quantitative, reason, summarize, support, text, visual* The student will perform basic processes, such as: • Summarize a grade-appropriate text or presented information using a teacher-provided template • Summarize the points a speaker makes (SL.5.3)
	Grade 4
Score 3.0	The student will: • Paraphrase portions of a grade-appropriate text read aloud or information presented in diverse grade-appropriate media and formats, including visually, quantitatively, and orally (SL.4.2) • Identify the reasons and evidence a speaker provides to support particular points (SL.4.3)
Score 2.0	The student will recognize or recall specific vocabulary, such as: • *Diverse, evidence, format, information, media, orally, paraphrase, point, quantitative, reason, support, text, visual* The student will perform basic processes, such as: • Paraphrase a grade-appropriate text or presented information using a teacher-provided template • Identify the reasons a speaker provides to support particular points

<table>
<tr><th colspan="2">Grade 3</th></tr>
<tr><td>Score 3.0</td><td>The student will:
• Determine the main ideas and supporting details of a grade-appropriate text read aloud or information presented in diverse grade-appropriate media and formats, including visually, quantitatively, and orally (SL.3.2)
• Ask and answer questions about information from a speaker, offering appropriate elaboration and detail (SL.3.3)</td></tr>
<tr><td>Score 2.0</td><td>The student will recognize or recall specific vocabulary, such as:
• Answer, ask, detail, diverse, elaboration, format, information, main idea, media, orally, quantitative, question, supporting detail, text, visual
The student will perform basic processes, such as:
• Identify the main ideas and supporting details of presentations in diverse grade-appropriate media and formats
• Answer teacher-provided questions about a grade-appropriate text read aloud or an oral presentation</td></tr>
<tr><th colspan="2">Grade 2</th></tr>
<tr><td>Score 3.0</td><td>The student will:
• Summarize key ideas or details from a grade-appropriate text read aloud or information presented orally or through other media (SL.2.2)
• Ask and answer questions about what a speaker says in order to clarify comprehension, gather additional information, or deepen understanding of a topic or issue (SL.2.3)</td></tr>
<tr><td>Score 2.0</td><td>The student will recognize or recall specific vocabulary, such as:
• Answer, ask, clarify, comprehension, detail, idea, information, issue, media, orally, question, summarize, text, topic
The student will perform basic processes, such as:
• Identify key ideas or details in a grade-appropriate text read aloud or an oral presentation
• Answer teacher-provided questions about a grade-appropriate text read aloud or an oral presentation</td></tr>
<tr><th colspan="2">Grade 1</th></tr>
<tr><td>Score 3.0</td><td>The student will:
• Ask and answer questions about key details in a grade-appropriate text read aloud or information presented orally or through other media (SL.1.2)
• Ask and answer questions about what a speaker says in order to gather additional information or clarify something that is not understood (SL.1.3)</td></tr>
<tr><td>Score 2.0</td><td>The student will recognize or recall specific vocabulary, such as:
• Answer, ask, clarify, detail, information, media, orally, question, text
The student will perform basic processes, such as:
• Answer teacher-provided questions about a grade-appropriate text read aloud or an oral presentation</td></tr>
<tr><th colspan="2">Kindergarten</th></tr>
<tr><td>Score 3.0</td><td>The student will:
• Ask and answer questions about key details and request clarification if something is not understood from text read aloud or information presented orally or through other grade-appropriate media (SL.K.2)
• Ask and answer questions in order to seek help, get information, or clarify something that is not understood (SL.K.3)</td></tr>
<tr><td>Score 2.0</td><td>The student will recognize or recall specific vocabulary, such as:
• Answer, ask, clarification, clarify, detail, information, media, orally, question, text
The student will perform basic processes, such as:
• Answer teacher-provided questions about a grade-appropriate text read aloud or an oral presentation</td></tr>
</table>

Speech Writing

Grades 11–12		
Score 4.0	In addition to score 3.0 performance, the student demonstrates in-depth inferences and applications that go beyond what was taught.	
	Score 3.5	*In addition to score 3.0 performance, partial success at score 4.0 content*
Score 3.0	The student will: • Present grade-appropriate information, findings, and supporting evidence, conveying a clear and distinct perspective, such that listeners can follow the line of reasoning (SL.11–12.4) • Address alternative or opposing perspectives (SL.11–12.4) • Use organization, development, substance, and style appropriate to purpose, audience, and task (SL.11–12.4)	
	Score 2.5	*No major errors or omissions regarding score 2.0 content, and partial success at score 3.0 content*
Score 2.0	The student will recognize or recall specific vocabulary, such as: • *Alternative, audience, convey, development, distinct, evidence, finding, information, opposing, organization, perspective, purpose, reasoning, style, substance, support, task* The student will perform basic processes, such as: • Write a grade-appropriate speech based on a teacher-provided template	
	Score 1.5	*Partial success at score 2.0 content, and major errors or omissions regarding score 3.0 content*
Score 1.0	With help, partial success at score 2.0 content and score 3.0 content	
	Score 0.5	*With help, partial success at score 2.0 content but not at score 3.0 content*
Score 0.0	Even with help, no success	
Grades 9–10		
Score 3.0	The student will: • Present grade-appropriate information, findings, and supporting evidence clearly, concisely, and logically such that listeners can follow the line of reasoning and the organization, development, substance, and style are appropriate to purpose, audience, and task (SL.9–10.4)	
Score 2.0	The student will recognize or recall specific vocabulary, such as: • *Audience, concise, development, evidence, finding, information, logical, organization, purpose, reasoning, style, substance, support, task* The student will perform basic processes, such as: • Write a grade-appropriate speech based on a teacher-provided template	
Grade 8		
Score 3.0	The student will: • Present grade-appropriate claims and findings, emphasizing salient points in a focused, coherent manner with relevant evidence, sound valid reasoning, and well-chosen details (SL.8.4)	
Score 2.0	The student will recognize or recall specific vocabulary, such as: • *Claim, coherent, detail, emphasize, evidence, finding, focus, point, reasoning, relevant, salient, sound, valid* The student will perform basic processes, such as: • Write a grade-appropriate speech using a teacher-provided graphic organizer or template	
Grade 7		
Score 3.0	The student will: • Present grade-appropriate claims and findings, emphasizing salient points in a focused, coherent manner with pertinent descriptions, facts, details, and examples (SL.7.4)	

<table>
<tr><td>Score 2.0</td><td>The student will recognize or recall specific vocabulary, such as:
• Claim, coherent, description, detail, emphasize, example, fact, finding, focus, pertinent, point, salient
The student will perform basic processes, such as:
• Write a grade-appropriate speech using a teacher-provided graphic organizer or template</td></tr>
<tr><td colspan="2">Grade 6</td></tr>
<tr><td>Score 3.0</td><td>The student will:
• Present grade-appropriate claims and findings, sequencing ideas logically and using pertinent descriptions, facts, and details to accentuate main ideas or themes (SL.6.4)</td></tr>
<tr><td>Score 2.0</td><td>The student will recognize or recall specific vocabulary, such as:
• Accentuate, claim, description, detail, fact, finding, idea, logical, main idea, pertinent, sequence, theme
The student will perform basic processes, such as:
• Write a grade-appropriate speech using a teacher-provided graphic organizer or template</td></tr>
<tr><td colspan="2">Grade 5</td></tr>
<tr><td>Score 3.0</td><td>The student will:
• Report on a grade-appropriate topic or text, or present an opinion, sequencing ideas logically and using appropriate facts and relevant, descriptive details to support main ideas or themes (SL.5.4)</td></tr>
<tr><td>Score 2.0</td><td>The student will recognize or recall specific vocabulary, such as:
• Descriptive, detail, fact, idea, logical, main idea, opinion, relevant, report, sequence, support, text, theme, topic
The student will perform basic processes, such as:
• Write a grade-appropriate speech using a teacher-provided graphic organizer or template</td></tr>
<tr><td colspan="2">Grade 4</td></tr>
<tr><td>Score 3.0</td><td>The student will:
• Report on a grade-appropriate topic or text, tell a story, or recount an experience in an organized manner with appropriate facts and relevant, descriptive details to support main ideas or themes (SL.4.4)</td></tr>
<tr><td>Score 2.0</td><td>The student will recognize or recall specific vocabulary, such as:
• Descriptive, detail, experience, fact, main idea, organized, recount, relevant, report, story, support, text, theme, topic
The student will perform basic processes, such as:
• Write a grade-appropriate speech using a teacher-provided graphic organizer or template</td></tr>
<tr><td colspan="2">Grade 3</td></tr>
<tr><td>Score 3.0</td><td>The student will:
• Report on a grade-appropriate topic or text, tell a story, or recount an experience with appropriate facts and relevant, descriptive details (SL.3.4)</td></tr>
<tr><td>Score 2.0</td><td>The student will recognize or recall specific vocabulary, such as:
• Descriptive, detail, experience, fact, recount, relevant, report, story, text, topic
The student will perform basic processes, such as:
• Write a grade-appropriate speech using a teacher-provided graphic organizer or template</td></tr>
<tr><td colspan="2">Grade 2</td></tr>
<tr><td>Score 3.0</td><td>The student will:
• Tell a grade-appropriate story or recount an experience with appropriate facts and relevant, descriptive details in an oral presentation (SL.2.4)</td></tr>
</table>

Score 2.0	The student will recognize or recall specific vocabulary, such as: • *Descriptive, detail, experience, fact, oral, recount, relevant, story* The student will perform basic processes, such as: • Write a grade-appropriate speech using a teacher-provided graphic organizer or template	
Grade 1		
Score 3.0	The student will: • Describe people, places, things, and events with relevant details in an oral presentation (SL.1.4)	
Score 2.0	The student will recognize or recall specific vocabulary, such as: • *Describe, detail, event, oral, relevant* The student will perform basic processes, such as: • Plan a speech to answer teacher-provided questions	
Kindergarten		
Score 3.0	The student will: • Describe familiar people, places, things, and events in an oral presentation (SL.K.4)	
Score 2.0	The student will recognize or recall specific vocabulary, such as: • *Describe, event, oral, question* The student will perform basic processes, such as: • Orally answer teacher-provided questions	

Presentation and Delivery

Grades 11–12		
Score 4.0	In addition to score 3.0 performance, the student demonstrates in-depth inferences and applications that go beyond what was taught.	
	Score 3.5	*In addition to score 3.0 performance, partial success at score 4.0 content*
Score 3.0	The student will demonstrate proper grade-appropriate oral presentation techniques: • Make strategic use of digital media (for example, textual, graphical, audio, visual, and interactive elements) in presentations to enhance understanding of findings, reasoning, and evidence and to add interest (SL.11–12.5) • Adapt speech to a variety of contexts and tasks, demonstrating a command of formal English when indicated or appropriate (SL.11–12.6)	
	Score 2.5	*No major errors or omissions regarding score 2.0 content, and partial success at score 3.0 content*
Score 2.0	The student will recognize or recall specific vocabulary, such as: • *Audio, context, digital, element, enhance, evidence, finding, formal English, graphical, interactive, interest, media, presentation, reasoning, strategic, task, textual, visual, visual aid* The student will perform basic processes, such as: • Incorporate a digital visual aid in a presentation • Adapt speech to a specified context	
	Score 1.5	*Partial success at score 2.0 content, and major errors or omissions regarding score 3.0 content*
Score 1.0	With help, partial success at score 2.0 content and score 3.0 content	
	Score 0.5	*With help, partial success at score 2.0 content but not at score 3.0 content*
Score 0.0	Even with help, no success	

Grades 9–10	
Score 3.0	The student will demonstrate proper grade-appropriate oral presentation techniques: • Make strategic use of digital media (for example, textual, graphical, audio, visual, and interactive elements) in presentations to enhance understanding of findings, reasoning, and evidence (SL.9–10.5) • Adapt speech to a variety of contexts and tasks, demonstrating command of formal English when indicated or appropriate (SL.9–10.6)
Score 2.0	The student will recognize or recall specific vocabulary, such as: • *Audio*, *context*, *digital*, *element*, *enhance*, *evidence*, *finding*, *formal English*, *graphical*, *interactive*, *media*, *presentation*, *reasoning*, *strategic*, *task*, *textual*, *visual*, *visual aid* The student will perform basic processes, such as: • Incorporate a digital visual aid in a presentation • Adapt speech to a specified context
Grade 8	
Score 3.0	The student will demonstrate proper grade-appropriate oral presentation techniques: • Use appropriate eye contact, adequate volume, and clear pronunciation (SL.8.4) • Integrate multimedia and visual displays into presentations to clarify information, strengthen claims and evidence, and add interest (SL.8.5) • Adapt speech to a variety of contexts and tasks, demonstrating command of formal English when indicated or appropriate (SL.8.6)
Score 2.0	The student will recognize or recall specific vocabulary, such as: • *Claim*, *clarify*, *context*, *evidence*, *eye contact*, *formal English*, *information*, *integrate*, *interest*, *multimedia*, *presentation*, *pronunciation*, *task*, *visual*, *visual aid*, *volume* The student will perform basic processes, such as: • Demonstrate speech to only one context • Use visual aids for presentation (for example, white board, pictures) • Describe the elements of effective presentations
Grade 7	
Score 3.0	The student will demonstrate proper grade-appropriate oral presentation techniques: • Use appropriate eye contact, adequate volume, and clear pronunciation (SL.7.4) • Include multimedia components and visual displays in presentations to clarify claims and findings and emphasize salient points (SL.7.5) • Adapt speech to a variety of contexts and tasks, demonstrating command of formal English when indicated or appropriate (SL.7.6)
Score 2.0	The student will recognize or recall specific vocabulary, such as: • *Claim*, *clarify*, *context*, *emphasize*, *eye contact*, *finding*, *formal English*, *multimedia*, *point*, *presentation*, *pronunciation*, *salient*, *task*, *visual*, *visual aid*, *volume* The student will perform basic processes, such as: • Demonstrate speech to only one context • Use visual aids for presentation (for example, white board, pictures) • Identify the elements of effective presentations

Grade 6	
Score 3.0	The student will demonstrate proper grade-appropriate oral presentation techniques: • Use appropriate eye contact, adequate volume, and clear pronunciation (SL.6.4) • Include multimedia components (for example, graphics, images, music, sound) and visual displays in presentations to clarify information (SL.6.5) • Adapt speech to a variety of contexts and tasks, demonstrating command of formal English when indicated or appropriate (SL.6.6)
Score 2.0	The student will recognize or recall specific vocabulary, such as: • *Clarify*, *context*, *eye contact*, *formal English*, *graphic*, *image*, *information*, *multimedia*, *presentation*, *pronunciation*, *task*, *visual*, *visual aid*, *volume* The student will perform basic processes, such as: • Demonstrate speech to only one context • Use visual aids for presentation (for example, white board, pictures) • Identify the elements of effective presentations
Grade 5	
Score 3.0	The student will demonstrate proper grade-appropriate oral presentation techniques: • Include multimedia components (for example, graphics, sound) and visual displays in presentations when appropriate to enhance the development of main ideas or themes (SL.5.5) • Adapt speech to a variety of contexts and tasks, using formal English when appropriate to task and situation (SL.5.6)
Score 2.0	The student will recognize or recall specific vocabulary, such as: • *Context*, *development*, *enhance*, *formal English*, *graphic*, *main idea*, *multimedia*, *pace*, *presentation*, *task*, *theme*, *visual*, *visual aid* The student will perform basic processes, such as: • Speak clearly at an understandable pace (SL.5.4) • Use a visual aid for presentations • Demonstrate speech to only one context
Grade 4	
Score 3.0	The student will demonstrate proper grade-appropriate oral presentation techniques: • Add audio recordings and visual displays to presentations when appropriate to enhance the development of main ideas or themes (SL.4.5) • Use formal English and informal discourse where appropriate (SL.4.6)
Score 2.0	The student will recognize or recall specific vocabulary, such as: • *Audio*, *context*, *development*, *differentiate*, *discourse*, *enhance*, *formal English*, *informal*, *main idea*, *pace*, *presentation*, *theme*, *visual*, *visual aid* The student will perform basic processes, such as: • Speak clearly at an understandable pace (SL.4.4) • Use a visual aid for presentations • Differentiate between contexts that call for formal English and informal discourse (SL.4.6)
Grade 3	
Score 3.0	The student will demonstrate proper grade-appropriate oral presentation techniques: • Demonstrate fluid oral reading (SL.3.5) • Add visual displays when appropriate to emphasize or enhance certain facts or details (SL.3.5) • Speak in complete sentences when appropriate to task and situation in order to provide requested detail or clarification (SL.3.6)

<table>
<tr><td>Score 2.0</td><td>The student will recognize or recall specific vocabulary, such as:<ul><li>Clarification, complete sentence, detail, emphasize, enhance, experience, fact, oral, pace, presentation, situation, task, visual</li></ul>The student will perform basic processes, such as:<ul><li>Retell or recount a simple experience</li><li>Speak clearly at an understandable pace (SL.3.4)</li></ul></td></tr>
<tr><td colspan="2">Grade 2</td></tr>
<tr><td>Score 3.0</td><td>The student will demonstrate proper grade-appropriate oral presentation techniques:<ul><li>Create audio recordings of stories or poems (SL.2.5)</li><li>Add drawings or other visual displays to stories or recounts of experiences when appropriate to clarify ideas, thoughts, and feelings (SL.2.5)</li><li>Produce complete sentences when appropriate to task and situation in order to provide requested detail or clarification (SL.2.6)</li></ul></td></tr>
<tr><td>Score 2.0</td><td>The student will recognize or recall specific vocabulary, such as:<ul><li>Audible, audio, clarification, clarify, coherent, complete sentence, detail, experience, feeling, idea, poem, presentation, sentence, situation, story, task, visual</li></ul>The student will perform basic processes, such as:<ul><li>Speak audibly in coherent sentences (SL.2.4)</li></ul></td></tr>
<tr><td colspan="2">Grade 1</td></tr>
<tr><td>Score 3.0</td><td>The student will demonstrate proper oral presentation techniques:<ul><li>Express ideas and feelings clearly (SL.1.4)</li><li>Add drawings or other visual displays to descriptions when appropriate to clarify ideas, thoughts, and feelings (SL.1.5)</li><li>Produce complete sentences when appropriate to task and situation (SL.1.6)</li></ul></td></tr>
<tr><td>Score 2.0</td><td>The student will recognize or recall specific vocabulary, such as:<ul><li>Audible, clarify, complete sentence, feeling, idea, presentation, story, visual</li></ul>The student will perform basic processes, such as:<ul><li>Add drawings to express basic understanding of a grade-appropriate text</li><li>Tell a brief story, speaking audibly in complete sentences</li></ul></td></tr>
<tr><td colspan="2">Kindergarten</td></tr>
<tr><td>Score 3.0</td><td>The student will demonstrate proper grade-appropriate oral presentation techniques:<ul><li>Use drawings or other visual displays (SL.K.5)</li><li>Clearly express thoughts, ideas, opinions, and feelings orally (SL.K.6)</li></ul></td></tr>
<tr><td>Score 2.0</td><td>The student will recognize or recall specific vocabulary, such as:<ul><li>Audibly, feeling, idea, opinion, visual</li></ul>The student will perform basic processes, such as:<ul><li>Speak audibly (SL.K.6)</li></ul></td></tr>
</table>

Language

Grammar

<table>
<tr><th colspan="3">Grades 11–12</th></tr>
<tr><td>Score 4.0</td><td colspan="2">In addition to score 3.0 performance, the student demonstrates in-depth inferences and applications that go beyond what was taught.</td></tr>
<tr><td></td><td>Score 3.5</td><td>In addition to score 3.0 performance, partial success at score 4.0 content</td></tr>
<tr><td>Score 3.0</td><td colspan="2">The student will demonstrate command of the conventions of standard grade-appropriate English grammar and usage in context when writing or speaking (L.11–12.1):
• Apply the understanding that usage is a matter of convention, can change over time, and is sometimes contested (L.11–12.1a)
• Resolve issues of complex or contested usage, consulting references (for example, Merriam-Webster's Dictionary of English Usage, Garner's Modern American Usage) as needed (L.11–12.1b)</td></tr>
<tr><td></td><td>Score 2.5</td><td>No major errors or omissions regarding score 2.0 content, and partial success at score 3.0 content</td></tr>
<tr><td>Score 2.0</td><td colspan="2">The student will recognize or recall specific vocabulary, such as:
• Complex, consult, contested, convention, grammar, reference, usage
The student will perform basic processes, such as:
• Use grade-appropriate grammar and usage in isolation</td></tr>
<tr><td></td><td>Score 1.5</td><td>Partial success at score 2.0 content, and major errors or omissions regarding score 3.0 content</td></tr>
<tr><td>Score 1.0</td><td colspan="2">With help, partial success at score 2.0 content and score 3.0 content</td></tr>
<tr><td></td><td>Score 0.5</td><td>With help, partial success at score 2.0 content but not at score 3.0 content</td></tr>
<tr><td>Score 0.0</td><td colspan="2">Even with help, no success</td></tr>
<tr><th colspan="3">Grades 9–10</th></tr>
<tr><td>Score 3.0</td><td colspan="2">The student will demonstrate command of the conventions of standard grade-appropriate English grammar and usage in context when writing or speaking (L.9–10.1):
• Use parallel structure (L.9–10.1a)
• Use various types of phrases (noun, verb, adjectival, adverbial, participial, prepositional, absolute) and clauses (independent, dependent, noun, relative, adverbial) to convey specific meanings (L.9–10.1b)</td></tr>
<tr><td>Score 2.0</td><td colspan="2">The student will recognize or recall specific vocabulary, such as:
• Absolute phrase, adjectival phrase, adverbial clause, adverbial phrase, convention, dependent clause, grammar, independent clause, noun clause, noun phrase, parallel, participial phrase, prepositional phrase, relative clause, structure, usage, verb phrase
The student will perform basic processes, such as:
• Use grade-appropriate grammar and usage in isolation</td></tr>
<tr><th colspan="3">Grade 8</th></tr>
<tr><td>Score 3.0</td><td colspan="2">The student will demonstrate command of the conventions of standard grade-appropriate English grammar and usage in context when writing or speaking (L.8.1):
• Explain the function of verbals (gerunds, participles, infinitives) in general and their function in particular sentences (L.8.1a)
• Form and use verbs in the active and passive voice (L.8.1b)
• Form and use verbs in the indicative, imperative, interrogative, conditional, and subjunctive mood (L.8.1c)
• Recognize and correct inappropriate shifts in verb voice and mood (L.8.1d)</td></tr>
</table>

Score 2.0	The student will recognize or recall specific vocabulary, such as: • *Active voice*, *conditional mood*, *convention*, *gerund*, *grammar*, *imperative mood*, *indicative mood*, *infinitive*, *interrogative mood*, *mood*, *participle*, *passive voice*, *sentence*, *subjunctive mood*, *usage*, *verb*, *verbal*, *voice* The student will perform basic processes, such as: • Use grade-appropriate grammar and usage in isolation
Grade 7	
Score 3.0	The student will demonstrate command of the conventions of standard grade-appropriate English grammar and usage in context when writing or speaking (L.7.1): • Explain the function of phrases and clauses in general and their function in specific sentences (L.7.1a) • Choose among simple, compound, complex, and compound-complex sentences to signal differing relationships among ideas (L.7.1b) • Place phrases and clauses within a sentence, recognizing and correcting misplaced and dangling modifiers (L.7.1c)
Score 2.0	The student will recognize or recall specific vocabulary, such as: • *Clause*, *complex sentence*, *compound sentence*, *compound-complex sentence*, *convention*, *dangling modifier*, *grammar*, *idea*, *misplaced modifier*, *phrase*, *relationship*, *sentence*, *simple sentence*, *usage* The student will perform basic processes, such as: • Use grade-appropriate grammar and usage in isolation
Grade 6	
Score 3.0	The student will demonstrate command of the conventions of standard grade-appropriate English grammar and usage in context when writing or speaking (L.6.1): • Ensure that pronouns are in the proper case (subjective, objective, possessive) (L.6.1a) • Use intensive pronouns (for example, *myself*, *ourselves*) (L.6.1b) • Recognize and correct inappropriate shifts in pronoun number and person (L.6.1c) • Recognize and correct vague pronouns (for example, ones with unclear or ambiguous antecedents) (L.6.1d) • Recognize variations from standard English in their own and others' writing and speaking, and identify and use strategies to improve expression in conventional language (L.6.1e)
Score 2.0	The student will recognize or recall specific vocabulary, such as: • *Ambiguous*, *antecedent*, *convention*, *conventional*, *expression*, *grammar*, *intensive pronoun*, *number*, *objective case*, *person*, *possessive case*, *pronoun*, *standard English*, *strategy*, *subjective case*, *usage*, *vague* The student will perform basic processes, such as: • Use grade-appropriate grammar and usage in isolation
Grade 5	
Score 3.0	The student will demonstrate command of the conventions of standard grade-appropriate English grammar and usage in context when writing or speaking (L.5.1): • Explain the function of conjunctions, prepositions, and interjections in general and their function in particular sentences (L.5.1a) • Form and use the perfect (for example, *I had walked*; *I have walked*; *I will have walked*) verb tenses (L.5.1b) • Use verb tense to convey various times, sequences, states, and conditions (L.5.1c) • Recognize and correct inappropriate shifts in verb tense (L.5.1d) • Use correlative conjunctions (for example, *either/or*, *neither/nor*) (L.5.1e)
Score 2.0	The student will recognize or recall specific vocabulary, such as: • *Condition*, *conjunction*, *convention*, *correlative conjunction*, *grammar*, *interjection*, *perfect verb tense*, *preposition*, *sentence*, *sequence*, *state*, *usage*, *verb tense* The student will perform basic processes, such as: • Use grade-appropriate grammar and usage in isolation

<table>
<tr><th colspan="2">Grade 4</th></tr>
<tr><td>Score 3.0</td><td>The student will demonstrate command of the conventions of standard grade-appropriate English grammar and usage in context when writing or speaking (L.4.1):<ul><li>Use relative pronouns (who, whose, whom, which, that) and relative adverbs (where, when, why) (L.4.1a)</li><li>Form and use the progressive (for example, I was walking; I am walking; I will be walking) verb tenses (L.4.1b)</li><li>Use modal auxiliaries (for example, can, may, must) to convey various conditions (L.4.1c)</li><li>Order adjectives within sentences according to conventional patterns (for example, a small red bag rather than a red small bag) (L.4.1d)</li><li>Form and use prepositional phrases (L.4.1e)</li></ul></td></tr>
<tr><td>Score 2.0</td><td>The student will recognize or recall specific vocabulary, such as:<ul><li>Adjective, condition, convention, conventional, grammar, modal auxiliary, prepositional phrase, progressive verb tense, relative adverb, relative pronoun, sentence, usage</li></ul>The student will perform basic processes, such as:<ul><li>Use grade-appropriate grammar and usage in isolation</li></ul></td></tr>
<tr><th colspan="2">Grade 3</th></tr>
<tr><td>Score 3.0</td><td>The student will demonstrate command of the conventions of standard grade-appropriate English grammar and usage in context when writing or speaking (L.3.1):<ul><li>Explain the function of nouns, pronouns, verbs, adjectives, and adverbs in general and their functions in particular sentences (L.3.1a)</li><li>Form and use regular and irregular plural nouns (L.3.1b)</li><li>Use abstract nouns (for example, childhood) (L.3.1c)</li><li>Form and use regular and irregular verbs (L.3.1d)</li><li>Form and use the simple (for example, I walked; I walk; I will walk) verb tenses (L.3.1e)</li><li>Ensure subject-verb and pronoun-antecedent agreement (L.3.1f)</li><li>Form and use comparative and superlative adjectives and adverbs, and choose between them depending on what is to be modified (L.3.1g)</li><li>Use coordinating and subordinating conjunctions (L.3.1h)</li></ul></td></tr>
<tr><td>Score 2.0</td><td>The student will recognize or recall specific vocabulary, such as:<ul><li>Abstract, adjective, adverb, comparative, convention, coordinating conjunction, grammar, irregular, modify, noun, plural, pronoun, pronoun-antecedent agreement, regular, sentence, simple verb tense, subject-verb agreement, subordinating conjunction, superlative, usage, verb</li></ul>The student will perform basic processes, such as:<ul><li>Use grade-appropriate grammar and usage in isolation</li></ul></td></tr>
<tr><th colspan="2">Grade 2</th></tr>
<tr><td>Score 3.0</td><td>The student will demonstrate command of the conventions of standard grade-appropriate English grammar and usage in context when writing or speaking (L.2.1):<ul><li>Use collective nouns (for example, group) (L.2.1a)</li><li>Form and use frequently occurring irregular plural nouns (for example, feet, children, teeth, mice, fish) (L.2.1b)</li><li>Use reflexive pronouns (for example, myself, ourselves) (L.2.1c)</li><li>Form and use the past tense of frequently occurring irregular verbs (for example, sat, hid, told) (L.2.1d)</li><li>Use adjectives and adverbs, and choose between them depending on what is to be modified (L.2.1e)</li></ul></td></tr>
<tr><td>Score 2.0</td><td>The student will recognize or recall specific vocabulary, such as:<ul><li>Adjective, adverb, collective, irregular, modify, noun, past tense, plural, reflexive pronoun, verb</li></ul>The student will perform basic processes, such as:<ul><li>Use grade-appropriate grammar and usage in isolation</li></ul></td></tr>
</table>

	Grade 1
Score 3.0	The student will demonstrate command of the conventions of standard grade-appropriate English grammar and usage in context when writing or speaking (L.1.1): • Use common, proper, and possessive nouns (L.1.1b) • Use singular and plural nouns with matching verbs in basic sentences (for example, *He hops*; *We hop*) (L.1.1c) • Use personal, possessive, and indefinite pronouns (for example, *I*, *me*, *my*, *they*, *them*, *their*, *anyone*, *everything*) (L.1.1d) • Use verbs to convey a sense of past, present, and future (for example, *Yesterday I walked home*; *Today I walk home*; *Tomorrow I will walk home*) (L.1.1e) • Use frequently occurring adjectives (L.1.1f) • Use frequently occurring conjunctions (for example, *and*, *but*, *or*, *so*, *because*) (L.1.1g) • Use frequently occurring determiners (for example, *a*, *an*, *the*, *this*, *those*, *my*, *your*, *his*) (L.1.1h) • Use frequently occurring prepositions (for example, *during*, *beyond*, *toward*) (L.1.1i)
Score 2.0	The student will recognize or recall specific vocabulary, such as: • *Adjective*, *common noun*, *conjunction*, *convey*, *determiner*, *future*, *indefinite pronoun*, *noun*, *past*, *personal pronoun*, *plural*, *possessive noun*, *possessive pronoun*, *preposition*, *present*, *proper noun*, *sentence*, *singular*, *verb* The student will perform basic processes, such as: • Use grade-appropriate grammar and usage in isolation
	Kindergarten
Score 3.0	The student will demonstrate command of the conventions of standard grade-appropriate English grammar and usage in context when writing or speaking (L.K.1): • Use frequently occurring nouns and verbs (L.K.1b) • Form regular plural nouns orally by adding /s/ or /es/ (for example, *dog*, *dogs*; *wish*, *wishes*) (L.K.1c) • Use the most frequently occurring prepositions (for example, *to*, *from*, *in*, *out*, *on*, *off*, *for*, *of*, *by*, *with*) (L.K.1e)
Score 2.0	The student will recognize or recall specific vocabulary, such as: • *Noun*, *plural*, *preposition*, *verb* The student will perform basic processes, such as: • Use grade-appropriate grammar and usage in isolation

Sentences

	Grades 11–12, 9–10, 8, 7, 6	
Score 3.0	Not applicable.	
Score 2.0	Not applicable.	
	Grade 5	
Score 4.0	In addition to score 3.0 performance, the student demonstrates in-depth inferences and applications that go beyond what was taught.	
	Score 3.5	*In addition to score 3.0 performance, partial success at score 4.0 content*
Score 3.0	The student will: • Expand, combine, and reduce grade-appropriate sentences for meaning, reader/listener interest, and style in context (L.5.3a)	
	Score 2.5	*No major errors or omissions regarding score 2.0 content, and partial success at score 3.0 content*

Score 2.0	The student will recognize or recall specific vocabulary, such as: • *Combine, expand, interest, meaning, reduce, sentence, style* The student will perform basic processes, such as: • Expand, combine, and reduce grade-appropriate sentences for meaning in isolation	
	Score 1.5	*Partial success at score 2.0 content, and major errors or omissions regarding score 3.0 content*
Score 1.0	With help, partial success at score 2.0 content and score 3.0 content	
	Score 0.5	*With help, partial success at score 2.0 content but not at score 3.0 content*
Score 0.0	Even with help, no success	
	Grade 4	
Score 3.0	The student will: • Produce complete grade-appropriate sentences, recognizing and correcting inappropriate fragments and run-ons in context (L.4.1f)	
Score 2.0	The student will recognize or recall specific vocabulary, such as: • *Complete sentence, fragment, run-on* The student will perform basic processes, such as: • Correct grade-appropriate sentences in isolation for inappropriate fragments and run-ons	
	Grade 3	
Score 3.0	The student will: • Produce simple, compound, and complex grade-appropriate sentences in context (L.3.1i)	
Score 2.0	The student will recognize or recall specific vocabulary, such as: • *Complex sentence, compound sentence, simple sentence* The student will perform basic processes, such as: • Produce simple, compound, and complex grade-appropriate sentences in isolation	
	Grade 2	
Score 3.0	The student will: • Produce, expand, and rearrange complete simple and compound grade-appropriate sentences in context (for example, *The boy watched the movie*; *The little boy watched the movie*; *The action movie was watched by the little boy*) (L.2.1f)	
Score 2.0	The student will recognize or recall specific vocabulary, such as: • *Complete sentence, compound sentence, expand, produce, rearrange, simple sentence* The student will perform basic processes, such as: • Produce, expand, and rearrange complete simple and compound grade-appropriate sentences in isolation	
	Grade 1	
Score 3.0	The student will: • Produce and expand complete simple and compound declarative, interrogative, imperative, and exclamatory grade-appropriate sentences in context (L.1.1j)	
Score 2.0	The student will recognize or recall specific vocabulary, such as: • *Complete sentence, compound sentence, declarative, exclamatory, imperative, interrogative, simple sentence* The student will perform basic processes, such as: • Produce and expand complete simple and compound declarative, interrogative, imperative, and exclamatory grade-appropriate sentences in isolation	

Kindergarten	
Score 3.0	The student will: • Understand and use question words (interrogatives) (for example, *who*, *what*, *where*, *when*, *why*, *how*) (L.K.1d) • Expand complete sentences in shared language activities (L.K.1f)
Score 2.0	The student will recognize or recall specific vocabulary, such as: • *Complete sentence*, *how*, *interrogative*, *question*, *what*, *when*, *where*, *who*, *why* The student will perform basic processes, such as: • Recognize or recall examples of question words • Produce complete sentences in shared language activities (L.K.1f)

Capitalization and Punctuation

Grades 11–12		
Score 4.0	In addition to score 3.0 performance, the student demonstrates in-depth inferences and applications that go beyond what was taught.	
	Score 3.5	*In addition to score 3.0 performance, partial success at score 4.0 content*
Score 3.0	The student will demonstrate command of the conventions of standard grade-appropriate English capitalization and punctuation in context when writing (L.11–12.2): • Observe hyphenation conventions (L.11–12.2a)	
	Score 2.5	*No major errors or omissions regarding score 2.0 content, and partial success at score 3.0 content*
Score 2.0	The student will recognize or recall specific vocabulary, such as: • *Convention*, *hyphenation* The student will perform basic processes, such as: • Demonstrate the use of grade-appropriate conventions in isolation	
	Score 1.5	*Partial success at score 2.0 content, and major errors or omissions regarding score 3.0 content*
Score 1.0	With help, partial success at score 2.0 content and score 3.0 content	
	Score 0.5	*With help, partial success at score 2.0 content but not at score 3.0 content*
Score 0.0	Even with help, no success	
Grades 9–10		
Score 3.0	The student will demonstrate command of the conventions of standard grade-appropriate English capitalization and punctuation in context when writing (L.9–10.2): • Use a semicolon (and perhaps a conjunctive adverb) to link two or more closely related independent clauses (L.9–10.2a) • Use a colon to introduce a list or quotation (L.9–10.2b)	
Score 2.0	The student will recognize or recall specific vocabulary, such as: • *Colon*, *conjunctive adverb*, *convention*, *independent clause*, *quotation*, *semicolon* The student will perform basic processes, such as: • Demonstrate the use of grade-appropriate conventions in isolation	
Grade 8		
Score 3.0	The student will demonstrate command of the conventions of standard grade-appropriate English capitalization and punctuation and context when writing (L.8.2): • Use punctuation (comma, ellipsis, dash) to indicate a pause or break (L.8.2a) • Use an ellipsis to indicate an omission (L.8.2b)	

Score 2.0	The student will recognize or recall specific vocabulary, such as: • *Break, comma, convention, dash, ellipsis, omission, pause, punctuation* The student will perform basic processes, such as: • Demonstrate the use of grade-appropriate conventions in isolation
	Grade 7
Score 3.0	The student will demonstrate command of the conventions of standard grade-appropriate English capitalization and punctuation in context when writing (L.7.2): • Use a comma to separate coordinate adjectives (for example, *It was a fascinating, enjoyable movie* but not *He wore an old[,] green shirt*) (L.7.2a)
Score 2.0	The student will recognize or recall specific vocabulary, such as: • *Comma, convention, coordinate adjective* The student will perform basic processes, such as: • Demonstrate the use of grade-appropriate conventions in isolation
	Grade 6
Score 3.0	The student will demonstrate command of the conventions of standard grade-appropriate English capitalization and punctuation in context when writing (L.6.2): • Use punctuation (commas, parentheses, dashes) to set off nonrestrictive/parenthetical elements (L.6.2a)
Score 2.0	The student will recognize or recall specific vocabulary, such as: • *Comma, convention, dash, element, nonrestrictive, parentheses, parenthetical, punctuation* The student will perform basic processes, such as: • Demonstrate the use of grade-appropriate conventions in isolation
	Grade 5
Score 3.0	The student will demonstrate command of the conventions of standard grade-appropriate English capitalization and punctuation in context when writing (L.5.2): • Use punctuation to separate items in a series (L.5.2a) • Use a comma to separate an introductory element from the rest of the sentence (L.5.2b) • Use a comma to set off the words *yes* and *no* (for example, *Yes, thank you*), to set off a tag question from the rest of the sentence (for example, *It's true, isn't it?*), and to indicate direct address (for example, *Is that you, Steve?*) (L.5.2c) • Use underlining, quotation marks, or italics to indicate titles of works (L.5.2d)
Score 2.0	The student will recognize or recall specific vocabulary, such as: • *Comma, convention, direct address, introductory element, italics, punctuation, quotation mark, sentence, series, tag question* The student will perform basic processes, such as: • Demonstrate the use of grade-appropriate conventions in isolation
	Grade 4
Score 3.0	The student will demonstrate command of the conventions of standard grade-appropriate English capitalization and punctuation in context when writing (L.4.2): • Use correct capitalization (L.4.2a) • Use commas and quotation marks to mark direct speech and quotations from a text (L.4.2b) • Use a comma before a coordinating conjunction in a compound sentence (L.4.2c)
Score 2.0	The student will recognize or recall specific vocabulary, such as: • *Capitalization, comma, compound sentence, convention, coordinating conjunction, direct speech, quotation, quotation mark* The student will perform basic processes, such as: • Demonstrate the use of grade-appropriate conventions in isolation

Grade 3	
Score 3.0	The student will demonstrate command of the conventions of standard grade-appropriate English capitalization and punctuation in context when writing (L.3.2): • Capitalize appropriate words in titles (L.3.2a) • Use commas in addresses (L.3.2b) • Use commas and quotation marks in dialogue (L.3.2c) • Form and use possessives (L.3.2d)
Score 2.0	The student will recognize or recall specific vocabulary, such as: • *Address*, *capitalize*, *comma*, *convention*, *dialogue*, *possessive*, *quotation mark*, *title* The student will perform basic processes, such as: • Demonstrate the use of grade-appropriate conventions in isolation
Grade 2	
Score 3.0	The student will demonstrate command of the conventions of standard grade-appropriate English capitalization and punctuation in context when writing (L.2.2): • Capitalize holidays, product names, and geographic names (L.2.2a) • Use commas in greetings and closings of letters (L.2.2b) • Use an apostrophe to form contractions and frequently occurring possessives (L.2.2c)
Score 2.0	The student will recognize or recall specific vocabulary, such as: • *Apostrophe*, *capitalize*, *closing*, *comma*, *contraction*, *greeting*, *possessive* The student will perform basic processes, such as: • Demonstrate the use of grade-appropriate conventions in isolation
Grade 1	
Score 3.0	The student will demonstrate command of the conventions of standard grade-appropriate English capitalization and punctuation in context when writing (L.1.2): • Capitalize dates and names of people (L.1.2a) • Use end punctuation for sentences (L.1.2b) • Use commas in dates and to separate single words in a series (L.1.2c)
Score 2.0	The student will recognize or recall specific vocabulary, such as: • *Capitalize*, *comma*, *end punctuation*, *sentence*, *series* The student will perform basic processes, such as: • Demonstrate the use of grade-appropriate conventions in isolation
Kindergarten	
Score 3.0	The student will demonstrate command of the conventions of standard grade-appropriate English capitalization and punctuation in context when writing (L.K.2): • Capitalize the first word in a sentence and the pronoun *I* (L.K.2a) • Recognize and name end punctuation (L.K.2b)
Score 2.0	The student will recognize or recall specific vocabulary, such as: • *Capitalize*, *end punctuation*, *pronoun*, *sentence* The student will perform basic processes, such as: • Demonstrate the use of grade-appropriate conventions in isolation

Spelling

Grades 11–12		
Score 4.0	In addition to score 3.0 performance, the student demonstrates in-depth inferences and applications that go beyond what was taught.	
	Score 3.5	*In addition to score 3.0 performance, partial success at score 4.0 content*
Score 3.0	The student will: • Spell grade-appropriate words correctly when writing (L.11–12.2b)	
	Score 2.5	*No major errors or omissions regarding score 2.0 content, and partial success at score 3.0 content*
Score 2.0	The student will perform basic processes, such as: • Spell grade-appropriate words correctly in isolation	
	Score 1.5	*Partial success at score 2.0 content, and major errors or omissions regarding score 3.0 content*
Score 1.0	With help, partial success at score 2.0 content and score 3.0 content	
	Score 0.5	*With help, partial success at score 2.0 content but not at score 3.0 content*
Score 0.0	Even with help, no success	
Grades 9–10		
Score 3.0	The student will: • Spell grade-appropriate words correctly when writing (L.9–10.2c)	
Score 2.0	The student will perform basic processes, such as: • Spell grade-appropriate words correctly in isolation	
Grade 8		
Score 3.0	The student will: • Spell grade-appropriate words correctly when writing (L.8.2c)	
Score 2.0	The student will perform basic processes, such as: • Spell grade-appropriate words correctly in isolation	
Grade 7		
Score 3.0	The student will: • Spell grade-appropriate words correctly when writing (L.7.2b)	
Score 2.0	The student will perform basic processes, such as: • Spell grade-appropriate words correctly in isolation	
Grade 6		
Score 3.0	The student will: • Spell grade-appropriate words correctly when writing (L.6.2b)	
Score 2.0	The student will perform basic processes, such as: • Spell grade-appropriate words correctly in isolation	
Grade 5		
Score 3.0	The student will: • Spell grade-appropriate words correctly when writing, consulting references as needed (L.5.2e)	
Score 2.0	The student will recognize or recall specific vocabulary, such as: • *References* The student will perform basic processes, such as: • Spell grade-appropriate words correctly in isolation	

<table>
<tr><th colspan="2">Grade 4</th></tr>
<tr><td>Score 3.0</td><td>The student will:
• Correctly use frequently confused grade-appropriate words (for example, to, too, two; there, their) (L.4.1g)
• Spell grade-appropriate words correctly when writing, consulting references as needed (L.4.2d)</td></tr>
<tr><td>Score 2.0</td><td>The student will recognize or recall specific vocabulary, such as:
• Confused, references
The student will perform basic processes, such as:
• Spell grade-appropriate words correctly in isolation</td></tr>
<tr><th colspan="2">Grade 3</th></tr>
<tr><td>Score 3.0</td><td>The student will:
• Use conventional spelling for high-frequency and other studied words and for adding suffixes to base words (for example, sitting, smiled, cries, happiness) (L.3.2e)
• Use spelling patterns and generalizations (for example, word families, position-based spellings, syllable patterns, ending rules, meaningful word parts) in writing words (L.3.2f)
• Consult reference materials, including beginning dictionaries, as needed to check and correct spellings (L.3.2g)</td></tr>
<tr><td>Score 2.0</td><td>The student will recognize or recall specific vocabulary, such as:
• Base word, dictionary, ending rule, generalization, pattern, position-based, reference, suffix, syllable, word family, word part
The student will perform basic processes, such as:
• Spell grade-appropriate words correctly in isolation</td></tr>
<tr><th colspan="2">Grade 2</th></tr>
<tr><td>Score 3.0</td><td>The student will:
• Generalize learned spelling patterns when writing words (L.2.2d)
• Consult reference materials, including beginning dictionaries, as needed to check and correct spellings (L.2.2e)</td></tr>
<tr><td>Score 2.0</td><td>The student will recognize or recall specific vocabulary, such as:
• Dictionary, generalize, pattern, reference
The student will perform basic processes, such as:
• Spell grade-appropriate words correctly in isolation</td></tr>
<tr><th colspan="2">Grade 1</th></tr>
<tr><td>Score 3.0</td><td>The student will:
• Use conventional spelling for words with common spelling patterns and for frequently occurring irregular words (L.1.2d)
• Spell untaught words phonetically, drawing on phonemic awareness and spelling conventions (L.1.2e)</td></tr>
<tr><td>Score 2.0</td><td>The student will recognize or recall specific vocabulary, such as:
• Convention, irregular, pattern
The student will perform basic processes, such as:
• Spell grade-appropriate words correctly in isolation</td></tr>
<tr><th colspan="2">Kindergarten</th></tr>
<tr><td>Score 3.0</td><td>The student will:
• Write a letter or letters for most consonant and short vowel sounds (phonemes) (L.K.2c)
• Spell grade-appropriate words phonetically, drawing on knowledge of sound-letter relationships (L.K.2d)</td></tr>
</table>

Score 2.0	The student will recognize or recall specific vocabulary, such as: • *Consonant, letter, short vowel, sound, word* The student will perform basic processes, such as: • Recognize or recall sound-letter relationships

Language Conventions

	Grades 11–12	
Score 4.0	In addition to score 3.0 performance, the student demonstrates in-depth inferences and applications that go beyond what was taught.	
	Score 3.5	*In addition to score 3.0 performance, partial success at score 4.0 content*
Score 3.0	The student will apply grade-appropriate knowledge of language to understand how language functions in different contexts, to make effective choices for meaning or style, and to comprehend more fully when reading or listening (L.11–12.3): • Vary syntax for effect, consulting references (for example, Tufte's *Artful Sentences*) for guidance as needed; apply an understanding of syntax to the study of complex texts when reading (L.11–12.3a)	
	Score 2.5	*No major errors or omissions regarding score 2.0 content, and partial success at score 3.0 content*
Score 2.0	The student will recognize or recall specific vocabulary, such as: • *Complex, context, effect, meaning, reference, style, syntax, text* The student will perform basic processes, such as: • Describe the impact of particular uses of syntax in a grade-appropriate text	
	Score 1.5	*Partial success at score 2.0 content, and major errors or omissions regarding score 3.0 content*
Score 1.0	With help, partial success at score 2.0 content and score 3.0 content	
	Score 0.5	*With help, partial success at score 2.0 content but not at score 3.0 content*
Score 0.0	Even with help, no success	
	Grades 9–10	
Score 3.0	The student will apply grade-appropriate knowledge of language to understand how language functions in different contexts, to make effective choices for meaning or style, and to comprehend more fully when reading or listening (L.9–10.3): • Write and edit work so that it conforms to the guidelines in a style manual (for example, *MLA Handbook*, Turabian's *Manual for Writers*) appropriate for the discipline and writing type (L.9–10.3a)	
Score 2.0	The student will recognize or recall specific vocabulary, such as: • *Conform, context, discipline, edit, guideline, meaning, style, style manual* The student will perform basic processes, such as: • Demonstrate the use of a style manual	
	Grade 8	
Score 3.0	The student will use grade-appropriate knowledge of language and its conventions when writing, speaking, reading, or listening (L.8.3): • Use verbs in the active and passive voice and in the conditional and subjunctive mood to achieve particular effects (for example, emphasizing the actor or the action; expressing uncertainty or describing a state contrary to fact) (L.8.3a)	

Score 2.0	The student will recognize or recall specific vocabulary, such as: • *Action*, *active voice*, *actor*, *conditional mood*, *contrary*, *effect*, *passive voice*, *subjunctive mood*, *uncertainty*, *verb* The student will perform basic processes, such as: • Identify examples of the use of active and passive voice and conditional and subjunctive mood to achieve particular effects
	Grade 7
Score 3.0	The student will use grade-appropriate knowledge of language and its conventions when writing, speaking, reading, or listening (L.7.3): • Choose language that expresses ideas precisely and concisely (L.7.3a)
Score 2.0	The student will recognize or recall specific vocabulary, such as: • *Concise*, *eliminate*, *idea*, *precise*, *redundancy*, *wordiness* The student will perform basic processes, such as: • Identify and eliminate wordiness and redundancy (L.7.3a)
	Grade 6
Score 3.0	The student will use grade-appropriate knowledge of language and its conventions when writing, speaking, reading, or listening (L.6.3): • Vary sentence patterns for meaning, reader/listener interest, and style (L.6.3a) • Maintain consistency in style and tone (L.6.3b)
Score 2.0	The student will recognize or recall specific vocabulary, such as: • *Consistency*, *interest*, *pattern*, *sentence*, *style*, *tone* The student will perform basic processes, such as: • Vary sentence patterns and maintain consistency in style and tone based on teacher and peer feedback
	Grade 5
Score 3.0	The student will use grade-appropriate knowledge of language and its conventions when writing, speaking, reading, or listening (L.5.3): • Compare and contrast the varieties of English (for example, dialects, registers) used in stories, dramas, or poems (L.5.3b)
Score 2.0	The student will recognize or recall specific vocabulary, such as: • *Compare*, *contrast*, *dialect*, *drama*, *poem*, *register*, *story*, *variety* The student will perform basic processes, such as: • Identify examples of the varieties of English used in stories, dramas, or poems
	Grade 4
Score 3.0	The student will use grade-appropriate knowledge of language and its conventions when writing, speaking, reading, or listening (L.4.3): • Choose words, phrases, and punctuation that convey ideas precisely (L.4.3a; L.4.3b) • Explain why certain contexts call for formal English (for example, presenting ideas) and why informal discourse is appropriate in other situations (for example, small-group discussion) (L.4.3c)
Score 2.0	The student will recognize or recall specific vocabulary, such as: • *Context*, *convey*, *discourse*, *discussion*, *formal English*, *idea*, *informal*, *phrase*, *precise*, *punctuation* The student will perform basic processes, such as: • Choose words, phrases, and punctuation based on teacher and peer feedback • Recognize or recall contexts that call for formal and informal uses of English

Grade 3	
Score 3.0	The student will use grade-appropriate knowledge of language and its conventions when writing, speaking, reading, or listening (L.3.3): • Choose words and phrases for effect (L.3.3a) • Describe differences between the conventions of spoken and written standard English (L.3.3b)
Score 2.0	The student will recognize or recall specific vocabulary, such as: • *Convention, effect, phrase, standard English* The student will perform basic processes, such as: • Choose words and phrases based on teacher and peer feedback • Identify differences between the conventions of spoken and written standard English
Grade 2	
Score 3.0	The student will use grade-appropriate knowledge of language and its conventions when writing, speaking, reading, or listening (L.2.3): • Compare formal and informal uses of English (L.2.3a)
Score 2.0	The student will recognize or recall specific vocabulary, such as: • *Compare, formal, informal* The student will perform basic processes, such as: • Identify examples of formal versus informal uses of English
Grade 1 and Kindergarten	
Score 3.0	Not applicable.
Score 2.0	Not applicable.

Context Clues

Grades 11–12		
Score 4.0	In addition to score 3.0 performance, the student demonstrates in-depth inferences and applications that go beyond what was taught.	
	Score 3.5	*In addition to score 3.0 performance, partial success at score 4.0 content*
Score 3.0	The student will: • Use context (for example, the overall meaning of a sentence, paragraph, or text; a word's position or function in a sentence) as a clue to the meaning of a grade-appropriate word or phrase (L.11–12.4a)	
	Score 2.5	*No major errors or omissions regarding score 2.0 content, and partial success at score 3.0 content*
Score 2.0	The student will recognize or recall specific vocabulary, such as: • *Clue, context, function, meaning, paragraph, phrase, position, sentence, text, word* The student will perform basic processes, such as: • Demonstrate the use of context clues using structured sentences in isolation	
	Score 1.5	*Partial success at score 2.0 content, and major errors or omissions regarding score 3.0 content*
Score 1.0	With help, partial success at score 2.0 content and score 3.0 content	
	Score 0.5	*With help, partial success at score 2.0 content but not at score 3.0 content*
Score 0.0	Even with help, no success	

Grades 9–10	
Score 3.0	The student will: • Use context (for example, the overall meaning of a sentence or paragraph; a word's position or function in a sentence) as a clue to the meaning of a grade-appropriate word or phrase (L.9–10.4a)
Score 2.0	The student will recognize or recall specific vocabulary, such as: • *Clue*, *context*, *function*, *meaning*, *paragraph*, *phrase*, *position*, *sentence*, *word* The student will perform basic processes, such as: • Demonstrate the use of context clues using structured sentences in isolation
Grade 8	
Score 3.0	The student will: • Use context (for example, the overall meaning of a sentence or paragraph; a word's position or function in a sentence) as a clue to the meaning of a grade-appropriate word or phrase (L.8.4a)
Score 2.0	The student will recognize or recall specific vocabulary, such as: • *Clue*, *context*, *function*, *meaning*, *paragraph*, *phrase*, *position*, *sentence*, *word* The student will perform basic processes, such as: • Demonstrate the use of context clues using structured sentences in isolation
Grade 7	
Score 3.0	The student will: • Use context (for example, the overall meaning of a sentence or paragraph; a word's position or function in a sentence) as a clue to the meaning of a grade-appropriate word or phrase (L.7.4a)
Score 2.0	The student will recognize or recall specific vocabulary, such as: • *Clue*, *context*, *function*, *meaning*, *paragraph*, *phrase*, *position*, *sentence*, *word* The student will perform basic processes, such as: • Demonstrate the use of context clues using structured sentences in isolation
Grade 6	
Score 3.0	The student will: • Use context (for example, the overall meaning of a sentence or paragraph; a word's position or function in a sentence) as a clue to the meaning of a grade-appropriate word or phrase (L.6.4a)
Score 2.0	The student will recognize or recall specific vocabulary, such as: • *Clue*, *context*, *function*, *meaning*, *paragraph*, *phrase*, *position*, *sentence*, *word* The student will perform basic processes, such as: • Demonstrate the use of context clues using structured sentences in isolation
Grade 5	
Score 3.0	The student will: • Use context (for example, cause/effect relationships and comparisons in text) as a clue to the meaning of a grade-appropriate word or phrase (L.5.4a) • Use context to confirm or self-correct word recognition and understanding (RF.5.4c)
Score 2.0	The student will recognize or recall specific vocabulary, such as: • *Cause/effect*, *clue*, *comparison*, *confirm*, *context*, *meaning*, *phrase*, *relationship*, *self-correct*, *text*, *word* The student will perform basic processes, such as: • Demonstrate the use of context clues using structured sentences in isolation

Grade 4	
Score 3.0	The student will: • Use context (for example, definitions, examples, or restatements in text) as a clue to the meaning of a grade-appropriate word or phrase (L.4.4a) • Use context to confirm or self-correct word recognition and understanding (RF.4.4c)
Score 2.0	The student will recognize or recall specific vocabulary, such as: • *Clue*, *confirm*, *context*, *definition*, *example*, *meaning*, *phrase*, *restatement*, *self-correct*, *text*, *word* The student will perform basic processes, such as: • Demonstrate the use of context clues using structured sentences in isolation
Grade 3	
Score 3.0	The student will: • Use sentence-level context as a clue to the meaning of a grade-appropriate word or phrase (L.3.4a) • Use context to confirm or self-correct word recognition and understanding (RF.3.4c)
Score 2.0	The student will recognize or recall specific vocabulary, such as: • *Clue*, *confirm*, *context*, *meaning*, *phrase*, *self-correct*, *sentence-level*, *word* The student will perform basic processes, such as: • Demonstrate the use of context clues using structured sentences in isolation
Grade 2	
Score 3.0	The student will: • Use sentence-level context as a clue to the meaning of a grade-appropriate word or phrase (L.2.4a) • Use context to confirm or self-correct word recognition and understanding (RF.2.4c)
Score 2.0	The student will recognize or recall specific vocabulary, such as: • *Clue*, *confirm*, *context*, *meaning*, *phrase*, *self-correct*, *sentence-level*, *word* The student will perform basic processes, such as: • Identify words that help to determine the meaning from context
Grade 1	
Score 3.0	The student will: • Use sentence-level context as a clue to the meaning of a grade-appropriate word or phrase (L.1.4a) • Use context to confirm or self-correct word recognition and understanding (RF.1.4c)
Score 2.0	The student will recognize or recall specific vocabulary, such as: • *Clue*, *confirm*, *context*, *meaning*, *phrase*, *self-correct*, *sentence-level*, *word* The student will perform basic processes, such as: • Identify words that help to determine the meaning from context
Kindergarten	
Score 3.0	The student will: • Apply new meanings to familiar words (for example, knowing *duck* is a bird and a verb) (L.K.4a)
Score 2.0	The student will recognize or recall specific vocabulary, such as: • *Familiar*, *meaning*, *word* The student will perform basic processes, such as: • Recognize new meanings for familiar words when pointed out by the teacher

Word Origins and Roots

	Grades 11–12	
Score 4.0	In addition to score 3.0 performance, the student demonstrates in-depth inferences and applications that go beyond what was taught.	
	Score 3.5	*In addition to score 3.0 performance, partial success at score 4.0 content*
Score 3.0	The student will: • Correctly use grade-appropriate patterns of word changes that indicate different meanings or parts of speech (for example, *conceive*, *conception*, *conceivable*) (L.11–12.4b)	
	Score 2.5	*No major errors or omissions regarding score 2.0 content, and partial success at score 3.0 content*
Score 2.0	The student will recognize or recall specific vocabulary, such as: • *Meaning*, *part of speech*, *pattern* The student will perform basic processes, such as: • Recognize patterns of word changes that indicate different meanings or parts of speech (L.11–12.4b)	
	Score 1.5	*Partial success at score 2.0 content, and major errors or omissions regarding score 3.0 content*
Score 1.0	With help, partial success at score 2.0 content and score 3.0 content	
	Score 0.5	*With help, partial success at score 2.0 content but not at score 3.0 content*
Score 0.0	Even with help, no success	
	Grades 9–10	
Score 3.0	The student will: • Correctly use grade-appropriate patterns of word changes that indicate different meanings or parts of speech (for example, *analyze*, *analysis*, *analytical*; *advocate*, *advocacy*) (L.9–10.4b)	
Score 2.0	The student will recognize or recall specific vocabulary, such as: • *Meaning*, *part of speech*, *pattern* The student will perform basic processes, such as: • Recognize patterns of word changes that indicate different meanings or parts of speech (L.9–10.4b)	
	Grade 8	
Score 3.0	The student will: • Use common, grade-appropriate Greek or Latin affixes and roots as clues to the meaning of a word (for example, *precede*, *recede*, *secede*) (L.8.4b)	
Score 2.0	The student will recognize or recall specific vocabulary, such as: • *Affix*, *clue*, *meaning*, *root*, *word* The student will perform basic processes, such as: • Recognize or recall the meanings of grade-appropriate Greek or Latin affixes and roots	
	Grade 7	
Score 3.0	The student will: • Use common, grade-appropriate Greek or Latin affixes and roots as clues to the meaning of a word (for example, *belligerent*, *bellicose*, *rebel*) (L.7.4b)	
Score 2.0	The student will recognize or recall specific vocabulary, such as: • *Affix*, *clue*, *meaning*, *root*, *word* The student will perform basic processes, such as: • Recognize or recall the meanings of grade-appropriate Greek or Latin affixes and roots	

Grade 6	
Score 3.0	The student will: • Use common, grade-appropriate Greek or Latin affixes and roots as clues to the meaning of a word (for example, *audience*, *auditory*, *audible*) (L.6.4b)
Score 2.0	The student will recognize or recall specific vocabulary, such as: • *Affix*, *clue*, *meaning*, *root*, *word* The student will perform basic processes, such as: • Recognize or recall the meanings of grade-appropriate Greek or Latin affixes and roots
Grade 5	
Score 3.0	The student will: • Use common, grade-appropriate Greek and Latin affixes and roots as clues to the meaning of a word (for example, *photograph*, *photosynthesis*) (L.5.4b)
Score 2.0	The student will recognize or recall specific vocabulary, such as: • *Affix*, *clue*, *meaning*, *root*, *word* The student will perform basic processes, such as: • Recognize or recall the meanings of grade-appropriate Greek and Latin affixes and roots
Grade 4	
Score 3.0	The student will: • Use common, grade-appropriate Greek and Latin affixes and roots as clues to the meaning of a word (for example, *telegraph*, *photograph*, *autograph*) (L.4.4b)
Score 2.0	The student will recognize or recall specific vocabulary, such as: • *Affix*, *clue*, *meaning*, *root*, *word* The student will perform basic processes, such as: • Recognize or recall the meanings of grade-appropriate Greek and Latin affixes and roots
Grade 3	
Score 3.0	The student will: • Determine the meaning of the new grade-appropriate word formed when a known affix is added to a known word (for example, *agreeable/disagreeable*, *comfortable/uncomfortable*, *care/careless*, *heat/preheat*) (L.3.4b) • Use a known root word as a clue to the meaning of an unknown word with the same root (for example, *company*, *companion*) (L.3.4c) • Know the meaning of the most common prefixes and derivational suffixes (RF.3.3a) • Decode words with common Latin suffixes (RF.3.3b)
Score 2.0	The student will recognize or recall specific vocabulary, such as: • *Affix*, *clue*, *derivational*, *meaning*, *prefix*, *root*, *suffix*, *word* The student will perform basic processes, such as: • Identify common prefixes and suffixes (RF.3.3a)
Grade 2	
Score 3.0	The student will: • Determine the meaning of the new grade-appropriate word formed when a known prefix is added to a known word (for example, *happy/unhappy*, *tell/retell*) (L.2.4b) • Use a known root word as a clue to the meaning of an unknown word with the same root (for example, *addition*, *additional*) (L.2.4c) • Use the knowledge of the meaning of individual words to predict the meaning of compound words (for example, *birdhouse*, *lighthouse*, *housefly*; *bookshelf*, *notebook*, *bookmark*) (L.2.4d) • Decode words with common prefixes and suffixes (RF.2.3d)

Score 2.0	The student will recognize or recall specific vocabulary, such as: • *Affix, clue, compound word, meaning, predict, prefix, root, suffix, word* The student will perform basic processes, such as: • Recognize or recall the meanings of grade-appropriate affixes and roots
Grade 1	
Score 3.0	The student will: • Use frequently occurring affixes as a clue to the meaning of a grade-appropriate word (L.1.4b) • Identify frequently occurring root words (for example, *look*) and their inflectional forms (for example, *looks, looked, looking*) (L.1.4c)
Score 2.0	The student will recognize or recall specific vocabulary, such as: • *Affix, clue, inflection, meaning, root, word* The student will perform basic processes, such as: • Recognize or recall the meanings of grade-appropriate affixes and roots
Kindergarten	
Score 3.0	The student will: • Use the most frequently occurring inflections and affixes (for example, *-ed, -s, re-, un-, pre-, -ful, -less*) as a clue to the meaning of an unknown grade-appropriate word (L.K.4b)
Score 2.0	The student will recognize or recall specific vocabulary, such as: • *Affix, clue, meaning, word* The student will perform basic processes, such as: • Identify frequently occurring inflections and affixes

Reference Materials

Grades 11–12		
Score 4.0	In addition to score 3.0 performance, the student demonstrates in-depth inferences and applications that go beyond what was taught.	
	Score 3.5	*In addition to score 3.0 performance, partial success at score 4.0 content*
Score 3.0	The student will: • Consult general and specialized grade-appropriate reference materials (for example, dictionaries, glossaries, thesauruses), both print and digital, to find the pronunciation of a word or determine or clarify its precise meaning, its part of speech, its etymology, or its standard usage (L.11–12.4c)	
	Score 2.5	*No major errors or omissions regarding score 2.0 content, and partial success at score 3.0 content*
Score 2.0	The student will recognize or recall specific vocabulary, such as: • *Clarify, dictionary, digital, etymology, general, glossary, meaning, part of speech, precise, print, pronunciation, reference, specialized, standard usage, thesaurus, word* The student will perform basic processes, such as: • Demonstrate the use of general and specialized grade-appropriate reference materials in isolation	
	Score 1.5	*Partial success at score 2.0 content, and major errors or omissions regarding score 3.0 content*
Score 1.0	With help, partial success at score 2.0 content and score 3.0 content	
	Score 0.5	*With help, partial success at score 2.0 content but not at score 3.0 content*
Score 0.0	Even with help, no success	

Grades 9–10	
Score 3.0	The student will: • Consult general and specialized grade-appropriate reference materials (for example, dictionaries, glossaries, thesauruses), both print and digital, to find the pronunciation of a word or determine or clarify its precise meaning, its part of speech, or its etymology (L.9–10.4c)
Score 2.0	The student will recognize or recall specific vocabulary, such as: • *Clarify, dictionary, digital, etymology, general, glossary, meaning, part of speech, precise, print, pronunciation, reference, specialized, thesaurus, word* The student will perform basic processes, such as: • Demonstrate the use of general and specialized grade-appropriate reference materials in isolation
Grade 8	
Score 3.0	The student will: • Consult general and specialized grade-appropriate reference materials (for example, dictionaries, glossaries, thesauruses), both print and digital, to find the pronunciation of a word or determine or clarify its precise meaning or its part of speech (L.8.4c)
Score 2.0	The student will recognize or recall specific vocabulary, such as: • *Clarify, dictionary, digital, general, glossary, meaning, part of speech, precise, print, pronunciation, reference, specialized, thesaurus, word* The student will perform basic processes, such as: • Demonstrate the use of general and specialized grade-appropriate reference materials in isolation
Grade 7	
Score 3.0	The student will: • Consult general and specialized grade-appropriate reference materials (for example, dictionaries, glossaries, thesauruses), both print and digital, to find the pronunciation of a word or determine or clarify its precise meaning or its part of speech (L.7.4c)
Score 2.0	The student will recognize or recall specific vocabulary, such as: • *Clarify, dictionary, digital, general, glossary, meaning, part of speech, precise, print, pronunciation, reference, specialized, thesaurus, word* The student will perform basic processes, such as: • Demonstrate the use of general and specialized grade-appropriate reference materials in isolation
Grade 6	
Score 3.0	The student will: • Consult grade-appropriate reference materials (for example, dictionaries, glossaries, thesauruses), both print and digital, to find the pronunciation of a word or determine or clarify its precise meaning or its part of speech (L.6.4c)
Score 2.0	The student will recognize or recall specific vocabulary, such as: • *Clarify, dictionary, digital, glossary, meaning, part of speech, precise, print, pronunciation, reference, thesaurus, word* The student will perform basic processes, such as: • Demonstrate the use of grade-appropriate reference materials in isolation
Grade 5	
Score 3.0	The student will: • Consult grade-appropriate reference materials (for example, dictionaries, glossaries, thesauruses), both print and digital, to find the pronunciation and determine or clarify the precise meaning of key words and phrases (L.5.4c)

Score 2.0	The student will recognize or recall specific vocabulary, such as: • *Clarify, dictionary, digital, glossary, meaning, phrase, precise, print, pronunciation, reference, thesaurus, word* The student will perform basic processes, such as: • Demonstrate the use of grade-appropriate reference materials in isolation
Grade 4	
Score 3.0	The student will: • Consult grade-appropriate reference materials (for example, dictionaries, glossaries, thesauruses), both print and digital, to find the pronunciation and determine or clarify the precise meaning of key words and phrases (L.4.4c)
Score 2.0	The student will recognize or recall specific vocabulary, such as: • *Clarify, dictionary, digital, glossary, meaning, phrase, precise, print, pronunciation, reference, thesaurus, word* The student will perform basic processes, such as: • Demonstrate the use of grade-appropriate reference materials in isolation
Grade 3	
Score 3.0	The student will: • Use grade-appropriate glossaries or beginning dictionaries, both print and digital, to determine or clarify the precise meaning of key words and phrases (L.3.4d)
Score 2.0	The student will recognize or recall specific vocabulary, such as: • *Clarify, dictionary, digital, glossary, meaning, phrase, precise, print, word* The student will perform basic processes, such as: • Demonstrate the use of grade-appropriate glossaries or beginning dictionaries in isolation
Grade 2	
Score 3.0	The student will: • Use grade-appropriate glossaries and beginning dictionaries, both print and digital, to determine or clarify the meaning of words and phrases (L.2.4e)
Score 2.0	The student will recognize or recall specific vocabulary, such as: • *Clarify, dictionary, digital, glossary, meaning, phrase, print, word* The student will perform basic processes, such as: • Demonstrate the use of grade-appropriate glossaries or beginning dictionaries in isolation
Grade 1 and Kindergarten	
Score 3.0	Not applicable.
Score 2.0	Not applicable.

Word Relationships

Grades 11–12 and 9–10		
Score 3.0	Not applicable.	
Score 2.0	Not applicable.	
Grade 8		
Score 4.0	In addition to score 3.0 performance, the student demonstrates in-depth inferences and applications that go beyond what was taught.	
	Score 3.5	*In addition to score 3.0 performance, partial success at score 4.0 content*
Score 3.0	The student will: • Use the relationship between particular grade-appropriate words to better understand each of the words (L.8.5b)	

	Score 2.5	*No major errors or omissions regarding score 2.0 content, and partial success at score 3.0 content*
Score 2.0	The student will recognize or recall specific vocabulary, such as: • *Relationship, word* The student will perform basic processes, such as: • Identify the relationship between particular grade-appropriate words	
	Score 1.5	*Partial success at score 2.0 content, and major errors or omissions regarding score 3.0 content*
Score 1.0	With help, partial success at score 2.0 content and score 3.0 content	
	Score 0.5	*With help, partial success at score 2.0 content but not at score 3.0 content*
Score 0.0	Even with help, no success	
Grade 7		
Score 3.0	The student will: • Use the relationship between particular grade-appropriate words (for example, synonym/antonym, analogy) to better understand each of the words (L.7.5b)	
Score 2.0	The student will recognize or recall specific vocabulary, such as: • *Analogy, antonym, relationship, synonym, word* The student will perform basic processes, such as: • Identify the relationship between particular grade-appropriate words (for example, synonym/antonym, analogy)	
Grade 6		
Score 3.0	The student will: • Use the relationship between particular grade-appropriate words (for example, cause/effect, part/whole, item/category) to better understand each of the words (L.6.5b)	
Score 2.0	The student will recognize or recall specific vocabulary, such as: • *Cause/effect, item/category, part/whole, relationship, word* The student will perform basic processes, such as: • Identify the relationship between particular grade-appropriate words (for example, cause/effect, part/whole, item/category)	
Grade 5		
Score 3.0	The student will: • Use the relationship between particular grade-appropriate words (for example, synonyms, antonyms, homographs) to better understand each of the words (L.5.5c)	
Score 2.0	The student will recognize or recall specific vocabulary, such as: • *Antonym, homograph, relationship, synonym, word* The student will perform basic processes, such as: • Identify the relationship between particular grade-appropriate words (for example, synonyms, antonyms, homographs)	
Grade 4		
Score 3.0	The student will: • Demonstrate understanding of grade-appropriate words by relating them to their opposites (antonyms) and to words with similar but not identical meanings (synonyms) (L.4.5c)	
Score 2.0	The student will recognize or recall specific vocabulary, such as: • *Antonym, identical, meaning, opposite, relate, similar, synonym, word* The student will perform basic processes, such as: • Recognize or recall antonyms and synonyms for grade-appropriate words	

	Grade 3
Score 3.0	The student will: • Explain the real-life connections between grade-appropriate words and their use (for example, describe people who are *friendly* or *helpful*) (L.3.5b)
Score 2.0	The student will recognize or recall specific vocabulary, such as: • *Connection*, *real-life*, *use*, *word* The student will perform basic processes, such as: • Identify examples of real-life connections between grade-appropriate words and their use (for example, identify people who are *friendly* or *helpful*)
	Grade 2
Score 3.0	The student will: • Explain the real-life connections between grade-appropriate words and their use (for example, describe foods that are *spicy* or *juicy*) (L.2.5a)
Score 2.0	The student will recognize or recall specific vocabulary, such as: • *Connection*, *real-life*, *use*, *word* The student will perform basic processes, such as: • Identify examples of real-life connections between grade-appropriate words and their use (for example, identify foods that are *spicy* or *juicy*)
	Grade 1
Score 3.0	The student will: • Sort words into categories (for example, colors, clothing) and describe each category (L.1.5a) • Explain the real-life connections between grade-appropriate words and their use (for example, describe places at home that are *cozy*) (L.1.5c)
Score 2.0	The student will recognize or recall specific vocabulary, such as: • *Category*, *connection*, *real-life*, *sort*, *use*, *word* The student will perform basic processes, such as: • Sort words into teacher-provided categories and describe each category • Identify examples of real-life connections between grade-appropriate words and their use (for example, identify places at home that are *cozy*)
	Kindergarten
Score 3.0	The student will: • Sort common objects into categories and describe each category (L.K.5a) • Demonstrate understanding of frequently occurring verbs and adjectives by relating them to their opposites (antonyms) (L.K.5b) • Explain the real-life connections between grade-appropriate words and their use (for example, describe places at school that are *colorful*) (L.K.5c)
Score 2.0	The student will recognize or recall specific vocabulary, such as: • *Adjective*, *antonym*, *category*, *connection*, *opposite*, *real life*, *relate*, *sort*, *use*, *verb* The student will perform basic processes, such as: • Sort common objects into teacher-provided categories and describe each category • Recognize opposites of frequently occurring verbs and adjectives • Identify examples of real-life connections between grade-appropriate words and their use (for example, identify places at school that are *colorful*)

Proficiency Scales for the Mathematics Common Core State Standards

MRL's scales for the Common Core State Standards were designed to include all of the mathematics standards from the CCSS. Here we include several notes about MRL's scales for the mathematics CCSS that may interest teachers and readers.

- In some cases, the CCSS present substandards for an overarching standard. For example, the overarching Geometry standard 8.G.A.1 has three substandards, labeled using a, b, and c. In cases like this, MRL used one of three approaches. We included (1) both the overarching standard and the substandards (if the overarching standard includes additional information), (2) the substandards but not the overarching standard (if the overarching standard does not include additional information), or (3) the overarching standard but not the substandards (if the substandards were simply examples of the overarching standard).
- MRL's scales for the CCSS include all of the standards without a (+) symbol (with one exception in the high school measurement topic Geometric Trigonometry). This is because the authors of the CCSS stated that "all standards without a (+) symbol should be in the common mathematics curriculum for all college and career ready students" (NGA & CCSSO, 2010d, p. 57).

The numbering system used to cite the Common Core standards used in each scale identifies mathematics standards by grade level first, domain name initials next, cluster letter next, and standard number last. The domain name initials for grades K–8 are as follows:

- Counting and cardinality = CC
- Operations and algebraic thinking = OA
- Number and operations in base ten = NBT
- Number and operations—fractions = NF
- Measurement and data = MD
- Geometry = G
- Ratios and proportional relationships = RP
- The number system = NS
- Expressions and equations = EE

- Statistics and probability = SP
- Functions = F

Clusters within each domain are lettered using A, B, C, or D. Therefore, 6.NS.A.1 (grade, domain, cluster, standard) represents the first standard of the first cluster in the domain *the number system* for sixth grade. At the high school level, the letters HS, a conceptual category initial (followed by a dash), and domain name initials are listed first. The initials for the conceptual categories and domains at the high school level are as follows:

- Number and Quantity = HSN
  - The real number system = HSN-RN
  - Quantities = HSN-Q
  - The complex number system = HSN-CN
- Algebra = HSA
  - Seeing structure in expressions = HSA-SSE
  - Arithmetic with polynomials and rational expressions = HSA-APR
  - Creating equations = HSA-CED
  - Reasoning with equations and inequalities = HSA-REI
- Functions = HSF
  - Interpreting functions = HSF-IF
  - Building functions = HSF-BF
  - Linear, quadratic, and exponential models = HSF-LE
  - Trigonometric functions = HSF-TF
- Geometry = HSG
  - Congruence = HSG-CO
  - Similarity, right triangles, and trigonometry = HSG-SRT
  - Circles = HSG-C
  - Expressing geometric properties with equations = HSG-GPE
  - Geometric measurement and dimension = HSG-GMD
  - Modeling with geometry = HSG-MG
- Statistics and probability = HSS
  - Interpreting categorical and quantitative data = HSS-ID
  - Making inferences and justifying conclusions = HSS-IC
  - Conditional probability and the rules of probability = HSS-CP
  - Using probability to make decisions = HSS-MD

For example, HSN-RN.A.1 denotes the high school conceptual category of Number and Quantity (HSN-), the domain of *the real number system* (RN), and the first cluster's (A) first standard (1) in that domain.

Teachers and readers should note that for each measurement topic, the scale for the highest grade level in the topic shows all the scores (including half-point scores). For all other grade levels, the scale shows scores 3.0 and 2.0 only, because the descriptors for the other scores do not change from grade level to grade level.

Number and Quantity

Number Names

High School and Grades 8, 7, 6, 5, 4, 3, 2		
Score 3.0	Not applicable.	
Score 2.0	Not applicable.	
Grade 1		
Score 4.0	In addition to score 3.0 performance, the student demonstrates in-depth inferences and applications that go beyond what was taught.	
	Score 3.5	*In addition to score 3.0 performance, partial success at score 4.0 content*
Score 3.0	The student will: • Count numbers to 120, starting at any number less than 120 (1.NBT.A.1) • Represent a number of objects with a written numeral (1.NBT.A.1)	
	Score 2.5	*No major errors or omissions regarding score 2.0 content, and partial success at score 3.0 content*
Score 2.0	The student will recognize or recall specific vocabulary, such as: • *Count, number, numeral* The student will perform basic processes, such as: • Count and write numbers up to 120 (1.NBT.A.1)	
	Score 1.5	*Partial success at score 2.0 content, and major errors or omissions regarding score 3.0 content*
Score 1.0	With help, partial success at score 2.0 content and score 3.0 content	
	Score 0.5	*With help, partial success at score 2.0 content but not at score 3.0 content*
Score 0.0	Even with help, no success	
Kindergarten		
Score 3.0	The student will: • Count forward beginning from a given number within the known sequence (K.CC.A.2) • Represent a number of objects between 0 and 20 with a written numeral (K.CC.A.3)	
Score 2.0	The student will recognize or recall specific vocabulary, such as: • *Count, number, numeral, ones, sequence, tens* The student will perform basic processes, such as: • Count to 100 by ones and tens (K.CC.A.1) • Write numbers from zero to 20 (K.CC.A.3)	

Counting

High School and Grades 8, 7, 6, 5, 4, 3, 2, 1	
Score 3.0	Not applicable.
Score 2.0	Not applicable.

Kindergarten		
Score 4.0	In addition to score 3.0 performance, the student demonstrates in-depth inferences and applications that go beyond what was taught.	
	Score 3.5	*In addition to score 3.0 performance, partial success at score 4.0 content*
Score 3.0	The student will: • Count groups of objects up to 20 (K.CC.B.5) • Given a number from one to 20, count out that many objects (K.CC.B.5)	
	Score 2.5	*No major errors or omissions regarding score 2.0 content, and partial success at score 3.0 content*
Score 2.0	The student will recognize or recall specific vocabulary, such as: • *Count, larger, last, number, number name, pairing, standard order* The student will perform basic processes, such as: • Say the number names in standard order (K.CC.B.4a) • Count objects by pairing one object with one number name (K.CC.B.4a) • Use the last number said (when counting) to determine the number of objects counted (K.CC.B.4b) • Explain that each successive number refers to a quantity that is one larger (K.CC.B.4c)	
	Score 1.5	*Partial success at score 2.0 content, and major errors or omissions regarding score 3.0 content*
Score 1.0	With help, partial success at score 2.0 content and score 3.0 content	
	Score 0.5	*With help, partial success at score 2.0 content but not at score 3.0 content*
Score 0.0	Even with help, no success	

Compare Numbers

High School and Grades 8, 7, 6, 5, 4, 3, 2, 1		
Score 3.0	Not applicable.	
Score 2.0	Not applicable.	
Kindergarten		
Score 4.0	In addition to score 3.0 performance, the student demonstrates in-depth inferences and applications that go beyond what was taught.	
	Score 3.5	*In addition to score 3.0 performance, partial success at score 4.0 content*
Score 3.0	The student will: • Compare two numbers between one and 10 presented as written numerals (K.CC.C.7)	
	Score 2.5	*No major errors or omissions regarding score 2.0 content, and partial success at score 3.0 content*
Score 2.0	The student will recognize or recall specific vocabulary, such as: • *Compare, counting strategy, equal to, greater than, less than, matching strategy, number, numeral, set* The student will perform basic processes, such as: • Identify sets of objects as greater than, less than, or equal to another set of objects using matching and counting strategies (K.CC.C.6)	
	Score 1.5	*Partial success at score 2.0 content, and major errors or omissions regarding score 3.0 content*
Score 1.0	With help, partial success at score 2.0 content and score 3.0 content	
	Score 0.5	*With help, partial success at score 2.0 content but not at score 3.0 content*
Score 0.0	Even with help, no success	

Place Value

<table>
<tr><th colspan="3">High School and Grades 8, 7, 6, 5</th></tr>
<tr><td>Score 3.0</td><td colspan="2">Not applicable.</td></tr>
<tr><td>Score 2.0</td><td colspan="2">Not applicable.</td></tr>
<tr><th colspan="3">Grade 4</th></tr>
<tr><td>Score 4.0</td><td colspan="2">In addition to score 3.0 performance, the student demonstrates in-depth inferences and applications that go beyond what was taught.</td></tr>
<tr><td></td><td>Score 3.5</td><td>In addition to score 3.0 performance, partial success at score 4.0 content</td></tr>
<tr><td>Score 3.0</td><td colspan="2">The student will:
• Compare two multidigit numbers based on meanings of the digits in each place using <, >, and = (4.NBT.A.2)
• Use place value understanding to round multidigit whole numbers to any place (4.NBT.A.3)</td></tr>
<tr><td></td><td>Score 2.5</td><td>No major errors or omissions regarding score 2.0 content, and partial success at score 3.0 content</td></tr>
<tr><td>Score 2.0</td><td colspan="2">The student will recognize or recall specific vocabulary, such as:
• Base-ten numeral, compare, digit, expanded form, multidigit number, number name, place, place value, round, whole number
The student will perform basic processes, such as:
• Recognize that in a multidigit whole number, a digit in one place represents ten times what it represents in the place to its right (4.NBT.A.1)
• Read and write multidigit whole numbers using base-ten numerals, number names, and expanded form (4.NBT.A.2)</td></tr>
<tr><td></td><td>Score 1.5</td><td>Partial success at score 2.0 content, and major errors or omissions regarding score 3.0 content</td></tr>
<tr><td>Score 1.0</td><td colspan="2">With help, partial success at score 2.0 content and score 3.0 content</td></tr>
<tr><td></td><td>Score 0.5</td><td>With help, partial success at score 2.0 content but not at score 3.0 content</td></tr>
<tr><td>Score 0.0</td><td colspan="2">Even with help, no success</td></tr>
<tr><th colspan="3">Grade 3</th></tr>
<tr><td>Score 3.0</td><td colspan="2">The student will:
• Use place value understanding to round whole numbers within 1,000 to the nearest 10 and 100 (3.NBT.A.1)</td></tr>
<tr><td>Score 2.0</td><td colspan="2">The student will recognize or recall specific vocabulary, such as:
• Nearest, place value, round, whole number
The student will perform basic processes, such as:
• Use place value understanding to round whole numbers within 1,000 to the nearest 10 and 100 with visual support</td></tr>
<tr><th colspan="3">Grade 2</th></tr>
<tr><td>Score 3.0</td><td colspan="2">The student will:
• Read and write numbers within 1,000 using base-ten numerals, number names, and expanded form (2.NBT.A.3)
• Compare two three-digit numbers based on the meanings of the hundreds, tens, and ones digits using <, >, and = (2.NBT.A.4)</td></tr>
<tr><td>Score 2.0</td><td colspan="2">The student will recognize or recall specific vocabulary, such as:
• Base-ten numeral, compare, count, decompose, digit, expanded form, hundreds, number, number name, ones, skip count, tens
The student will perform basic processes, such as:
• Decompose the three digits of a three-digit number into hundreds, tens, and ones (2.NBT.A.1)
• Count within 1,000 (2.NBT.A.2)
• Skip count by 5s, 10s, and 100s (2.NBT.A.2)</td></tr>
</table>

Grade 1	
Score 3.0	The student will: • Compare and order two-digit numbers based on meanings of the tens and ones using <, >, or = (1.NBT.B.3) • Given a two-digit number, mentally find 10 more or 10 less (1.NBT.C.5)
Score 2.0	The student will recognize or recall specific vocabulary, such as: • *Amount, compare, digit, less, mentally, more, number, ones, order, tens* The student will perform basic processes, such as: • Recognize symbols, such as <, >, and = • Represent the two digits of a two-digit number as amounts of tens and ones (1.NBT.B.2)
Kindergarten	
Score 3.0	The student will: • Compose numbers from 11 to 19 into ten ones and further ones (for example, using objects or drawings) (K.NBT.A.1) • Decompose numbers from 11 to 19 into ten ones and further ones (for example, using objects or drawings) (K.NBT.A.1) • Record compositions and decompositions using a drawing or equation (K.NBT.A.1)
Score 2.0	The student will recognize or recall specific vocabulary, such as: • *Add, compose, composition, decompose, decomposition, equation, number, ones, record* The student will perform basic processes, such as: • Decompose numbers (less than or equal to 10) in more than one way (for example, using objects, drawings) and record using a drawing or equation (K.OA.A.3) • Find the number that makes 10 when added to any number from one to 10 (for example, using objects or drawings) and record the answer with a drawing or equation (K.OA.A.4)

Foundations of Fractions

High School and Grades 8, 7, 6, 5, 4		
Score 3.0	Not applicable.	
Score 2.0	Not applicable.	
Grade 3		
Score 4.0	In addition to score 3.0 performance, the student demonstrates in-depth inferences and applications that go beyond what was taught.	
	Score 3.5	*In addition to score 3.0 performance, partial success at score 4.0 content*
Score 3.0	The student will: • Represent fractions 1/*b* and *a/b* on a number line (3.NF.A.2a; 3.NF.A.2b)	
	Score 2.5	*No major errors or omissions regarding score 2.0 content, and partial success at score 3.0 content*
Score 2.0	The student will recognize or recall specific vocabulary, such as: • *Divided, equal, fraction, number line, part, quantity, size, whole* The student will perform basic processes, such as: • Describe zero to one on a number line as one whole • Describe a fraction 1/*b* as the quantity formed by one part when a whole is divided into *b* equal parts (3.NF.A.1) • Describe a fraction *a/b* as the quantity formed by *a* parts of size 1/*b* (3.NF.A.1)	

	Score 1.5	*Partial success at score 2.0 content, and major errors or omissions regarding score 3.0 content*
Score 1.0	With help, partial success at score 2.0 content and score 3.0 content	
	Score 0.5	*With help, partial success at score 2.0 content but not at score 3.0 content*
Score 0.0	Even with help, no success	
Grades 2, 1, and Kindergarten		
Score 3.0	Not applicable.	
Score 2.0	Not applicable.	

Fractions

High School and Grades 8, 7, 6, 5		
Score 3.0	Not applicable.	
Score 2.0	Not applicable.	
Grade 4		
Score 4.0	In addition to score 3.0 performance, the student demonstrates in-depth inferences and applications that go beyond what was taught.	
	Score 3.5	*In addition to score 3.0 performance, partial success at score 4.0 content*
Score 3.0	The student will: • Compare two fractions with different numerators and different denominators using <, >, and =, and justify the comparison (4.NF.A.2)	
	Score 2.5	*No major errors or omissions regarding score 2.0 content, and partial success at score 3.0 content*
Score 2.0	The student will recognize or recall specific vocabulary, such as: • *Compare, comparison, denominator, equivalent, fraction, generate, justify, numerator* The student will perform basic processes, such as: • Recognize and generate equivalent fractions (4.NF.A.1)	
	Score 1.5	*Partial success at score 2.0 content, and major errors or omissions regarding score 3.0 content*
Score 1.0	With help, partial success at score 2.0 content and score 3.0 content	
	Score 0.5	*With help, partial success at score 2.0 content but not at score 3.0 content*
Score 0.0	Even with help, no success	
Grade 3		
Score 3.0	The student will: • Generate simple equivalent fractions (for example, 1/2 = 2/4; 4/6 = 2/3) and explain why they are equivalent (3.NF.A.3b) • Express whole numbers as fractions (3.NF.A.3c) • Use comparison symbols (<, >, and =) to compare fractions and justify the comparison of two fractions with the same numerator or same denominator (3.NF.A.3d)	
Score 2.0	The student will recognize or recall specific vocabulary, such as: • *Compare, comparison, denominator, equivalent, express, fraction, generate, justify, model, numerator, simple fraction, visual, whole number* (3.NF.A.3a) The student will perform basic processes, such as: • Recognize simple equivalent fractions with a visual model (3.NF.A.3b) • Recognize fractions that are equivalent to whole numbers (3.NF.A.3c) • Compare two fractions with the same numerator or same denominator using visual fraction models (3.NF.A.3d)	

Grades 2, 1, and Kindergarten	
Score 3.0	Not applicable.
Score 2.0	Not applicable.

Adding and Subtracting Fractions

High School and Grades 8, 7, 6		
Score 3.0	Not applicable.	
Score 2.0	Not applicable.	
Grade 5		
Score 4.0	In addition to score 3.0 performance, the student demonstrates in-depth inferences and applications that go beyond what was taught.	
	Score 3.5	*In addition to score 3.0 performance, partial success at score 4.0 content*
Score 3.0	The student will: • Solve word problems involving the addition and subtraction of fractions referring to the same whole, including cases of unlike denominators (5.NF.A.2) • Use benchmark fractions to estimate answers and check for reasonableness (5.NF.A.2)	
	Score 2.5	*No major errors or omissions regarding score 2.0 content, and partial success at score 3.0 content*
Score 2.0	The student will recognize or recall specific vocabulary, such as: • *Add, addition, benchmark fraction, denominator, estimate, fraction, mixed number, reasonableness, refer, subtract, subtraction, unlike, whole, word problem* The student will perform basic processes, such as: • Add and subtract fractions with unlike denominators, including mixed numbers (5.NF.A.1)	
	Score 1.5	*Partial success at score 2.0 content, and major errors or omissions regarding score 3.0 content*
Score 1.0	With help, partial success at score 2.0 content and score 3.0 content	
	Score 0.5	*With help, partial success at score 2.0 content but not at score 3.0 content*
Score 0.0	Even with help, no success	
Grade 4		
Score 3.0	The student will: • Add and subtract mixed numbers with like denominators (4.NF.B.3c) • Solve word problems involving addition and subtraction of fractions referring to the same whole and having the same denominator (4.NF.B.3d) • Add two fractions with denominators 10 and 100 by making the denominators equivalent (4.NF.C.5)	
Score 2.0	The student will recognize or recall specific vocabulary, such as: • *Add, addition, decompose, denominator, equivalent, express, fraction, join, mixed number, part, refer, separate, subtract, subtraction, sum, whole, word problem* The student will perform basic processes, such as: • Describe addition and subtraction of fractions as joining and separating parts referring to the same whole (4.NF.B.3a) • Decompose a fraction into a sum of fractions with the same denominator in a variety of ways (for example, 3/8 = 1/8 + 1/8 + 1/8) (4.NF.B.3b) • Express a fraction with denominator 10 as an equivalent fraction with denominator 100 (4.NF.C.5)	

Grades 3, 2, 1, and Kindergarten	
Score 3.0	Not applicable.
Score 2.0	Not applicable.

Multiplying and Dividing Fractions

High School and Grades 8, 7		
Score 3.0	Not applicable.	
Score 2.0	Not applicable.	
Grade 6		
Score 4.0	In addition to score 3.0 performance, the student demonstrates in-depth inferences and applications that go beyond what was taught.	
	Score 3.5	*In addition to score 3.0 performance, partial success at score 4.0 content*
Score 3.0	The student will: • Solve word problems involving the division of fractions by fractions (6.NS.A.1)	
	Score 2.5	*No major errors or omissions regarding score 2.0 content, and partial success at score 3.0 content*
Score 2.0	The student will recognize or recall specific vocabulary, such as: • *Compute, division, equation, fraction, interpret, model, quotient, visual, word problem* The student will perform basic processes, such as: • Interpret quotients of fractions (6.NS.A.1) • Compute quotients of fractions by using visual fraction models and equations to represent the problem (6.NS.A.1)	
	Score 1.5	*Partial success at score 2.0 content, and major errors or omissions regarding score 3.0 content*
Score 1.0	With help, partial success at score 2.0 content and score 3.0 content	
	Score 0.5	*With help, partial success at score 2.0 content but not at score 3.0 content*
Score 0.0	Even with help, no success	
Grade 5		
Score 3.0	The student will: • Solve real-world problems involving multiplication of fractions and mixed numbers (5.NF.B.6) • Solve real-world problems involving division of unit fractions by nonzero whole numbers and division of whole numbers by unit fractions (5.NF.B.7c)	
Score 2.0	The student will recognize or recall specific vocabulary, such as: • *Denominator, divide, division, fraction, greater than, interpret, less than, mixed number, multiplication, multiply, number, numerator, product, real world, scaling, unit fraction, whole number* The student will perform basic processes, such as: • Interpret a fraction as division of the numerator by the denominator and determine the location of the fraction between two whole numbers (5.NF.B.3) • Multiply a fraction by a whole number or a fraction (5.NF.B.4) • Interpret multiplication as scaling (for example, multiplying a given number by a fraction greater than 1 results in a product greater than the given number; multiplying a given number by a fraction less than 1 results in a product smaller than the given number) (5.NF.B.5) • Divide unit fractions by whole numbers and whole numbers by unit fractions (5.NF.B.7a; 5.NF.B.7b)	

Grade 4		
Score 3.0	The student will: • Solve word problems involving the multiplication of a fraction by a whole number using fraction models and equations (4.NF.B.4c)	
Score 2.0	The student will recognize or recall specific vocabulary, such as: • *Equation, fraction, model, multiple, multiplication, multiply, whole number, word problem* The student will perform basic processes, such as: • Describe a fraction *a*/*b* as a multiple of 1/*b* (4.NF.B.4a) • Multiply a fraction by a whole number using the understanding that a multiple of *a*/*b* is a multiple of 1/*b* (4.NF.B.4b)	
Grades 3, 2, 1, and Kindergarten		
Score 3.0	Not applicable.	
Score 2.0	Not applicable.	

Decimal Concepts

High School and Grades 8, 7, 6		
Score 3.0	Not applicable.	
Score 2.0	Not applicable.	
Grade 5		
Score 4.0	In addition to score 3.0 performance, the student demonstrates in-depth inferences and applications that go beyond what was taught.	
	Score 3.5	*In addition to score 3.0 performance, partial success at score 4.0 content*
Score 3.0	The student will: • Use whole number exponents to denote powers of 10 (5.NBT.A.2) • Compare two decimals to thousandths (5.NBT.A.3b) • Round decimals to any place (5.NBT.A.4)	
	Score 2.5	*No major errors or omissions regarding score 2.0 content, and partial success at score 3.0 content*
Score 2.0	The student will recognize or recall specific vocabulary, such as: • *Base-ten numeral, compare, decimal, decimal point, digit, divide, expanded form, exponent, multiply, number, number name, pattern, place, powers of 10, round, thousandth, value, whole number* The student will perform basic processes, such as: • Describe the value of digits in a multidigit number (for example, a digit in one place represents 10 times as much as it represents in the place to its right and 1/10 of what it represents in the place to its left) (5.NBT.A.1) • Explain patterns in the number of zeroes and the decimal point when multiplying or dividing by powers of 10 (5.NBT.A.2) • Read and write decimals to thousandths using base-ten numerals, number names, and expanded form (5.NBT.A.3a)	
	Score 1.5	*Partial success at score 2.0 content, and major errors or omissions regarding score 3.0 content*
Score 1.0	With help, partial success at score 2.0 content and score 3.0 content	
	Score 0.5	*With help, partial success at score 2.0 content but not at score 3.0 content*
Score 0.0	Even with help, no success	

Grade 4	
Score 3.0	The student will: • Compare and justify the comparison of two decimals to hundredths (4.NF.C.7)
Score 2.0	The student will recognize or recall specific vocabulary, such as: • *Compare, comparison, decimal, denominator, fraction, hundredth, justify, notation* The student will perform basic processes, such as: • Use decimal notation for fractions with denominators of 10 or 100 (4.NF.C.6)
Grades 3, 2, 1, and Kindergarten	
Score 3.0	Not applicable.
Score 2.0	Not applicable.

Ratios and Unit Rates

High School and Grade 8		
Score 3.0	Not applicable.	
Score 2.0	Not applicable.	
Grade 7		
Score 4.0	In addition to score 3.0 performance, the student demonstrates in-depth inferences and applications that go beyond what was taught.	
	Score 3.5	*In addition to score 3.0 performance, partial success at score 4.0 content*
Score 3.0	The student will: • Compute unit rates associated with ratios of fractions measured in like or unlike units (7.RP.A.1) • Explain what a point (*x*, *y*) on the graph of a proportional relationship means in terms of the situation, with special attention to the points (0, 0) and (1, *r*) where *r* is the unit rate (7.RP.A.2d) • Use proportional relationships to solve multistep ratio and percent problems (for example, simple interest, tax, markups and markdowns, gratuities and commissions, fees, percent increase and decrease, percent error) (7.RP.A.3)	
	Score 2.5	*No major errors or omissions regarding score 2.0 content, and partial success at score 3.0 content*
Score 2.0	The student will recognize or recall specific vocabulary, such as: • *Commission problem, compute, constant of proportionality, equation, fee problem, fraction, graph, gratuity problem, like, markdown problem, markup problem, percent, percent decrease problem, percent error problem, percent increase problem, point, proportional relationship, quantity, ratio, simple interest problem, tax problem, unit, unit rate, unlike* The student will perform basic processes, such as: • Decide whether two quantities are in a proportional relationship (7.RP.A.2a) • Identify the constant of proportionality or unit rate (7.RP.A.2b) • Represent proportional relationships by equations (7.RP.A.2c)	
	Score 1.5	*Partial success at score 2.0 content, and major errors or omissions regarding score 3.0 content*
Score 1.0	With help, partial success at score 2.0 content and score 3.0 content	
	Score 0.5	*With help, partial success at score 2.0 content but not at score 3.0 content*
Score 0.0	Even with help, no success	

Grade 6		
Score 3.0	The student will: • Solve real-world and mathematical problems using ratios and unit rates (6.RP.A.3)	
Score 2.0	The student will recognize or recall specific vocabulary, such as: • *Equivalent, mathematical, quantity, rate, ratio, real world, relationship, representation, unit rate* The student will perform basic processes, such as: • Use ratio language to describe a ratio relationship between two quantities (6.RP.A.1) • Use rate language in the context of a ratio relationship (6.RP.A.2) • Recognize multiple equivalent representations of ratios (for example, 1:2, 1 to 2, 1/2)	
Grades 5, 4, 3, 2, 1, and Kindergarten		
Score 3.0	Not applicable.	
Score 2.0	Not applicable.	

Rational and Irrational Numbers

High School		
Score 4.0	In addition to score 3.0 performance, the student demonstrates in-depth inferences and applications that go beyond what was taught.	
	Score 3.5	*In addition to score 3.0 performance, partial success at score 4.0 content*
Score 3.0	The student will: • Explain why the sum or product of two rational numbers is rational (HSN-RN.B.3) • Explain why the sum of a rational number and an irrational number is irrational (HSN-RN.B.3) • Explain why the product of a nonzero rational number and an irrational number is irrational (HSN-RN.B.3)	
	Score 2.5	*No major errors or omissions regarding score 2.0 content, and partial success at score 3.0 content*
Score 2.0	The student will recognize or recall specific vocabulary, such as: • *Irrational number, product, property, rational number, sum* The student will perform basic processes, such as: • Recognize or recall the properties of rational and irrational numbers	
	Score 1.5	*Partial success at score 2.0 content, and major errors or omissions regarding score 3.0 content*
Score 1.0	With help, partial success at score 2.0 content and score 3.0 content	
	Score 0.5	*With help, partial success at score 2.0 content but not at score 3.0 content*
Score 0.0	Even with help, no success	
Grade 8		
Score 3.0	The student will: • Use rational approximations to compare the size of irrational numbers and estimate the value of expressions (8.NS.A.2)	
Score 2.0	The student will recognize or recall specific vocabulary, such as: • *Approximation, compare, convert, decimal, estimate, expansion, expression, irrational number, nonrepeating, nonterminating, number line, rational, rational number, size, value* The student will perform basic processes, such as: • Convert a decimal expansion which repeats into a rational number (8.NS.A.1) • Locate irrational numbers (using rational approximations) on a number line (8.NS.A.2) • Recognize or recall examples of irrational numbers such as π, $\sqrt{2}$, and nonrepeating, nonterminating decimals	

Grade 7	
Score 3.0	Not applicable.
Score 2.0	Not applicable.
Grade 6	
Score 3.0	The student will: • Write, interpret, and explain statements of order for rational numbers in real-world contexts (for example, writing -3°C > -7°C to express the fact that -3°C is warmer than -7°C) (6.NS.C.7b) • Interpret absolute value as a magnitude for a positive or negative quantity in a real-world situation (6.NS.C.7c) • Distinguish comparisons of absolute value from statements about order (6.NS.C.7d)
Score 2.0	The student will recognize or recall specific vocabulary, such as: • *Absolute value, comparison, diagram, inequality, integer, interpret, magnitude, negative, number, number line, opposite, order, positive, quantity, rational number, real world, relative, represent, sign* The student will perform basic processes, such as: • Use positive and negative numbers to represent quantities in real-world context explaining the meaning of zero in each situation (6.NS.C.5) • Recognize opposite signs of numbers as indicating locations on opposite sides of 0 on the number line (6.NS.C.6a) • Recognize that the opposite of the opposite of a number is the number itself (for example, -(-3) = 3) (6.NS.C.6a) • Find and position rational numbers, including integers, on a number line (6.NS.C.6c) • Interpret statements of inequality as statements about the relative position of two numbers on a number line diagram (6.NS.C.7a)
Grades 5, 4, 3, 2, 1, and Kindergarten	
Score 3.0	Not applicable.
Score 2.0	Not applicable.

Exponents and Roots

High School		
Score 4.0	In addition to score 3.0 performance, the student demonstrates in-depth inferences and applications that go beyond what was taught.	
	Score 3.5	*In addition to score 3.0 performance, partial success at score 4.0 content*
Score 3.0	The student will: • Rewrite expressions involving radicals and rational exponents using the properties of exponents (HSN-RN.A.2)	
	Score 2.5	*No major errors or omissions regarding score 2.0 content, and partial success at score 3.0 content*
Score 2.0	The student will recognize or recall specific vocabulary, such as: • *Exponent, expression, integer, property, radical, rational* The student will perform basic processes, such as: • Apply the meaning of rational exponents (HS-RN.A.1) • Apply properties of integer exponents (HSN-RN.A.1)	
	Score 1.5	*Partial success at score 2.0 content, and major errors or omissions regarding score 3.0 content*
Score 1.0	With help, partial success at score 2.0 content and score 3.0 content	
	Score 0.5	*With help, partial success at score 2.0 content but not at score 3.0 content*
Score 0.0	Even with help, no success	

Grade 8	
Score 3.0	The student will: • Evaluate square roots of small perfect squares and cube roots of small perfect cubes (8.EE.A.2) • Use reasoning to compare very large or small quantities using numbers expressed in the form of a single digit times an integer power of 10 (8.EE.A.3) • Perform operations with numbers expressed in scientific notation, including problems where both decimal and scientific notation are used (8.EE.A.4)
Score 2.0	The student will recognize or recall specific vocabulary, such as: • *Compare, cube root, decimal, digit, equation, equivalent, evaluate, exponent, expression, integer, large, measurement, number, numerical, operation, perfect cube, perfect square, power of 10, quantity, reasoning, scientific notation, small, solution, square root, symbol* The student will perform basic processes, such as: • Apply the properties of integer exponents to generate equivalent numerical expressions (8.EE.A.1) • Use square and cube root symbols to represent solutions to equations of the form $x^2 = p$ and $x^3 = p$ (8.EE.A.2) • Use scientific notation for measurements of very large and very small quantities (8.EE.A.4)
Grades 7, 6, 5, 4, 3, 2, 1, and Kindergarten	
Score 3.0	Not applicable.
Score 2.0	Not applicable.

Quantities

High School		
Score 4.0	In addition to score 3.0 performance, the student demonstrates in-depth inferences and applications that go beyond what was taught.	
	Score 3.5	*In addition to score 3.0 performance, partial success at score 4.0 content*
Score 3.0	The student will: • Define appropriate quantities for the purpose of descriptive modeling (HSN-Q.A.2) • Choose a level of accuracy appropriate to limitations on measurement when reporting quantities (HSN-Q.A.3)	
	Score 2.5	*No major errors or omissions regarding score 2.0 content, and partial success at score 3.0 content*
Score 2.0	The student will recognize or recall specific vocabulary, such as: • *Data display, descriptive, formula, graph, interpret, level of accuracy, limitation, measurement, modeling, origin, quantity, report, scale, solution, unit* The student will perform basic processes, such as: • Use units as a way to understand problems and to guide the solution of multistep problems (HSN-Q.A.1) • Choose and interpret the scale and the origin in graphs and data displays (HSN-Q.A.1) • Choose and interpret units consistently in formulas (HSN-Q.A.1)	
	Score 1.5	*Partial success at score 2.0 content, and major errors or omissions regarding score 3.0 content*
Score 1.0	With help, partial success at score 2.0 content and score 3.0 content	
	Score 0.5	*With help, partial success at score 2.0 content but not at score 3.0 content*
Score 0.0	Even with help, no success	
Grades 8, 7, 6, 5, 4, 3, 2, 1, and Kindergarten		
Score 3.0	Not applicable.	
Score 2.0	Not applicable.	

Operations With Complex Numbers

High School		
Score 4.0	In addition to score 3.0 performance, the student demonstrates in-depth inferences and applications that go beyond what was taught.	
	Score 3.5	*In addition to score 3.0 performance, partial success at score 4.0 content*
Score 3.0	The student will: • Add and subtract complex numbers (HSN-CN.A.2) • Multiply complex numbers using the relation $i^2 = -1$ and the commutative, associative, and distributive properties (HSN-CN.A.2)	
	Score 2.5	*No major errors or omissions regarding score 2.0 content, and partial success at score 3.0 content*
Score 2.0	The student will recognize or recall specific vocabulary, such as: • *Add, associative property, commutative property, complex number, distributive property, multiply, real number, relation, subtract* The student will perform basic processes, such as: • Recognize or recall complex number form: $a + bi$ (a and b are real) (HSN.CN.A.1)	
	Score 1.5	*Partial success at score 2.0 content, and major errors or omissions regarding score 3.0 content*
Score 1.0	With help, partial success at score 2.0 content and score 3.0 content	
	Score 0.5	*With help, partial success at score 2.0 content but not at score 3.0 content*
Score 0.0	Even with help, no success	
Grades 8, 7, 6, 5, 4, 3, 2, 1, and Kindergarten		
Score 3.0	Not applicable.	
Score 2.0	Not applicable.	

Polynomial Identities and Equations

High School		
Score 4.0	In addition to score 3.0 performance, the student demonstrates in-depth inferences and applications that go beyond what was taught.	
	Score 3.5	*In addition to score 3.0 performance, partial success at score 4.0 content*
Score 3.0	The student will: • Solve quadratic equations with real coefficients that have complex solutions (HSN-CN.C.7)	
	Score 2.5	*No major errors or omissions regarding score 2.0 content, and partial success at score 3.0 content*
Score 2.0	The student will recognize or recall specific vocabulary, such as: • *Coefficient, complex number, quadratic equation, real number, solution, solve* The student will perform basic processes, such as: • Explain the steps required to solve quadratic equations with real solutions	
	Score 1.5	*Partial success at score 2.0 content, and major errors or omissions regarding score 3.0 content*
Score 1.0	With help, partial success at score 2.0 content and score 3.0 content	
	Score 0.5	*With help, partial success at score 2.0 content but not at score 3.0 content*
Score 0.0	Even with help, no success	
Grades 8, 7, 6, 5, 4, 3, 2, 1, and Kindergarten		
Score 3.0	Not applicable.	
Score 2.0	Not applicable.	

Operations and Algebra

Addition and Subtraction

High School and Grade 8		
Score 3.0	Not applicable.	
Score 2.0	Not applicable.	
Grade 7		
Score 4.0	In addition to score 3.0 performance, the student demonstrates in-depth inferences and applications that go beyond what was taught.	
	Score 3.5	*In addition to score 3.0 performance, partial success at score 4.0 content*
Score 3.0	The student will: • Apply properties of operations as strategies to add and subtract rational numbers (7.NS.A.1d) • Solve real-world and mathematical problems involving the addition and subtraction of rational numbers (7.NS.A.3)	
	Score 2.5	*No major errors or omissions regarding score 2.0 content, and partial success at score 3.0 content*
Score 2.0	The student will recognize or recall specific vocabulary, such as: • *Add, addition, diagram, difference, horizontal, integer, interpret, mathematical, number line, operation, property, rational number, real world, represent, strategy, subtract, subtraction, sum, vertical* The student will perform basic processes, such as: • Represent addition and subtraction with rational numbers on a horizontal or vertical number line diagram (7.NS.A.1) • Interpret sums and differences in real-world contexts (7.NS.A.1a; 7.NS.A.1b; 7.NS.A.1c) • Apply properties of operations as strategies to add and subtract integers	
	Score 1.5	*Partial success at score 2.0 content, and major errors or omissions regarding score 3.0 content*
Score 1.0	With help, partial success at score 2.0 content and score 3.0 content	
	Score 0.5	*With help, partial success at score 2.0 content but not at score 3.0 content*
Score 0.0	Even with help, no success	
Grade 6		
Score 3.0	The student will: • Solve real-world and word problems involving multidigit decimals	
Score 2.0	The student will recognize or recall specific vocabulary, such as: • *Add, algorithm, decimal, digit, real world, subtract, word problem* The student will perform basic processes, such as: • Add and subtract multidigit decimals using the standard algorithm (6.NS.B.3)	
Grade 5		
Score 3.0	The student will: • Add and subtract decimals to hundredths and explain the strategies and reasoning used (5.NBT.B.7)	
Score 2.0	The student will recognize or recall specific vocabulary, such as: • *Add, decimal, hundredth, model, reasoning, strategy, subtract* The student will perform basic processes, such as: • Add and subtract decimals to hundredths using concrete models or drawings (5.NBT.B.7)	

Grade 4	
Score 3.0	The student will: • Fluently add and subtract multidigit whole numbers using the standard algorithm (4.NBT.B.4)
Score 2.0	The student will recognize or recall specific vocabulary, such as: • *Add, algorithm, digit, model, subtract, whole number* The student will perform basic processes, such as: • Add and subtract multidigit whole numbers using concrete models or drawings
Grade 3	
Score 3.0	The student will: • Fluently add and subtract within 1,000 using strategies and algorithms based on place value, properties of operations, and/or the relationship between addition and subtraction (3.NBT.A.2)
Score 2.0	The student will recognize or recall specific vocabulary, such as: • *Add, addition, algorithm, model, operation, place value, property, relationship, strategy, subtract, subtraction* The student will perform basic processes, such as: • Add and subtract within 1,000 using concrete models or drawings
Grade 2	
Score 3.0	The student will: • Use addition and subtraction within 100 to solve one- or two-step word problems including problems involving lengths that are given in the same units (2.OA.A.1; 2.MD.B.5) • Add and subtract within 1,000, using concrete models or drawings and strategies based on place value, properties of operations, and/or the relationship between addition and subtraction (2.NBT.B.7) • Mentally add or subtract 10 or 100 to or from a given number between 100 and 900 (2.NBT.B.8) • Explain why addition and subtraction strategies work, using place value and the properties of operations (2.NBT.B.9)
Score 2.0	The student will recognize or recall specific vocabulary, such as: • *Add, addition, diagram, difference, digit, length, mental, model, number, number line, operation, place value, property, relationship, represent, strategy, subtract, subtraction, sum, unit, whole number, word problem* The student will perform basic processes, such as: • Fluently add and subtract within 20 using mental strategies (2.OA.B.2) • Know from memory all sums of two one-digit numbers (2.OA.B.2) • Fluently add and subtract within 100 (2.NBT.B.5) • Add up to four two-digit numbers using strategies based on place value and properties of operations (2.NBT.B.6) • Represent whole-number sums and differences within 100 on a number line diagram (2.MD.B.6)
Grade 1	
Score 3.0	The student will: • Solve word problems involving addition and subtraction within 20, using objects, drawings, and equations to represent the problem (1.OA.A.1) • Solve word problems involving addition of three whole numbers (sum less than or equal to 20) using objects, drawings, and equations (1.OA.A.2) • Determine the unknown whole number in an addition or subtraction equation relating three whole numbers (1.OA.D.8) • Add within 100, including adding a two-digit number to a one-digit number and adding a two-digit number and a multiple of 10, and explain the strategies and reasoning used (1.NBT.C.4) • Subtract multiples of 10 in the range of 10 to 90 from multiples of 10 in the range of 10 to 90 and explain the strategies and reasoning used (1.NBT.C.6)

Score 2.0	The student will recognize or recall specific vocabulary, such as: • *Add, addition, count, decompose, digit, equal sign, equation, equivalent, false, model, multiple, number, reasoning, relate, relationship, strategy, subtract, subtraction, sum, true, unknown, whole number, word problem* The student will perform basic processes, such as: • Recognize symbols, such as +, –, and = • Relate counting to addition and subtraction (for example, counting on by two to add two) (1.OA.C.5) • Add and subtract within 20 (strategies may include using objects and drawings, counting on, making 10, decomposing a number leading to a 10, using the relationship between addition and subtraction, or creating equivalent but easier or known sums) (1.OA.C.6) • Add and subtract fluently within 10 (1.OA.C.6) • Understand the meaning of the equal sign and determine if equations involving addition and subtraction are true or false (1.OA.D.7) • Add a two-digit number to a one-digit number using concrete models (1.NBT.C.4) • Subtract multiples of 10 in the range of 10 to 90 using concrete models (1.NBT.C.6)	
Kindergarten		
Score 3.0	The student will: • Solve addition and subtraction word problems (K.OA.A.2) • Solve addition and subtraction within 10 (for example, using objects or drawings to represent problems) (K.OA.A.2) • Fluently add and subtract within five (K.OA.A.5)	
Score 2.0	The student will recognize or recall specific vocabulary, such as: • *Add, addition, equation, explanation, expression, mental image, represent, subtract, subtraction, verbal, word problem* The student will perform basic processes, such as: • Recognize symbols, such as +, –, and = • Represent addition and subtraction (for example, using objects, fingers, mental images, drawings, sounds, acting out, verbal explanations, expressions, or equations) (K.OA.A.1)	

Multiplication and Division

High School and Grade 8		
Score 3.0	Not applicable.	
Score 2.0	Not applicable.	
Grade 7		
Score 4.0	In addition to score 3.0 performance, the student demonstrates in-depth inferences and applications that go beyond what was taught.	
	Score 3.5	*In addition to score 3.0 performance, partial success at score 4.0 content*
Score 3.0	The student will: • Interpret the products and quotients of rational numbers in real-world contexts (7.NS.A.2a; 7.NS.A.2b) • Apply properties of operations as strategies to multiply and divide rational numbers (7.NS.A.2c) • Solve real-world and mathematical problems involving the multiplication and division of rational numbers (7.NS.A.3)	
	Score 2.5	*No major errors or omissions regarding score 2.0 content, and partial success at score 3.0 content*

<table>
<tr><td>Score 2.0</td><td colspan="2">The student will recognize or recall specific vocabulary, such as:
• Decimal, divide, division, divisor, integer, interpret, mathematical, multiplication, multiply, operation, product, property, quotient, rational number, real world, repeating, strategy, terminating
The student will perform basic processes, such as:
• Interpret the products and quotients of integers in real-world contexts
• Know that rational numbers must have a nonzero divisor (7.NS.A.2b)
• Apply properties of operations as strategies to multiply and divide with integers
• Know rational numbers can be written as terminating or repeating decimals (7.NS.A.2d)</td></tr>
<tr><td></td><td>Score 1.5</td><td>Partial success at score 2.0 content, and major errors or omissions regarding score 3.0 content</td></tr>
<tr><td>Score 1.0</td><td colspan="2">With help, partial success at score 2.0 content and score 3.0 content</td></tr>
<tr><td></td><td>Score 0.5</td><td>With help, partial success at score 2.0 content but not at score 3.0 content</td></tr>
<tr><td>Score 0.0</td><td colspan="2">Even with help, no success</td></tr>
<tr><td colspan="3">Grade 6</td></tr>
<tr><td>Score 3.0</td><td colspan="2">The student will:
• Use the distributive property to express a sum of two whole numbers between one and 100 with a common factor as a multiple of a sum of two whole numbers with no common factor (6.NS.B.4)</td></tr>
<tr><td>Score 2.0</td><td colspan="2">The student will recognize or recall specific vocabulary, such as:
• Algorithm, common, decimal, digit, distributive property, divide, express, factor, greatest common factor, least common multiple, multiple, multiply, number, sum, whole number
The student will perform basic processes, such as:
• Divide multidigit numbers using the standard algorithm (6.NS.B.2)
• Multiply and divide multidigit decimals using the standard algorithm (6.NS.B.3)
• Find greatest common factor (≤100) and least common multiple (≥12) for two whole numbers (6.NS.B.4)</td></tr>
<tr><td colspan="3">Grade 5</td></tr>
<tr><td>Score 3.0</td><td colspan="2">The student will:
• Illustrate and explain the multiplication and division of whole numbers using equations, rectangular arrays, and/or area models (5.NBT.B.5; 5.NBT.B.6)
• Multiply and divide decimals to hundredths and explain the strategies and reasoning used (5.NBT.B.7)</td></tr>
<tr><td>Score 2.0</td><td colspan="2">The student will recognize or recall specific vocabulary, such as:
• Area model, decimal, digit, divide, dividend, division, divisor, equation, hundredth, illustrate, model, multiplication, multiply, reasoning, rectangular array, strategy, whole number
The student will perform basic processes, such as:
• Multiply whole numbers and divide whole numbers with up to four-digit dividends and two-digit divisors (5.NBT.B.5; 5.NBT.B.6)
• Multiply and divide decimals to hundredths using concrete models or drawings (5.NBT.B.7)</td></tr>
<tr><td colspan="3">Grade 4</td></tr>
<tr><td>Score 3.0</td><td colspan="2">The student will:
• Multiply or divide to solve word problems involving multiplicative comparisons (for example, by using drawings and equations with a symbol for the unknown number to represent the problem, distinguishing multiplicative comparison from additive comparison) (4.OA.A.2)
• Solve multistep word problems posed with whole numbers and having whole number answers using the four operations, including division word problems in which remainders must be interpreted (4.OA.A.3)
• Illustrate and explain calculations using strategies based on place value, properties of operations, equations, and/or models (4.NBT.B.5)</td></tr>
</table>

<table>
<tr><td>Score 2.0</td><td>The student will recognize or recall specific vocabulary, such as:
• Additive, array, calculation, comparison, digit, distinguish, divide, dividend, division, divisor, equation, illustrate, interpret, model, multiplication, multiplicative, multiply, number, operation, place value, property, remainder, represent, quotient, strategy, symbol, unknown, verbal, whole number, word problem
The student will perform basic processes, such as:
• Interpret a multiplication equation as a comparison (4.OA.A.1)
• Represent verbal statements of multiplicative comparisons as multiplication equations (4.OA.A.1)
• Multiply a whole number of up to four digits by a one-digit whole number, and multiply two two-digit whole numbers (4.NBT.B.5)
• Find whole number quotients and remainders with up to four-digit dividends and one-digit divisors (4.NBT.B.6)
• Use arrays and/or models to solve multiplication and division problems</td></tr>
<tr><td colspan="2">Grade 3</td></tr>
<tr><td>Score 3.0</td><td>The student will:
• Use multiplication and division within 100 to solve word problems (for example, using drawings and equations with a symbol for the unknown number to represent the problem) (3.OA.A.3)
• Determine the unknown whole number in a multiplication or division equation relating three whole numbers (for example, $8 \times \_\_ = 45$, $5 = \_\_ \div 3$) (3.OA.A.4)
• Solve division problems as unknown-factor problems (for example, finding $32 \div 8$ by finding the number that makes 32 when multiplied by 8) (3.OA.B.6)
• Multiply one-digit whole numbers by multiples of 10 in the range of 10 to 90 using strategies based on place value and properties of whole numbers (3.NBT.A.3)</td></tr>
<tr><td>Score 2.0</td><td>The student will recognize or recall specific vocabulary, such as:
• Digit, divide, division, equation, interpret, multiplication, multiple, multiply, number, place value, product, property, quotient, relate, represent, strategy, symbol, unknown, unknown-factor problem, whole number, word problem
The student will perform basic processes, such as:
• Interpret products of whole numbers (for example, understanding 5×7 as the total number of objects in five groups of seven) (3.OA.A.1)
• Interpret whole-number quotients of whole numbers (for example, understanding $56 \div 8$ as the number of objects in each share when 56 objects are divided into equal shares of 8 objects each) (3.OA.A.2)
• Fluently multiply and divide within 100 (3.OA.C.7)
• Know from memory all products of two one-digit numbers (3.OA.C.7)</td></tr>
<tr><td colspan="2">Grade 2</td></tr>
<tr><td>Score 3.0</td><td>The student will:
• Use addition to find the total number of objects arranged in rectangular arrays with up to five rows and up to five columns; write an equation to express the total as a sum of equal addends (2.OA.C.4)</td></tr>
<tr><td>Score 2.0</td><td>The student will recognize or recall specific vocabulary, such as:
• Addend, addition, column, equal, equation, even, member, number, odd, rectangular array, row, sum, total
The student will perform basic processes, such as:
• Determine whether a group of objects (up to 20) has an odd or even number of members; if the total is even, write an equation to express the total as a sum of two equal addends (2.OA.C.3)</td></tr>
<tr><td colspan="2">Grade 1 and Kindergarten</td></tr>
<tr><td>Score 3.0</td><td>Not applicable.</td></tr>
<tr><td>Score 2.0</td><td>Not applicable.</td></tr>
</table>

Properties of Operations

<table>
<tr><th colspan="3">High School and Grades 8, 7, 6, 5, 4</th></tr>
<tr><td>Score 3.0</td><td colspan="2">Not applicable.</td></tr>
<tr><td>Score 2.0</td><td colspan="2">Not applicable.</td></tr>
<tr><th colspan="3">Grade 3</th></tr>
<tr><td>Score 4.0</td><td colspan="2">In addition to score 3.0 performance, the student demonstrates in-depth inferences and applications that go beyond what was taught.</td></tr>
<tr><td></td><td>Score 3.5</td><td>In addition to score 3.0 performance, partial success at score 4.0 content</td></tr>
<tr><td>Score 3.0</td><td colspan="2">The student will:
• Apply properties of operations as strategies to multiply and divide (for example, commutative, associative, distributive*) (3.OA.B.5)
• Explain arithmetic patterns (addition or multiplication table) using the properties of operations (3.OA.D.9)</td></tr>
<tr><td></td><td>Score 2.5</td><td>No major errors or omissions regarding score 2.0 content, and partial success at score 3.0 content</td></tr>
<tr><td>Score 2.0</td><td colspan="2">The student will recognize or recall specific vocabulary, such as:
• Addition, arithmetic, divide, multiplication, multiply, operation, pattern, property, strategy, table
The student will perform basic processes, such as:
• Recognize or recall the properties of multiplication (for example, commutative, associative, distributive*)
• Identify arithmetic patterns in the addition and multiplication tables (3.OA.D.9)</td></tr>
<tr><td></td><td>Score 1.5</td><td>Partial success at score 2.0 content, and major errors or omissions regarding score 3.0 content</td></tr>
<tr><td>Score 1.0</td><td colspan="2">With help, partial success at score 2.0 content and score 3.0 content</td></tr>
<tr><td></td><td>Score 0.5</td><td>With help, partial success at score 2.0 content but not at score 3.0 content</td></tr>
<tr><td>Score 0.0</td><td colspan="2">Even with help, no success</td></tr>
<tr><th colspan="3">Grade 2</th></tr>
<tr><td>Score 3.0</td><td colspan="2">Not applicable.</td></tr>
<tr><td>Score 2.0</td><td colspan="2">Not applicable.</td></tr>
<tr><th colspan="3">Grade 1</th></tr>
<tr><td>Score 3.0</td><td colspan="2">The student will:
• Apply properties of operations as strategies to add and subtract (for example, commutative, associative*) (1.OA.B.3)
• Solve subtraction problems as unknown addend problems (for example, subtracting 10 – 8 by finding the number that makes 10 when added to 8) (1.OA.B.4)</td></tr>
<tr><td>Score 2.0</td><td colspan="2">The student will recognize or recall specific vocabulary, such as:
• Add, addend, operation, property, strategy, subtract, subtraction, unknown
The student will perform basic processes, such as:
• Recognize examples of the commutative and associative properties*</td></tr>
<tr><th colspan="3">Kindergarten</th></tr>
<tr><td>Score 3.0</td><td colspan="2">Not applicable.</td></tr>
<tr><td>Score 2.0</td><td colspan="2">Not applicable.</td></tr>
</table>

*Note: Students do not need to use the formal terms for these properties.

Expressions and Equations

High School and Grade 8		
Score 3.0	Not applicable.	
Score 2.0	Not applicable.	
Grade 7		
Score 4.0	In addition to score 3.0 performance, the student demonstrates in-depth inferences and applications that go beyond what was taught.	
	Score 3.5	*In addition to score 3.0 performance, partial success at score 4.0 content*
Score 3.0	The student will: • Apply properties of operations as strategies to add, subtract, factor, and expand linear expressions with rational coefficients (7.EE.A.1) • Rewrite expressions in different forms in a problem context to demonstrate how quantities are related (for example, $a + 0.05a = 1.05a$ means that "increase by 5%" is the same as "multiply by 1.05") (7.EE.A.2)	
	Score 2.5	*No major errors or omissions regarding score 2.0 content, and partial success at score 3.0 content*
Score 2.0	The student will recognize or recall specific vocabulary, such as: • *Add, coefficient, expand, expression, factor, linear, operation, property, quantity, rational, relate, strategy, subtract* The student will perform basic processes, such as: • Apply properties of operations to simplify linear expressions with rational coefficients	
	Score 1.5	*Partial success at score 2.0 content, and major errors or omissions regarding score 3.0 content*
Score 1.0	With help, partial success at score 2.0 content and score 3.0 content	
	Score 0.5	*With help, partial success at score 2.0 content but not at score 3.0 content*
Score 0.0	Even with help, no success	
Grade 6		
Score 3.0	The student will: • Evaluate expressions at specific values of their variables including whole-number exponents (6.EE.A.1; 6.EE.A.2c) • Generate equivalent expressions using the properties of operations (6.EE.A.3)	
Score 2.0	The student will recognize or recall specific vocabulary, such as: • *Equivalent, exponent, expression, generate, mathematical, number, operation, part, property, term, value, variable, whole number* The student will perform basic processes, such as: • Write expressions involving exponents, numbers, and letters standing for numbers (6.EE.A.1; 6.EE.A.2a) • Identify parts of an expression using mathematical terms (6.EE.A.2b) • Identify when two expressions are equivalent (6.EE.A.4)	
Grade 5		
Score 3.0	The student will: • Write linguistically-expressed calculations using symbols (for example, expressing "add eight and seven, then multiply by two" as $2 \times [8 + 7]$) (5.OA.A.2) • Interpret numerical expressions without evaluating them (for example, $3 \times [183 + 921]$ is three times as large as $183 + 921$) (5.OA.A.2)	

Score 2.0	The student will recognize or recall specific vocabulary, such as: • *Brace, bracket, calculation, evaluate, express, expression, linguistic, numerical, parentheses, symbol* The student will perform basic processes, such as: • Evaluate expressions with parentheses, brackets, or braces (5.OA.A.1)
Grade 4	
Score 3.0	The student will: • Solve multistep word problems involving the four operations posed with whole numbers with a symbol for the unknown number (4.OA.A.3)
Score 2.0	The student will recognize or recall specific vocabulary, such as: • *Equation, number, operation, quantity, represent, symbol, unknown, whole number, word problem* The student will perform basic processes, such as: • Represent word problems using equations with a letter standing for the unknown quantity (4.OA.A.3)
Grade 3	
Score 3.0	The student will: • Solve two-step word problems using the four operations with a letter standing for the unknown quantity (3.OA.D.8) • Assess the reasonableness of answers using mental computation and estimation strategies (3.OA.D.8)
Score 2.0	The student will recognize or recall specific vocabulary, such as: • *Computation, equation, estimation, mental, operation, quantity, reasonableness, strategy, unknown, word problem* The student will perform basic processes, such as: • Represent two-step word problems using equations with a letter standing for the unknown quantity (3.OA.D.8)
Grades 2, 1, and Kindergarten	
Score 3.0	Not applicable.
Score 2.0	Not applicable.

Factors and Multiples

High School and Grades 8, 7, 6, 5		
Score 3.0	Not applicable.	
Score 2.0	Not applicable.	
Grade 4		
Score 4.0	In addition to score 3.0 performance, the student demonstrates in-depth inferences and applications that go beyond what was taught.	
	Score 3.5	*In addition to score 3.0 performance, partial success at score 4.0 content*
Score 3.0	The student will: • Determine whether a given whole number in the range of 1 to 100 is prime or composite (4.OA.B.4) • Determine whether a given whole number in the range of 1 to 100 is a multiple of a given one-digit number (4.OA.B.4)	
	Score 2.5	*No major errors or omissions regarding score 2.0 content, and partial success at score 3.0 content*

Score 2.0	The student will recognize or recall specific vocabulary, such as: • *Composite, digit, factor pair, multiple, number, prime, whole number* The student will perform basic processes, such as: • Find all factor pairs for a whole number in the range of 1 to 100 (4.OA.B.4)	
	Score 1.5	*Partial success at score 2.0 content, and major errors or omissions regarding score 3.0 content*
Score 1.0	With help, partial success at score 2.0 content and score 3.0 content	
	Score 0.5	*With help, partial success at score 2.0 content but not at score 3.0 content*
Score 0.0	Even with help, no success	
Grades 3, 2, 1, and Kindergarten		
Score 3.0	Not applicable.	
Score 2.0	Not applicable.	

Patterns

High School and Grades 8, 7, 6		
Score 3.0	Not applicable.	
Score 2.0	Not applicable.	
Grade 5		
Score 4.0	In addition to score 3.0 performance, the student demonstrates in-depth inferences and applications that go beyond what was taught.	
	Score 3.5	*In addition to score 3.0 performance, partial success at score 4.0 content*
Score 3.0	The student will: • Form ordered pairs from numerical patterns (5.OA.B.3) • Interpret the relationship between patterns by graphing ordered pairs on a coordinate plane (5.OA.B.3)	
	Score 2.5	*No major errors or omissions regarding score 2.0 content, and partial success at score 3.0 content*
Score 2.0	The student will recognize or recall specific vocabulary, such as: • *Coordinate plane, generate, graph, interpret, numerical, ordered pair, pattern, relationship, rule* The student will perform basic processes, such as: • Generate numerical patterns using given rules (5.OA.B.3)	
	Score 1.5	*Partial success at score 2.0 content, and major errors or omissions regarding score 3.0 content*
Score 1.0	With help, partial success at score 2.0 content and score 3.0 content	
	Score 0.5	*With help, partial success at score 2.0 content but not at score 3.0 content*
Score 0.0	Even with help, no success	
Grade 4		
Score 3.0	The student will: • Describe the features of a number or shape pattern including those that are not explicit in the rule itself (4.OA.C.5)	
Score 2.0	The student will recognize or recall specific vocabulary, such as: • *Number, pattern, rule, shape* The student will perform basic processes, such as: • Generate a number or shape pattern that follows a given rule (4.OA.C.5)	

Grades 3, 2, 1, and Kindergarten	
Score 3.0	Not applicable.
Score 2.0	Not applicable.

Equations and Inequalities

High School		
Score 4.0	In addition to score 3.0 performance, the student demonstrates in-depth inferences and applications that go beyond what was taught.	
	Score 3.5	*In addition to score 3.0 performance, partial success at score 4.0 content*
Score 3.0	The student will: • Solve linear equations in one variable with coefficients represented by letters (HSA-REI.B.3) • Solve linear inequalities in one variable with coefficients represented by letters (HSA-REI.B.3)	
	Score 2.5	*No major errors or omissions regarding score 2.0 content, and partial success at score 3.0 content*
Score 2.0	The student will recognize or recall specific vocabulary, such as: • *Coefficient, equation, inequality, linear, represent, variable* The student will perform basic processes, such as: • Solve given linear equations in one variable (HSA-REI.B.3) • Solve given linear inequalities in one variable (HSA-REI.B.3)	
	Score 1.5	*Partial success at score 2.0 content, and major errors or omissions regarding score 3.0 content*
Score 1.0	With help, partial success at score 2.0 content and score 3.0 content	
	Score 0.5	*With help, partial success at score 2.0 content but not at score 3.0 content*
Score 0.0	Even with help, no success	
Grade 8		
Score 3.0	The student will: • Solve linear equations with rational number coefficients where there is one solution, infinitely many solutions, or no solution (8.EE.C.7)	
Score 2.0	The student will recognize or recall specific vocabulary, such as: • *Coefficient, distributive property, equation, example, infinite, integer, like, linear, rational number, solution, term* The student will perform basic processes, such as: • Solve linear equations with integer coefficients where there is one solution • Recognize examples of linear equations with rational number coefficients where there is one solution, infinitely many solutions, or no solution (8.EE.C.7a) • Transform the given equation into simpler forms (an equivalent equation of the form $x = a$, $a = a$, or $a = b$) (8.EE.C.7a) • Use the distributive property and collect like terms when solving linear equations (8.EE.C.7b)	
Grade 7		
Score 3.0	The student will: • Solve multistep real-world and mathematical problems posed with rational numbers in any form (7.EE.B.3) • Assess the reasonableness of answers using mental computation and estimation strategies (7.EE.B.3) • Solve word problems leading to equations of the form $px + q = r$ and $p(x + q) = r$ (7.EE.B.4a) • Solve and graph word problems leading to inequalities of the form $px + q > r$ and $px + q < r$ (7.EE.B.4b)	

Score 2.0	The student will recognize or recall specific vocabulary, such as: • *Computation, convert, decimal, equation, estimation, fraction, graph, inequality, integer, mathematical, mental, percent, rational number, real world, reasonableness, strategy, word problem* The student will perform basic processes, such as: • Solve multistep real-world and mathematical problems posed with integers in any form • Convert among fraction, decimal, and percent as appropriate (7.EE.B.3)
Grade 6	
Score 3.0	The student will: • Solve real-world and mathematical equations of the form $x + p = q$ and $px = q$ when all variables are nonnegative, rational numbers (6.EE.B.7) • Write an inequality of the form $x > c$ or $x < c$ to represent a constraint or condition of a real-world or mathematical problem (6.EE.B.8)
Score 2.0	The student will recognize or recall specific vocabulary, such as: • *Condition, constraint, diagram, equation, expression, inequality, mathematical, negative, number, number line, rational number, real world, represent, solution, substitution, true, variable* The student will perform basic processes, such as: • Use substitution to determine whether a given number makes an equation or inequality true (6.EE.B.5) • Use variables to represent numbers and write expressions (6.EE.B.6) • Represent solutions of inequalities on number line diagrams (6.EE.B.8)
Grades 5, 4, 3, 2, 1, and Kindergarten	
Score 3.0	Not applicable.
Score 2.0	Not applicable.

Dependent and Independent Variables

High School and Grades 8, 7		
Score 3.0	Not applicable.	
Score 2.0	Not applicable.	
Grade 6		
Score 4.0	In addition to score 3.0 performance, the student demonstrates in-depth inferences and applications that go beyond what was taught.	
	Score 3.5	*In addition to score 3.0 performance, partial success at score 4.0 content*
Score 3.0	The student will: • Analyze the relationship between the independent and dependent variable using graphs, tables, and equations (6.EE.C.9)	
	Score 2.5	*No major errors or omissions regarding score 2.0 content, and partial success at score 3.0 content*
Score 2.0	The student will recognize or recall specific vocabulary, such as: • *Analyze, dependent, equation, graph, independent, quantity, relationship, table, variable* The student will perform basic processes, such as: • Write an equation to express one quantity (dependent variable) in terms of the other quantity (independent variable) (6.EE.C.9)	
	Score 1.5	*Partial success at score 2.0 content, and major errors or omissions regarding score 3.0 content*
Score 1.0	With help, partial success at score 2.0 content and score 3.0 content	
	Score 0.5	*With help, partial success at score 2.0 content but not at score 3.0 content*

Score 0.0	Even with help, no success	
Grades 5, 4, 3, 2, 1, and Kindergarten		
Score 3.0	Not applicable.	
Score 2.0	Not applicable.	

Slope

High School		
Score 3.0	Not applicable.	
Score 2.0	Not applicable.	
Grade 8		
Score 4.0	In addition to score 3.0 performance, the student demonstrates in-depth inferences and applications that go beyond what was taught.	
	Score 3.5	*In addition to score 3.0 performance, partial success at score 4.0 content*
Score 3.0	The student will: • Derive the equation $y = mx + b$ for a line given two distinct nonvertical points (8.EE.B.5) • Explain why the slope m is the same between any two distinct points on a nonvertical line in the coordinate plane using similar triangles (8.EE.B.6) • Derive the equation $y = mx$ for a line through the origin and the equation $y = mx + b$ for a line intersecting the vertical axis at b (8.EE.B.6)	
	Score 2.5	*No major errors or omissions regarding score 2.0 content, and partial success at score 3.0 content*
Score 2.0	The student will recognize or recall specific vocabulary, such as: • *Axis, compare, coordinate plane, equation, graph, interpret, intersect, line, origin, point, proportional relationship, similar, slope, table, triangle, unit rate, vertical* The student will perform basic processes, such as: • Graph proportional relationships (8.EE.B.5) • Interpret slope as the unit rate of the graph (8.EE.B.5) • Compare proportional relationships displayed in different ways (for example, graph, table, equation) (8.EE.B.5)	
	Score 1.5	*Partial success at score 2.0 content, and major errors or omissions regarding score 3.0 content*
Score 1.0	With help, partial success at score 2.0 content and score 3.0 content	
	Score 0.5	*With help, partial success at score 2.0 content but not at score 3.0 content*
Score 0.0	Even with help, no success	
Grades 7, 6, 5, 4, 3, 2, 1, and Kindergarten		
Score 3.0	Not applicable.	
Score 2.0	Not applicable.	

Systems of Equations

High School		
Score 4.0	In addition to score 3.0 performance, the student demonstrates in-depth inferences and applications that go beyond what was taught.	
	Score 3.5	*In addition to score 3.0 performance, partial success at score 4.0 content*

Score 3.0	The student will: • Solve systems of linear equations (focusing on pairs of linear equations in two variables) exactly and approximately (for example, using graphs) (HSA-REI.C.6) • Solve a simple system consisting of a linear equation and a quadratic equation in two variables algebraically and graphically (HSA-REI.C.7)	
	Score 2.5	*No major errors or omissions regarding score 2.0 content, and partial success at score 3.0 content*
Score 2.0	The student will recognize or recall specific vocabulary, such as: • *Algebraic, approximately, equation, graph, graphic, linear, multiple, pair, quadratic equation, simple, solution, sum, system, variable* The student will perform basic processes, such as: • Prove that, given a system of two equations in two variables, replacing one equation by the sum of that equation and a multiple of the other produces a system with the same solutions (HSA-REI.C.5)	
	Score 1.5	*Partial success at score 2.0 content, and major errors or omissions regarding score 3.0 content*
Score 1.0	With help, partial success at score 2.0 content and score 3.0 content	
	Score 0.5	*With help, partial success at score 2.0 content but not at score 3.0 content*
Score 0.0	Even with help, no success	
Grade 8		
Score 3.0	The student will: • Solve systems of linear equations with rational solutions (8.EE.C.8b) • Solve real-world and mathematical problems leading to two linear equations in two variables (8.EE.C.8c)	
Score 2.0	The student will recognize or recall specific vocabulary, such as: • *Algebraic, equation, estimate, graph, infinite, integer, linear, mathematical, rational, real world, solution, system, variable* (8.EE.C.8a) The student will perform basic processes, such as: • Solve systems of two linear equations with integer solutions in two variables algebraically (8.EE.C.8b) • Estimate the solutions of systems of linear equations by graphing (8.EE.C.8b) • Recognize that systems of linear equations may have one, infinitely many, or no solutions	
Grades 7, 6, 5, 4, 3, 2, 1, and Kindergarten		
Score 3.0	Not applicable.	
Score 2.0	Not applicable.	

Structure of Expressions

High School		
Score 4.0	In addition to score 3.0 performance, the student demonstrates in-depth inferences and applications that go beyond what was taught.	
	Score 3.5	*In addition to score 3.0 performance, partial success at score 4.0 content*
Score 3.0	The student will: • Interpret complicated expressions by viewing one or more of their parts as a single entity (HSA-SSE.A.1b) • Rewrite expressions based on the structure of the expression (HSA-SSE.A.2)	
	Score 2.5	*No major errors or omissions regarding score 2.0 content, and partial success at score 3.0 content*

Score 2.0	The student will recognize or recall specific vocabulary, such as: • *Complicated, entity, expression, interpret, part, single, structure* The student will perform basic processes, such as: • Identify the parts of an expression (HSA-SSE.A.1a)	
	Score 1.5	*Partial success at score 2.0 content, and major errors or omissions regarding score 3.0 content*
Score 1.0	With help, partial success at score 2.0 content and score 3.0 content	
	Score 0.5	*With help, partial success at score 2.0 content but not at score 3.0 content*
Score 0.0	Even with help, no success	
Grades 8, 7, 6, 5, 4, 3, 2, 1, and Kindergarten		
Score 3.0	Not applicable.	
Score 2.0	Not applicable.	

Equivalent Expressions

High School		
Score 4.0	In addition to score 3.0 performance, the student demonstrates in-depth inferences and applications that go beyond what was taught.	
	Score 3.5	*In addition to score 3.0 performance, partial success at score 4.0 content*
Score 3.0	The student will: • Choose equivalent forms of an expression to reveal and explain properties of the quantity represented by the expression (HSA-SSE.B.3) • Complete the square of a quadratic expression to reveal the maximum or minimum value of the function it defines (HSA-SSE.B.3b) • Derive the formula for the sum of a finite geometric series and use the formula to solve problems (HSA-SSE.B.4)	
	Score 2.5	*No major errors or omissions regarding score 2.0 content, and partial success at score 3.0 content*
Score 2.0	The student will recognize or recall specific vocabulary, such as: • *Complete the square, define, derive, equivalent, exponent, exponential function, expression, factor, finite, formula, function, geometric, maximum, minimum, property, quadratic expression, quantity, series, sum, transform, value, zeroes* The student will perform basic processes, such as: • Produce equivalent forms of an expression (HSA-SSE.B.3) • Factor a quadratic expression to reveal the zeroes of the function it defines (HSA-SSE.B.3a) • Use the properties of exponents to transform expressions for exponential functions (HSA-SSE.B.3c) • Recognize equivalent expressions • Use given formulas for the sum of a finite geometric series	
	Score 1.5	*Partial success at score 2.0 content, and major errors or omissions regarding score 3.0 content*
Score 1.0	With help, partial success at score 2.0 content and score 3.0 content	
	Score 0.5	*With help, partial success at score 2.0 content but not at score 3.0 content*
Score 0.0	Even with help, no success	
Grades 8, 7, 6, 5, 4, 3, 2, 1, and Kindergarten		
Score 3.0	Not applicable.	
Score 2.0	Not applicable.	

Arithmetic Operations on Polynomials

High School		
Score 4.0	In addition to score 3.0 performance, the student demonstrates in-depth inferences and applications that go beyond what was taught.	
	Score 3.5	*In addition to score 3.0 performance, partial success at score 4.0 content*
Score 3.0	The student will: • Add, subtract, and multiply polynomials (HSA-APR.A.1)	
	Score 2.5	*No major errors or omissions regarding score 2.0 content, and partial success at score 3.0 content*
Score 2.0	The student will recognize or recall specific vocabulary, such as: • *Add, addition, closed, multiplication, multiply, operation, polynomial, subtract, subtraction* The student will perform basic processes, such as: • Understand that polynomials are closed under the operations of addition, subtraction, and multiplication (HSA-APR.A.1)	
	Score 1.5	*Partial success at score 2.0 content, and major errors or omissions regarding score 3.0 content*
Score 1.0	With help, partial success at score 2.0 content and score 3.0 content	
	Score 0.5	*With help, partial success at score 2.0 content but not at score 3.0 content*
Score 0.0	Even with help, no success	
Grades 8, 7, 6, 5, 4, 3, 2, 1, and Kindergarten		
Score 3.0	Not applicable.	
Score 2.0	Not applicable.	

Zeroes and Factors of Polynomials

High School		
Score 4.0	In addition to score 3.0 performance, the student demonstrates in-depth inferences and applications that go beyond what was taught.	
	Score 3.5	*In addition to score 3.0 performance, partial success at score 4.0 content*
Score 3.0	The student will: • Apply the Remainder Theorem (HSA-APR.B.2) • Use the zeroes of polynomials to construct a rough graph of the function defined by the polynomial (HSA-APR.B.3)	
	Score 2.5	*No major errors or omissions regarding score 2.0 content, and partial success at score 3.0 content*
Score 2.0	The student will recognize or recall specific vocabulary, such as: • *Factor, function, graph, polynomial, Remainder Theorem, zero of a polynomial* The student will perform basic processes, such as: • Recall the Remainder Theorem (HSA-APR.B.2) • Identify zeroes of polynomials when suitable factoring is available (HSA-APR.B.3)	
	Score 1.5	*Partial success at score 2.0 content, and major errors or omissions regarding score 3.0 content*
Score 1.0	With help, partial success at score 2.0 content and score 3.0 content	
	Score 0.5	*With help, partial success at score 2.0 content but not at score 3.0 content*
Score 0.0	Even with help, no success	

Grades 8, 7, 6, 5, 4, 3, 2, 1, and Kindergarten		
Score 3.0	Not applicable.	
Score 2.0	Not applicable.	

Polynomial Identities

High School		
Score 4.0	In addition to score 3.0 performance, the student demonstrates in-depth inferences and applications that go beyond what was taught.	
	Score 3.5	*In addition to score 3.0 performance, partial success at score 4.0 content*
Score 3.0	The student will: • Use polynomial identities to describe numerical relationships (HSA-APR.C.4)	
	Score 2.5	*No major errors or omissions regarding score 2.0 content, and partial success at score 3.0 content*
Score 2.0	The student will recognize or recall specific vocabulary, such as: • *Numerical, polynomial identity, prove, relationship* The student will perform basic processes, such as: • Prove polynomial identities (HSA-APR.C.4)	
	Score 1.5	*Partial success at score 2.0 content, and major errors or omissions regarding score 3.0 content*
Score 1.0	With help, partial success at score 2.0 content and score 3.0 content	
	Score 0.5	*With help, partial success at score 2.0 content but not at score 3.0 content*
Score 0.0	Even with help, no success	
Grades 8, 7, 6, 5, 4, 3, 2, 1, and Kindergarten		
Score 3.0	Not applicable.	
Score 2.0	Not applicable.	

Rational Expressions

High School		
Score 4.0	In addition to score 3.0 performance, the student demonstrates in-depth inferences and applications that go beyond what was taught.	
	Score 3.5	*In addition to score 3.0 performance, partial success at score 4.0 content*
Score 3.0	The student will: • Write $a(x)/b(x)$ in the form $q(x) + r(x)/b(x)$ where $a(x)$, $b(x)$, $q(x)$, and $r(x)$ are polynomials with the degree of $r(x)$ less than the degree of $b(x)$ using inspection, long division, or computer algebra systems (HSA-APR.D.6)	
	Score 2.5	*No major errors or omissions regarding score 2.0 content, and partial success at score 3.0 content*
Score 2.0	The student will recognize or recall specific vocabulary, such as: • *Algebra, common, degree, denominator, expression, inspection, less than, long division, polynomial, rational* The student will perform basic processes, such as: • Recognize common denominators for rational expressions • Rewrite simple rational expressions in different forms (HSA-APR.D.6)	
	Score 1.5	*Partial success at score 2.0 content, and major errors or omissions regarding score 3.0 content*

Score 1.0	With help, partial success at score 2.0 content and score 3.0 content	
	Score 0.5	*With help, partial success at score 2.0 content but not at score 3.0 content*
Score 0.0	Even with help, no success	
Grades 8, 7, 6, 5, 4, 3, 2, 1, and Kindergarten		
Score 3.0	Not applicable.	
Score 2.0	Not applicable.	

Creating Equations

High School		
Score 4.0	In addition to score 3.0 performance, the student demonstrates in-depth inferences and applications that go beyond what was taught.	
	Score 3.5	*In addition to score 3.0 performance, partial success at score 4.0 content*
Score 3.0	The student will: • Create equations in two or more variables to represent relationships between quantities (HSA-CED.A.2) • Graph equations on coordinate axes with labels and scales (HSA-CED.A.2) • Represent constraints by equations or inequalities and by systems of equations and/or inequalities (HSA-CED.A.3) • Interpret solutions as viable or nonviable options in a modeling context (HSA-CED.A.3)	
	Score 2.5	*No major errors or omissions regarding score 2.0 content, and partial success at score 3.0 content*
Score 2.0	The student will recognize or recall specific vocabulary, such as: • *Constraint, coordinate axes, equation, exponential, formula, function, graph, inequality, interest, interpret, label, linear, model, quadratic, quantity, rational, relationship, represent, scale, solution, system, variable, viable* The student will perform basic processes, such as: • Create linear equations and inequalities in one variable and use them to solve problems including quadratic functions and simple rational and exponential functions (HSA.CED.A.1) • Rearrange formulas to highlight a quantity of interest (HSA-CED.A.4)	
	Score 1.5	*Partial success at score 2.0 content, and major errors or omissions regarding score 3.0 content*
Score 1.0	With help, partial success at score 2.0 content and score 3.0 content	
	Score 0.5	*With help, partial success at score 2.0 content but not at score 3.0 content*
Score 0.0	Even with help, no success	
Grades 8, 7, 6, 5, 4, 3, 2, 1, and Kindergarten		
Score 3.0	Not applicable.	
Score 2.0	Not applicable.	

Reasoning to Solve Equations

High School		
Score 4.0	In addition to score 3.0 performance, the student demonstrates in-depth inferences and applications that go beyond what was taught.	
	Score 3.5	*In addition to score 3.0 performance, partial success at score 4.0 content*

Score 3.0	The student will: • Solve simple rational and radical equations in one variable and identify extraneous solutions (HSA-REI.A.2) • Construct a viable argument to justify a solution method (HSA-REI.A.2)	
	Score 2.5	*No major errors or omissions regarding score 2.0 content, and partial success at score 3.0 content*
Score 2.0	The student will recognize or recall specific vocabulary, such as: • *Argument, equation, extraneous, justify, linear, radical, rational, solution, variable, viable* The student will perform basic processes, such as: • Explain each step in solving a simple linear equation (HSA-REI.A.1)	
	Score 1.5	*Partial success at score 2.0 content, and major errors or omissions regarding score 3.0 content*
Score 1.0	With help, partial success at score 2.0 content and score 3.0 content	
	Score 0.5	*With help, partial success at score 2.0 content but not at score 3.0 content*
Score 0.0	Even with help, no success	
Grades 8, 7, 6, 5, 4, 3, 2, 1, and Kindergarten		
Score 3.0	Not applicable.	
Score 2.0	Not applicable.	

Solving Quadratic Equations

High School		
Score 4.0	In addition to score 3.0 performance, the student demonstrates in-depth inferences and applications that go beyond what was taught.	
	Score 3.5	*In addition to score 3.0 performance, partial success at score 4.0 content*
Score 3.0	The student will: • Solve quadratic equations in one variable using inspection, taking square roots, the quadratic formula, and factoring (HSA-REI.B.4b) • Write complex solutions as $a \pm bi$ for real numbers a and b (HSA-REI.B.4b)	
	Score 2.5	*No major errors or omissions regarding score 2.0 content, and partial success at score 3.0 content*
Score 2.0	The student will recognize or recall specific vocabulary, such as: • *Complete the square, complex, derive, equation, factor, inspection, method, quadratic equation, quadratic formula, real number, solution, square root, transform, variable* The student will perform basic processes, such as: • Use the method of completing the square to transform any quadratic equation in x into an equation of the form $(x - p)^2 = q$ that has the same solutions (HSA-REI.B.4a) • Derive the quadratic formula using the method of completing the square (HSA-REI.B.4a)	
	Score 1.5	*Partial success at score 2.0 content, and major errors or omissions regarding score 3.0 content*
Score 1.0	With help, partial success at score 2.0 content and score 3.0 content	
	Score 0.5	*With help, partial success at score 2.0 content but not at score 3.0 content*
Score 0.0	Even with help, no success	
Grades 8, 7, 6, 5, 4, 3, 2, 1, and Kindergarten		
Score 3.0	Not applicable.	
Score 2.0	Not applicable.	

Graphs of Equations and Inequalities

High School		
Score 4.0	In addition to score 3.0 performance, the student demonstrates in-depth inferences and applications that go beyond what was taught.	
	Score 3.5	*In addition to score 3.0 performance, partial success at score 4.0 content*
Score 3.0	The student will: • Explain why the *x*-coordinates of the points where the graphs of the equations $y = f(x)$ and $y = g(x)$ intersect are the solutions of the equation $f(x) = g(x)$ (HSA-REI.D.11) • Find the approximate solutions of linear, polynomial, rational, absolute value, exponential, and logarithmic functions using technology, tables of values, or successive approximations (HSA-REI.D.11) • Graph the solution set to a system of linear inequalities in two variables as the intersection of the corresponding half planes (HSA-REI.D.12)	
	Score 2.5	*No major errors or omissions regarding score 2.0 content, and partial success at score 3.0 content*
Score 2.0	The student will recognize or recall specific vocabulary, such as: • *Absolute value function, approximate, approximation, boundary, coordinate, coordinate plane, corresponding, curve, equation, exponential function, graph, half plane, inequality, intersect, intersection, line, linear function, logarithmic function, plot, point, polynomial function, rational function, set, solution, successive, system, table of values, technology, variable* The student will perform basic processes, such as: • Understand that the graph of an equation in two variables is a set of all its solutions plotted in the coordinate plane, often forming a curve (which could be a line) (HSA-REI.D.10) • Graph the solutions to a linear inequality in two variables as a half plane (excluding the boundary in the case of a strict inequality) (HSA-REI.D.12)	
	Score 1.5	*Partial success at score 2.0 content, and major errors or omissions regarding score 3.0 content*
Score 1.0	With help, partial success at score 2.0 content and score 3.0 content	
	Score 0.5	*With help, partial success at score 2.0 content but not at score 3.0 content*
Score 0.0	Even with help, no success	
Grades 8, 7, 6, 5, 4, 3, 2, 1, and Kindergarten		
Score 3.0	Not applicable.	
Score 2.0	Not applicable.	

Functions

Functions

High School		
Score 4.0	In addition to score 3.0 performance, the student demonstrates in-depth inferences and applications that go beyond what was taught.	
	Score 3.5	*In addition to score 3.0 performance, partial success at score 4.0 content*
Score 3.0	The student will: • Interpret statements that use function notation in terms of a context (HSF-IF.A.2) • Evaluate functions for inputs in their domains (HSF-IF.A.2) • Recognize that sequences are functions, sometimes defined recursively, whose domain is a subset of the integers (HSF-IF.A.3)	
	Score 2.5	*No major errors or omissions regarding score 2.0 content, and partial success at score 3.0 content*
Score 2.0	The student will recognize or recall specific vocabulary, such as: • *Define, denote, domain, element, equation, evaluate, function, graph, input, integer, interpret, notation, output, range, recursive, sequence, set, subset* The student will perform basic processes, such as: • Understand that a function from one set (called the domain) to another set (called the range) assigns to each element of the domain exactly one element of the range (HSF-IF.A.1) • Understand that if f is a function and x is an element of its domain, then $f(x)$ denotes the output of f corresponding to the input of x (HSF-IF.A.1) • Understand that the graph of f is the graph of the equation $y = f(x)$ (HSF-IF.A.1) • Use function notation (HSF-IF.A.2)	
	Score 1.5	*Partial success at score 2.0 content, and major errors or omissions regarding score 3.0 content*
Score 1.0	With help, partial success at score 2.0 content and score 3.0 content	
	Score 0.5	*With help, partial success at score 2.0 content but not at score 3.0 content*
Score 0.0	Even with help, no success	
Grade 8		
Score 3.0	The student will: • Compare properties of two functions represented in different ways (algebraically, numerically in tables, graphically, or by verbal description) (8.F.A.2)	
Score 2.0	The student will recognize or recall specific vocabulary, such as: • *Algebraic, compare, equation, example, function, graphic, interpret, linear, numeric, property, represent, table, verbal* (8.F.A.1) The student will perform basic processes, such as: • Interpret the equation $y = mx + b$ as defining a linear function (8.F.A.3) • Give examples of functions that are not linear (8.F.A.3)	
Grades 7, 6, 5, 4, 3, 2, 1, and Kindergarten		
Score 3.0	Not applicable.	
Score 2.0	Not applicable.	

Interpret Functions

High School		
Score 4.0	In addition to score 3.0 performance, the student demonstrates in-depth inferences and applications that go beyond what was taught.	
	Score 3.5	*In addition to score 3.0 performance, partial success at score 4.0 content*
Score 3.0	The student will: • Interpret key features of graphs and tables of functions in terms of the two quantities modeled by the functional relationship (for example, intercepts; intervals where the function is increasing, decreasing, positive, or negative; relative maximums and minimums; symmetries; end behavior; and periodicity) (HSF-IF.B.4) • Sketch graphs showing key features given a verbal description of the relationship (for example, intercepts; intervals where the function is increasing, decreasing, positive, or negative; relative maximums and minimums; symmetries; end behavior; and periodicity) (HSF-IF.B.4) • Relate the domain of a function to its graph and, where applicable, to the quantitative relationship it describes (HSF-IF.B.5) • Calculate and interpret the average rate of change of a function over a specified interval (HSF-IF.B.6) • Estimate the rate of change from a graph (HSF-IF.B.6)	
	Score 2.5	*No major errors or omissions regarding score 2.0 content, and partial success at score 3.0 content*
Score 2.0	The student will recognize or recall specific vocabulary, such as: • *Average, calculate, decrease, domain, end behavior, estimate, function, functional relationship, graph, increase, intercept, interpret, interval, maximum, minimum, model, negative, periodicity, positive, quantitative, quantity, rate of change, relationship, relative, sketch, symmetry, table, verbal* The student will perform basic processes, such as: • Identify key features of graphs and tables of functions (for example, intercepts; intervals where the function is increasing, decreasing, positive, or negative; relative maximums and minimums; symmetries; end behavior; and periodicity) (HSF-IF.B.4)	
	Score 1.5	*Partial success at score 2.0 content, and major errors or omissions regarding score 3.0 content*
Score 1.0	With help, partial success at score 2.0 content and score 3.0 content	
	Score 0.5	*With help, partial success at score 2.0 content but not at score 3.0 content*
Score 0.0	Even with help, no success	
Grade 8		
Score 3.0	The student will: • Determine the rate of change and initial value of a function from a description of a relationship or from two (*x*, *y*) values (8.F.B.4) • Describe qualitatively the functional relationship between two quantities by analyzing a graph (for example, where the function is increasing or decreasing, linear or nonlinear) (8.F.B.5)	
Score 2.0	The student will recognize or recall specific vocabulary, such as: • *Analyze, decrease, function, functional relationship, graph, increase, initial, linear, model, nonlinear, qualitative, quantity, rate of change, relationship, sketch, value* The student will perform basic processes, such as: • Given the rate of change and initial value, determine the function that models the situation (8.F.B.4) • Sketch a graph that exhibits the qualitative features of a function (8.F.B.5)	
Grades 7, 6, 5, 4, 3, 2, 1, and Kindergarten		
Score 3.0	Not applicable.	
Score 2.0	Not applicable.	

Graph Functions

High School		
Score 4.0	In addition to score 3.0 performance, the student demonstrates in-depth inferences and applications that go beyond what was taught.	
	Score 3.5	*In addition to score 3.0 performance, partial success at score 4.0 content*
Score 3.0	The student will graph functions expressed symbolically (HSF-IF.C.7): • Linear and quadratic functions showing intercepts, maxima, and minima (HSF-IF.C.7a) • Square root, cube root, and piecewise defined functions, including step functions and absolute value functions (HSF-IF.C.7b) • Polynomial functions, identifying zeroes when suitable factorizations are available, and showing end behavior (HSF-IF.7C.c) • Exponential and logarithmic functions, showing intercepts and end behavior (HSF-IF.C.7e) • Trigonometric functions, showing period, midline, and amplitude (HSF-IF.C.7e)	
	Score 2.5	*No major errors or omissions regarding score 2.0 content, and partial success at score 3.0 content*
Score 2.0	The student will recognize or recall specific vocabulary, such as: • *Absolute value function, amplitude, cube root function, end behavior, exponential function, factorization, function, graph, intercept, linear function, logarithmic function, maxima, midline, minima, period, piecewise defined function, polynomial function, quadratic function, square root function, step function, trigonometric function, zero* The student will perform basic processes, such as: • Identify features of a variety of graphs (for example, intercepts, maxima, minima, period, midline, amplitude, zeroes, end behavior) (HSF-IF.C.7; HSF-IF.C.7a; HSF-IF.C.7b; HSF-IF.C.7c; HSF-IF.C.7e)	
	Score 1.5	*Partial success at score 2.0 content, and major errors or omissions regarding score 3.0 content*
Score 1.0	With help, partial success at score 2.0 content and score 3.0 content	
	Score 0.5	*With help, partial success at score 2.0 content but not at score 3.0 content*
Score 0.0	Even with help, no success	
Grades 8, 7, 6, 5, 4, 3, 2, 1, and Kindergarten		
Score 3.0	Not applicable.	
Score 2.0	Not applicable.	

Properties of Functions

High School		
Score 4.0	In addition to score 3.0 performance, the student demonstrates in-depth inferences and applications that go beyond what was taught.	
	Score 3.5	*In addition to score 3.0 performance, partial success at score 4.0 content*
Score 3.0	The student will: • Interpret zeroes, extreme values, and symmetry of a quadratic function in terms of a context (HSF-IF.C.8a) • Use the properties of exponents to interpret expressions for exponential functions (HSF-IF.C.8b) • Compare properties of two functions each represented in a different way (algebraically, graphically, numerically in tables, or by verbal descriptions) (HSF-IF.C.9)	
	Score 2.5	*No major errors or omissions regarding score 2.0 content, and partial success at score 3.0 content*

Score 2.0	The student will recognize or recall specific vocabulary, such as: • *Algebraic, compare, complete the square, exponent, exponential function, expression, extreme value, factor, function, graph, graphic, interpret, numeric, property, quadratic function, represent, symmetry, table, verbal, zero* The student will perform basic processes, such as: • Show zeroes, extreme values, and symmetry of the graph using the process of factoring and completing the square (HSF-IF.C.8a)	
	Score 1.5	*Partial success at score 2.0 content, and major errors or omissions regarding score 3.0 content*
Score 1.0	With help, partial success at score 2.0 content and score 3.0 content	
	Score 0.5	*With help, partial success at score 2.0 content but not at score 3.0 content*
Score 0.0	Even with help, no success	
Grades 8, 7, 6, 5, 4, 3, 2, 1, and Kindergarten		
Score 3.0	Not applicable.	
Score 2.0	Not applicable.	

Model Relationships

High School		
Score 4.0	In addition to score 3.0 performance, the student demonstrates in-depth inferences and applications that go beyond what was taught.	
	Score 3.5	*In addition to score 3.0 performance, partial success at score 4.0 content*
Score 3.0	The student will: • Combine standard function types using arithmetic operations (HSF-BF.A.1b) • Write arithmetic and geometric sequences both recursively and with an explicit formula, use them to model situations, and translate between the two forms (HSF-BF.A.2)	
	Score 2.5	*No major errors or omissions regarding score 2.0 content, and partial success at score 3.0 content*
Score 2.0	The student will recognize or recall specific vocabulary, such as: • *Arithmetic, calculation, explicit, expression, formula, function, geometric, graph, model, operation, quantity, recursive, relationship, sequence, table, translate* The student will perform basic processes, such as: • Write a function that describes a relationship between two quantities (from a table or a graph) (HSF-BF.A.1) • Determine an explicit expression, recursive process, or steps for calculation from a context (HSF-BF.A.1a)	
	Score 1.5	*Partial success at score 2.0 content, and major errors or omissions regarding score 3.0 content*
Score 1.0	With help, partial success at score 2.0 content and score 3.0 content	
	Score 0.5	*With help, partial success at score 2.0 content but not at score 3.0 content*
Score 0.0	Even with help, no success	
Grades 8, 7, 6, 5, 4, 3, 2, 1, and Kindergarten		
Score 3.0	Not applicable.	
Score 2.0	Not applicable.	

Building New Functions

High School		
Score 4.0	In addition to score 3.0 performance, the student demonstrates in-depth inferences and applications that go beyond what was taught.	
	Score 3.5	*In addition to score 3.0 performance, partial success at score 4.0 content*
Score 3.0	The student will: • Solve an equation of the form $f(x) = c$ for a simple function f that has an inverse and write an expression for the inverse (HSF-BF.B.4a)	
	Score 2.5	*No major errors or omissions regarding score 2.0 content, and partial success at score 3.0 content*
Score 2.0	The student will recognize or recall specific vocabulary, such as: • *Algebraic, effect, equation, even, expression, function, graph, inverse, negative, odd, positive, simple function, value* The student will perform basic processes, such as: • Identify the effect on the graph of replacing $f(x)$ by $f(x) + k$, $kf(x)$, $f(kx)$, and $f(x + k)$ for specific values of k (both positive and negative); find the value of k given the graphs (HSF-BF.B.3) • Recognize odd and even functions from their graphs and algebraic expressions for them (HSF-BF.B.3)	
	Score 1.5	*Partial success at score 2.0 content, and major errors or omissions regarding score 3.0 content*
Score 1.0	With help, partial success at score 2.0 content and score 3.0 content	
	Score 0.5	*With help, partial success at score 2.0 content but not at score 3.0 content*
Score 0.0	Even with help, no success	
Grades 8, 7, 6, 5, 4, 3, 2, 1, and Kindergarten		
Score 3.0	Not applicable.	
Score 2.0	Not applicable.	

Linear and Exponential Models

High School		
Score 4.0	In addition to score 3.0 performance, the student demonstrates in-depth inferences and applications that go beyond what was taught.	
	Score 3.5	*In addition to score 3.0 performance, partial success at score 4.0 content*
Score 3.0	The student will: • Construct linear and exponential functions, including arithmetic and geometric sequences, given a graph, a description of a relationship, or two input-output pairs (including reading these from a table) (HSF-LE.A.2) • Observe using graphs and tables that a quantity increasing exponentially eventually exceeds a quantity increasing linearly, quadratically, or as a polynomial function (HSF-LE.A.3) • Express as a logarithm, the solution to $ab^{ct} = d$ *where* a, c, and d are numbers and the base b is 2, 10, or e; evaluate using technology (HSF-LE.A.4)	
	Score 2.5	*No major errors or omissions regarding score 2.0 content, and partial success at score 3.0 content*

Score 2.0	The student will recognize or recall specific vocabulary, such as: • *Arithmetic, base, constant, construct, decay, difference, equal, evaluate, exceed, exponential, exponential function, express, factor, geometric, graph, grow, increase, input-output pair, interval, linear, linear function, logarithm, model, number, percent, polynomial function, prove, quadratic, quantity, rate, relationship, relative, sequence, solution, table, technology, unit* The student will perform basic processes, such as: • Distinguish between situations that can be modeled with linear functions and with exponential functions (HSF-LE.A.1) • Prove that linear functions grow by equal differences over equal intervals and that exponential functions grow by equal factors over equal intervals (HSF-LE.A.1a) • Recognize situations in which one quantity changes at a constant rate per unit interval relative to another (HSF-LE.A.1b) • Recognize situations in which a quantity grows or decays by a constant percent rate per unit interval relative to another (HSF-LE.A.1c)	
	Score 1.5	*Partial success at score 2.0 content, and major errors or omissions regarding score 3.0 content*
Score 1.0	With help, partial success at score 2.0 content and score 3.0 content	
	Score 0.5	*With help, partial success at score 2.0 content but not at score 3.0 content*
Score 0.0	Even with help, no success	
	Grades 8, 7, 6, 5, 4, 3, 2, 1, and Kindergarten	
Score 3.0	Not applicable.	
Score 2.0	Not applicable.	

Interpret Linear and Exponential Functions

	High School	
Score 4.0	In addition to score 3.0 performance, the student demonstrates in-depth inferences and applications that go beyond what was taught.	
	Score 3.5	*In addition to score 3.0 performance, partial success at score 4.0 content*
Score 3.0	The student will: • Interpret the parameters in a linear or exponential function in terms of a context (HSF-LE.B.5)	
	Score 2.5	*No major errors or omissions regarding score 2.0 content, and partial success at score 3.0 content*
Score 2.0	The student will recognize or recall specific vocabulary, such as: • *Exponential function, interpret, linear function, parameters* The student will perform basic processes, such as: • Identify the parameters of linear and exponential functions	
	Score 1.5	*Partial success at score 2.0 content, and major errors or omissions regarding score 3.0 content*
Score 1.0	With help, partial success at score 2.0 content and score 3.0 content	
	Score 0.5	*With help, partial success at score 2.0 content but not at score 3.0 content*
Score 0.0	Even with help, no success	
	Grades 8, 7, 6, 5, 4, 3, 2, 1, and Kindergarten	
Score 3.0	Not applicable.	
Score 2.0	Not applicable.	

Trigonometric Functions

High School		
Score 4.0	In addition to score 3.0 performance, the student demonstrates in-depth inferences and applications that go beyond what was taught.	
	Score 3.5	*In addition to score 3.0 performance, partial success at score 4.0 content*
Score 3.0	The student will: • Explain how the unit circle in the coordinate plane enables the extension of trigonometric functions to all real numbers, interpreted as radian measures of angles transversed counterclockwise around the unit circle (HSF-TF.A.2)	
	Score 2.5	*No major errors or omissions regarding score 2.0 content, and partial success at score 3.0 content*
Score 2.0	The student will recognize or recall specific vocabulary, such as: • *Angle, arc, coordinate plane, counterclockwise, extension, interpret, length, radian measure, real number, subtend, transverse, trigonometric function, unit circle* The student will perform basic processes, such as: • Describe the radian measure of an angle as the length of the arc on the unit circle subtended by the angle (HSF-TF.A.1)	
	Score 1.5	*Partial success at score 2.0 content, and major errors or omissions regarding score 3.0 content*
Score 1.0	With help, partial success at score 2.0 content and score 3.0 content	
	Score 0.5	*With help, partial success at score 2.0 content but not at score 3.0 content*
Score 0.0	Even with help, no success	
Grades 8, 7, 6, 5, 4, 3, 2, 1, and Kindergarten		
Score 3.0	Not applicable.	
Score 2.0	Not applicable.	

Periodic Phenomena

High School		
Score 4.0	In addition to score 3.0 performance, the student demonstrates in-depth inferences and applications that go beyond what was taught.	
	Score 3.5	*In addition to score 3.0 performance, partial success at score 4.0 content*
Score 3.0	The student will: • Choose trigonometric functions to model periodic phenomena with specified amplitude, frequency, and midline (HSF-TF.B.5)	
	Score 2.5	*No major errors or omissions regarding score 2.0 content, and partial success at score 3.0 content*
Score 2.0	The student will recognize or recall specific vocabulary, such as: • *Amplitude, cosine, frequency, midline, model, periodic, phenomena, sine, tangent, trigonometric function* The student will perform basic processes, such as: • Describe the periodic phenomena for the trigonometric functions sine, cosine, and tangent	
	Score 1.5	*Partial success at score 2.0 content, and major errors or omissions regarding score 3.0 content*
Score 1.0	With help, partial success at score 2.0 content and score 3.0 content	
	Score 0.5	*With help, partial success at score 2.0 content but not at score 3.0 content*

Score 0.0	Even with help, no success
Grades 8, 7, 6, 5, 4, 3, 2, 1, and Kindergarten	
Score 3.0	Not applicable.
Score 2.0	Not applicable.

Trigonometric Identities

High School		
Score 4.0	In addition to score 3.0 performance, the student demonstrates in-depth inferences and applications that go beyond what was taught.	
	Score 3.5	*In addition to score 3.0 performance, partial success at score 4.0 content*
Score 3.0	The student will: • Prove the Pythagorean identity $\sin^2(\theta) + \cos^2(\theta) = 1$ (HSF-TF.C.8)	
	Score 2.5	*No major errors or omissions regarding score 2.0 content, and partial success at score 3.0 content*
Score 2.0	The student will recognize or recall specific vocabulary, such as: • *Angle, cosine, prove, Pythagorean identity, quadrant, sine, tangent* The student will perform basic processes, such as: • Use the Pythagorean identity $\sin^2(\theta) + \cos^2(\theta) = 1$ to find $\sin(\theta)$, $\cos(\theta)$, or $\tan(\theta)$ given $\sin(\theta)$, $\cos(\theta)$, or $\tan(\theta)$ and the quadrant of the angle (HSF-TF.C.8)	
	Score 1.5	*Partial success at score 2.0 content, and major errors or omissions regarding score 3.0 content*
Score 1.0	With help, partial success at score 2.0 content and score 3.0 content	
	Score 0.5	*With help, partial success at score 2.0 content but not at score 3.0 content*
Score 0.0	Even with help, no success	
Grades 8, 7, 6, 5, 4, 3, 2, 1, and Kindergarten		
Score 3.0	Not applicable.	
Score 2.0	Not applicable.	

Geometry

Shapes

High School		
Score 4.0	In addition to score 3.0 performance, the student demonstrates in-depth inferences and applications that go beyond what was taught.	
	Score 3.5	*In addition to score 3.0 performance, partial success at score 4.0 content*
Score 3.0	The student will: • Identify three-dimensional objects generated by rotations of two-dimensional objects (HSG-GMD.B.4)	
	Score 2.5	*No major errors or omissions regarding score 2.0 content, and partial success at score 3.0 content*
Score 2.0	The student will recognize or recall specific vocabulary, such as: • *Cross section, rotation, shape, three dimensional, two dimensional* The student will perform basic processes, such as: • Identify shapes of two-dimensional cross sections of three-dimensional objects (HSG-GMD.B.4)	
	Score 1.5	*Partial success at score 2.0 content, and major errors or omissions regarding score 3.0 content*
Score 1.0	With help, partial success at score 2.0 content and score 3.0 content	
	Score 0.5	*With help, partial success at score 2.0 content but not at score 3.0 content*
Score 0.0	Even with help, no success	
Grade 8		
Score 3.0	Not applicable.	
Score 2.0	Not applicable.	
Grade 7		
Score 3.0	The student will: • Describe the two-dimensional figures that result from slicing three-dimensional figures (7.G.A.3)	
Score 2.0	The student will recognize or recall specific vocabulary, such as: • *Condition, figure, geometric, multiple, set, slice, three dimensional, triangle, two dimensional, unique* The student will perform basic processes, such as: • Recognize that no triangle, a unique triangle, or multiple triangles can be formed from a given set of conditions (7.G.A.2) • Construct geometric figures with given conditions (7.G.A.2)	
Grade 6		
Score 3.0	Not applicable.	
Score 2.0	Not applicable.	
Grade 5		
Score 3.0	The student will: • Classify two-dimensional figures in a hierarchy based on properties (5.G.B.4)	
Score 2.0	The student will recognize or recall specific vocabulary, such as: • *Classify, figure, hierarchy, property, two dimensional* The student will perform basic processes, such as: • Describe the properties of two-dimensional figures (5.G.B.3)	

Grade 4	
Score 3.0	The student will: • Classify shapes based on the presence or absence of parallel or perpendicular lines (4.G.A.2) • Classify shapes based on the presence or absence of angles of a specified size (4.G.A.2)
Score 2.0	The student will recognize or recall specific vocabulary, such as: • *Absence, angle, classify, line, parallel, perpendicular, presence, right triangle, shape, size* The student will perform basic processes, such as: • Identify right triangles (4.G.A.2)
Grade 3	
Score 3.0	The student will: • Classify quadrilaterals into categories based on their attributes (3.G.A.1)
Score 2.0	The student will recognize or recall specific vocabulary, such as: • *Attribute, category, classify, quadrilateral* The student will perform basic processes, such as: • Identify the attributes of various quadrilaterals
Grade 2	
Score 3.0	The student will: • Draw shapes that have specific attributes, such as a number of equal faces or number of equal angles (2.G.A.1)
Score 2.0	The student will recognize or recall specific vocabulary, such as: • *Angle, attribute, cube, equal, face, hexagon, number, pentagon, quadrilateral, shape, triangle* The student will perform basic processes, such as: • Identify triangles, quadrilaterals, pentagons, hexagons, and cubes (2.G.A.1)
Grade 1	
Score 3.0	The student will: • Distinguish between the defining and nondefining attributes of a variety of shapes (for example, defining attributes of triangles: closed, three-sided; nondefining attributes include color, orientation, and overall size) (1.G.A.1)
Score 2.0	The student will recognize or recall specific vocabulary, such as: • *Attribute, closed, color, defining, distinguish, nondefining, orientation, shape, size, three sided, triangle* The student will perform basic processes, such as: • Identify the attributes of various shapes
Kindergarten	
Score 3.0	The student will: • Analyze and compare a variety of two- and three-dimensional shapes using informal language to describe similarities, differences, component parts (for example, number of sides and vertices/"corners") and other attributes (for example, having sides of equal length) (K.G.B.4)
Score 2.0	The student will recognize or recall specific vocabulary, such as: • *Analyze, attribute, compare, corner, difference, number, part, shape, side, similarity, three dimensional, two dimensional* The student will perform basic processes, such as: • Use the names of shapes to describe objects in the environment (K.G.A.1) • Describe the relative position of objects (for example, using terms such as *above, below, beside, in front of, behind, next to*) (K.G.A.1) • Name shapes regardless of orientation or size (K.G.A.2) • Identify shapes as two dimensional (lying in plane, flat) or three dimensional (solid) (K.G.A.3) • Identify attributes of two- and three-dimensional shapes

Compose and Decompose Shapes

High School and Grades 8, 7, 6, 5, 4		
Score 3.0	Not applicable.	
Score 2.0	Not applicable.	
Grade 3		
Score 4.0	In addition to score 3.0 performance, the student demonstrates in-depth inferences and applications that go beyond what was taught.	
	Score 3.5	*In addition to score 3.0 performance, partial success at score 4.0 content*
Score 3.0	The student will: • Express the area of each part of a partitioned shape as a unit fraction of the whole (3.G.A.2)	
	Score 2.5	*No major errors or omissions regarding score 2.0 content, and partial success at score 3.0 content*
Score 2.0	The student will recognize or recall specific vocabulary, such as: • *Area, equal, express, part, partition, shape, unit fraction, whole* The student will perform basic processes, such as: • Partition shapes into parts with equal areas (3.G.A.2)	
	Score 1.5	*Partial success at score 2.0 content, and major errors or omissions regarding score 3.0 content*
Score 1.0	With help, partial success at score 2.0 content and score 3.0 content	
	Score 0.5	*With help, partial success at score 2.0 content but not at score 3.0 content*
Score 0.0	Even with help, no success	
Grade 2		
Score 3.0	The student will: • Describe the shares of a partitioned circle or rectangle using the words *halves*, *thirds*, *half of*, and *a third of*, and so on (2.G.A.3) • Describe the whole as two halves, three thirds, and four fourths (2.G.A.3) • Determine that equal shares of identical wholes need not have the same shape (2.G.A.3)	
Score 2.0	The student will recognize or recall specific vocabulary, such as: • *Circle, column, count, equal, fourth, half, identical, number, partition, rectangle, row, shape, share, size, square, third, total, whole* The student will perform basic processes, such as: • Partition a rectangle into rows and columns of the same size squares and count to find the total number (2.G.A.2) • Partition circles and rectangles into two, three, or four equal shares (2.G.A.3)	
Grade 1		
Score 3.0	The student will: • Create composite shapes by composing three-dimensional shapes (cubes, right rectangular prisms, right circular cones, and right circular cylinders) (1.G.A.2) • Describe the shares of partitioned circles and rectangles using the words *halves*, *fourths*, and *quarters* (1.G.A.3)	
Score 2.0	The student will recognize or recall specific vocabulary, such as: • *Circle, compose, composite, cube, equal, fourth, half, half-circle, partition, quarter, quarter-circle, rectangle, right circular cone, right circular cylinder, right rectangular prism, shape, share, square, three dimensional, trapezoid, triangle, two dimensional* The student will perform basic processes, such as: • Create two-dimensional shapes (rectangles, squares, trapezoids, triangles, half-circles, and quarter-circles) • Partition circles and rectangles into two and four equal shares (1.G.A.3)	

Kindergarten		
Score 3.0	The student will: • Compose simple shapes to form larger shapes (for example, joining two triangles to make a rectangle) (K.G.B.6)	
Score 2.0	The student will recognize or recall specific vocabulary, such as: • *Build, compose, larger, model, rectangle, shape, triangle* The student will perform basic processes, such as: • Model shapes in the real world by building shapes from components and drawing shapes (K.G.B.5)	

Lines and Symmetry

High School and Grades 8, 7, 6, 5		
Score 3.0	Not applicable.	
Score 2.0	Not applicable.	
Grade 4		
Score 4.0	In addition to score 3.0 performance, the student demonstrates in-depth inferences and applications that go beyond what was taught.	
	Score 3.5	*In addition to score 3.0 performance, partial success at score 4.0 content*
Score 3.0	The student will: • Draw points, lines, line segments, rays, angles, and perpendicular and parallel lines (4.G.A.1) • Draw all possible lines of symmetry in two-dimensional figures (4.G.A.3)	
	Score 2.5	*No major errors or omissions regarding score 2.0 content, and partial success at score 3.0 content*
Score 2.0	The student will recognize or recall specific vocabulary, such as: • *Angle, example, figure, line, line segment, line-symmetric, parallel, perpendicular, point, ray, symmetry, two dimensional* The student will perform basic processes, such as: • Identify examples of points, lines, line segments, rays, angles, and perpendicular and parallel lines in two-dimensional figures (4.G.A.1) • Identify line-symmetric figures (4.G.A.3)	
	Score 1.5	*Partial success at score 2.0 content, and major errors or omissions regarding score 3.0 content*
Score 1.0	With help, partial success at score 2.0 content and score 3.0 content	
	Score 0.5	*With help, partial success at score 2.0 content but not at score 3.0 content*
Score 0.0	Even with help, no success	
Grades 3, 2, 1, and Kindergarten		
Score 3.0	Not applicable.	
Score 2.0	Not applicable.	

Coordinate System

High School		
Score 4.0	In addition to score 3.0 performance, the student demonstrates in-depth inferences and applications that go beyond what was taught.	
	Score 3.5	*In addition to score 3.0 performance, partial success at score 4.0 content*

<table>
<tr><td>Score 3.0</td><td colspan="2">The student will:
• Use the slope criteria of parallel and perpendicular lines to solve geometric problems (HSG-GPE.B.5)
• Find the point on a directed line segment between two given points that partitions the segment in a given ratio (HSG-GPE.B.6)
• Use coordinates to compute perimeters of polygons and areas of triangles and rectangles (HSG-GPE.B.7)</td></tr>
<tr><td></td><td>Score 2.5</td><td>No major errors or omissions regarding score 2.0 content, and partial success at score 3.0 content</td></tr>
<tr><td>Score 2.0</td><td colspan="2">The student will recognize or recall specific vocabulary, such as:
• Algebraic, area, compute, coordinate, criteria, directed, geometric, line, line segment, parallel, partition, perimeter, perpendicular, point, polygon, prove, ratio, rectangle, slope, theorem, triangle
The student will perform basic processes, such as:
• Use coordinates to prove simple geometric theorems algebraically (HSG-GPE.B.4)
• Prove the slope criteria for parallel and perpendicular lines (HSG-GPE.B.5)</td></tr>
<tr><td></td><td>Score 1.5</td><td>Partial success at score 2.0 content, and major errors or omissions regarding score 3.0 content</td></tr>
<tr><td>Score 1.0</td><td colspan="2">With help, partial success at score 2.0 content and score 3.0 content</td></tr>
<tr><td></td><td>Score 0.5</td><td>With help, partial success at score 2.0 content but not at score 3.0 content</td></tr>
<tr><td>Score 0.0</td><td colspan="2">Even with help, no success</td></tr>
<tr><td colspan="3" align="center">Grades 8 and 7</td></tr>
<tr><td>Score 3.0</td><td colspan="2">Not applicable.</td></tr>
<tr><td>Score 2.0</td><td colspan="2">Not applicable.</td></tr>
<tr><td colspan="3" align="center">Grade 6</td></tr>
<tr><td>Score 3.0</td><td colspan="2">The student will:
• Use coordinates and absolute value to find distances between points with the same first coordinate or the same second coordinate (6.NS.C.8)
• Use coordinates to find the length of a side joining points with the same first coordinate or the same second coordinate (6.G.A.3)</td></tr>
<tr><td>Score 2.0</td><td colspan="2">The student will recognize or recall specific vocabulary, such as:
• Absolute value, axis, coordinate, coordinate plane, distance, graph, integer, join, length, location, mathematical, ordered pair, point, polygon, position, quadrant, rational number, real world, reflection, side, sign, vertex
The student will perform basic processes, such as:
• Draw polygons in the coordinate plane given coordinates for the vertices (6.G.A.3)
• Find and position rational numbers, including integers, on a coordinate plane (6.NS.C.6)
• Understand signs of numbers in ordered pairs as indicating locations in quadrants of the coordinate plane; recognize that when two ordered pairs differ only by signs, the locations of the points are related by reflection across one or both axes (6.NS.C.6b)
• Graph points (including rational numbers) in all four quadrants of the coordinate plane to solve real-world and mathematical problems (6.NS.C.6; 6.NS.C.8; 6.G.A.3)</td></tr>
<tr><td colspan="3" align="center">Grade 5</td></tr>
<tr><td>Score 3.0</td><td colspan="2">The student will:
• Graph points in the first quadrant of the coordinate plane (5.G.A.2)
• Interpret the coordinate points according to the context (5.G.A.2)</td></tr>
</table>

Score 2.0	The student will recognize or recall specific vocabulary, such as: • *Axis, coordinate, coordinate plane, coordinate system, graph, interpret, number, number line, ordered pair, perpendicular, plane, point, position, quadrant* The student will perform basic processes, such as: • Describe the coordinate system as a set of perpendicular number lines (5.G.A.1) • Describe how to find a given point on the plane (for example, using an ordered pair of numbers corresponding to a position on each number line or axis) (5.G.A.1)	
	Grades 4, 3, 2, 1, and Kindergarten	
Score 3.0	Not applicable.	
Score 2.0	Not applicable.	

Area

	High School and Grade 8	
Score 3.0	Not applicable.	
Score 2.0	Not applicable.	
	Grade 7	
Score 4.0	In addition to score 3.0 performance, the student demonstrates in-depth inferences and applications that go beyond what was taught.	
	Score 3.5	*In addition to score 3.0 performance, partial success at score 4.0 content*
Score 3.0	The student will: • Use the formulas for the area and circumference of a circle to solve problems (7.G.B.4) • Solve real-world and mathematical problems involving the area of two- and three-dimensional shapes composed of triangles, quadrilaterals, polygons, cubes, and right prisms (7.G.B.6)	
	Score 2.5	*No major errors or omissions regarding score 2.0 content, and partial success at score 3.0 content*
Score 2.0	The student will recognize or recall specific vocabulary, such as: • *Area, calculate, circle, circumference, cube, figure, formula, mathematical, polygon, quadrilateral, real world, right prism, scale drawing, shape, three dimensional, triangle, two dimensional* The student will perform basic processes, such as: • Recognize or recall the formulas for the area and circumference of a circle • Recognize or recall the formulas for the area of two- and three-dimensional figures • Calculate area using scale drawings (7.G.A.1)	
	Score 1.5	*Partial success at score 2.0 content, and major errors or omissions regarding score 3.0 content*
Score 1.0	With help, partial success at score 2.0 content and score 3.0 content	
	Score 0.5	*With help, partial success at score 2.0 content but not at score 3.0 content*
Score 0.0	Even with help, no success	
	Grade 6	
Score 3.0	The student will: • Solve real-world or mathematical problems involving the area of polygons (6.G.A.1)	

Score 2.0	The student will recognize or recall specific vocabulary, such as: • *Area, compose, decompose, mathematical, polygon, quadrilateral, real world, rectangle, right triangle, shape, triangle* The student will perform basic processes, such as: • Find the area of right triangles, other triangles, special quadrilaterals, and polygons by composing into rectangles or decomposing into triangles and other shapes (6.G.A.1)
Grade 5	
Score 3.0	Not applicable.
Score 2.0	Not applicable.
Grade 4	
Score 3.0	The student will: • Apply the area formula for rectangles in real-world and word problems (4.MD.A.3)
Score 2.0	The student will recognize or recall specific vocabulary, such as: • *Area, formula, mathematical, real world, rectangle, word problem* The student will perform basic processes, such as: • Apply the area formula for rectangles in mathematical problems (4.MD.A.3)
Grade 3	
Score 3.0	The student will: • Solve real-world problems involving rectangular and rectilinear area (3.MD.C.7b; 3.MD.C.7d) • Use tiling to demonstrate the distributive property by showing that the area of a rectangle with side lengths a and $b + c$ is the sum of $a \times b$ and $a \times c$ (3.MD.C.7c) • Calculate areas of rectilinear figures by decomposing them into nonoverlapping rectangles and adding the area (3.MD.C.7d)
Score 2.0	The student will recognize or recall specific vocabulary, such as: • *Add, area, calculate, concept, count, decompose, distributive property, figure, length, measure, measurement, multiply, overlap, real world, rectangle, rectangular, rectilinear, side, square unit, sum, tiling* The student will perform basic processes, such as: • Explain concepts of area measurement (3.MD.C.5) • Measure area by counting square units (cm, m, in., ft.) (3.MD.C.6) • Demonstrate that area can be found by tiling a rectangular area and that it is the same as multiplying the side lengths (3.MD.C.7a)
Grades 2, 1, and Kindergarten	
Score 3.0	Not applicable.
Score 2.0	Not applicable.

Perimeter

High School and Grades 8, 7, 6, 5	
Score 3.0	Not applicable.
Score 2.0	Not applicable.

Grade 4		
Score 4.0	In addition to score 3.0 performance, the student demonstrates in-depth inferences and applications that go beyond what was taught.	
	Score 3.5	*In addition to score 3.0 performance, partial success at score 4.0 content*
Score 3.0	The student will: • Apply the perimeter formula for rectangles in real-world and word problems (4.MD.A.3)	
	Score 2.5	*No major errors or omissions regarding score 2.0 content, and partial success at score 3.0 content*
Score 2.0	The student will recognize or recall specific vocabulary, such as: • *Formula, mathematical, perimeter, real world, rectangle, word problem* The student will perform basic processes, such as: • Apply the perimeter formula for rectangles in mathematical problems (4.MD.A.3)	
	Score 1.5	*Partial success at score 2.0 content, and major errors or omissions regarding score 3.0 content*
Score 1.0	With help, partial success at score 2.0 content and score 3.0 content	
	Score 0.5	*With help, partial success at score 2.0 content but not at score 3.0 content*
Score 0.0	Even with help, no success	
Grade 3		
Score 3.0	The student will: • Solve real-world and mathematical problems involving perimeters of polygons (3.MD.D.8) • Compare rectangles with the same area and different perimeters, as well as rectangles with the same perimeters and different areas (3.MD.D.8) • Solve for an unknown side length given the perimeter of a polygon (3.MD.D.8)	
Score 2.0	The student will recognize or recall specific vocabulary, such as: • *Area, compare, different, length, mathematical, perimeter, polygon, real world, rectangle, same, side, unknown* The student will perform basic processes, such as: • Find the perimeter of polygons given the side lengths (3.MD.D.8)	
Grades 2, 1, and Kindergarten		
Score 3.0	Not applicable.	
Score 2.0	Not applicable.	

Surface Area

High School and Grade 8		
Score 3.0	Not applicable.	
Score 2.0	Not applicable.	
Grade 7		
Score 4.0	In addition to score 3.0 performance, the student demonstrates in-depth inferences and applications that go beyond what was taught.	
	Score 3.5	*In addition to score 3.0 performance, partial success at score 4.0 content*
Score 3.0	The student will: • Solve real-world and mathematical problems involving the surface area of two- and three-dimensional shapes composed of triangles, quadrilaterals, polygons, cubes, and right prisms (7.G.B.6)	
	Score 2.5	*No major errors or omissions regarding score 2.0 content, and partial success at score 3.0 content*

Score 2.0	The student will recognize or recall specific vocabulary, such as: • *Compose, cube, figure, formula, mathematical, polygon, quadrilateral, real world, right prism, surface area, three dimensional, triangle, two dimensional* The student will perform basic processes, such as: • Recognize or recall the formulas for the surface area of two- and three-dimensional figures	
	Score 1.5	*Partial success at score 2.0 content, and major errors or omissions regarding score 3.0 content*
Score 1.0	With help, partial success at score 2.0 content and score 3.0 content	
	Score 0.5	*With help, partial success at score 2.0 content but not at score 3.0 content*
Score 0.0	Even with help, no success	
Grade 6		
Score 3.0	The student will: • Solve real-world and mathematical problems involving the surface area of a right prism (6.G.A.4) • Use nets to find the surface area of the figure (6.G.A.4)	
Score 2.0	The student will recognize or recall specific vocabulary, such as: • *Figure, mathematical, net, real world, rectangle, right prism, surface area, three dimensional, triangle* The student will perform basic processes, such as: • Represent three-dimensional figures using nets made up of rectangles and triangles (6.G.A.4)	
Grades 5, 4, 3, 2, 1, and Kindergarten		
Score 3.0	Not applicable.	
Score 2.0	Not applicable.	

Volume

High School		
Score 4.0	In addition to score 3.0 performance, the student demonstrates in-depth inferences and applications that go beyond what was taught.	
	Score 3.5	*In addition to score 3.0 performance, partial success at score 4.0 content*
Score 3.0	The student will: • Use the volume formulas for cylinders, pyramids, cones, and spheres to solve problems (HSG-GMD.A.3)	
	Score 2.5	*No major errors or omissions regarding score 2.0 content, and partial success at score 3.0 content*
Score 2.0	The student will recognize or recall specific vocabulary, such as: • *Area, argument, circle, circumference, cone, cylinder, formula, pyramid, sphere, volume* The student will perform basic processes, such as: • Give informal arguments for the formulas for the circumference of a circle, area of a circle, and the volume of a cylinder, pyramid, and cone (HSG-GMD.A.1)	
	Score 1.5	*Partial success at score 2.0 content, and major errors or omissions regarding score 3.0 content*
Score 1.0	With help, partial success at score 2.0 content and score 3.0 content	
	Score 0.5	*With help, partial success at score 2.0 content but not at score 3.0 content*
Score 0.0	Even with help, no success	
Grade 8		
Score 3.0	The student will: • Use the volumes of cones, spheres, and cylinders to solve real-world and mathematical problems (8.G.C.9)	

Score 2.0	The student will recognize or recall specific vocabulary, such as: • *Cone*, *cylinder*, *formula*, *mathematical*, *real world*, *sphere*, *volume* The student will perform basic processes, such as: • Recognize or recall the formulas for the volumes of cones, spheres, and cylinders (8.G.C.9)
Grade 7	
Score 3.0	The student will: • Solve real-world and mathematical problems involving volume of three-dimensional shapes composed of cubes and right prisms (7.G.B.6)
Score 2.0	The student will recognize or recall specific vocabulary, such as: • *Compose*, *cube*, *formula*, *mathematical*, *real world*, *right prism*, *shape*, *three dimensional*, *volume* The student will perform basic processes, such as: • Recognize or recall the formulas for volume of cubes and right prisms
Grade 6	
Score 3.0	The student will: • Apply the formulas $V = lwh$ and $V = bh$ to find the volume of a right rectangular prism with fractional edge lengths in the context of solving real-world and mathematical problems (6.G.A.2)
Score 2.0	The student will recognize or recall specific vocabulary, such as: • *Edge*, *formula*, *fractional*, *length*, *mathematical*, *real world*, *right rectangular prism*, *unit cube*, *volume* The student will perform basic processes, such as: • Find the volume of a right rectangular prism by packing it with unit cubes of the appropriate fractional edge length (6.G.A.2)
Grade 5	
Score 3.0	The student will solve real-world and mathematical problems involving volume (5.MD.C.5): • Apply the formula $V = l \times w \times h$ to find the volume of right rectangular prisms (5.MD.C.5b) • Find volumes of solid figures composed of two nonoverlapping right rectangular prisms by adding the volumes of the parts (5.MD.C.5c)
Score 2.0	The student will recognize or recall specific vocabulary, such as: • *Add*, *attribute*, *centimeter*, *count*, *cube*, *cubic*, *foot*, *figure*, *formula*, *improvised*, *inch*, *measure*, *overlap*, *part*, *relationship*, *right rectangular prism*, *solid*, *sum*, *unit cube*, *volume* The student will perform basic processes, such as: • Explain that volume is an attribute of solid figures (5.MD.C.3) • Measure volume by counting unit cubes, using cubic centimeters, cubic inches, cubic feet, and improvised units and understand the relationship between the sum of the cubes and the volume formula, $V = l \times w \times h$ (5.MD.C.4; 5.MD.C.5a)
Grades 4, 3, 2, 1, and Kindergarten	
Score 3.0	Not applicable.
Score 2.0	Not applicable.

Scale Drawings

High School and Grade 8	
Score 3.0	Not applicable.
Score 2.0	Not applicable.

Grade 7		
Score 4.0	In addition to score 3.0 performance, the student demonstrates in-depth inferences and applications that go beyond what was taught.	
	Score 3.5	*In addition to score 3.0 performance, partial success at score 4.0 content*
Score 3.0	The student will: • Solve problems involving scale drawings of geometric figures (7.G.A.1) • Compute real distances from a scale drawing (7.G.A.1)	
	Score 2.5	*No major errors or omissions regarding score 2.0 content, and partial success at score 3.0 content*
Score 2.0	The student will recognize or recall specific vocabulary, such as: • *Distance, figure, geometric, scale, scale drawing* The student will perform basic processes, such as: • Reproduce a scale drawing at a different scale (7.G.A.1)	
	Score 1.5	*Partial success at score 2.0 content, and major errors or omissions regarding score 3.0 content*
Score 1.0	With help, partial success at score 2.0 content and score 3.0 content	
	Score 0.5	*With help, partial success at score 2.0 content but not at score 3.0 content*
Score 0.0	Even with help, no success	
Grades 6, 5, 4, 3, 2, 1, and Kindergarten		
Score 3.0	Not applicable.	
Score 2.0	Not applicable.	

Angles

High School		
Score 3.0	Not applicable.	
Score 2.0	Not applicable.	
Grade 8		
Score 4.0	In addition to score 3.0 performance, the student demonstrates in-depth inferences and applications that go beyond what was taught.	
	Score 3.5	*In addition to score 3.0 performance, partial success at score 4.0 content*
Score 3.0	The student will: • Use informal arguments to establish facts about the angle sum and exterior angles of triangles, about the angles created when parallel lines are cut by a transversal, and about the angle-angle criterion for similarity of triangles (8.G.A.5)	
	Score 2.5	*No major errors or omissions regarding score 2.0 content, and partial success at score 3.0 content*
Score 2.0	The student will recognize or recall specific vocabulary, such as: • *Angle, angle sum, angle-angle criterion, argument, cut, exterior angle, fact, line, parallel, similarity, transversal, triangle* The student will perform basic processes, such as: • Recognize or recall facts about angle sum and exterior angles of triangles, the angles created when parallel lines are cut by a transversal, and the angle-angle criterion for similarity of triangles	
	Score 1.5	*Partial success at score 2.0 content, and major errors or omissions regarding score 3.0 content*
Score 1.0	With help, partial success at score 2.0 content and score 3.0 content	

	Score 0.5	*With help, partial success at score 2.0 content but not at score 3.0 content*
Score 0.0	Even with help, no success	
Grade 7		
Score 3.0	The student will: • Use facts about supplementary, complementary, vertical, and adjacent angles in a multistep problem to write and solve simple equations for an unknown angle in a figure (7.G.B.5)	
Score 2.0	The student will recognize or recall specific vocabulary, such as: • *Adjacent, angle, complementary, equation, fact, feature, figure, simple, supplementary, unknown, vertical* The student will perform basic processes, such as: • Recognize or recall the features of complementary, supplementary, vertical, and adjacent angles	
Grades 6, 5		
Score 3.0	Not applicable.	
Score 2.0	Not applicable.	
Grade 4		
Score 3.0	The student will: • Solve addition and subtraction problems to find unknown angles on a diagram (4.MD.C.7)	
Score 2.0	The student will recognize or recall specific vocabulary, such as: • *Addition, angle, degree, diagram, measure, protractor, subtraction, unknown, whole number* (4.MD.C.5; 4.MD.C.5a; 4.MD.C.5b) The student will perform basic processes, such as: • Measure angles in whole number degrees using a protractor (4.MD.C.6)	
Grades 3, 2, 1, and Kindergarten		
Score 3.0	Not applicable.	
Score 2.0	Not applicable.	

Pythagorean Theorem

High School		
Score 3.0	Not applicable.	
Score 2.0	Not applicable.	
Grade 8		
Score 4.0	In addition to score 3.0 performance, the student demonstrates in-depth inferences and applications that go beyond what was taught.	
	Score 3.5	*In addition to score 3.0 performance, partial success at score 4.0 content*
Score 3.0	The student will: • Explain the converse of a proof of the Pythagorean theorem (8.G.B.6) • Use the Pythagorean theorem to determine unknown side lengths and solve problems in three dimensions (8.G.B.7)	
	Score 2.5	*No major errors or omissions regarding score 2.0 content, and partial success at score 3.0 content*

Score 2.0	The student will recognize or recall specific vocabulary, such as: • *Converse, coordinate system, dimension, distance, length, point, proof, Pythagorean theorem, side, unknown* The student will perform basic processes, such as: • Explain a proof of the Pythagorean theorem (8.G.B.6) • Use the Pythagorean theorem to determine unknown side lengths and solve problems in two dimensions (8.G.B.7) • Use the Pythagorean theorem to find the distance between two points in a coordinate system (8.G.B.8)	
	Score 1.5	*Partial success at score 2.0 content, and major errors or omissions regarding score 3.0 content*
Score 1.0	With help, partial success at score 2.0 content and score 3.0 content	
	Score 0.5	*With help, partial success at score 2.0 content but not at score 3.0 content*
Score 0.0	Even with help, no success	
	Grades 7, 6, 5, 4, 3, 2, 1, and Kindergarten	
Score 3.0	Not applicable.	
Score 2.0	Not applicable.	

Congruence and Similarity

	High School	
Score 4.0	In addition to score 3.0 performance, the student demonstrates in-depth inferences and applications that go beyond what was taught.	
	Score 3.5	*In addition to score 3.0 performance, partial success at score 4.0 content*
Score 3.0	The student will: • Show that two triangles are congruent if and only if corresponding pairs of sides and corresponding pairs of angles are also congruent (HSG-CO.B.7) • Explain how the criteria for triangle congruence (ASA, SAS, and SSS) follow from the definition of congruence in terms of rigid motions (HSG-CO.B.8) • Explain, using similarity transformations, the meaning of similarity for triangles as the equality of all corresponding pairs of angles and the proportionality of all corresponding pairs of sides (HSG-SRT.A.2) • Establish the AA criterion for two triangles to be similar using the properties of similarity transformations (HSG-SRT.A.3)	
	Score 2.5	*No major errors or omissions regarding score 2.0 content, and partial success at score 3.0 content*
Score 2.0	The student will recognize or recall specific vocabulary, such as: • *AA criterion, angle, ASA criterion, congruence, congruent, corresponding, criteria, equality, figure, pair, property, proportionality, rigid motion, SAS criterion, side, similar, similarity, similarity transformation, SSS criterion, transformation, triangle* The student will perform basic processes, such as: • Use the definition of congruence in terms of rigid motions to decide if two figures are congruent (HSG-CO.B.6) • Determine if two figures are similar using transformations (HSG-SRT.A.2)	
	Score 1.5	*Partial success at score 2.0 content, and major errors or omissions regarding score 3.0 content*
Score 1.0	With help, partial success at score 2.0 content and score 3.0 content	
	Score 0.5	*With help, partial success at score 2.0 content but not at score 3.0 content*
Score 0.0	Even with help, no success	

Grade 8	
Score 3.0	The student will: • Describe a sequence of transformations that exhibits the similarity between two similar two-dimensional figures (8.G.A.4)
Score 2.0	The student will recognize or recall specific vocabulary, such as: • *Congruence, congruent, exhibit, figure, sequence, similar, similarity, transformation, two dimensional* The student will perform basic processes, such as: • Describe the sequence of transformations that exhibits the congruence between two congruent figures (8.G.A.2)
Grades 7, 6, 5, 4, 3, 2, 1, and Kindergarten	
Score 3.0	Not applicable.
Score 2.0	Not applicable.

Transformations

High School		
Score 4.0	In addition to score 3.0 performance, the student demonstrates in-depth inferences and applications that go beyond what was taught.	
	Score 3.5	*In addition to score 3.0 performance, partial success at score 4.0 content*
Score 3.0	The student will: • Describe the rotations and reflections that carry a given rectangle, parallelogram, trapezoid, or regular polygon on to itself (HSG-CO.A.3) • Develop definitions of rotations, reflections, and translations in terms of angles, circles, perpendicular lines, parallel lines, and line segments (HSG-CO.A.4) • Specify the sequence of transformations that will carry a given figure onto another (HSG-CO.A.5) • Use geometric descriptions of rigid motions to transform figures and to predict the effect of a given rigid motion on a given figure (HSG-CO.B.6)	
	Score 2.5	*No major errors or omissions regarding score 2.0 content, and partial success at score 3.0 content*
Score 2.0	The student will recognize or recall specific vocabulary, such as: • *Angle, circle, definition, distance, figure, function, geometric, graph paper, horizontal stretch, input, line, line segment, output, parallel, parallelogram, perpendicular, plane, point, polygon, predict, preserve, rectangle, reflection, regular, represent, rigid motion, rotation, sequence, software, tracing paper, transform, transformation, translation, trapezoid* (HSG-CO.A.1) The student will perform basic processes, such as: • Describe transformations as functions that take points in the plane as inputs and give other points as outputs (HSG-CO.A.2) • Represent transformations in the plane using, for example, transparencies and geometry software (HSG-CO.A.2) • Compare transformations that preserve distance and angle to those that do not (for example, translation vs. horizontal stretch) (HSG-CO.A.2) • Given a geometric figure and a rotation, reflection, or translation, draw the transformed figure using, for example, graph paper, tracing paper, or geometry software (HSG-CO.A.5)	
	Score 1.5	*Partial success at score 2.0 content, and major errors or omissions regarding score 3.0 content*
Score 1.0	With help, partial success at score 2.0 content and score 3.0 content	
	Score 0.5	*With help, partial success at score 2.0 content but not at score 3.0 content*
Score 0.0	Even with help, no success	

Grade 8	
Score 3.0	The student will: • Describe the effect of dilations, translations, rotations, and reflections on two-dimensional figures using coordinates (8.G.A.3)
Score 2.0	The student will recognize or recall specific vocabulary, such as: • *Coordinate, dilation, experimental, figure, property, reflection, rotation, translation, two dimensional, verify* The student will perform basic processes, such as: • Verify experimentally the properties of rotations, reflections, and translations (8.G.A.1)
Grades 7, 6, 5, 4, 3, 2, 1, and Kindergarten	
Score 3.0	Not applicable.
Score 2.0	Not applicable.

Geometric Theorems

High School		
Score 4.0	In addition to score 3.0 performance, the student demonstrates in-depth inferences and applications that go beyond what was taught.	
	Score 3.5	*In addition to score 3.0 performance, partial success at score 4.0 content*
Score 3.0	The student will: • Prove theorems about lines and angles (HSG-CO.C.9) • Prove theorems about triangles (HSG-CO.C.10) • Prove theorems about parallelograms (HSG-CO.C.11)	
	Score 2.5	*No major errors or omissions regarding score 2.0 content, and partial success at score 3.0 content*
Score 2.0	The student will recognize or recall specific vocabulary, such as: • *Angle, line, parallelogram, prove, theorem, triangle* The student will perform basic processes, such as: • Recognize or recall theorems about lines and angles, triangles, and parallelograms	
	Score 1.5	*Partial success at score 2.0 content, and major errors or omissions regarding score 3.0 content*
Score 1.0	With help, partial success at score 2.0 content and score 3.0 content	
	Score 0.5	*With help, partial success at score 2.0 content but not at score 3.0 content*
Score 0.0	Even with help, no success	
Grades 8, 7, 6, 5, 4, 3, 2, 1, and Kindergarten		
Score 3.0	Not applicable.	
Score 2.0	Not applicable.	

Geometric Constructions

High School		
Score 4.0	In addition to score 3.0 performance, the student demonstrates in-depth inferences and applications that go beyond what was taught.	
	Score 3.5	*In addition to score 3.0 performance, partial success at score 4.0 content*

Score 3.0	The student will: • Construct an equilateral triangle, a square, and a regular hexagon inscribed in a circle (HSG-CO.D.13)	
	Score 2.5	*No major errors or omissions regarding score 2.0 content, and partial success at score 3.0 content*
Score 2.0	The student will recognize or recall specific vocabulary, such as: • *Circle, compass, construct, construction, equilateral, formal, hexagon, method, paper folding, reflective device, regular, software, square, straightedge, string, tool, triangle* The student will perform basic processes, such as: • Make formal constructions with a variety of tools and methods (for example, compass, straightedge, string, reflective devices, paper folding, software) (HSG-CO.D.12)	
	Score 1.5	*Partial success at score 2.0 content, and major errors or omissions regarding score 3.0 content*
Score 1.0	With help, partial success at score 2.0 content and score 3.0 content	
	Score 0.5	*With help, partial success at score 2.0 content but not at score 3.0 content*
Score 0.0	Even with help, no success	
Grades 8, 7, 6, 5, 4, 3, 2, 1, and Kindergarten		
Score 3.0	Not applicable.	
Score 2.0	Not applicable.	

Dilations

High School		
Score 4.0	In addition to score 3.0 performance, the student demonstrates in-depth inferences and applications that go beyond what was taught.	
	Score 3.5	*In addition to score 3.0 performance, partial success at score 4.0 content*
Score 3.0	The student will: • Verify experimentally that a dilation takes a line not passing through the center of the dilation to a parallel line, and leaves a line passing through the center unchanged (HSG-SRT.A.1a) • Verify experimentally that a dilation of a line segment is longer or shorter in the ratio given by the scale factor (HSG-SRT.A.1b)	
	Score 2.5	*No major errors or omissions regarding score 2.0 content, and partial success at score 3.0 content*
Score 2.0	The student will recognize or recall specific vocabulary, such as: • *Center, dilation, experimental, line, line segment, parallel, ratio, scale factor, verify* The student will perform basic processes, such as: • Demonstrate dilations of a line segment	
	Score 1.5	*Partial success at score 2.0 content, and major errors or omissions regarding score 3.0 content*
Score 1.0	With help, partial success at score 2.0 content and score 3.0 content	
	Score 0.5	*With help, partial success at score 2.0 content but not at score 3.0 content*
Score 0.0	Even with help, no success	
Grades 8, 7, 6, 5, 4, 3, 2, 1, and Kindergarten		
Score 3.0	Not applicable.	
Score 2.0	Not applicable.	

Theorems Involving Similarity

	High School	
Score 4.0	In addition to score 3.0 performance, the student demonstrates in-depth inferences and applications that go beyond what was taught.	
	Score 3.5	*In addition to score 3.0 performance, partial success at score 4.0 content*
Score 3.0	The student will: • Prove theorems about triangles, including: a line parallel to one side of a triangle divides the other two sides proportionally, and conversely, the Pythagorean theorem proved using triangle similarity (HSG-SRT.B.4) • Use congruence and similarity criteria for triangles to solve problems and to prove relationships in geometric figures (HSG-SRT.B.5)	
	Score 2.5	*No major errors or omissions regarding score 2.0 content, and partial success at score 3.0 content*
Score 2.0	The student will recognize or recall specific vocabulary, such as: • *Congruence, converse, criteria, divide, figure, geometric, line, parallel, proportional, prove, Pythagorean theorem, relationship, side, similarity, theorem, triangle* The student will perform basic processes, such as: • Recognize or recall theorems about triangles	
	Score 1.5	*Partial success at score 2.0 content, and major errors or omissions regarding score 3.0 content*
Score 1.0	With help, partial success at score 2.0 content and score 3.0 content	
	Score 0.5	*With help, partial success at score 2.0 content but not at score 3.0 content*
Score 0.0	Even with help, no success	
	Grades 8, 7, 6, 5, 4, 3, 2, 1, and Kindergarten	
Score 3.0	Not applicable.	
Score 2.0	Not applicable.	

Trigonometric Ratios

	High School	
Score 4.0	In addition to score 3.0 performance, the student demonstrates in-depth inferences and applications that go beyond what was taught.	
	Score 3.5	*In addition to score 3.0 performance, partial success at score 4.0 content*
Score 3.0	The student will: • Use trigonometric ratios and the Pythagorean theorem to solve right triangles in applied problems (HSG-SRT.C.8)	
	Score 2.5	*No major errors or omissions regarding score 2.0 content, and partial success at score 3.0 content*
Score 2.0	The student will recognize or recall specific vocabulary, such as: • *Acute angle, applied, complementary angle, cosine, property, Pythagorean theorem, relationship, right triangle, side ratio, similarity, sine, trigonometric ratio* The student will perform basic processes, such as: • Understand that by similarity, side ratios in right triangles are properties of the acute angles of the right triangles, leading to definitions of trigonometric ratios (HSG-SRT.C.6) • Explain the relationship between the sine and cosine of complementary angles (HSG-SRT.C.7)	

	Score 1.5	*Partial success at score 2.0 content, and major errors or omissions regarding score 3.0 content*
Score 1.0	With help, partial success at score 2.0 content and score 3.0 content	
	Score 0.5	*With help, partial success at score 2.0 content but not at score 3.0 content*
Score 0.0	Even with help, no success	
Grades 8, 7, 6, 5, 4, 3, 2, 1, and Kindergarten		
Score 3.0	Not applicable.	
Score 2.0	Not applicable.	

Geometric Trigonometry

High School		
Score 4.0	In addition to score 3.0 performance, the student demonstrates in-depth inferences and applications that go beyond what was taught.	
	Score 3.5	*In addition to score 3.0 performance, partial success at score 4.0 content*
Score 3.0	The student will: • Prove the Laws of Sines and Cosines (HSG-SRT.D.10) • Apply the Laws of Sines and Cosines to find unknown measurements in right and nonright triangles (HSG-SRT.D.11)	
	Score 2.5	*No major errors or omissions regarding score 2.0 content, and partial success at score 3.0 content*
Score 2.0	The student will recognize or recall specific vocabulary, such as: • *Law of Cosines, Law of Sines, measurement, nonright triangle, prove, right triangle, unknown* The student will perform basic processes, such as: • Recognize and recall the Laws of Sines and Cosines	
	Score 1.5	*Partial success at score 2.0 content, and major errors or omissions regarding score 3.0 content*
Score 1.0	With help, partial success at score 2.0 content and score 3.0 content	
	Score 0.5	*With help, partial success at score 2.0 content but not at score 3.0 content*
Score 0.0	Even with help, no success	
Grades 8, 7, 6, 5, 4, 3, 2, 1, and Kindergarten		
Score 3.0	Not applicable.	
Score 2.0	Not applicable.	

Circle Theorems

High School		
Score 4.0	In addition to score 3.0 performance, the student demonstrates in-depth inferences and applications that go beyond what was taught.	
	Score 3.5	*In addition to score 3.0 performance, partial success at score 4.0 content*
Score 3.0	The student will: • Describe relationships among inscribed angles, radii, and chords (HSG-C.A.2) • Construct the inscribed and circumscribed circles of a triangle and prove properties of angles for a quadrilateral inscribed in a circle (HSG-C.A.3)	

	Score 2.5	*No major errors or omissions regarding score 2.0 content, and partial success at score 3.0 content*
Score 2.0	The student will recognize or recall specific vocabulary, such as: • *Angle, central, chord, circle, circumscribe, construct, inscribe, line, property, prove, quadrilateral, radius, relationship, similar, tangent, triangle* The student will perform basic processes, such as: • Prove that all circles are similar (HSG-C.A.1) • Identify central, inscribed, and circumscribed angles, radii, chords, and tangent lines (HSG-C.A.2)	
	Score 1.5	*Partial success at score 2.0 content, and major errors or omissions regarding score 3.0 content*
Score 1.0	With help, partial success at score 2.0 content and score 3.0 content	
	Score 0.5	*With help, partial success at score 2.0 content but not at score 3.0 content*
Score 0.0	Even with help, no success	
Grades 8, 7, 6, 5, 4, 3, 2, 1, and Kindergarten		
Score 3.0	Not applicable.	
Score 2.0	Not applicable.	

Arc Length and Sectors

High School		
Score 4.0	In addition to score 3.0 performance, the student demonstrates in-depth inferences and applications that go beyond what was taught.	
	Score 3.5	*In addition to score 3.0 performance, partial success at score 4.0 content*
Score 3.0	The student will: • Derive, using similarity, the fact that the length of the arc intercepted by an angle is proportional to the radius (HSG-C.B.5) • Derive the formula for the area of a sector (HSG-C.B.5)	
	Score 2.5	*No major errors or omissions regarding score 2.0 content, and partial success at score 3.0 content*
Score 2.0	The student will recognize or recall specific vocabulary, such as: • *Angle, arc, area, calculate, constant of proportionality, derive, formula, intercept, length, proportional, radian measure, radius, sector, similarity* The student will perform basic processes, such as: • Define the radian measure of the angle as the constant of proportionality (HSG-C.B.5) • Calculate arc length	
	Score 1.5	*Partial success at score 2.0 content, and major errors or omissions regarding score 3.0 content*
Score 1.0	With help, partial success at score 2.0 content and score 3.0 content	
	Score 0.5	*With help, partial success at score 2.0 content but not at score 3.0 content*
Score 0.0	Even with help, no success	
Grades 8, 7, 6, 5, 4, 3, 2, 1, and Kindergarten		
Score 3.0	Not applicable.	
Score 2.0	Not applicable.	

Conic Sections

High School		
Score 4.0	In addition to score 3.0 performance, the student demonstrates in-depth inferences and applications that go beyond what was taught.	
	Score 3.5	*In addition to score 3.0 performance, partial success at score 4.0 content*
Score 3.0	The student will: • Derive the equation of a parabola given a focus and directrix (HSG-GPE.A.2)	
	Score 2.5	*No major errors or omissions regarding score 2.0 content, and partial success at score 3.0 content*
Score 2.0	The student will recognize or recall specific vocabulary, such as: • *Center, circle, complete the square, derive, directrix, equation, focus, parabola, Pythagorean theorem, radius* The student will perform basic processes, such as: • Derive the equation of a circle of given center and radius using the Pythagorean theorem (HSG-GPE.A.1) • Complete the square to find the center and radius of a circle given by an equation (HSG-GPE.A.1)	
	Score 1.5	*Partial success at score 2.0 content, and major errors or omissions regarding score 3.0 content*
Score 1.0	With help, partial success at score 2.0 content and score 3.0 content	
	Score 0.5	*With help, partial success at score 2.0 content but not at score 3.0 content*
Score 0.0	Even with help, no success	
Grades 8, 7, 6, 5, 4, 3, 2, 1, and Kindergarten		
Score 3.0	Not applicable.	
Score 2.0	Not applicable.	

Geometric Modeling

High School		
Score 4.0	In addition to score 3.0 performance, the student demonstrates in-depth inferences and applications that go beyond what was taught.	
	Score 3.5	*In addition to score 3.0 performance, partial success at score 4.0 content*
Score 3.0	The student will: • Apply concepts of density based on area and volume in modeling situations (HSG-MG.A.2) • Apply geometric methods to solve design problems (HSG-MG.A.3)	
	Score 2.5	*No major errors or omissions regarding score 2.0 content, and partial success at score 3.0 content*
Score 2.0	The student will recognize or recall specific vocabulary, such as: • *Area, concept, density, design, geometric, measure, method, model, property, shape, volume* The student will perform basic processes, such as: • Use geometric shapes, their measures, and their properties to describe objects (HSG-MG.A.1)	
	Score 1.5	*Partial success at score 2.0 content, and major errors or omissions regarding score 3.0 content*
Score 1.0	With help, partial success at score 2.0 content and score 3.0 content	
	Score 0.5	*With help, partial success at score 2.0 content but not at score 3.0 content*
Score 0.0	Even with help, no success	
Grades 8, 7, 6, 5, 4, 3, 2, 1, and Kindergarten		
Score 3.0	Not applicable.	
Score 2.0	Not applicable.	

Measurement, Data, Statistics, and Probability

Measurement

High School and Grades 8, 7, 6		
Score 3.0	Not applicable.	
Score 2.0	Not applicable.	
Grade 5		
Score 4.0	In addition to score 3.0 performance, the student demonstrates in-depth inferences and applications that go beyond what was taught.	
	Score 3.5	*In addition to score 3.0 performance, partial success at score 4.0 content*
Score 3.0	The student will: • Use conversions to solve multistep word problems (5.MD.A.1)	
	Score 2.5	*No major errors or omissions regarding score 2.0 content, and partial success at score 3.0 content*
Score 2.0	The student will recognize or recall specific vocabulary, such as: • *Centimeter, conversion, foot, measurement, meter, unit, word problem, yard* The student will perform basic processes, such as: • Convert among different-sized standard measurement units within a given measurement system (for example, feet to yards, centimeters to meters) (5.MD.A.1)	
	Score 1.5	*Partial success at score 2.0 content, and major errors or omissions regarding score 3.0 content*
Score 1.0	With help, partial success at score 2.0 content and score 3.0 content	
	Score 0.5	*With help, partial success at score 2.0 content but not at score 3.0 content*
Score 0.0	Even with help, no success	
Grade 4		
Score 3.0	The student will: • Use the four operations to solve word problems involving distance, intervals of time, liquid volumes, masses of objects, and money, including problems that involve simple fractions or decimals and problems that require expressing measurements given in a larger unit in terms of a smaller unit (4.MD.A.2)	
Score 2.0	The student will recognize or recall specific vocabulary, such as: • *Centimeter, decimal, distance, express, fraction, gram, hour, interval, kilogram, kilometer, liquid, liter, mass, measurement, meter, milliliter, minute, money, operation, ounce, pound, second, time, unit, volume, word problem* The student will perform basic processes, such as: • Express measurements in a larger unit in terms of a smaller unit (for example, km, m, cm, kg, g, lb, oz, l, ml, hr, min, sec) (4.MD.A.1)	
Grade 3		
Score 3.0	The student will: • Solve one-step word problems involving masses or volumes that are given in the same units (3.MD.A.2)	

Score 2.0	The student will recognize or recall specific vocabulary, such as: • *Estimate, gram, kilogram, liquid, liter, mass, measure, unit, volume, word problem* The student will perform basic processes, such as: • Measure and estimate liquid volumes and masses of objects using standard units of grams, kilograms, and liters (3.MD.A.2)
	Grade 2
Score 3.0	The student will: • Estimate length using units of feet, inches, centimeters, and meters (2.MD.A.3) • Measure to determine how much longer one object is than another, expressing the difference in standard units (2.MD.A.4)
Score 2.0	The student will recognize or recall specific vocabulary, such as: • *Centimeter, compare, estimate, express, foot, inch, length, measure, measurement, measuring tape, meter, meter stick, ruler, tool, unit, yardstick* The student will perform basic processes, such as: • Measure length by selecting and using standard tools (for example, rulers, yardsticks, meter sticks, and measuring tapes) (2.MD.A.1) • Compare two measurements of the same object made using different units (2.MD.A.2)
	Grade 1
Score 3.0	The student will: • Express the length of an object as a whole number of length units (1.MD.A.2)
Score 2.0	The student will recognize or recall specific vocabulary, such as: • *Compare, indirect, length, order, unit, whole number* The student will perform basic processes, such as: • Order three objects by length (1.MD.A.1) • Compare the length of two objects indirectly by using a third object (1.MD.A.1)
	Kindergarten
Score 3.0	The student will: • Compare and describe the difference between two objects with a measureable attribute in common (K.MD.A.2)
Score 2.0	The student will recognize or recall specific vocabulary, such as: • *Attribute, common, compare, length, measure, weight* The student will perform basic processes, such as: • Describe several measurable attributes of an object (for example, length and weight) (K.MD.A.1)

Represent and Interpret Data

	High School and Grades 8, 7, 6	
Score 3.0	Not applicable.	
Score 2.0	Not applicable.	
	Grade 5	
Score 4.0	In addition to score 3.0 performance, the student demonstrates in-depth inferences and applications that go beyond what was taught.	
	Score 3.5	*In addition to score 3.0 performance, partial success at score 4.0 content*

Score 3.0	The student will: • Use operations to solve problems involving line plots with data in fractions of a unit (5.MD.B.2)	
	Score 2.5	*No major errors or omissions regarding score 2.0 content, and partial success at score 3.0 content*
Score 2.0	The student will recognize or recall specific vocabulary, such as: • *Data, fraction, line plot, measurement, operation, unit* The student will perform basic processes, such as: • Make a line plot of measurement data in fractions of a unit (5.MD.B.2)	
	Score 1.5	*Partial success at score 2.0 content, and major errors or omissions regarding score 3.0 content*
Score 1.0	With help, partial success at score 2.0 content and score 3.0 content	
	Score 0.5	*With help, partial success at score 2.0 content but not at score 3.0 content*
Score 0.0	Even with help, no success	
	Grade 4	
Score 3.0	The student will: • Solve problems using a line plot of measurement data in fractions of a unit (1/2, 1/4, 1/8) (4.MD.B.4)	
Score 2.0	The student will recognize or recall specific vocabulary, such as: • *Data, fraction, line plot, measurement, unit* The student will perform basic processes, such as: • Make a line plot of measurement data in fractions of a unit (1/2, 1/4, 1/8) (4.MD.B.4)	
	Grade 3	
Score 3.0	The student will: • Draw a scaled picture graph and a scaled bar graph to represent a data set (3.MD.B.3) • Solve two-step problems using information from scaled bar graphs (3.MD.B.3) • Represent measurement data in halves and fourths of an inch on a line plot (3.MD.B.4)	
Score 2.0	The student will recognize or recall specific vocabulary, such as: • *Bar graph, data, data set, fourth, generate, half, inch, interpret, length, less, line plot, measure, measurement, more, picture graph, represent, scaled* The student will perform basic processes, such as: • Interpret a scaled picture graph and bar graph • Solve one-step problems (for example, "how many more" and "how many less") using information from scaled bar graphs (3.MD.B.3) • Generate data by measuring lengths to the half and fourth of an inch (3.MD.B.4)	
	Grade 2	
Score 3.0	The student will: • Make a line plot in whole number units to display data (2.MD.D.9) • Solve simple put-together and take-apart problems and compare problems using information presented in a bar graph (2.MD.D.10)	
Score 2.0	The student will recognize or recall specific vocabulary, such as: • *Bar graph, category, compare problem, data, line plot, picture graph, put-together problem, scale, take-apart problem, unit, whole number* The student will perform basic processes, such as: • Draw a picture graph and a bar graph with a single unit scale and up to four categories (2.MD.D.10) • Interpret a picture graph and a bar graph	

Grade 1		
Score 3.0	The student will: • Represent and interpret data with up to three categories (1.MD.C.4)	
Score 2.0	The student will recognize or recall specific vocabulary, such as: • *Category, data, interpret, less, more, number, organize, point, question, represent, representation* The student will perform basic processes, such as: • Organize data into up to three categories (1.MD.C.4) • Ask and answer questions about data and representations of data (for example, total number of data points, number in each category, how many more or less in one category) (1.MD.C.4)	
Kindergarten		
Score 3.0	The student will: • Classify and sort objects into given categories (each category should contain 10 or fewer objects) (K.MD.B.3)	
Score 2.0	The student will recognize or recall specific vocabulary, such as: • *Category, classify, sort* The student will perform basic processes, such as: • Recognize the appropriate category for an object when given options	

Time

High School and Grades 8, 7, 6, 5, 4		
Score 3.0	Not applicable.	
Score 2.0	Not applicable.	
Grade 3		
Score 4.0	In addition to score 3.0 performance, the student demonstrates in-depth inferences and applications that go beyond what was taught.	
	Score 3.5	*In addition to score 3.0 performance, partial success at score 4.0 content*
Score 3.0	The student will: • Solve word problems involving addition and subtraction of time intervals in minutes (3.MD.A.1)	
	Score 2.5	*No major errors or omissions regarding score 2.0 content, and partial success at score 3.0 content*
Score 2.0	The student will recognize or recall specific vocabulary, such as: • *Addition, elapsed, minute, nearest, subtraction, time, time interval, word problem* The student will perform basic processes, such as: • Tell and write time to the nearest minute (3.MD.A.1) • Measure time intervals in minutes (elapsed time) (3.MD.A.1)	
	Score 1.5	*Partial success at score 2.0 content, and major errors or omissions regarding score 3.0 content*
Score 1.0	With help, partial success at score 2.0 content and score 3.0 content	
	Score 0.5	*With help, partial success at score 2.0 content but not at score 3.0 content*
Score 0.0	Even with help, no success	
Grade 2		
Score 3.0	The student will: • Tell and write time from analog clocks to the nearest five minutes (2.MD.C.7)	

Score 2.0	The student will recognize or recall specific vocabulary, such as: • *Analog, clock, digital, minute, nearest, time* The student will perform basic processes, such as: • Tell and write time from digital clocks to the nearest five minutes (2.MD.C.7)	
Grade 1		
Score 3.0	The student will: • Tell time in hours and half hours using an analog clock (1.MD.B.3)	
Score 2.0	The student will recognize or recall specific vocabulary, such as: • *Analog, clock, digital, half hour, hour, time* The student will perform basic processes, such as: • Tell time to the hour and half hour using a digital clock (1.MD.B.3)	
Kindergarten		
Score 3.0	Not applicable.	
Score 2.0	Not applicable.	

Money

High School and Grades 8, 7, 6, 5, 4, 3		
Score 3.0	Not applicable.	
Score 2.0	Not applicable.	
Grade 2		
Score 4.0	In addition to score 3.0 performance, the student demonstrates in-depth inferences and applications that go beyond what was taught.	
	Score 3.5	*In addition to score 3.0 performance, partial success at score 4.0 content*
Score 3.0	The student will: • Solve word problems involving dollar bills, quarters, dimes, nickels, and pennies using symbols appropriately (2.MD.C.8)	
	Score 2.5	*No major errors or omissions regarding score 2.0 content, and partial success at score 3.0 content*
Score 2.0	The student will recognize or recall specific vocabulary, such as: • *Dime, dollar bill, nickel, penny, quarter, symbol, value, word problem* The student will perform basic processes, such as: • Recognize symbols, such as $, ., and ¢ • Recognize or recall the values of dollar bills, quarters, dimes, nickels, and pennies	
	Score 1.5	*Partial success at score 2.0 content, and major errors or omissions regarding score 3.0 content*
Score 1.0	With help, partial success at score 2.0 content and score 3.0 content	
	Score 0.5	*With help, partial success at score 2.0 content but not at score 3.0 content*
Score 0.0	Even with help, no success	
Grade 1 and Kindergarten		
Score 3.0	Not applicable.	
Score 2.0	Not applicable.	

Data Distributions

High School		
Score 4.0	In addition to score 3.0 performance, the student demonstrates in-depth inferences and applications that go beyond what was taught.	
	Score 3.5	*In addition to score 3.0 performance, partial success at score 4.0 content*
Score 3.0	The student will: • Interpret differences in shape, center, and spread in the context of the data sets, accounting for possible effects of extreme data points (outliers) (HSS-ID.A.3) • Use the mean and standard deviation of a data set to fit it to a normal distribution and to estimate population percentages and recognize that there are data sets for which such a procedure is not appropriate (HSS-ID.A.4) • Use calculators, spreadsheets, and tables to estimate areas under the normal curve (HSS-ID.A.4)	
	Score 2.5	*No major errors or omissions regarding score 2.0 content, and partial success at score 3.0 content*
Score 2.0	The student will recognize or recall specific vocabulary, such as: • *Box plot, calculator, center, compare, data, data point, data set, distribution, dot plot, effect, estimate, extreme, histogram, interpret, interquartile range, mean, median, normal curve, normal distribution, outlier, plot, population percentage, real number line, represent, shape, spread, spreadsheet, standard deviation, statistics, table* The student will perform basic processes, such as: • Represent data with plots on the real number line (dot plots, histograms, and box plots) (HSS-ID.A.1) • Use statistics appropriate to the shape of the data distribution to compare center (median, mean) and spread (interquartile range, standard deviation) of two or more different data sets (HSS-ID.A.2)	
	Score 1.5	*Partial success at score 2.0 content, and major errors or omissions regarding score 3.0 content*
Score 1.0	With help, partial success at score 2.0 content and score 3.0 content	
	Score 0.5	*With help, partial success at score 2.0 content but not at score 3.0 content*
Score 0.0	Even with help, no success	
Grade 8		
Score 3.0	Not applicable.	
Score 2.0	Not applicable.	
Grade 7		
Score 3.0	The student will: • Use measures of center and measures of variability for numerical data from random samples to draw informal comparative inferences about two populations (7.SP.B.4)	
Score 2.0	The student will recognize or recall specific vocabulary, such as: • *Assess, comparative, data, degree, distribution, inference, informal, measure of center, measure of variability, numerical, overlap, population, random sample, visual* The student will perform basic processes, such as: • Informally assess the degree of visual overlap of two numerical data distributions (7.SP.B.3)	
Grade 6		
Score 3.0	The student will: • Calculate quantitative measures of center (median, mean) and variability (interquartile range, mean absolute deviation) (6.SP.B.5c) • Describe patterns and deviations from patterns in the data (6.SP.B.5c) • Choose the appropriate measure of center and variability based on the shape of the data distribution and the context in which the data were gathered (6.SP.B.5d)	

Score 2.0	The student will recognize or recall specific vocabulary, such as: • *Attribute, box plot, calculate, center, context, data, data set, deviation, distribution, histogram, interquartile range, mean, mean absolute deviation, measure, measure of center, measure of variability, measurement, median, numerical, observation, pattern, quantitative, shape, spread, surface feature, unit* (6.SP.A.1; 6.SP.A.3) The student will perform basic processes, such as: • Describe the distribution of a set of data by center, spread, and overall shape (6.SP.A.2) • Display numerical data on a histogram and a box plot (6.SP.B.4) • Describe surface features of numerical data sets (for example, number of observations, how the attribute was measured, units of measurement) (6.SP.B.5a; 6.SP.B.5b)	
Grades 5, 4, 3, 2, 1, and Kindergarten		
Score 3.0	Not applicable.	
Score 2.0	Not applicable.	

Random Sampling

High School		
Score 4.0	In addition to score 3.0 performance, the student demonstrates in-depth inferences and applications that go beyond what was taught.	
	Score 3.5	*In addition to score 3.0 performance, partial success at score 4.0 content*
Score 3.0	The student will: • Develop a margin of error through the use of simulation models for random sampling, sample surveys, experiments, and observational studies (HSS-IC.B.4) • Compare two treatments using data from a randomized experiment (HSS-IC.B.5) • Use simulations to decide if differences between parameters are significant (HSS-IC.B.5) • Evaluate reports based on data (HSS-IC.B.6)	
	Score 2.5	*No major errors or omissions regarding score 2.0 content, and partial success at score 3.0 content*
Score 2.0	The student will recognize or recall specific vocabulary, such as: • *Data, compare, consistent, estimate, evaluate, experiment, inference, margin of error, model, observational study, parameter, population, population mean, population parameter, population proportion, random sample, randomization, randomized experiment, report, result, sample survey, significant, simulation, statistics, treatment* The student will perform basic processes, such as: • Understand that statistics is a process for making inferences about population parameters based on a random sample from that population (HSS-IC.A.1) • Decide if a specified model is consistent with results from a given data-generating process (for example, using simulation) (HSS-IC.A.2) • Recognize the purposes of and differences among sample surveys, experiments, and observational studies (HSS-IC.B.3) • Explain how randomization applies to sample surveys, experiments, and observational studies (HSS-IC.B.3) • Estimate a population mean or proportion using data from sample surveys, experiments, and observational studies (HSS-IC.B.4)	
	Score 1.5	*Partial success at score 2.0 content, and major errors or omissions regarding score 3.0 content*
Score 1.0	With help, partial success at score 2.0 content and score 3.0 content	
	Score 0.5	*With help, partial success at score 2.0 content but not at score 3.0 content*
Score 0.0	Even with help, no success	

Grade 8		
Score 3.0	Not applicable.	
Score 2.0	Not applicable.	
Grade 7		
Score 3.0	The student will: • Recognize that different random samples from a population may yield different inferences (7.SP.A.1) • Draw inferences about a population using data from a random sample (7.SP.A.2) • Analyze variation of multiple samples (7.SP.A.2)	
Score 2.0	The student will recognize or recall specific vocabulary, such as: • *Analyze, data, estimate, gauge, generate, inference, population, prediction, random sampling, reasonable, sample, size, variation* The student will perform basic processes, such as: • Recognize reasonable inferences about a population • Generate multiple samples of the same size to gauge the variation in estimates or predictions (7.SP.A.2)	
Grades 6, 5, 4, 3, 2, 1, and Kindergarten		
Score 3.0	Not applicable.	
Score 2.0	Not applicable.	

Probability

High School		
Score 4.0	In addition to score 3.0 performance, the student demonstrates in-depth inferences and applications that go beyond what was taught.	
	Score 3.5	*In addition to score 3.0 performance, partial success at score 4.0 content*
Score 3.0	The student will: • Understand the conditional probability of *A* given *B* as *P*(*A* and *B*)/*P*(*B*), and interpret independence of *A* and *B* as saying that the conditional probability of *A* given *B* is the same as the probability of *A*, and the conditional probability of *B* given *A* is the same as the probability of *B* (HSS-CP.A.3) • Interpret two-way frequency tables of data when two categories are associated with each object being classified (HSS-CP.A.4) • Use a two-way table as a sample space to decide if the events are independent and approximate conditional probabilities (HSS-CP.A.4) • Explain the concepts of conditional probability and independence in everyday language and situations (HSS-CP.A.5)	
	Score 2.5	*No major errors or omissions regarding score 2.0 content, and partial success at score 3.0 content*
Score 2.0	The student will recognize or recall specific vocabulary, such as: • *Approximate, category, characteristic, classify, complement, concept, conditional probability, construct, data, event, independence, independent, interpret, intersection, outcome, probability, product, sample space, subset, two-way frequency table, two-way table, union* The student will perform basic processes, such as: • Describe events as subsets of a sample space (the set of outcomes) using characteristics (or categories) of the outcomes, or as unions, intersections, or complements of other events (*or, and, not*) (HSS-CP.A.1) • Understand that two events *A* and *B* are independent if the probability of *A* and *B* occurring together is the product of their probabilities, and use this characterization to determine if they are independent (HSS-CP.A.2) • Construct two-way frequency tables of data (HSS-CP.A.4) • Recognize examples of conditional probability and independence in everyday situations and language (HSS-CP.A.5)	

<table>
<tr><td></td><td>Score 1.5</td><td>Partial success at score 2.0 content, and major errors or omissions regarding score 3.0 content</td></tr>
<tr><td>Score 1.0</td><td colspan="2">With help, partial success at score 2.0 content and score 3.0 content</td></tr>
<tr><td></td><td>Score 0.5</td><td>With help, partial success at score 2.0 content but not at score 3.0 content</td></tr>
<tr><td>Score 0.0</td><td colspan="2">Even with help, no success</td></tr>
<tr><td colspan="3" align="center">Grade 8</td></tr>
<tr><td>Score 3.0</td><td colspan="2">Not applicable.</td></tr>
<tr><td>Score 2.0</td><td colspan="2">Not applicable.</td></tr>
<tr><td colspan="3" align="center">Grade 7</td></tr>
<tr><td>Score 3.0</td><td colspan="2">The student will:<ul><li>Develop a probability model and use it to find probabilities of events (7.SP.C.7)</li><li>Compare probabilities from a model to observed frequency and reason about differences between the model and observed frequency (7.SP.C.7)</li><li>Find probabilities of compound events using organized lists, tables, tree diagrams, and simulation (7.SP.C.8)</li></ul></td></tr>
<tr><td>Score 2.0</td><td colspan="2">The student will recognize or recall specific vocabulary, such as:<ul><li>Chance process, compound event, data, event, frequency, list, model, observed, organize, predict, probability, reason, simulation, table, tree diagram (7.SP.C.5)</li></ul>The student will perform basic processes, such as:<ul><li>Collect data on a chance process and predict probability (7.SP.C.6)</li></ul></td></tr>
<tr><td colspan="3" align="center">Grades 6, 5, 4, 3, 2, 1, and Kindergarten</td></tr>
<tr><td>Score 3.0</td><td colspan="2">Not applicable.</td></tr>
<tr><td>Score 2.0</td><td colspan="2">Not applicable.</td></tr>
</table>

Multivariable Data Distributions

<table>
<tr><td colspan="3" align="center">High School</td></tr>
<tr><td>Score 4.0</td><td colspan="2">In addition to score 3.0 performance, the student demonstrates in-depth inferences and applications that go beyond what was taught.</td></tr>
<tr><td></td><td>Score 3.5</td><td>In addition to score 3.0 performance, partial success at score 4.0 content</td></tr>
<tr><td>Score 3.0</td><td colspan="2">The student will:<ul><li>Interpret relative frequencies (for example, joint, marginal, and conditional) in the context of data in two-way frequency tables and recognize possible associations and trends in the data (HSS-ID.B.5)</li><li>Fit a function to the data (emphasize linear, quadratic, and exponential models) (HSS-ID.B.6a)</li><li>Use functions fitted to the data to solve problems (HSS-ID.B.6a)</li><li>Plot and analyze residuals to informally assess the fit of a function (HSS-ID.B.6b)</li><li>Fit a linear function for a scatter plot that suggests a linear association (HSS-ID.B.6c)</li></ul></td></tr>
<tr><td></td><td>Score 2.5</td><td>No major errors or omissions regarding score 2.0 content, and partial success at score 3.0 content</td></tr>
<tr><td>Score 2.0</td><td colspan="2">The student will recognize or recall specific vocabulary, such as:<ul><li>Analyze, assess, association, categorical data, category, conditional, data, exponential model, fit, frequency, function, informal, interpret, joint, linear, linear model, marginal, plot, quadratic model, quantitative, relative, residual, scatter plot, summarize, trend, two-way frequency table, variable</li></ul>The student will perform basic processes, such as:<ul><li>Summarize categorical data for two categories in two-way frequency tables (HSS-ID.B.5)</li><li>Represent data on two quantitative variables on a scatter plot (HSS-ID.B.6)</li></ul></td></tr>
</table>

	Score 1.5	*Partial success at score 2.0 content, and major errors or omissions regarding score 3.0 content*
Score 1.0	With help, partial success at score 2.0 content and score 3.0 content	
	Score 0.5	*With help, partial success at score 2.0 content but not at score 3.0 content*
Score 0.0	Even with help, no success	
	Grade 8	
Score 3.0	The student will: • Use the equation of a linear model to solve problems in the context of bivariate measurement data, interpreting the slope and intercept (8.SP.A.3) • Interpret patterns of association by displaying frequencies and relative frequencies in a two-way table; describe associations between variables (8.SP.A.4)	
Score 2.0	The student will recognize or recall specific vocabulary, such as: • *Assess, association, bivariate, construct, data, equation, frequency, informal, intercept, interpret, line, linear, measurement, model, pattern, quantitative, relationship, relative, scatter plot, slope, two-way table, variable* The student will perform basic processes, such as: • Construct and interpret scatter plots for bivariate measurement data (8.SP.A.1) • Use straight lines to informally model and assess relationships between two quantitative variables (8.SP.A.2)	
	Grades 7, 6, 5, 4, 3, 2, 1, and Kindergarten	
Score 3.0	Not applicable.	
Score 2.0	Not applicable.	

Linear Models

	High School	
Score 4.0	In addition to score 3.0 performance, the student demonstrates in-depth inferences and applications that go beyond what was taught.	
	Score 3.5	*In addition to score 3.0 performance, partial success at score 4.0 content*
Score 3.0	The student will: • Compute (using technology) and interpret the correlation coefficient of a linear fit (HSS-ID.C.8) • Distinguish between correlation and causation in a data set (HSS-ID.C.9)	
	Score 2.5	*No major errors or omissions regarding score 2.0 content, and partial success at score 3.0 content*
Score 2.0	The student will recognize or recall specific vocabulary, such as: • *Causation, compute, constant, correlation, correlation coefficient, data, data set, distinguish, fit, intercept, interpret, linear, linear model, rate of change, slope, technology, term* The student will perform basic processes, such as: • Interpret the slope (rate of change) and the intercept (constant term) of a linear model in the context of the data (HSS-ID.C.7)	
	Score 1.5	*Partial success at score 2.0 content, and major errors or omissions regarding score 3.0 content*
Score 1.0	With help, partial success at score 2.0 content and score 3.0 content	
	Score 0.5	*With help, partial success at score 2.0 content but not at score 3.0 content*
Score 0.0	Even with help, no success	
	Grades 8, 7, 6, 5, 4, 3, 2, 1, and Kindergarten	
Score 3.0	Not applicable.	
Score 2.0	Not applicable.	

Rules of Probability

High School		
Score 4.0	In addition to score 3.0 performance, the student demonstrates in-depth inferences and applications that go beyond what was taught.	
	Score 3.5	*In addition to score 3.0 performance, partial success at score 4.0 content*
Score 3.0	The student will: • Find the conditional probability of *A* given *B* as the fraction of *B*'s outcomes that also belong to *A* and interpret the answer in terms of the model (HSS-CP.B.6) • Apply the Addition rule, $P(A \text{ or } B) = P(A) + P(B) - P(A \text{ and } B)$, and interpret the answer in terms of the model (HSS-CP.B.7)	
	Score 2.5	*No major errors or omissions regarding score 2.0 content, and partial success at score 3.0 content*
Score 2.0	The student will recognize or recall specific vocabulary, such as: • *Addition rule, conditional probability, fraction, interpret, model, outcome* The student will perform basic processes, such as: • Recognize or recall the Addition rule, $P(A \text{ or } B) = P(A) + P(B) - P(A \text{ and } B)$	
	Score 1.5	*Partial success at score 2.0 content, and major errors or omissions regarding score 3.0 content*
Score 1.0	With help, partial success at score 2.0 content and score 3.0 content	
	Score 0.5	*With help, partial success at score 2.0 content but not at score 3.0 content*
Score 0.0	Even with help, no success	
Grades 8, 7, 6, 5, 4, 3, 2, 1, and Kindergarten		
Score 3.0	Not applicable.	
Score 2.0	Not applicable.	

References and Resources

Bell, B. (2011). Structures for supporting all learners. In *Navigating implementation of the Common Core State Standards* (pp. 111–126). Englewood, CO: Lead and Learn Press.

Costa, A. L., & Kallick, B. (Eds.). (2009). *Habits of mind across the curriculum: Practical and creative strategies for teachers.* Alexandria, VA: Association for Supervision and Curriculum Development.

Daggett, W. R., & Gendron, S. (2010). *Common Core State Standards Initiative: Classroom implications for 2014.* Rexford, NY: International Center for Leadership in Education.

Daro, P., Mosher, F. A., & Corcoran, T. (2011). *Learning trajectories in mathematics: A foundation for standards, curriculum, assessment, and instruction.* Accessed at www.cpre.org/learning-trajectories-mathematics-foundation-standards-curriculum-assessment-and-instruction on April 17, 2012.

Dweck, C. S. (2000). *Self-theories: Their role in motivation, personality, and development.* New York: Psychology Press.

Hattie, J. (1984). An empirical study of various indices for determining unidimensionality. *Multivariate Behavioral Research, 19,* 49–78.

Hattie, J. (1985). Methodology review: Assessing the unidimensionality of tests and items. *Applied Psychological Measurement, 9*(2), 139–164.

Heritage, M. (2008). *Learning progressions: Supporting instruction and formative assessment.* Washington, DC: Council of Chief State School Officers.

Johnson, D. W., & Johnson, R. T. (2005). *Teaching students to be peacemakers* (4th ed.). Edina, MN: Interaction.

K–12 Center at ETS. (2012). *Coming together to raise achievement: New assessments for the Common Core State Standards.* Austin, TX: Educational Testing Service.

Kendall, J. (2011). *Understanding Common Core State Standards.* Alexandria, VA: Association for Supervision and Curriculum Development.

Kendall, J. S., & Marzano, R. J. (2000). *Content knowledge: A compendium of standards and benchmarks for K–12 education.* Alexandria, VA: Association for Supervision and Curriculum Development.

Kober, N., & Rentner, D. S. (2011). *Common Core State Standards: Progress and challenges in school districts' implementation.* Washington, DC: Center on Education Policy.

Kober, N., & Rentner, D. S. (2012). *Year two of implementing the Common Core State Standards: States' progress and challenges.* Washington, DC: Center on Education Policy.

Lord, F. M. (1959). Problems in mental test theory arising from errors of measurement. *Journal of the American Statistical Association, 54*(286), 472–479.

Loveless, T. (2012). *The 2012 Brown Center report on American education: How well are American students learning?* Washington, DC: Brown Center on Education Policy.

Marzano, R. J. (2006). *Classroom assessment and grading that work.* Alexandria, VA: Association for Supervision and Curriculum Development.

Marzano, R. J. (2007). *The art and science of teaching: A comprehensive framework for effective instruction.* Alexandria, VA: Association for Supervision and Curriculum Development.

Marzano, R. J. (2009). *Designing and teaching learning goals and objectives.* Bloomington, IN: Marzano Research Laboratory.

Marzano, R. J. (2010). *Formative assessment and standards-based grading.* Bloomington, IN: Marzano Research Laboratory.

Marzano, R. J., Brandt, R. S., Hughes, C. S., Jones, B. F., Presseisen, B. Z., Rankin, S. C., et al. (1988). *Dimensions of thinking: A framework for curriculum and instruction.* Alexandria, VA: Association for Supervision and Curriculum Development.

Marzano, R. J., & Haystead, M. W. (2008). *Making standards useful in the classroom.* Alexandria, VA: Association for Supervision and Curriculum Development.

Marzano, R. J., & Heflebower, T. (2012). *Teaching and assessing 21st century skills.* Bloomington, IN: Marzano Research Laboratory.

Marzano, R. J., & Kendall, J. S. (with Gaddy, B. B.). (1999). *Essential knowledge: The debate over what American students should know.* Aurora, CO: Mid-continent Research for Education and Learning.

Marzano, R. J., & Pickering, D. J. (1997). *Dimensions of learning: Teacher's manual* (2nd ed.). Alexandria, VA: Association for Supervision and Curriculum Development.

Marzano, R. J., & Pollock, J. E. (2001). Standards-based thinking and reasoning skills. In A. L. Costa (Ed.), *Developing minds: A resource book for teaching thinking* (3rd ed., pp. 29–34). Alexandria, VA: Association for Supervision and Curriculum Development.

Marzano, R. J., & Waters, T. (2009). *District leadership that works: Striking the right balance.* Bloomington, IN: Solution Tree Press.

National Council of Teachers of Mathematics. (1989). *Curriculum and evaluation standards for school mathematics.* Reston, VA: Author.

National Council of Teachers of Mathematics. (2000). *Principles and standards for school mathematics.* Reston, VA: Author.

National Governors Association Center for Best Practices, & Council of Chief State School Officers. (2010a). *Common Core State Standards for English language arts & literacy in history/social studies, science, and technical subjects.* Washington, DC: Authors.

National Governors Association Center for Best Practices, & Council of Chief State School Officers. (2010b). *Common Core State Standards for English language arts & literacy in history/social studies, science, and technical subjects—Appendix A: Research supporting key elements of the standards and glossary of key terms.* Washington, DC: Authors.

National Governors Association Center for Best Practices, & Council of Chief State School Officers. (2010c). *Common Core State Standards for English language arts & literacy in history/social studies, science, and technical subjects—Appendix B: Text exemplars and sample performance tasks.* Washington, DC: Authors.

National Governors Association Center for Best Practices, & Council of Chief State School Officers. (2010d). *Common Core State Standards for mathematics.* Washington, DC: Authors.

National Governors Association Center for Best Practices, & Council of Chief State School Officers. (2010e). *Reaching higher: The Common Core State Standards validation committee.* Washington, DC: National Governors Association.

Nichols, P. D. (2010). *What is a learning progression?* Accessed at www.pearsonassessments.com/NR/rdonlyres/6C8F4D6F-EFB1-47CE-9247-3712D274190F/0/Bulletin_12.pdf on April 24, 2012.

Partnership for 21st Century Skills. (2012). *Framework for 21st century learning.* Accessed at www.p21.org/overview on June 6, 2012.

Phillips, V., & Wong, C. (2010). Tying together the Common Core of standards, instruction, and assessments. *Phi Delta Kappan, 91*(5), 37–42.

Polikoff, M. S., Porter, A. C., & Smithson, J. (2011). How well aligned are state assessments of student achievement with state content standards? *American Educational Research Journal, 48*(4), 965–995.

Porter, A., McMaken, J., Hwang, J., & Yang, R. (2011a). Assessing the Common Core standards: Opportunities for improving measures of instruction. *Educational Researcher, 40*(4), 186–188.

Porter, A., McMaken, J., Hwang, J., & Yang, R. (2011b). Common Core standards: The new U.S. intended curriculum. *Educational Researcher, 40*(3), 103–116.

Porter, A. C., & Polikoff, M. S. (2009). The time for national content standards. *Education Week, 28*(35). Accessed at www.edweek.org/ew/articles/2009/06/11/35porter.h28.html on March 30, 2012.

Porter, A. C., Polikoff, M. S., & Smithson, J. (2009). Is there a de facto national intended curriculum? Evidence from state content standards. *Educational Evaluation and Policy Analysis, 31*(3), 238–268.

Reynolds, A. J., Chen, C-C., & Herbers, J. E. (2009, June). *School mobility and educational success: A research synthesis and evidence on prevention.* Paper presented at the Workshop on the Impact of Mobility and Change on the Lives of Young Children, Schools, and Neighborhoods, Board on Children, Youth, and Families, National Research Council, Washington, DC.

Rothman, R. (2011). *Something in common: The Common Core standards and the next chapter in American education.* Cambridge, MA: Harvard Education Press.

Schoenfeld, A., & Burkhardt, H. (2012). *Content specifications for the summative assessment of the Common Core State Standards for mathematics.* Accessed at www.smarterbalanced.org/wordpress/wp-content/uploads/2011/12/MathContentSpecifications.pdf on June 7, 2012.

U.S. Department of Labor, Secretary's Commission on Achieving Necessary Skills. (1991). *What work requires of schools: A SCANS report for America 2000.* Washington, DC: Author. Accessed at http://wdr.doleta.gov/SCANS/whatwork/whatwork.pdf on January 7, 2011.

Wiggs, M. D. (2011). Gaining a deeper understanding of the Common Core State Standards: The big picture. In *Navigating implementation of the Common Core State Standards* (pp. 23–58). Englewood, CO: Lead and Learn Press.

Index

D

E

N

Q

R

S

T

U

V

W

Y

Z